AF413657

BY THE SAME AUTHOR

[NON-FICTION]

Promises of Betrayals: The History That Shaped the Iranian Shia Clerics,
Revived Failure: Iran's Reality After the American Withdrawal of the Nuclear Deal,
Why Ukraine Matters,
Hallucinating Stewards: A Potential Financial Crisis,
With Blood and Flame: How the British Empire changed Bengal,

[FICTION]

With Dark Understandings: A Novel,
The Other Side of Eden: A Novel,
Never Among Equals: A WWI Novel,
The Secrets We Live In: A Novel,

UKRAINE AT ANY PRICE

A WAR AGAINST THE WEST

FAZLE CHOWDHURY

FABREZAN & PHILLIPE

for Ukrainians,

Don't lose hope.

"Ukraine is not merely a country. It's a vital component of a larger defense of democracy and the West. Without Ukraine, Russia ceases to be an empire in Eurasia"

— Henry Kissinger
United States Secretary of State (1973-1977)

CONTENTS

AUTHOR'S NOTE

Some of the subjects in this book have their beginnings from my undergraduate thesis. Back then, my submission did not win the mind or the heart of my now long-deceased thesis advisor. No matter the endless research and the sleepless nights or the agonies of my circumstances back then, I had hoped my efforts would have something I could take with me as I neared the day of my graduation. That would not be so. I was denied the $50 prize, which instead went to another contemporary who had written about a much less interesting subject. I had desperately sought the approval and admiration of my advisor and when I did not find it, all hopes of putting my thesis into a book had been squashed. Looking back, the subject of Ukraine was very distant to me. The only thing close to it was the tales of an old family friend who had worked in the railways in the Donbas in 1956. He proudly said to me that as an engineer who neither spoke Russian nor Ukrainian, what was on display in the designs on paper, spoke volumes than the language of interaction. It was a story that stayed with me since.

In the fall of 2004, things were heating up in Eurasia. At the time, I was living and working in Baku, Azerbaijan, and soon found myself among a group of acquaintances who kept on pressing me to explore events that were shaping around us. Tashkent was in the news, at the time the British ambassador was asked to leave. I took little interest in the subject but it was big news in the company I kept. The construction of the Baku-Tblisi-Pipeline was also a topic of much discussion, many of my colleagues believed it was so important for this project to be complete, as it would provide, at the very least, an independent economic lifeline to Azerbaijan. Events in Iraq was much more central to me. I had organized and protested against the 2003 American invasion on 18th January 2003 at the National Mall in Washington DC, but with no success. Since then I had taken a less of an interest in foreign affairs. However, the people I had come to know later did bring me back to take interest on what was happening in Ukraine. Some believed since 2002, the country was shifting further to the West. I did get a chance to visit Kyiv in October 2004. It was a trip I would not have otherwise taken but only accepted at the very last minute and will forever remain in my memory. The adventure, the stormy weather and the company of colleagues whom I had known for a very short time and many who would later become lifelong friends.

For four days in the cold, I spoke to young people like me (at least at the time) who told me about their desires to study and work in Western European capitals in Berlin, Paris, and London. That Ukraine's future lay with the West and not Russia. That narrative changed as I met others outside the city, who had the opposite view. For some of them, at least one family member worked in some surrounding area of Moscow. This was not a temporary arrangement but something that had been the case for some Ukrainian Russian-speaking populations that continued even after the disbanding of the Soviet Union. Ukraine would see political upheaval but that would calm down after the 2005 election. The political upheaval did calm down but only temporarily. I had little idea how much Russia would change its tone afterward.

For two decades, I kept a very distant view of the events in Ukraine. However, in the fall of 2021, a friend contacted me about her safety in Estonia. She sensed there could be problems to come as Russian troops were taking positions in Belarus and along the borders of Ukraine. Thankfully, she was able to travel safely back to her home in London only days prior to the Russian invasion of Ukraine. For me, those interactions gave life to the two-decade-long void and gave me a feeling to bring back to life a thesis that I wrote two decades back. I was fortunate that I was pressed by long-time friends to contribute to a subject few had known little about.

Today, the situation in Ukraine presents a stark contrast to the relatively peaceful environments of Canada, Western Europe, and the United States. In Ukraine, civilians face the daily realities of Russian aggression, marked by attacks, abductions, and the systematic destruction of their cultural heritage. President Vladimir Putin's actions, which include bombing schools and hospitals and targeting civilians, amount to massacres. Despite these hardships, Ukrainians have demonstrated remarkable resilience, confronting Russian forces and inflicting significant setbacks.

Ukraine is not decisively winning the war but it is not losing either. Skepticism persists regarding American military and economic assistance and critics question the United States' financial commitment to a distant conflict, especially given past military withdrawals from Afghanistan and Iraq and pressing domestic issues like border security and crime.

For President Zelenskyy, maintaining American support is crucial, especially as 2024 approaches, a critical year with potential shifts in U.S., and European political leadership and escalating Russian military threats. Russia's ambitions extend beyond Ukraine, aiming to annex additional territories and influence European backers, thereby straining NATO and European Union (EU) unity.

Throughout this conflict, I have maintained that Ukraine's struggle is a bulwark against potential Russian escalations in regions such as the Baltics, Germany, Moldova, and Poland. A Ukrainian victory could also deter China from considering an invasion of Taiwan and discourage rogue regimes from pursuing aggressive ambitions. *Ukraine At Any Price* argues that American and European financial and military aid alone is insufficient; a Russian occupation of Ukraine would undermine the credibility of the West, which is why supporting Ukraine is so crucial.

Putin is not the first Russian leader to invade a peaceful country, justifying his actions by alleging NATO's eastward expansion through a "Nazi-controlled" Ukraine. Despite the failure of his "special military operation," he has found allies in China, India, and some European states. As the war nears its third year, public opinion is shifting, and war fatigue is becoming a significant issue, raising questions about what a future against Russia will look like, especially with the possibility of a newly elected U.S. president in November 2024.

Reflecting on Otto von Bismarck, the architect of Prussian foreign policy and the chief creator of the formation and unification of Germany, "The secret of politics? Make a good treaty with Russia," it is evident that cooperation with Russia has historically been seen as essential for European stability. Nevertheless, I diverge from Bismarck's 19th century Realpolitik in advocating for a more assertive stance that requires a nuclear-armed Russia to retreat to Ukraine's pre-2022 borders before any negotiations can commence.

To make my case in this book, there are a host of people I would like to extend my heartfelt gratitude, especially to my friends and former colleagues from Kyiv and Moscow, who have a deep love for their countries, and their invaluable insights significantly enriched my research.

My intention is not to alter the reader's opinion but to offer a different viewpoint, recognizing fully well that I may not have every detail of history as I have demonstrated the thoughtful examination that I have put before you.

May 2024,
Fazle Chowdhury

PREFACE

The story of Rusalka and Vodyanoy is a compelling piece of folklore that has endured through centuries, illustrating the intricate interplay between myth and morality. According to the legend, Rusalka is a figure of haunting beauty and vengeance, often portrayed as a drowned maiden sorceress who entices humans to watery graves. She is emblematic of lush, verdant landscapes and flowing rivers, embodying both the allure and peril of the natural world. Her counterpart, Vodyanoy is a malevolent water demon presiding over the depths of southern lakes and rivers. Depicted as a wrinkled, frog-like entity, Vodyanoy is a symbol of the eerie and foreboding aspects of aquatic realms. The epic takes a pivotal turn one winter when an unusual event occurs: warm water falls from the sky, invigorating Vodyanoy amidst a frozen landscape. Intrigued by the source of this warmth, she journeys westward, only to find that the warmth persists solely on one side of her body.

This mysterious phenomenon is soon attributed to the experiments of Vespucci's wizards from the West, who inadvertently create this unnatural warmth. However, the ground beneath Vodyanoy abruptly turns to ice, a transformation she recognizes as the work of her adversary, Rusalka. The confrontation between them escalates, with Rusalka seemingly intent on war. In a desperate bid for self-preservation, Vodyanoy attempts to defend by carving a protective circle, yet she remains vulnerable on one side.

The tale leaves the ultimate outcome of their clash unresolved, instead offering an emphasis that even under siege, vigilance and resilience, can ensure that not all is lost. This enduring folklore suggests that remnants of the past persist. Through the allegorical struggle between Rusalka and Vodyanoy, the story imparts wisdom on the enduring nature of the subtle balance between life, preservation, death, and destruction. While the tale does not specifically say that Vodyanoy is Ukraine, there are similarities.

The war in Ukraine, which began in 2014 and escalated significantly in 2022, has deep historical roots and significant geopolitical implications. President Voldomyr Zelenskyy has kept Ukrainians' faith alive and his armed forces continue to fight the Russian army despite unable to take back large parts of the east.

The man who began the "special military operation" on 17 March 2024, President Vladimir Putin, celebrated his re-election with a victory speech. It was a moment he issued a stark warning to Western powers about a direct confrontation between Russia and NATO. Putin's words come as a stark reminder of how the biggest European conflict since World War II could escalate into massive consequences. The Russian President's words may be directed at the West, but its impact will most certainly be felt all over the world.

The Ukraine war has triggered the deepest crisis in Russian-Western relations since the 1962 Cuban Missile Crisis, a pivotal moment in the Cold War, characterized by a 13-day confrontation between the United States and the Soviet Union over the placement of nuclear missiles in Cuba. The episode is regarded as the closest the world has ever come to nuclear war.

Ukraine was always a Russian "red line," and Putin's threat is a warning to the West after years of repeated declarations that NATO should not expand eastwards. Putin has singled out the Aegis Ashore missile defense system in Poland and Romania, as evidence of NATO's duplicity. Deployed on naval vessels and developed by Lockheed Martin, the system is designed to intercept and destroy ballistic missiles, short to intermediate-range during their midcourse and terminal phases of flight. It is unclear why the Russian President saw Aegis as an attacking weapon against Russia, especially since its use is defensive in nature against non-Russian adversaries. Yet he kept on with his warnings, signaling his serious intentions to have them removed.

The decision to deploy a missile defense system by the United States in close coordination with European allies was part of NATO's broader effort to enhance its ballistic missile defense capabilities. It is in response to evolving security threats, particularly from ballistic missiles originating from outside Europe. The announcement initially came from then Obama administration as part of the European Phased Adaptive Approach (EPAA) in September 2009. The EPAA aimed to deploy a flexible and adaptive missile defense system to protect NATO member-states and enhance the alliance's collective security. Poland and Romania were chosen as host countries due to their strategic locations and their willingness to host the missile defense installations. The sites are equipped with the Aegis Combat System and SM-3 interceptor missiles, providing capabilities to detect, track, and intercept ballistic missile threats. For Putin, the situation mirrored another instance where NATO was reneging on its commitments.

The decision to enlarge NATO eastwards was taken during the July 1997 NATO Summit in Madrid. It was at this summit that NATO leaders formally invited three Central and Eastern European countries to begin the process of joining the alliance: Poland, Hungary, and the Czech Republic. On 12 March 1999, all three joined NATO. The decision marked the first round of NATO enlargement since the end of the Cold War and represented a significant expansion of the alliance's membership into former Warsaw Pact countries. The process of NATO enlargement continued in subsequent years. In 2004, seven former communist bloc countries joined the defense alliance. Bulgaria, Estonia, Latvia, Lithuania, Romania, Slovakia, and Slovenia all joined. Additional rounds of expansion continued throughout the years. Montenegro officially became the 29th member of NATO on 5 June 2017, marking a strong NATO foothold in the Western Balkans. Sweden and Finland requested to join the alliance after the 24 February 2022 Russian invasion of Ukraine.

The decision to expand NATO eastwards was a result of American strategic considerations, a part of the Clinton administration's view as a means to promote stability, democracy, and security in Central and Eastern Europe. Clinton's leadership was instrumental in initiating and implementing the first round of NATO enlargement in 1999. Madeleine Albright, the U.S. Ambassador to the United Nations and later Secretary of State, was a vocal advocate for NATO expansion.

She believed in the importance of integrating former Soviet bloc countries into Western institutions as a path of consolidating democratic reforms and enhancing regional security in these former Soviet states, benefiting Europe. However, several prominent individuals within the American establishment expressed their reservations. George F. Kennan, best known for his role in the strategic containment of the Soviet Union in shaping U.S. foreign policy during the Cold War, was against it. He believed that it was unnecessary, provocative, and risked alienating Russia. Henry Kissinger, former Secretary of State to President Nixon and President Gerald Ford, expressed skepticism. While not outright opposing enlargement, Kissinger raised concerns about Russia's security interests, emphasizing the need for a cooperative approach to European security that involved Russia as a partner. Brent Scowcroft, a respected foreign policy expert who served as National Security Advisor to Presidents Gerald Ford and George H.W. Bush, also questioned the decision. He cautioned that it could provoke a negative reaction from Russia and undermine stability in Europe. Zbigniew Brzezinski, a former National Security Advisor under President Jimmy Carter, expressed mixed views. While supportive of the principle of NATO enlargement as a means of promoting stability and democracy in Europe, he also warned against alienating Russia and advocated for measures to address Russia's security concerns. Brzezinski emphasized the importance of engaging Russia in a constructive dialogue to build a cooperative security framework in Europe.

NATO, as Putin saw it, was the arm of the United States. It was not Berlin nor Paris but Washington that wanted Ukraine as part of NATO. Ukraine had expressed its interest in joining the alliance as far back as 1991. Within the first decade, Ukraine's prospects appeared promising. The country engaged in several rounds of talks, joined the Partnership for Peace program, participated in NATO's Planning and Review Process, and established the joint NATO-Ukraine Commission in 1998, bringing it close to NATO membership. However, the subsequent decade saw little to no progress. Then came the 2008 Bucharest Summit, when the roadmap for Ukraine to become a NATO member was brought to the table. Supporters of Ukraine's President Viktor Yushchenko had little to no interest in joining a military alliance; their priority was geared toward membership to the economically prosperous European Union (EU). Since the February 2014 Russian annexation of Crimea, the sentiment to join NATO has gone through a thorough U-turn. The majority of Ukrainians want to join a pro-West military alliance. On 30 September 2022, Ukraine formally applied to join NATO.

Putin's objections to Ukraine's NATO membership became more pronounced following the 21 November 2004 Orange Revolution. Europe was deaf to the peaceful protests of that winter, and America had little interest. It was the first sign of troubles within Ukraine, where a Russian-speaking population of the country's east first came to international attention. They were backed by the Kremlin against a larger, younger, Ukrainian population that saw their futures not in Moscow but in Berlin, London, New York, and Paris. Ukraine's media too, broke the shackles of Soviet-era censorship and became fiercely independent to produce a new defiant form of journalism. The darker threats around this episode marked the beginning of Putin's strong suspicion that the West was interfering in Russia's own neighborhood.

The election of a pro-West Viktor Yushchenko at the conclusion of the Orange Revolution brought the start of a war against the West. As part of its "Russia First" policy, the first since the Brezhnev era (1964-82), the Kremlin launched the first Russian-owned English-speaking channel, Russia Today (RT). It was the arm to fight the information war with hostility against the West. Most importantly, it carried an anti-Western messaging platform to give political life to those who were nostalgic for the Soviet era against the West's capitalism and democracy propaganda. Russia Today was only the beginning of a slow progression to authority and continuity with the Soviet past, galvanizing other strategically important European and Central Asian states to look the other way of its former communist-era crimes and focus on a future with Russia.

The 2004 Orange Revolution also paved the way for increased suppression. Domestically, the Kremlin began to crack down on any group or opposition to Putin. It targeted NGOs with ties to the West as "foreign agents." Within Russia, it created youth groups that mirrored the actions of the historical National Socialist German Workers' Party in "Putin's Youth" called Nashi.

By 2007, Russia continued to benefit from high global oil and gas prices, leading to strong economic growth and increased government revenues. The economic prosperity, coupled with domestic and energy policies aimed at stabilizing the Russian economy after the tumultuous, barren 1990s, helped to bolster Putin's popularity among many Europeans and Russians. Feeling secure, the Russian President no longer needed the West. Putin's 2007 Munich speech indicated Russia was back.

When it came to Ukraine, after the 2014 Revolution of Dignity, Putin was confident that as the United States and its allies conducted themselves in former Soviet client states like Syria, they were similarly going to meddle in Ukraine.

Putin viewed Ukraine's pursuit of NATO membership as the cardinal excuse after winning his rigged 2012 Russian Presidential election. The 2014 EU deal with Ukraine brought the urgency right to his doorstep, threatening the Kremlin's economic interest. By invading the only former Soviet state that had historical and biblical links between "Mother Russia" and the present Russia, which also had the longest border to industrial Russian areas, Putin hoped to galvanize his supporters who longed nostalgically for the past. NATO provided the larger excuse to undermine regional stability and security, but there was no way a defensive alliance was any threat to a much larger, military-capable Russia. NATO was the excuse, Ukraine was the target, and the message to the West was, this is Russia's, not yours.

"The collapse of the Soviet Union was the greatest geopolitical catastrophe of the century," a statement from Putin's annual address to the Federal Assembly of Russia in April 2005. It is an accurate assessment of how Putin sees the West. It is also an indication of what the Russian President witnessed during his time in East Germany (GDR). An outcome of American victory over the Soviet Union, followed by subsequent events in former Soviet states in the 21st century in replacing former Soviet strongmen with American proxies.

In Georgia, the 2003 Rose Revolution overthrew President Eduard Shevardnadze's government and the rise of American-educated Mikheil Saakashvili as President. In Kyrgyzstan, the 2005 Revolution led to the ousting of the Soviet-era President Askar Akayev. In Moldova, the 2009 Revolution led to the ousting of the communist government and the election of a pro-European coalition. Ukraine was Putin's red line. In 2014, when Putin's ally, Victor Yanukovych was no longer in power in Ukraine, Russian forces invaded Crimea in

February, an act that he may have implemented after the conclusion of the 2004 Orange Revolution. Nonetheless, 2004 was still a year when Putin wanted to improve his relations with the West and grow the Russian economy after nearly a decade of stagnation. A military invasion of Ukraine in 2004 would have likely led to heightened tensions with the United States, something he could not afford to do at the time. However, since the successes of Russia's interventions in Georgia in 2008, Syria in 2015, Libya in 2022, and America's exit from Iraq in 2011 and Afghanistan in 2021, Putin found confidence.

Only days before the Russian 2024 Presidential elections, France's President Emmanuel Macron had made the case that sending Western troops to Ukraine should not be ruled out. As Putin secured a fifth term in office, it is almost certain that the war in Ukraine will see escalations in what looks to be catastrophic consequences with neither side backing down. Putin's "red line," and a potential nuclear response, is a danger the West cannot ignore.

Putin's threats are as misaligned as the hypocrisy of his own election credentials. His main opponent, 46-year-old Alexei Navalny, had died at Yamalo-Nenets prison in Western Siberia. His Central Election Commission (CEC) rejected the candidacies of Sergey Malinkovich (Communists of Russia) and Boris Nadezhdin (Civic Initiative), the only candidate who made ending the Ukraine war his chief campaign pledge. The CEC approved Duma representatives Vladislav Davankov, Leonid Slutsky, and Nikolay Kharitonov, all of whom combined, produced votes accumulating less than 14% compared to that of Putin.

For Putin, America is the laughing stock for elections, with a highly polarized electorate, presenting Russia, in contrast, orderly and stable. He may concede that Russia's elections are not democratic, but he believes Russians approve of him.

Beyond electoral approval, Putin's election result shows that without an unlikely Russian revolution, the Russian war in Ukraine will continue for years, maybe even decades. Ukraine can't win the war outright without extensive manpower and Western support, but a victory for Russia is also unlikely.

Only four days after Putin's election victory on 21 March 2024, Kyiv experienced numerous overnight blasts across the city. Falling debris came down as the residential buildings were hit. In estimates,

11 strategic bombers and close to 31 Russian missiles with separate drones descended in waves, unseen in Ukraine for the previous 44 days. The city's population took shelter at the Kyiv Metro as Ukraine's air defense tried to shield off the Russian assault. The worrying factor was many cruise ballistic missiles and also a Kh-47M2 Kinzhal hypersonic missile, referred to as the "Dagger," which is very difficult to intercept, descended into Ukraine.

Fortunately, many were intercepted, but Kyiv was damaged. Businesses, power infrastructure, a few injuries, including two children, and the destruction of buildings were a fearful awakening.

It is a Russian retaliation to the attacks on Belgorod Oblast, a region bordering Ukraine to the northeast. Already, fighting was intensifying, where heavy bombardment and shelling were ongoing, but it was particularly affecting the Russian Belgorod areas, where evacuation measures had to be taken. Schools in nearby areas had to be closed, and homes were destroyed as Russian forces struggled to defend. In the 2024 Russian Presidential election, Belgorod Oblast voted 90.66% for Putin, and he quickly responded.

"There is a lot to do and we will do everything which depends on us," he said at a televised meeting at the Kremlin. "Of course, the primary task is to ensure safety. There are different ways to do this. They are not easy, but we will do it."

Previously, Ukrainian attacks have remained confined to Russian oil facilities to disrupt the Kremlin's main cash flow. Belgorod was not alone; Engels, a port city in the Saratov Oblast, located on the Volga River in Ukraine's east, witnessed similar attacks. It is home to a Russian air base for strategic bombers.

Six months of delayed Western aid has shown European leaders that their most reliable ally, the United States, also has limits. Russian forces made advances during those months. When the aid finally reaches Ukraine, there is hope that Ukraine's forces can push the Russians back. Most Western military analysts believe that American aid will only strengthen Ukraine's defense posture, but there is also a dangerous ticking clock. The issue of delay in reality, may very well have given Russia what it wanted: enough time to advance and occupy more Ukrainian territories. Europe too, will have to speed up in supplying Ukraine with air defense systems and financial support. The awful reality is Ukrainians have no choice but to remain quiet as forces out of their control determine their fate. It is a horrible feeling that Ukraine's allies are doing too little, and are unaware of the consequences on the Ukrainian population.

When the American aid was still debated, Prime Minister Petr Fiala's Center-right Conservative Eurosceptic Czech government provided the much-needed 300,000 artillery shells. However, Ukraine won't receive them until June of 2024. It is a Ukranian frustration that is all too visible. The reality is Ukraine is dependent on aid against Russian attacks at its front line. Its fortifications are going to include anti-tank obstacles, trenches, and minefields. Ukraine needs its own military-industrial complex. Without it, will be forced to make concessions. As a consequence, Ukrainian forces will have to continue to be on the defensive mode when additional Western aid fails to arrive on time.

Kupiansk, an important city known for its railroad junction in the Kharkiv Oblast in eastern Ukraine, was first occupied in February 2022 when the Russian invasion of Ukraine began. Most of the city has been destroyed even though it was liberated by Ukrainian forces after nearly six months. Locals are preparing for the threat of an upcoming Russian attack as air raid sirens are part of daily life. The city's hospitals are staffed by limited numbers of doctors who have remained to carry out the exhaustive regular tasks. The few inhabitants who remain are looking to leave if the fighting intensifies.

In early 2024, Russian forces shelled nearby areas, causing inhabitants to flee. In Hrakove, a village in Kharkiv Oblast, there is a sight of large ruins. There is a fear that other Ukrainian villages will meet a similar fate. Shops, houses, and schools have been flattened and have remained so since February 2022. The only building that glows is the golden dome, but just barely. Inhabitants live in dire conditions, either in basements or in shattered buildings. Russian forces left the area in September 2022 as a result of Ukraine's counteroffensive. The prospect of another Russian occupation still unleashes fears among the neighboring towns and villages.

Under the first Russian occupation, windows were shattered, and filthy food packets remained scattered. Refrigerators and TVs were stolen. Ukrainians were regularly searched, and their mobile phones were often checked for anything anti-Russian. It was later revealed that Russian forces were aggressively searching for any evidence that might give away their positions. Mass arrests, killings, shootings, and abductions continued. Large amounts of trash and destroyed roads are a common sight. Shortage of food and water is a persistent problem, and only now much of it is delivered from outside areas.

As the details of conditions in Russian-occupied areas became known, the Baltic states and Poland, a key group of Ukrainian allies, became significantly alarmed. Their support for Ukraine may very well be the reason why Russian forces may never take Kyiv. Previously, areas that Russian forces occupied and lost quickly now will be harder to take on, especially with support from these states, but Ukraine still has to deal with internal problems.

President Zelenskyy's government has struggled to raise significant combat numbers and secure additional future aid. Failure on these two urgencies, will lead to difficulties for Ukraine's forces to defend.

2022 and 2023 were the hard years for the Russian army, but they learned their lessons. In 2024, there is an increase in Russian combat numbers. The ratio of 6:1 favoring Russia and with a much greater supply lines will produce better results than previous years, but a lot of that remains to be seen after the summer of 2024.

Ukraine is also captive to the results of the June 2024 European parliamentary elections and the November 2024 American elections. In the interim, Ukraine's forces will have no choice but to conduct themselves more defensively as they endure Russian assault.

Putin has already bid his time and waited for the Western appetite to arm Ukraine to weaken. The war has taken a heavy toll on the Russian treasury, but it has found ways to sustain itself. The "special military operation" has drained its economic and military resources while also fueling domestic social tensions, forcing the Kremlin to ruthlessly crack down on dissent. In 2023 summer, Putin faced the most serious challenge to his authority when the Wagner Group chief Yevgeny Prigozhin ordered his troops to march on to Moscow to oust top military leaders. The brief mutiny ended with a deal for Prigozhin, to move to Belarus. His death in a suspicious plane crash two months later was widely seen as Putin doesn't tolerate rebellion among the ranks. Prigozhin's death shored up the Russian President's authority and cemented loyalty among the elite, but the episode showed a key fragility: all layers of power are channeled to Putin.

Russia has already sown the seeds of an internal crisis against

Ukraine's main backer, the United States. During the 2016 American presidential election, the Russian security services conducted a campaign to interfere with the electoral process and influence the outcome of the election in favor of then-candidate Donald Trump, which will give Putin some leverage should the former President win in 2024 November.

The psychological dynamic is what the Kremlin uses to sway American leaders through their propaganda, to convince Ukraine's supporters that the Ukrainians can't do it alone, that they are corrupt, divided, and Western-backed sanctions are only hurting Europe and the United States, not Russia. This propaganda has worked in limited terms.

Already, there are American politicians that are advocating and producing materials that come directly from Russian propaganda sites, calling Ukrainians "Nazis" and using similar language of the Kremlin. There are elements within the American political establishment that have moved into a space where, in their public debates, the Russian disinformation has found credibility. For instance, a fake news article, debunked by AP, was released on President Zelenskyy purchasing two multimillion-dollar yachts despite the devastating conflict.

To nullify the Russian disinformation requires persistence from Western politicians who believe in Ukraine. For instance, Ukraine's aid only came to the Congress floor for a vote after several consultations with British and European leaders with former President Trump. Only after he had given the green light that the situation produced a vote and then approval in Congress.

The absence of six months of American aid to Ukraine did not change the situation in the Black Sea. It is where the Russians feel a serious blow to their war efforts. The Russian blockade has weakened as Ukraine's handful of small Navy vessels has sunk Russia's Black Sea Fleet flagship, the Moskva. It has liberated Snake Island, a strategic point, and continued to cause problems for Russia with its drone strikes on facilities in Russian-occupied Crimea.

Ukraine's marine drone fleet, with the help of British and French-supplied cruise missiles, caused damages to the Russian port of Novorossiysk in the eastern Black Sea. Additional successes followed in the destruction of a Russian submarine and a warship undergoing maintenance in Crimea's Sevastopol, the traditional home port of

Russia's Black Sea Fleet.

The attack on the Tsezar Kunikov was the second successful naval operation. Named after a Soviet Naval Infantry officer and with a history of successful operations in the 2008 Russia-Georgian War and the Syrian Civil War, it saw its end in February 2024, along with another high-profile ship, the Ivanovets, which also carried large missile cutters.

The Russian Navy has struggled to find success in the Black Sea's northwest and has forced a withdrawal of fleets from Crimea to safer Russian ports. As a result, the Russian army's logistics have become unsettled in Crimea and Ukraine's south. Today, Ukraine's Navy's success have led to the resumption of Ukrainian exports to the global markets, giving a valuable financial lifeline.

Where Ukraine is still vulnerable is in its land warfare. It has managed to defend itself with limited supplies of cruise missiles, but it will do far better after the Americans and Europeans deliver long-range missiles.

Under Western-backed sanctions, Russian finances have found new life. The Kremlin began using the price floor for oil sales, the lowest price at which oil can be sold by producers. When the cost of extracting and processing oil varies depending on the location and the method of extraction, producers typically aim to sell oil above their production costs to ensure profitability. For some producers, especially those with high production costs, there may be a de facto price floor determined by these costs. In some cases, a government may set a minimum price for oil sales through regulatory measures or production agreements among oil-producing nations (e.g. OPEC). These agreements may include production quotas or price targets aimed at stabilizing oil prices. Since oil prices are also influenced by global supply and demand dynamics, geopolitical factors, economic conditions, and other market forces play a role. While there may not be an official price floor set by governments, market conditions can create a de facto floor by discouraging producers from selling oil below certain price levels. When oil prices drop significantly, it may become economically unfeasible for producers to sell oil at such low prices. Instead, they may opt to store oil until prices recover, effectively establishing a de facto price floor determined by storage costs. This is what the Kremlin was patiently waiting for and now has nearly doubled its energy revenues. The decision to activate the price floor came after the price of Russia's crude fell due to tougher Western sanctions.

Western sanctions, however, set a price cap of $60 a barrel on Russian oil, which also helped keep a lid on prices and the Kremlin's oil revenues, but the imposed restrictions don't restrict anyone from buying as long as they don't use Western insurance and shipping services. To its benefit, the Kremlin managed to pivot to buyers in Africa, India, and China, managing to get around the Western-sanctioned price cap by using intermediaries to launder and sell its oil and gas.

The oil price cap influenced the foreign policies of both producing and consuming countries, leading to diplomatic efforts to secure favorable alliances with oil-producing countries. Conversely, oil-exporting countries like Russia used oil as a tool for forming strategic partnerships based on energy cooperation. This is where the United States fell uncomfortably at a direct confrontation with Russia.

As the United States gravitates slowly to the European obsession with keeping migrants out, Europe is witnessing another calamity. European far-right groups have found momentum in spreading Russian disinformation and carry attractive propaganda that supports narratives that influence public opinion. In extreme cases, they can seek to destabilize governments or create social unrest, which could indirectly affect policy toward Ukraine by diverting attention, something both American and European leaders are realizing. The war in Ukraine has surfaced ideological differences (e.g., democracy vs. authoritarianism), and that has heightened the need among pro-Ukrainian supporters to petition Western governments to back Ukraine beyond military support.

The consequences of six months of no military aid are resonating on the battlefield. In February 2024, Avdiivka, a city in Donetsk Oblast, in Ukraine's east, fell to Russian forces. Ukraine's east is becoming the epitome of a successful Russian resurgent advance, part of a shift on the battlefield, coming faster than previously predicted.

Like Avdiivka, many towns and villages are on route to the Russian advance. Ukraine's forces are in a state of defensive mode until American aid takes effect. The Kremlin has taken full advantage of the no-aid window until Ukraine is rearmed by the West. It has pushed Ukraine's line further southwest and now has a foothold in areas it can use for future campaigns.

Previous Russian advances meant the total destruction of Ukrainian cities, towns, and villages, and this time, it's no different. The problem with Ukrainian forces retreating in the hopes of saving boots on the ground may look like a temporary viable decision, but for the Russian advance, that is exactly what it wants. Russian pilots have provided significant assistance to the ground troops during the offensive. They placed glide bombs, munitions suited for specific areas, and precision air strikes. That is not to say they did not incur losses. Ukrainians have shot down some Sukhoi-34s and a Sukhoi-35 over Donetsk, more than one plane a day.

Russian aircover assisted troops entering Avdiivka along a railway line as it passed through relatively peaceful areas under disguise. The ploy led to a faster means of mobilizing large forces over long distances, bypassing potential obstacles such as rough terrains and congested road networks to ensure a steady enhancement for combat effectiveness. Russian forces will not be able to repeat the same formula in other areas that helped them capture Avdiivka. The city is located in close proximity to pro-Russian separatist forces, which would only mean that future Russian advances will be slow.

Dnipro, formerly known as Dnipropetrovsk, is a city in central Ukraine located on the Dnieper River. It is situated in the heart of Ukraine and serves as a major transportation hub along important east-west and north-south transport routes, including railroads and highways, making it a vital logistical center. Historically, the city has been an industrial powerhouse, particularly in heavy machinery, metallurgy, aerospace, and defense. It has been a center of trade, industry, and culture since ancient times, and its historical legacy adds to its strategic importance. The city's industrial infrastructure and capabilities make it strategically important for Ukraine's economy and defense sector. Controlling the city for the Russians would provide strategic defensive capabilities and logistical support for military operations. For a defensive Ukrainian army, halting the fall of Dnipropetrovsk should be a key priority. If Ukraine's forces lose the city, it will signal the first of irreversible consequences of the delay in American aid.

In the latter part of 2023, Ukrainian forces complained that there were not enough numbers to defend and not enough shells to use against the advancing Russian forces. Unverifiable reports claimed that during the siege, wounded Ukrainian soldiers were shot dead in cold blood by Russian forces.

President Zelenskyy may have to get used to more of this kind of outcome. He continues to put on a brave face, but he is at the mercy of his Western backers. Ukraine is finally getting American aid after six months, but even as those cheering in Congress for aid bill to pass, in April, Kharkiv, Ukraine's second-largest city faced a wide array of drone and missile strikes. To convert the grim scenario in the frontline and whether Ukraine will be able to change the shift in the battlefield is something many in Europe are looking at with extreme nervousness.

Chapter 1

VIGILANCE

2024 is a year when a majority of Europeans are pessimistic about a Ukrainian victory in the war. A survey from 12 European countries by the European Council on Foreign Relations says only 10% of respondents think that Ukraine can win, with 20% believing Russia to have the upper hand. 41%, however, want European leaders to pressure Ukraine to negotiate with Russia. There are two other important events that can play as key deciding factors: the results of the June 2024 European parliamentary elections and the November 2024 American elections. Europeans are also hesitant about who can backfill the American leadership role. The Americans are providing funds, material, and political leadership to support Ukraine and bring an international coalition of support, but who can match that in Europe if the political priorities change in 2025?

Pacifist Europe is also quarreling with inflation levels despite energy prices going back to pre-2022 levels. Europeans may not believe in Ukraine's military victory but also don't want to antagonize President Putin. That does not necessarily mean they want a Russian victory, far from it. There is a feeling that Europeans believe that the war will end in a negotiated political settlement, with a sizable portion of Ukraine's east occupied by Russia. The war has produced a stalemate so far, but recent developments show Russia gaining ground in very slow and limited expansions.

The war has shown Ukraine lacks the manpower and the funds,

while Russia lacks the strategic depth and logistics expertise. A deal on Russian terms is not something Ukrainians are willing to accept, and a surrender of Ukraine will not end Russia's "special military operation." Most importantly, Ukraine will not allow a permanent Russian takeover of their industrial rich areas of Donbas and Luhansk, as well as occupied Crimea, home to Ukraine's hydrocarbon resources and eighty percent of Ukraine's oil and gas deposits in the Black Sea.

Leaders in Brussels are hoping to include a "durable peace," mirroring what the Swiss government is working to bring together, a large coalition of countries as part of the peace between Russia and Ukraine. It hopes to recognize Ukraine's territorial integrity and political sovereignty, which are backed by the international community.

Negotiations after two years of war may appear challenging but it had begun from the very beginning of the war. Four days after the Russian invasion, on 28 February 2022, Russian and Ukrainian officials came together in Gomel, a city in Belarus, to start negotiating. Interactions continued for a month before being called off but what got the Russians to come to the table was their inability to take Kyiv.

Ukraine demanded that the Kremlin own its actions over war crimes and withdraw from all captured Ukrainian territory, including Crimea, and wanted war reparations. These were absolutely unacceptable for Putin, who instead wanted Ukraine to recognize Russian-annexed Crimea as a "permanent neutrality" status for Ukraine and autonomy for the Russian-occupied Ukraine's east and south. Putin's demands were unacceptable to President Volodymyr Zelenskyy. Despite the unwavering stances on both sides, talks continued, and after 2023 summer, it looked like Ukraine was willing to accept a key Kremlin demand, "neutrality" in its constitution.

Events however, took a different turn. On 10 March 2024, Belarus was no longer the setting of negotiations. The talks moved to Antalya, the Turkish seaside city with its extravagant hotels and non-stop entertainment. Chaired by Turkish Foreign Minister Mevlut Cavusogiu, it was a forum for the Russian and Ukrainian foreign ministers Sergey Lavrov and Dmytro Kuleba to meet for the first time since the war started, with a firm importance on humanitarian corridors. Ukraine claims the talks broke down over Russian commitments without expressed approval from Putin. The Russians claim Ukraine "devalued the existing negotiations." A few more unsuccessful rounds of talks continued until a breakthrough on 29 March. Ukraine put forth the Russian demand for neutrality and non-nuclear status in return for Russian security guarantees supported by China, Britain, and France. It also meant Ukraine would begin a 15-year negotiation over the status of Crimea. In return, Russia would "drastically reduce" military activity near Kyiv to "create the necessary conditions for further negotiations." After a successful Ukraine counter-offensive, the Russians withdrew from their offer on 29 March. On 17 June 2023, Putin waved a "peace agreement" before Russian TV cameras, claiming Ukraine "trashed" what was a Russian demand, among others, for "permanent neutrality."

The talks revealed that even during the ongoing war, both sides were willing to make some compromises. It was certainly a better development than the previous agreements brokered by France and Germany, known as the September 2014 Minsk I and Minsk II agreements related to occupied Crimea. It was facilitated by the Organization for Security and Co-operation in Europe (OSCE). The agreements were intended to give the Russian-occupied provinces a degree of autonomy within Ukraine.

Despite the ceasefire agreement, both Ukrainian forces and the separatists frequently violated the terms. The conflict continued with sporadic skirmishes and clashes. The OSCE was tasked with monitoring the ceasefire, but their mission was hampered by limited access to conflict zones and restricted movement, making it difficult to verify compliance. The Minsk I agreement had vague provisions and lacked clarity on several key issues, such as the precise boundaries of the buffer zone and the withdrawal of heavy weaponry. This vagueness led to different interpretations by the involved parties. There was a significant lack of trust between the Ukrainian government and the separatist forces, as well as between Russia and the West. This mistrust undermined the willingness of parties to fully commit to the agreement. Similar to Minsk I, the Minsk II agreement also saw numerous violations of the ceasefire from the outset. Fighting continued in strategic areas, particularly around Debaltseve, which was not explicitly mentioned in the agreement. There were no robust mechanisms to enforce compliance or penalize violations. The absence of a strong international peacekeeping force meant that breaches of the agreement went largely unchecked. Key provisions of the Minsk II agreement, such as the holding of local elections in the Donbas region under Ukrainian law and the restoration of control over the border to the Ukrainian government, were contentious. Disagreements over the sequencing and implementation of these steps led to a deadlock. The role of Russia was critical in the agreements. While Russia was a signatory and was expected to influence the separatists to adhere to the agreements, there were accusations that Russia continued to provide military support to the separatists, thus undermining the peace process. The agreements collapsed in 2015.

Two factors have plagued the present negotiations despite some success. One, the Russian atrocities conducted during the first months of the war in rapes, murders, massacres, looting, indiscriminate bombings, and excess war crimes. It was especially in Azovstal, Bucha, Borodianka, and Irpin, episodes which remain an open wound for the Zelenskyy government.

The second is a little more complicated. On 6 April 2022, then British Prime Minister Boris Johnson arrived in Kyiv to deliver Ukraine's President a message: That Putin should be "pressured" not negotiated with and Ukraine could sign an agreement with Russia but NATO won't. The British PM also promised Zelenskyy $130 million of military equipment and $500 million in financial aid.

Johnson would be ousted by September 2024 as PM by his Tory party, but more importantly, his message had no validation or endorsement from NATO powers. Ukraine could have had a peace deal, but how much Russia would honor such an agreement is questionable. Two years into the war, the decision to achieve peace looks unlikely between Putin and Zelenskyy.

What is even more evident is the Kremlin view that Ukraine's foreign policy is not compatible with Russia. President Putin still believes that the Kremlin owns Ukraine, even when Ukraine has moved far away from Russia's orbit of influence.

As talks continue, neither side has the capability to win this war outright militarily. Putin has been threatening to use nuclear bombs if NATO doesn't pull back, but NATO isn't pulling back. Before his recent election win, he told Rossiya-1 television and news agency RIA that Russia was technically ready for nuclear war. It was a response to the possibility of NATO sending troops to Ukraine. But he also said that there was "no need" for the use of nuclear weapons in Ukraine. His words did not bear the entire truth.

During the first months of the war, as Ukraine's forces were putting up a strong defense and pushing back Russian forces, there was a feeling in the United States that the Russian President may opt to use his nuclear arsenal under a state of what looked like a military defeat. The first such intelligence report arrived towards the end of the summer of 2022 and worried the Biden administration.

Ukrainian forces successfully moved to the south, and not only were thousands of Russian forces looking to face defeat, but their humiliation was going to go viral. A calculation was made in Washington that a Ukraine victory would ensure a Russian strike and response with nuclear weapons.

The target was the southern city of Kherson. The city was founded in 1778 by Grigory Potemkin, a Russian military leader and statesman, during the reign of Empress Catherine the Great. A strategic fortress with a naval base to secure Russian interests in the Black Sea and to facilitate trade with the Ottoman Empire, Kherson's importance hasn't dimmed in the modern day as an important military stronghold.

In the late 18th and early 19th centuries, Kherson experienced rapid growth and development as a major center of trade, shipbuilding, and agriculture, attracting settlers from various ethnic backgrounds, including Russians, Ukrainians, Greeks, Germans, and Jews, contributing to its cultural diversity.

During Soviet times, Kherson experienced significant upheaval and transformation, including Nazi occupation, destruction, and loss of life, but also contributed to the Soviet war effort through its strategic location and industrial capabilities. After the disbanding of the Soviet Union in 1991, Kherson became part of independent Ukraine. Putin wanted Kherson at any cost. Once Russian forces occupied it, he declared it was now part of Russia itself.

Kherson looked to be the first to witness the effects of a Russian nuclear attack. That October, Russia's defense minister, Sergei Shoigu, communicated to his counterparts in Paris, London, Ankara, and Washington, "concerned about possible provocations by Kyiv involving the use of a dirty bomb."

While everyone knew that the Ukrainians were not going to use a dirty bomb, Western leaders, through their intelligence assessments, understood the Russian pretext. The response to which they feared, especially as reports emerged of discussions of an actual use of a nuclear strike by the Kremlin. There was no verification of whether Russia was actually moving tactical nuclear weapons into place, but when reports of drills to practice the launch and use of tactical nuclear weapons emerged, the Biden administration used all channels available to reach out to those who could sway Putin. Indian Prime Minister Narendra Modi and Chinese President Xi Jinping proved to help reduce the tensions.

In December 2023, the President of Belarus, Aleksandr Lukashenko, made the announcement that Russia had moved short-range tactical nuclear weapons inside Belarus in October. Lukashenko clarified that it was meant to deter NATO-member Poland against possible attacks on his country.

Putin reiterated the use of nuclear weapons in the Kremlin's nuclear doctrine, which sets out the conditions under which it would use such a weapon: broadly, a response to an attack using nuclear or other weapons of mass destruction or the use of conventional weapons against Russia "when the very existence of the state is put under threat." His Russian generals are testing the waters in Estonia and Poland, looking to see how NATO responds.

The Kremlin is conducting the war without major allies but with a few rogue states like Belarus, Iran, and North Korea. Minsk and its surrounding areas allowed Russia to stage part of the Ukraine invasion, giving Russia the shortest possible land route to Kyiv. Tehran provided drones, and Pyongyang provided artillery shells, missiles, and other equipments. However, all these pariah states are embroiled in other conflicts of their own. Belarus has been subjected to European and international sanctions, primarily due to concerns over human rights abuses, democratic backsliding, and political repression under the leadership of President Lukashenko. He is criticized for his crackdown on opposition figures, journalists, and civil society activists, particularly following his own disputed presidential election in August 2020, which saw widespread protests amid allegations of electoral fraud. The European Union (EU), the United States, and other countries have imposed targeted sanctions on Belarusian officials deemed responsible for human rights violations, electoral fraud, and repression of dissent. These sanctions include travel bans, asset freezes, and restrictions on financial transactions. Additionally, Belarus has faced increased scrutiny and pressure from the international community following the forced diversion of a commercial flight in May 2021 to arrest journalist Roman Protasevich, which drew condemnation from European governments and led to further sanctions.

Iran is engaged in a post-shadow war status against Israel. North Korea has suspicious eyes on both South Korea and Japan. Russia's senior partner, China, has its hands full with its own economy, balancing its domestic economic demands and its challenges on the global stage.

Chinese President Xi Jinping has been a critical ally of Putin, and he has become one of Russia's largest trading partners. China has been instrumental in providing crucial supplies to Russia in a climate of Western-backed sanctions. There is a feeling that China wants to use Russia to enhance the value of its own currency, the Chinese Yuan, to dethrone the U.S. dollar as the world's reserve currency. China also wants to test some of its most lethal weapons through Russia as it cautiously and delicately takes steps to invade Taiwan.

For Russia, the more the demand for weapons becomes a factor, the less likely they are to get them from China. Beijing looks to be slowly calculating the timing of such a move as it treads carefully around Western-backed sanctions and shields its economy, which it desperately needs Washington's help to rebound.

Like Washington, Beijing too looks to be concerned with Russia's calculations on using nuclear weapons. Questions remain how well has the Kremlin serviced their stockpiles? Does it have the capability? And most importantly, how soon is it operational?

During the Cold War, a system of deterrence kept the priorities of the two nuclear powers in check. Today, there are more than two nuclear powers and fewer safeguards. The nuclear order, arms control, and treaties all have a scope to exercise limits and find options. If the 20th century marked disarmament, then the 21st century marked its end. Nuclear stockpiles are growing.

During the Cold War, it reached its peak at 70,000 as part of the arms race between the Soviet Union and the United States. More than 2,000 nuclear tests were conducted in the Soviet Union. The fear of retaliation prevented both the United States and the Soviet Union from pushing the button first, in what was called: "the mutually assured destruction."

There was a series of arms control treaties, including the 1968 Treaty on the Non-Proliferation of Nuclear Weapons (NPT), which entered into force in 1970. Its intent was to prevent the spread of nuclear weapons and promote peaceful uses of nuclear energy, resulting in two categories; nuclear-weapon states (NWS) and the other, non-nuclear-weapon states (NNWS). The treaty required the NWS to pursue disarmament while the NNWS agreed not to acquire nuclear weapons. Then came the Strategic Arms Limitation Talks (SALT I and II), signed in 1972, the first major treaty between the United States and the Soviet Union. Its aim to limit strategic nuclear arms. SALT II, signed in 1979, un-ratified by the U.S. Senate, aimed to further reduce strategic arms, but its provisions were largely observed by both parties. The Intermediate-Range Nuclear Forces Treaty (INF), signed in 1987 between the United States and the Soviet Union, eliminated ground-launched ballistic and cruise missiles with ranges between 500 and 5,500 kilometers. The treaty collapsed in 2019 due to mutual accusations of non-compliance. The Strategic Arms Reduction Treaty (START I, II, and New START), aimed to enhance global security, promote strategic stability, and reduce the risk of nuclear war. START I, signed in 1991, was the first treaty to reduce strategic nuclear arms between the two nuclear powers. START II, signed in 1993 but never ratified, aimed for deeper cuts. New START, signed by Russia in 2010 and extended in 2021, limits the number of deployed strategic nuclear warheads and delivery systems between the U.S. and Russia. The Comprehensive Nuclear Test Ban Treaty (CTBT), signed in 1996, banned all nuclear explosions for any purpose. While it has been signed by 185 countries and ratified by 170, it has not entered into force because some key countries, including the United States, China, and North Korea, have not ratified it. The Chemical Weapons Convention (CWC) entered into force in 1997, prohibits the development, production, stockpiling, and use of chemical weapons and requires their destruction. Crucially, the Biological Weapons Convention (BWC), signed in 1972 and entered into force in 1975, prohibited the development, production, and stockpiling of biological and toxin weapons. While it lacks verification mechanisms, it serves as a key norm against biological weapons. After the disbanding of the Soviet Union came massive disarmament, and massive numbers of nuclear warheads decreased.

Today, nine countries have nuclear weapons. Most keep the exact size of their arsenal secret, while the United States and Russia are still the big players. China's arsenal is much smaller but is steadily growing. Countries like India, Pakistan, France, and Britain have kept a limited inventory. Israel is believed to be one of those but has never officially confirmed its status, and North Korea has periodically tested its nuclear warheads. Under the current state, a new nuclear arms race has started.

By threatening to break the nuclear taboo, Putin is throwing the system of deterrence off-balance. In 2023, for the first time, Russia sent nuclear weapons outside of its own territory to store at a military depot in central Belarus. It was seen as a threat to NATO's eastern members, but Russia is believed to already have another set in Kaliningrad, at its western exclave. Kaliningrad would provide a similar reach over NATO territory, and the Belarus move is seen to heighten the temperature and make NATO feel that the risk of nuclear war is increasing. To deter Russia, NATO began rattling its own nuclear sabers. In Europe, only Britain and France have their own limited piles. There are still some 100 American nuclear warheads deployed to bases in Belgium, the Netherlands, Germany, Italy, and Turkey. Washington maintains control over the weapons, but in a conflict, the bombs would be mounted on host nation warplanes.

Now preparations are running high to put American nuclear missiles at a British airbase just 100 km northeast of London. The maneuvers initially began after Russia's annexation of Crimea in February 2014. The United States is also bringing nuclear submarines and bombers like the B-52 over Stockholm to Europe. The Americans are going further east and into areas where they didn't use to go before. In March 2023, an American B-52 bomber conducted maneuvers over Europe, heading towards St. Petersburg and turning around just before it got to Russian airspace. Previously, Russia conducted a similar exercise in 2021 over the Baltic Sea, turning around just before it got to NATO airspace.

In the past, the U.S. and Russia had at least notified each other in advance, but now that is not the case. There are no treaties that limit their bomber exercises. The New START Treaty did address such issues. It also kept the lid on the number of strategic nuclear weapons designed to build trust through verification and have Russia and the U.S. to reduce their stockpiles. The war in Ukraine changed all that. Russia suspended participation in the treaty.

In 2019, President Donald Trump took the U.S. out of the treaty, banning mid-range missiles between tactical and strategic weapons as he was unhappy that the treaty did not include U.S. rivals China and North Korea. It comes at a time when other countries are increasing their arsenal. Today, six out of the nine nuclear states are adding to their stockpiles. China is rapidly building up its own nuclear arsenal and modernizing, and so far, refusing to be engaged in arms control talks, arguing for parity with the United States and Russia.

China has built more than 100 new silos, consisting of storage and launching sites for Intercontinental Ballistic Missiles (ICBMs). Since the rise of Xi Jinping, China has doubled its nuclear inventory. It is estimated that the country now has around 500 warheads and is projected to grow further.

China has never explained why it is expanding its arsenal and how far it wants to go. Analysts believe Beijing considered its arsenal too vulnerable to an attack, which means the "mutually assured destruction" will be much harder with three players instead of two.

The old system of deterrence is beginning to falter. Getting levels under control will be even harder. There is no telling how a multi-factor nuclear arms control agreement can work. The salience of nuclear weapons and their value in the minds of military and political leaders is increasing. The circumstances also send a message to non-nuclear states. There are more countries in Asia, in the Middle East, and even in Europe thinking about whether they might need a nuclear weapons capability of their own. The new nuclear arms race is picking up speed and has very few rules to keep all players in check.

For Putin, nuclear weapons are an option but not the answer to destabilize the Zelenskyy government in Kyiv. That would be very hard to do, given how Ukraine's intelligence agencies have maneuvered security around their capital. Putin knows he cannot install another proxy like Viktor Yanukovych. Having gone through a few rounds previously, even a pro-Russian government in Kyiv will be limited in what it can do for the Kremlin. Dangerously, time is still on the side of the septuagenarian Putin.

Most analysts believe that a Putin successor is unlikely to continue the war. That is not necessarily true. A January 2024 survey showed that 63% of Russians support Putin's "special military operation" in Ukraine. What does this say?

Since Joseph Stalin, every Soviet leader, including Boris Yeltsin and Putin, has had a deep political vein linked to Ukraine. Stalin saw Ukraine as an agricultural breadbasket and its fertile soil and favorable climate for his plans to industrialize his Soviet Union. Ukraine produced wheat, barley, and maize, and controlling those productions allowed the Soviet dictator to ensure a stable food supply for his labor to industrialize. Ukraine also possessed valuable industrial resources, including coal, iron ore, and manganese. The Donbas region, in particular, was rich in coal and became a major center for steel production. The Ukrainian SSR (Soviet Socialist Republic) was one of the largest and most populous republics within the Soviet Union, making it strategically important for any Soviet leader to maintain centralized control from Moscow.

One figure Stalin was particularly wary of was Nikita Khrushchev. Khrushchev's father, Sergei, was employed in a number of positions in the Donbas. Khrushchev, though born in the Russian Kursk Oblast on 15 April 1894 (6.8 miles east of Ukraine's border), had Ukrainian parents. He rose to become the First Secretary of the Communist Party of the Soviet Union (CPSU) and held leadership positions in the Ukrainian SSR, including serving as the First Secretary of the Communist Party of Ukraine (1938 to 1949). Khrushchev's tenure in Ukraine coincided with Stalin's Great Purges and Holodomor, a state-made famine facilitated by Stalin that resulted in the loss of approximately 3.9 million Ukrainian lives (*source:*Ukrainer). Khrushchev's Ukrainian background and his relatively moderate stance on certain issues made him a potential rival in Stalin's eyes. After Stalin's death in 1953, Khrushchev implemented significant reforms and pursued a policy of de-Stalinization, which included denouncing Stalin's cult of personality and acknowledging some of the atrocities committed during his rule. Khrushchev too, had a complex relationship with Ukraine throughout his political career.

He transferred the Crimean Peninsula from the Russian Soviet Federative Socialist Republic (RSFSR) to the Ukrainian Soviet Socialist Republic (Ukrainian SSR) in 1954. At the time of the transfer,

Crimea was heavily dependent on water, energy, and other resources supplied by Ukraine. By incorporating Crimea into the Ukrainian SSR, Khrushchev wanted to streamline administrative and economic management by consolidating these resources within a single republic. Political considerations of bolstering his own power base and gaining support from Ukrainian leaders in the early stages of his leadership also played a part in his decision. Some historians suggest Khrushchev's decision was motivated by a desire to leave a lasting legacy and assert his own influence on Soviet policy. By making a bold and unexpected move, Khrushchev aimed to distinguish himself as a visionary, willing to challenge conventional thinking within the Soviet hierarchy. His de-Stalinization efforts had significant implications for Ukraine, allowing for greater cultural and linguistic rights for Ukrainians. However, Khrushchev supported Stalin's regime and played a role in suppressing dissent and Ukrainian nationalism during his tenure. He cracked down on Ukrainian nationalists and continued to promote Russification policies in Ukraine, aiming to maintain centralized control from Moscow. In October 1964, during a closed session of the Central Committee of the CPSU, Khrushchev was confronted with a letter signed by several high-ranking party officials calling for his resignation. Prominent figures such as Leonid Brezhnev, Alexei Kosygin, and Nikolai Podgorny, among others, were dissatisfied with Khrushchev's leadership, his economic management and foreign policy. The discontented members of the Politburo and Central Committee saw the event as an opportunity to act collectively to remove him.

Facing pressure and fearing a potential coup, Khrushchev announced his retirement from the position of First Secretary of the CPSU and stepped down from all other official positions. On 14 October 1964, Khrushchev's petition for a "voluntary" retirement due to "advanced age and ill health" led to his political end. In retirement, he became depressed and then died of a heart attack on 11 September 1971.

Khrushchev's exit in 1964 paved the way for his successor, Leonid Brezhnev, to assume the leadership of the Soviet Union. Brezhnev, along with other members of the collective leadership, would go on to reverse many of Khrushchev's policies and consolidate their own power within the party and the state.

Brezhnev was born in then Yekaterinoslav on 19 December 1906 to a Ukrainian mother. His birthplace is an area comprising of Luhansk, Donetsk, Dnipropetrovsk, and Zaporizhzhia of modern Ukraine. Like all other Soviet officials of his generation, he maintained tight political control over Ukraine. Like his predecessors, Brezhnev promoted Russification policies in Ukraine aimed at fostering cultural assimilation and strengthening ties with the Russian-speaking population. Russian was promoted as the lingua franca of the Soviet Union, and Ukrainians faced pressure to assimilate into the broader Soviet identity.

For more than a decade, the Ukrainian SSR received significant Soviet investments in heavy industry, agriculture, and infrastructure. Industrial centers such as Donetsk, Dnipropetrovsk, and Kharkiv were further developed, solidifying the republic's role as a major industrial hub. Until 1973, the Soviet Union made strides in technological innovation, particularly in sectors like space exploration, defense, and nuclear energy. It had a large and relatively well-educated workforce, which contributed to its industrial output. Investments in education and training programs (initiated during the Khrushchev era) helped to expand the skilled labor force, driving productivity gains in key sectors of the economy. The Soviet Union was rich in natural resources, including oil, natural gas, coal, and minerals. The exploitation of these resources provided a significant source of revenue and contributed to economic growth during this period. Despite its inefficiencies, the centrally planned economy allowed for rapid mobilization of resources towards strategic priorities, such as heavy industry and defense. It was also helped by the global economy, which had been relatively stable since the 1960s, with a strong demand for Soviet exports, particularly energy and raw materials. The external demand provided a favorable environment for Soviet economic growth and contributed to increased revenues from exports.

Brezhnev's leadership also saw an "Era of Stagnation." Many historians believe the Soviet stagnation actually began in 1962 during Khrushchev's reign. Others consider 1973 to be the starting point of economic problems that continued to advance until the Soviet Union disbanded in 1991.

By 1973, the Soviet economy began to show signs of slowing down. The period of rapid industrial growth experienced in the 1950s and

1960s had tapered off, and the Soviet economy started to suffer from inefficiency, lack of innovation, and a heavy reliance on extensive rather than intensive growth.

The 1973 oil crisis temporarily masked some of the Soviet economic issues as high oil prices boosted Soviet revenues from oil exports. This also led to complacency and a lack of necessary economic reforms, exacerbating long-term structural problems in the economy.

The central planning system, which had driven Soviet industrialization, became increasingly unwieldy and ineffective. The bureaucratic nature of the planned economy stifled innovation and productivity. The lack of incentives for individual and enterprise-level efficiency further contributed to the weakening of the economy.

By 1980, the Soviet leadership became increasingly gerontocratic, with aging leaders clinging to power and resisting change. Corruption and nepotism became widespread within the Communist party and government institutions.

On 10 November 1982, Brezhnev died of a heart attack, making way for Yuri Andropov as the new General Secretary of the Communist Party of the Soviet Union (CPSU). Andropov's time was relatively brief, lasting from November 1982 until his death in February 1984. At the time, the Soviet Union faced significant economic challenges, including stagnation, inefficiency, and a growing budget deficit. These economic difficulties also affected Ukraine, which struggled with issues such as industrial inefficiency, agricultural problems, and environmental degradation.

His successor, Konstantin Chernenko, also had Ukrainian parents and served a shorter time than his predecessor, lasting from February 1984 until his death in March 1985.

Chernenko's successor, Mikhail Gorbachev, decentralized power within the Soviet Union and gave more autonomy to its constituent republics, including Ukraine. As a result, a more assertive Ukrainian national identity emerged with increased demands for greater political and economic autonomy. Ukrainian intellectuals, activists, and politicians began to openly advocate for greater autonomy and independence from Moscow.

The positive aspects of the movement were overshadowed by the tragic Chornobyl nuclear disaster in April 1986. The catastrophic nuclear accident at the Chernobyl Nuclear Power Plant near the town of Pripyat, in the north of the Ukrainian SSR, is considered one of the most frightening episodes in history. The incident involved a combination of reactor design flaws and operator errors, which led to an uncontrolled nuclear reaction. A sudden power surge caused a series of explosions, resulting in a fire that sent a massive plume of radioactive isotopes into the atmosphere.

The mishandling of the disaster highlighted the shortcomings of the Soviet system and raised questions about the transparency and effectiveness of Soviet governance. The aftermath of the disaster had significant environmental, health, and economic consequences for Ukrainians and contributed to growing discontent with the Soviet regime.

In August 1991, a group of hardline communists staged a coup against Gorbachev in Moscow. By this time, a key rivalry emerged that would forever change the course of the Soviet Union. Gorbachev, as the General Secretary of the Communist Party of the Soviet Union (CPSU), sought to modernize and revitalize the Soviet Union, but he also aimed to preserve its territorial integrity and socialist system. In contrast, his rival Boris Yeltsin, the President of the Russian Soviet Federative Socialist Republic (RSFSR), advocated for more radical reforms and a better version of a centralized economy.

As Gorbachev's reforms progressed, Yeltsin emerged as a rival, challenging Gorbachev's authority and advocating for greater autonomy for the Russian republic. Yeltsin's outspoken criticism of Gorbachev's leadership and his calls for greater democratization and sovereignty for Russia placed him at odds with the Soviet leadership. Their rivalry came to a head during the August 1991 attempted coup. Yeltsin famously stood on a tank in Moscow to resist the coup attempt and rallied public support for the defense of democratic institutions. His defiance and leadership during the crisis bolstered his popularity and weakened Gorbachev's authority, ultimately contributing to the collapse of the coup and further undermining Gorbachev's position.

To destroy Gorbachev's authority completely, Yeltsin signed the Belavezha Accords on 8 December 1991, along with the leaders of Belarus (Stanislav Shushkevich) and Ukraine (Leonid Kravchuk), which effectively disbanded the Soviet Union and established the Commonwealth of Independent States (CIS). Ukraine had already declared its independence from the Soviet Union on 24 August 1991, following a referendum in which the majority of Ukrainians voted in favor of independence. It set off a domino effect in the Baltics and other Soviet republics.

Yeltsin became the first Russian leader to vocally advocate for the sovereignty and independence of Ukraine from the Soviet Union. During his Presidency, he recognized Ukraine's independence and established diplomatic relations with the newly formed Ukrainian state. However, despite his overtures, relations between Russia and Ukraine were strained. Disputes over issues such as territorial boundaries, economic cooperation, language rights, historical narratives, and cultural heritage of the Russian-speaking population in Ukraine's east contributed to tensions. Yeltsin's efforts to maintain Russian influence in the post-Soviet era sometimes clashed with Ukraine's desire to assert its own sovereignty and pursue its own independent foreign policy objectives. In response, Yeltsin sought to promote economic cooperation, recognizing the importance of bilateral trade and economic ties. However, the transition from a centrally planned economy to a market-oriented system in both countries was fraught with challenges. Disagreements over energy prices, trade tariffs, and debt obligations continued to be a stumbling block.

Yeltsin made official visits to Kyiv and other Ukrainian cities, intended to strengthen ties between Russia and Ukraine to demonstrate goodwill, but the reality dictated otherwise. Economics and politics did not tie Kyiv and Moscow together, but what did was religion.

Kyiv, in Russian textbooks, is called "the mother of Russia" as the birthplace of Russian Orthodox Christianity. This was created by the Varangians, a group of Norse warriors, traders, and adventurers who were active during the Viking Age, roughly from the late 8th century to the mid-11th century, primarily from what is modern-day Sweden, Norway, and Denmark. The Varangians had seafaring skills and the willingness to travel great distances in search of trade, plunder, or employment as mercenaries. They traveled along the Dnieper, Volga, and Dniester rivers, establishing trade routes and settlements. One of their most significant ventures was the establishment of the Kyivan Rus', a federation of Slavic and Norse peoples in modern-day Kyiv.

According to some historical accounts, the Varangian warrior Rurik is said to have founded the first ruling dynasty of Kyivan Rus' in the late 9th century. He converted to Orthodox Christianity with the assistance of Byzantines. His followers later expanded their population centers in what is today Belarus and Russia, creating a state centered on the surrounding areas of Kyiv. They based their architecture on Byzantine art in Christian structures. For instance, the Saint Sophia's Cathedral in Kyiv during the reign of Grand Prince Yaroslav the Wise in the 11th century rivaled the Hagia Sophia and the Golden Gate in then Constantinople, as well as the Monastery of the Caves (also known as the Kievo-Pecherska Lavra, located on the banks of the Dniepro River). These architectures spread Christian Orthodox across the Slavic north.

In Novgorod, there was another Saint Sophia's Cathedral built by Prince Vladimir. The exact date of its construction is uncertain, with estimates ranging from the late 10th to 11th century. Vladimir was a member of the Rurikids dynasty and is sometimes referred to as Vladimir the Great. He was known for the Orthodox Christianization of the Kyivan Rus. Despite everything else that was to come in Ukraine's history, it is the Orthodox church that has survived and has had an ecumenical relationship between populations in modern-day Moscow and Kyiv.

After the death of Yaroslav the Wise in 1054, the Kyivan Rus experienced a period of political fragmentation as power struggles ensued among his descendants. It led to the division of several principalities, weakening the centralized authority of Kyiv. The Mongol invasion in 1223, which defeated a coalition of Kyivan Rus' forces at the Battle of Kalka River, further destroyed Kyivan Rus.

Within two decades, the Mongol Batu Khan devastated major cities, including Kyiv, leading to loss of life and the decline in the city's trade routes that were disrupted, and their agricultural lands devastated. The imposition of tribute payments to the Mongol overlords further strained the economy. Within the principalities, princely feuds and power struggles undermined political stability, contributing to the overall decline of the Kyiv state.

The rise of the Grand Duchy of Lithuania and the emergence of the Moscow state by Prince Yuri Dolgorukiy, who is credited with establishing the city in 1147, further fragmented economic and political dynamics in Kyivan Rus.

Throughout its history, Russia has had several capitals due to shifts in political power and territorial expansion. Kyiv, Vladimir, and Moscow were all capitals during different periods. St. Petersburg too, was a capital under Tsar Peter the Great. It was founded in 1703 and became the new capital of the Russian empire in 1712 until the Bolsheviks in 1917 reverted back to Moscow as their capital.

Many Western journalists assert that President Putin's admiration of Peter the Great (1682-1725) and further say, that he is trying to emulate the Tsar's actions within his own reign. The Tsar was known for centralizing his control over all territories within the Russian Empire, implementing reforms that significantly reduced regional autonomy and brought extensive areas under direct imperial administration. However, he was notably cautious in his approach to the local powers governing the former Kyivan Rus territories. During his reign, his primary rivals included the Swedish Empire, which maintained a strong presence in the Baltics, and the Ottoman Empire, which controlled substantial portions of what is now Ukraine.

The Tsar made his mark in the 1721 Treaty of Nystad, ending the two-decades-long Great Northern War, caused mainly by the death of Charles XI of Sweden in 1697 and the ascension of the young and inexperienced Charles XII. Sensing an opportunity to weaken Sweden's dominance in Europe, a Denmark-Norway coalition with the Polish-Lithuanian Commonwealth, backed by Russia, defeated the powerful Swedish empire. Parts of the Baltic Sea, parts of modern-day Estonia and Latvia, the southeastern shore of modern-day Gulf of Finland stretching to the east, all were now under the firm control of Russia. The result of the war not only indirectly impacted the Polish-Lithuanian Commonwealth but changed the balance of power in Eastern Europe.

The Tsar was already supporting various factions within the Polish-Lithuanian Commonwealth (the empire that occupied most of the Kyivan Rus) to maintain influence over its internal affairs. Peter frequently intervened in the Commonwealth's politics to stabilize his preferred rulers (i.e., King Augustus II) to keep the Commonwealth as a buffer state against Western European powers and to prevent it from becoming a strong independent state that could threaten Russian interests. By the end of Peter's reign, the Polish-Lithuanian Commonwealth had become more dependent on Russia, setting the stage for further Russian influence and eventual partitions in the late 18th century. This is precisely what the Russian President is aiming to do in Ukraine.

For Putin, while Europe and the West served his purpose of rebuilding Russia after the reckless near-decade rule of his predecessor, Ukraine remained crucially sensitive for one key reason. The Russian Orthodox Church views the religious schism in Ukraine as a challenge to its political interests. The Moscow Patriarchate has historically supported Russian government policies, including its actions in Ukraine, such as the annexation of Crimea and involvement in the Donbas region. As a result, any shift in religious allegiance in Ukraine can be seen as part of a broader pro-Western, anti-Russian movement. This resonates to the Russian President. He has publicly spoken and has been photographed attending Russian Orthodox Christian services and participating in religious rituals, depicting the significant aspects of his public image and political identity, which is often emphasized in the role of Russian Orthodox Christianity in Russian culture and society. The Russian President portrays himself as a defender of traditional values. The public expressions of faith are also intertwined with political considerations and realities in Russia, where the Russian Orthodox Church holds significant influence. Putin's alignment with the church is critical to his popularity and legitimacy among conservatives, nationalists and Soviet-nostalgic segments of the Russian population. Russian nationalism often includes the idea of a greater Russian nation that encompasses Ukraine which emphasizes a version of history where Ukraine has always been a part of Russia, downplaying periods of Ukrainian independence and Ukraine's unique national identity.

During the Soviet era, Ukraine offered employment opportunities. It was home to several industrial centers, including cities like Kyiv, Kharkiv, Donetsk, Dnipropetrovsk, and Zaporizhzhia, which had jobs for Russians in steel production, machinery manufacturing, chemical production, and mining. Ukraine was also home to numerous universities, research institutes, and scientific centers that offered opportunities, part of a modernizing initiative that began during Khrushchev's reign.

The most prominent among them was the Taras Shevchenko National University of Kyiv, named after the famous Ukrainian poet and artist Taras Shevchenko. The university has a rich history dating back to its establishment in 1834, but there are also others. The Kharkiv National University, Lviv University, Odesa University, and Kharkiv Polytechnic Institute. Ukraine also offered a relatively high standard of living, with the exception of East Germany (GDR), compared to some other Soviet republics, with access to amenities such as healthcare, education, housing, and cultural institutions. While living conditions varied depending on location and socio-economic status, many Russians found Ukraine to be a comfortable and hospitable place to live and work. All that changed on 24 August 1991, when Ukrainians held a referendum in favor of independence.

The Kremlin narrative that Ukraine should have never been independent in the first place and that Ukraine belongs to Russia is a message that resonated with Soviet-era nostalgists. The Russian propaganda that Ukraine is actually attacking Russia at the behest of the West is indeed a false one, but many Russians are convinced that they are under attack.

The accusations of endangering the Russian-speaking population in Ukraine's east and that Ukraine's Jewish President is a Nazi, is a narrative that the Kremlin will not compromise on. Putin is very clear that he is not willing to negotiate with the Ukrainian President. But Zelenskyy's pacifist European backers would like the war to end as soon as possible on unrealistic terms. They are neglecting the root causes of it, which has very little to do with Ukraine and its desire to join NATO. Leaders in Europe continue to believe Putin's demand for de-Nazification, de-militarization, and neutral status of Ukraine would suit the Russian demands, but what about Ukrainians?

One factor that is hardly spoken about is the demands the Kremlin made to Washington through the American Secretary of State on 15 December 2021. They were draft agreements on security guarantees that included larger demands beyond Ukraine. The language of the document centered around former Soviet Republics returning to the Russian fold, and when it came to Ukraine, it was the Kremlin not Kyiv, would determine its priorities in economics and foreign policy. There are further Russian demands for the withdrawal of NATO troops from Europe's east and a ban on the deployment of nuclear weapons stationed in Europe. Russia also wanted a ban on further NATO enlargement, restrictions on military exercises, and further limitations on military presence in the former Soviet bloc, which would mean NATO would go back to December 1991 levels. In addition, Russia wanted Central Europe as a security buffer, but most importantly, wanted the withdrawal of the United States from Europe. The de facto understanding is that U.S. withdrawal would also mean the removal of American soldiers, nuclear weapons, and American economic and political links to Europe. If that happens, the Baltic states, Poland, Moldova, Romania and Ukraine, will all be defenseless.

Following the American withdrawal from Afghanistan and Iraq and maintaining a limited involvement in Syria, the Russians believed that the United States was retreating into isolationism after several decades in leading globalization. The Kremlin was convinced that the U.S. would not entertain another war. For additional assurance, on 4 February 2022, under the pretext of attending the Beijing Olympics, Putin visited China to seek support for his impending war on Ukraine. Beijing saw the Russian adventure in Ukraine in the prism of their own future in the Pacific. The Chinese equation looked more at how the war plays out in Europe which will determine the future of its own actions in Taiwan. China, like other countries are sympathetic to Russia's concerns of NATO. It has its own concerns with American allies in the Pacific. Geographically, Singapore, South Korea, Japan and Taiwan encircle China in the Pacific, although they do not pose any military threat.

Russia has always claimed that the enlargement of NATO to include among other former Soviet-bloc states has violated Russia's security apparatus; however, the problem is based on a Russian perspective, not International law. For instance, much of International law references the Vienna Document, an agreement aimed at fostering transparency and confidence-building measures among participating states in Europe regarding military activities. It was initially negotiated and adopted in 1990 as part of the Organization for Security and Co-operation in Europe (OSCE). The document outlines various provisions related to military transparency, notification of military activities, and conducting inspections among OSCE participating states. Its primary objectives include reducing the risk of military conflict, enhancing mutual trust, and promoting cooperation in security matters among OSCE members. Many articles include mutual trust and security, with measures that will increase the transparency of military actions, including holding unannounced military exercises, inviting observers to carry out mutual inspections, declarations of arms-level verification missions, and others.

The Russian perspective in the 21st century is that they have the right to prevent former Soviet bloc countries from joining Western military alliances, political and economic unions. The idea of a former Soviet bloc member having a strong military and a thriving economy supported by democratic institutions and elections is deeply troubling to Putin. In his view, it is a "security threat," but surely, even the Russian President realizes that NATO is not a real threat but a convenient excuse.

NATO was designed to defend against a Soviet threat. The Russian Federation, the successor, has now achieved a similar, perhaps even a better standing than the Soviet Union, something that was not previously envisioned by Europeans. Russia has broken some agreements with Europe and continues to take aggressive measures against some of the former members of the Soviet bloc. The Kremlin has demanded the right to waive some of its special commitments and certain regulations from European law in energy policy and its relations with specific central European countries. Under the pretext of defending "legitimate" Russian interests to preserve influence, Moscow is using convenient measures to make a stand against the West. Ukraine falls within this Russian equation. The Kremlin wants to subjugate Ukraine, the second-largest country in Europe by land area at approximately 603,500 square kilometers, and without control over this area, and its decisive link to Europe, Russia cannot fully consider itself, in its own terms, a great power.

Putin still believes that the key to the Russian annexation of Ukraine lies in the reduced support from Europe and the United States. When that happens, the Russian military will maneuver expansive operations into Ukraine. He further believes Europe and NATO will concede to Russian blackmail over their use of nuclear weapons. What the Russian President hasn't yet calculated is that Ukraine, at any price, is determined to withstand the Russian aggression.

Ukraine faces a complex and uncertain future as the ongoing conflict shows little sign of resolution. Both Moscow and Kyiv appear to lack strategic foresight on how to end the war, while key powers like the United States and China remain focused on their own internal priorities. There are three potential outcomes: One, Ukraine may have to cede some territory in exchange for peace. However, the critical question remains whether Ukrainians can trust Putin to honor such an agreement. Two, a decisive victory or complete collapse of one side, which currently seems improbable. Finally, the war could evolve into a protracted frozen conflict, similar to the situation between North and South Korea since 1953 and which always has the potential to get out of control and for Ukraine, similar realities may be a part of its future.

Chapter 2

CHANGE OF FORTUNES

In February 2024, Avdiivka in eastern Ukraine, near the separatist-controlled city of Donetsk in Ukraine's east, fell to Russian forces. The fall of the city is Russia's biggest gain since it captured the city of Bakhmut in May 2023. Avdiivka is strategically important due to its proximity to the Donetsk Filtration Station, which supplies water to both government-controlled and separatist-controlled areas.

After the failure of Ukraine to pierce Russian lines in 2023, Moscow has been trying to grind down Ukrainian forces just as Kyiv ponders new measures of mobilization. Avdiivka is a city that has seen a decade of conflict. President Joe Biden had warned that Avdiivka could fall to Russian forces because of ammunition shortages following months of Republican congressional opposition to a new U.S. military aid package for Kyiv. Now that has passed, it remains to be seen whether Ukraine's forces can take it back.

Capturing Avdiivka is likely to provide a morale boost for Russia. It is also another step towards securing the Kremlin's hold on the regional center of Donetsk. Ukraine's east is becoming the epitome of a successful Russian resurgence and the start of a permanent occupation. There is a shift on the battlefield and the change is coming faster than previously predicted.

Six months of no American aid has produced avoidable setbacks. Units in Ukraine's military have complained that they need ammunition, and this is particularly a concern in Ukraine's east, where Russian forces are gaining ground. Kharkiv and Sumy Oblast are under constant shelling and attacks. Large numbers of civilians have already died, and the rest need to be evacuated. These are huge challenges for the Zelenskyy government in defending its population, as he knows the lack of ammunition is affecting the morale of his men. His parliament is working on new legislation to mobilize more troops. However, there is another problem brewing. Unverified surveys show domestic solidarity in Ukraine is decreasing. The government is less trusted, and Ukrainians are getting tired of the war. It is also reflected in the volunteers on battlefields and those who are living under the constant toll of war. There is further doubt that after ten years of war against Russia, there will be signs of some fatigue among the ranks. To credit Ukraine's armed forces, they have done a fantastic job of limiting Russia's advances but Russia still occupies approximately 17% of rich, resourced industrial areas of Ukraine's east.

Unlike previous campaigns in Georgia and Syria, in Ukraine, the Russian Air Force has struggled. It is unable to assist ground forces without the assistance of separatists from the east. They have strained to take total control of the air and are unable to stop ammunition supplies coming in from Ukraine's ally, Poland. The air non-superiority has also fettered in the Black Sea, where nearly 30% of Russian ships are underwater, with the remaining having to pull back from Sevastopol in Crimea.

Ukraine's successful attacks on Russian oil and gas infrastructure are common occurrences. Almost every week, there is news of some attack on an installation. Nearly 10% of Russian infrastructure has already been hit and destroyed. The Western-backed sanctions on Russia may not have done enough to destroy the oil and gas industry, but they have had an effect on Russian railways. The sanctions limited the ability to procure spare parts, equipment, and technology necessary for the maintenance and upkeep of railway infrastructure, leading to deteriorating conditions of tracks, bridges, signaling systems, and rolling stock. Delays and cancellations of projects in improving efficiency have had an impact on the supply chain for critical components such as fuel, lubricants, and maintenance materials.

The successful Russian advance is a test of will for Ukrainian soldiers. Many reports on the war have indicated most Russian soldiers don't want to be in this war. Many that are dying on the battlefield are non-Russian mercenaries from abroad. The war has become an industrial competition. What Ukraine really needs is the $61 billion of American aid to kick in and fast so that Ukraine's forces can take on the Russian advance with Western technology and firepower.

Six months of lack of funding have had a significant impact on Ukraine's air defense systems. Kyiv had warned its Western allies that munitions for some of its air defense systems could end by March of 2024. The lack of air defense missiles had a significant effect on defending the urban centers.

Since the fall of 2022, Russia began to concentrate on its weapons based technology rather than place boots on the ground. A successful strike by a Soviet era S300 air defense system deployed in Donetsk Oblast on the early side of March 2023 further validated Russia's Defense Ministry's successful tactic in penetrating Ukrainian lines. In May 2024, President Putin removed Sergei Shoigu from his position as Defense Minister, a position he has held since 2012. Shoigu will now take a less prominent seat as Secretary of the Security Council of Russia, replacing the veteran KGB and FSB head, 72-year-old Nikolai Patrushev. For Russian military analysts, the removal of Shoigu had been in the works for some time. The early Russian military setback in Ukraine did start the clock to his dismissal, but what escalated his removal was how Shoigu's Russian Defense Ministry conducted itself as the war dragged on.

History dictates that changing the most senior general during a time of war is considered a move that will lead to consequences. It is, in effect, to cancel out the ongoing strategic plans of the war. Replacing a top general will disrupt ongoing operations, affecting the forces on the ground. A sudden change will make commanders and troops feel uncertain and affect their performance, especially in following orders.

Putin's actions have echoed in Russian history. At the outset of World War I, Grand Duke Nicholas Nikolaevich, uncle of Tsar Nicholas II, was appointed as the commander-in-chief of the Russian forces. He was a respected military leader and had previously served with distinction. However, the Russian army faced numerous difficulties, including logistical problems, shortages of supplies and munitions, and heavy casualties. By the summer of 1915, the situation for Russia on the Eastern front had become increasingly dire. The Russian army had suffered significant defeats, particularly in the Gorlice-Tarnów offensive, where the Central Powers, led by the

German Empire, achieved a decisive victory. The series of losses forced Russian forces to retreat from modern-day Polish areas, causing further instability and a crisis of confidence in the Russian military leadership. Under a state of military setbacks and growing domestic unrest, Tsar Nicholas II decided to take personal command of the Russian armed forces. On 23 August 1915, he relieved Grand Duke Nicholas Nikolaevich of his command. By assuming the role of commander-in-chief himself, Nicholas II hoped to change the tide of the war. The move created problems both domestically and on the Russian war front. The Tsar lacked military expertise and experience. His decision to take direct command did not lead to any substantial improvements. The Russian army continued to suffer heavy losses and faced serious logistical and organizational challenges. The most dire consequence of the decision was the weakening of the Tsarist regime. Nicholas II's inability to reverse the fortunes of war contributed to the February 1917 Revolution, which led to his abdication and the eventual collapse of his Romanov dynasty.

Putin may suffer a similar fate, but the change of direction after 51 months of war does show that the Russian President and his inner circle are unsatisfied with how the war is going. An escalation to change the type of war from a purely military one to an economic-military categorical campaign appears to be Putin's new preference.

Sergei Shoigu did not come up the ranks of the military. Raised by a Ukrainian-born Russian mother in the Tuvan Oblast, he graduated from the Krasnoyarsk Polytechnic Institute in 1977 with a civil engineering degree. He came to the attention of former Russian President Boris Yeltsin during his time in the state Construction Committee, a place where the former President too, made his name. Shoigu made his name at the Russian Ministry of Emergency Situations (EMERCOM). His success in managing numerous high-profile emergencies, such as earthquakes, floods, and large-scale industrial accidents, garnered him widespread acclaim. His leadership in the successful management of the aftermath of the 1995 Neftegorsk earthquake and various other natural disasters throughout the 1990s and 2000s proved his ability to coordinate swift and effective relief efforts. Putin gave him the defense portfolio in 2012 despite having no military background, which infuriated the Russian military establishment.

Under Putin, Russia has consistently maintained a civilian head of the military, eschewing the appointment of an active-duty general to this pivotal role. The strategic decision aligns with the broader principle of civilian control over the military, a concept traditionally aimed at ensuring that no single individual within the military establishment garners excessive power and influence. However, in the context of Putin's governance, this policy serves additional, nuanced purposes that bolster his own authority. By appointing a civilian as the head of the military, Putin effectively prevents any single general from amassing significant power. A move that mitigates the risk of a military leader developing a loyal following within the armed forces that could challenge or undermine Putin's authority. The dispersion of power within the military ensures that no general can leverage the institution as a personal power base. The appointment of a civilian leader fosters a degree of division within the military hierarchy. Different factions, often loyal to various leaders, create an environment where power is diffused. The internal division makes it difficult for any military leader to unify the armed forces under a single command that could potentially threaten the Russian President. Maintaining a civilian head of the military allows Putin to retain significant leverage over the institution. Civilian leaders, typically appointed due to their loyalty to Putin, act as intermediaries who ensure that the military remains aligned with the Kremlin's directives. The structure places the ultimate control firmly in Putin's hands, who can maneuver through these civilian appointees to exert influence over military affairs without direct military involvement. This tactic is crucial in a political system where power struggles and factionalism can lead to significant instability. Putin's ability to keep military leaders in check ensures his position remains unchallenged. A civilian head of the military acts as a balancing force within the Russian power structure. The role helps to maintain a balance between different state institutions, preventing the military from becoming an overpowering force that could dominate other aspects of governance.

Shoigu's predecessor also did not come from the military ranks. A trained economist, Anatoly Serdyukov's rise to the Russian Defense Ministry came from the personal relationship of his father-in-law, Viktor Zubkov, with President Putin. A chairman of Gazprom and later Prime Minister, Zubkov was seen as a potential Russian President in

2008. He was eventually bypassed, and the position went to Dmitry Medvedev. Serdyukov had made his name as the Minister of Taxes (2004-07), successfully having court decisions go in favor of his ministry, winning him many admirers in the Kremlin, especially Putin's aide, former KGB Viktor Ivanov.

Putin had appointed Serdyukov to fight bribery and incompetence in the Russian Armed Forces. However, from the beginning, tensions between prominent Russian generals soon consumed Serdyukov's time. Chief of the General Staff General Yuri Baluyevsky, who would go on to make a name for himself in military reform and modernization of the Russian military, particularly led a group of generals to force the inexperienced military chief, at the very least, to understand the Russian military. He proposed for the Russian Defense Minister to take "preparatory training," an episode that further created the heightened tensions Serdyukov had to endure. Less than nine months into his time in office, Serdyukov submitted his first of a few attempted resignations. Putin would not permit him. Serdyukov got his wish in 2012, not by falling on Putin's bad side, but rather on his father-in-law's. After discovering an adulterous affair, Zubkov urged Putin to fire Serdyukov. Twelve days later, in November 2012, Serdyukov was replaced by Sergei Shoigu.

Shoigu too, met a similar condition to his predecessor. Tensions between prominent Russian generals continued during his time in office. There have been instances of high-profile resignations and reassignments within the Russian military hierarchy that suggest underlying tensions. The most prominent among them was General Andrei Kartapolov. A senior Russian military officer with an extensive career in the Russian Armed Forces, including Deputy Chief of the General Staff and commander of the Western Military District, Kartapolov's resignation in 2021 came at a time of increased military activity and reform efforts within the Russian Armed Forces. While official reasons for his resignation were not detailed, it was widely speculated that internal disagreements and strategic differences played a role. As a key figure in Shoigu's reforms, particularly in overseeing the military's political and ideological education, Kartapolov's departure might have impacted the continuity and implementation of these reforms. It underscored the challenges Shoigu faced in maintaining cohesion and support among senior military leaders.

Following his resignation, Kartapolov transitioned to a political role, becoming a deputy in the State Duma (the lower house of the Russian parliament). At the end of 2021, he was appointed Chairman of the State Duma Defense Committee, where he continues to influence defense policy as a legislator.

Kartapolov was not alone, other generals too opposed Shoigu's approach to consolidating control over military decisions and centralizing command structures. This has occasionally led to tensions with generals who prefer more decentralized decision-making and greater autonomy in their respective areas of command. The real impact from smaller to bigger disagreements materialized in 2023.

Wagner mercenary chief Yevgeny Prigozhin had become furious with the way Shoigu and his generals conducted themselves in the Ukraine war. The mercenary group provided extensive resources to the Russian military, such as manpower, technology, and weapons. As the war went on, the group found itself neither commanding any campaigns nor leading any specific, small, or large operations. The war became a conflict of control between Wagner and the Russian Defense Ministry. Prigozhin called the Russian Defense Minister a "dirtbag" and an "elderly clown," a message that was very visible in news and social media outlets around the world. In June 2023, he was even more infuriated when Shoigu ordered his mercenaries to sign contracts with the military before 1 July, a move that would turn Wagner into a contracting sub-unit of the Russian military. The deaths of hundreds of mercenaries from the Wagner group, which Prigozhin accused the Russian armed forces, further escalated the rift. For Prigozhin, it was his red line.

At the end of June 2023, the Wagner group invaded and captured the Russian city of Rostov-on-Don. The area approximately 665 miles south of Moscow is a major transportation hub, with an airport, extensive railway, and river connections. Putin addressed the nation on state TV, calling the actions "treason" and promising "harsh steps" to confront the invaders. Prigozhin response was clear. His aim was not to remove the Russian President but his Defense Minister, including General Valery Gerasimov, the Chief of the General Staff and First Deputy Minister of Defence.

The confrontation came to some normalcy after Chief of the Presidential Administration of Russia Anton Vaino, Secretary of the

Security Council of Russia Nikolai Patrushev, the Russian ambassador to Belarus Boris Gryzlov, along with President Alexander Lukashenko of Belarus, mediated on behalf of Putin. Legal accusations of high treason were dropped, and in return, the Wagner Group halted its actions to take Moscow. For the first time, the episode reflected a threateningly true dissension within Putin's inner circle. Prigozhin was not just a Putin ally but had a close affiliation with the Russian President for nearly 32 years. During that period, he had risen from chef to commander of one of the influential arms of Russia. It was a blessing in disguise for Putin when Prigozhin died in a plane crash just two months later. Prigozhin had previously alleged that the invasion of Ukraine was designed to further the interests of elements within the Ministry of Defence and Russian oligarchs.

Prigozhin death produced a set of realities that Putin and the Kremlin could not ignore. Within a year, Deputy Defense Minister Timur Ivanov was arrested on corruption charges. The Anti-Corruption Foundation (ACF) accused Ivanov of profiting from construction projects in the Ukrainian port city of Mariupol, much of which was destroyed by Russian bombing in the months following the full-scale invasion of Ukraine. It was an indication that Ivanov took the fall of a behind-the-scenes scheme Shoigu's Defense Ministry was conducting behind the Kremlin's back.

The new Russian Defense Minister, 65-year-old Andrei Belousov, is not too different from the usual Putin choice. Like Putin, he is a devout Russian Orthodox with a passion for martial arts. A trained Keynesian Economist from Moscow State University, specializing in Economic cybernetics, a field that applies principles of science concerned with control and communication in complex systems to economic systems and processes. Almost a two-decade-long Putin ally, Belousov previously served for long tenures in the Ministry of Economic Development, as an aide to Putin during his time in the Presidential Administration, and as the First Deputy Prime Minister. The choice of Belousov is part of a re-direction in harmonizing the alignment between his Russian economy and the war in Ukraine, making Russia's economic policy similar to the 1980s Soviet Union. A similar change came in Ukraine.

Three months earlier, Ukraine's President Zelenskyy fired his top

General, Valerii Zaluzhnyi. A month later, Zaluzhnyi took up his new role as Ukraine's Ambassador to Britain. Military analysts believe it is a result of the failure of Ukraine's counter-offensives from June 2023 summer, an aim to push the Russian forces south to the Sea of Azov, splitting the invading forces into several splintering units and cutting the Russian land bridge to Crimea. The real reason for the General's dismissal appears to be in the differences between Zelenskyy's 2024 and 2022 aims, which are much different. The General and the President also had differences on whether Ukraine needed a mass mobilization effort. Zaluzhnyi wanted close to five hundred thousand new recruits, which Zelenskyy did not want to entertain such a politically divisive issue. The sacking of the top General appears to be a result of a clash of personalities rather than objectives on the battlefield. There is a feeling that President Zelenskyy did not want to enhance the spotlight on his General, who not only commands the allegiance of the armed forces but to some degree, encroaches on his own media spotlight. Zelenskyy is presiding past his term and not holding a due Presidential election in 2024, citing unsuitable conditions at a time of war. There is a feeling that among the Ukrainian electorate, the former General is more popular and favorable than the Ukrainian president, with some polls that support such realities.

General Zaluzhnyi had risen up from the military ranks in the post-Soviet era. He had made a name for himself in the conflict in Ukraine's east, serving as commander in the Donetsk People's Republic (DPR), a separatist entity in Ukraine. Zaluzhnyi has been reported to have held significant roles in military operations and strategic planning within the DPR forces, particularly during periods of intense conflict in the Donetsk region. In 2021, he was appointed army chief by the same President that sacked him. Zaluzhnyi led Ukraine's forces to flush out Russian forces from Kyiv in 2022 and took back much of the south and east of Russian-occupied areas. It looked like by 2023, Zaluzhnyi's forces would flush out more Russian troops from Ukraine's territories, but after six months of no American aid, without ammunition and manpower, success on the battlefield proved elusive.

Zaluzhnyi's replacement is 59-year-old General Oleksandr Syrskyi. A graduate of the elite Moscow Higher Military Command School, and unlike his predecessor, he served in Afghanistan, Tajikistan, and former Czechoslovakia under the Soviet army. Most recently, he has served as the Commander of Ukrainian Land Forces since 2019. Like Zaluzhnyi, he rose through the ranks of the Ukrainian armed forces and, similarly, fought Russian forces in the eastern Donbas region. During the 24 February 2022 Russian invasion, Syrskyi led the successful defense of Kyiv and the effective counter-offensive in Kharkiv. What is evident is that Syrskyi is less of a media personality than Zaluzhnyi, but whether he will be a better General for Ukraine is hard to predict, especially as Russia still occupies nearly 17% of Ukraine and is looking to consolidate key cities like Kharkiv and Zaporizhzhia. The change at the top of the military will have an impact on Ukraine as it defends with limited means.

As Ukraine struggles, its allies are conducting military exercises on their own, in preparation to aid Ukraine or for their own purposes. On 24 January 2024, Britain conducted joint drills at the North Sea. HMS Prince of Wales has been pictured leading a NATO Fleet as the alliance carries out its largest joint drills in decades. The Royal Navy aircraft carrier led 14 vessels through an exercise as part of the Nordic response to reinforce Europe's northern frontiers. The 65,000-ton ship was seen flanked by the American Destroyer USS Paul Ignacius and Spain's Esps Almiranti Juan Duon Frot as Swedish and Finnish fighters flew over, operating around Norway's fleet. The carrier strike group will practice defensive maneuvers and amphibious landings to recapture allied territory in a defensive exercise. It is the largest NATO exercise since the Cold War, bringing together more than 90,000 troops from all 32 NATO countries to train. NATO has decided to boost its capabilities in response to threats made by Putin to the Baltics. At the same time, NATO launched Steadfast Defender 24, scheduled to last until 31 May, bringing together some 990,000 troops from 32 NATO member-states and no fewer than 1,100 armored vehicles, including 166 battle tanks. The exercises take place mainly on the plains of Poland and Norway but also in Germany, the Baltic states, Romania, Finland, Slovakia, Greece, and Sweden. While these exercises are a ceremonial gesture of preparation to show that they are behind Ukraine, they are far from the realities of what Ukraine's soldiers are presently battling on the ground.

Germany, Ukraine's second largest backer, will provide a further €500 million as part of its aid package. It is mere pennies compared to what Ukraine actually needs to defend its positions which is becoming increasingly difficult as the odds stack up against them.

In Donetsk Oblast, Ukrainian soldiers are using multiple rocket launchers made from the Soviet era as part of their defense. There are a few grenades, but there have not been enough of them since the war began. In Kharkiv, civilians are building more fortifications against the advancing Russian forces who are heavily bombarding them.

Ukraine is also dealing with soldier burnout. The majority of its fighters have been fighting for more than two years, and some units have for almost a decade. They carry injuries; some have Post-Traumatic Stress Disorder (PTSD), depression, anxiety disorders, Traumatic Brain Injury (TBI), chronic pain, and physical disabilities. Soldiers are suffering from sleep disorders, chronic pain, and physical disabilities due to injuries sustained during combat, such as limb amputations, spinal cord injuries, and musculoskeletal injuries. There is a feeling that Ukraine's forces are exhausted at a time when new recruitment is badly needed.

Defense officials in Ukraine have described claims of corruption within its army recruitment as shameful and unacceptable. It comes after President Zelenskyy recently sacked every regional recruitment head after officials were accused of using intimidation and taking bribes. Previously, Ukraine's military wanted their citizens to give their details so they can be called on if needed. When some didn't, recruitments not only fell short but changed drastically.

Some Ukrainians are unhappy with how the army finds its soldiers. It is still like a Soviet-era recruitment process. Mobilization is why most men under the age of 60 can't leave Ukraine. Military officers hand out notices and order citizens to sign up. Ukraine is constantly trying to increase its combat numbers as thousands are killed on the battlefield. Demand for additional soldiers is not being met. There are big questions over how Ukraine calls up fighting-age men, with officials being accused of intimidation and helping some escape the country for cash. There are exemptions, including poor health, but not for just not wanting to fight. It is written in the Ukrainian constitution that all male citizens must fight during times of war. Among the young and others, there is a feeling that this is not in line with their values. Thousands have already tried to avoid the draft, either through tip-offs or leaving the country illegally. When they are caught, the consequences are calamitous. It is a sensitive subject, and the young are afraid of fighting on the front lines. They are also anxious about a recruitment system that's been accused of corruption and not always following the law. The reality is that Ukraine needs new energized fighters and volunteers to defeat the Russian advance. There are estimates of nearly 2 million Ukrainians, including women and young men, that are of military age. The difficulty is Zelenskyy's government has to convince young Ukrainians to join the armed forces. It is Zelenskyy and not the army that has to do the job of changing the necessary law. The transparent message should include that the Ukrainian Armed Forces will not send its citizens to death. Those who join will have the right to uniform, training, and assigned unit that has rotations. Beyond that, there are benefits that are lacking in a cash-strapped country like Ukraine.

As recruitment remains an issue, so does the ability of Ukraine to have a military-industrial complex. Presently, Russia produces 3 million units of artillery ammunition annually, while the entire NATO alliance can only produce not even half of that. Despite Western-backed sanctions, Russia is still able to maintain its military-industrial complex by creating a military-industrial economy. Today, Russia has a significant portion of its industrial output, technological innovation, and workforce dedicated to the production and maintenance of military equipment, weaponry, and infrastructure centered on the "special military operation." The result is that the military and the defense sector play a central role in driving economic activity, investment, and employment in Russia.

While this may look like a numbers game, there is another side. The Chinese military strategist Sun Tzu, who wrote "The Art of War," while not explicitly stating a numerical ratio, emphasized the importance of strategy, deception, and exploiting weaknesses to achieve victory, even when facing a larger opponent. One of the key principles applies to a scenario of "knowing your enemy and knowing yourself." Understanding the strengths and weaknesses of one's own forces and those of the enemy allows for the development of effective strategies that can benefit the aggressor. Sun Tzu emphasizes the importance of avoiding direct confrontation when facing a stronger enemy. Instead, focus on indirect approaches, such as attacking the enemy's weaknesses, exploiting vulnerabilities in their defenses, or maneuvering to outflank them. To employ tactics to deceive the enemy and create confusion is one key priority. It could involve feints, false movements, or other forms of misdirection to make the enemy believe you are stronger or positioned differently than you actually are. One can utilize the natural landscape and the environmental factors to advantage. Positioning forces in areas that offer defensive advantages or where the enemy's larger numbers can be negated by difficult terrain is advisable. Sun Tzu stresses the importance of morale and psychological factors in warfare. To use tactics to undermine the enemy's morale, sow dissent among their ranks, or create fear and uncertainty through psychological warfare techniques. More importantly, to remain flexible and adaptable in tactics and strategy while also continuously assessing the war aims, adjusting plans as needed, and being prepared to exploit any opportunities that arise during the course of the conflict.

Diplomatic and political strategies to build alliances or divide the enemy's forces are crucial. Forming coalitions with other powers or exploiting internal divisions within the enemy's camp can help offset numerical disadvantages. Target the enemy's economic resources and supply lines to weaken their ability to sustain their larger forces. Disrupting their logistics, seizing key resources, or conducting economic warfare can undermine the ability to maintain their numerical advantage. Russia has employed all such measures but so has Ukraine.

For Ukraine, when additional aid arrives from the U.S., and Ukraine's forces have access to artillery rounds, and with the help of precision-guided missiles that can go as far as 300km, Ukraine will have some advantage but will need time and additional numbers to take back Russian-occupied areas. For Ukraine to get the upper hand now, Berlin, Paris, and Washington really need to go all out to support Ukraine, something which has not happened so far.

In the last two years, the European Union (EU) and its institutions have given Ukraine almost €85 billion ($92 billion) in military, financial, and humanitarian aid, with individual member states giving billions more. By comparison, the United States has given a total of €71.4 billion ($77 billion). By October 2023, there was a 90 percent reduction. Its just not the Biden administration but the EU that is struggling too.

There are internal dissensions within Europe. Tension between

Hungary's Prime Minister Viktor Orbán and Ukraine's President Zelenskyy primarily revolves around issues related to ethnic Hungarian minorities in Ukraine, particularly in the Transcarpathian region, and differences in their respective approaches to nationalism, minority rights, and regional geopolitics.

Like the Biden Administration which was previously trying to sort out its border security bill in return for Republican votes to send nearly $61 billion in aid to Ukraine, Orbán is using the Hungarian minority in Ukraine to get financial concessions from the EU over his support to the EU to pay for weapons and munitions for Ukraine. Hungary, along with Slovakia are also frustrated with Ukraine's decision to halt the flow of Russian oil, which they desperately rely on. Ukraine's strict enforcement of Western-backed sanctions against Russia has created a toxic divide among EU members.

Most EU members reluctantly support Ukraine politically, but where they stand militarily is questionable. Germany's Chancellor Olaf Scholz has kept his promises to Kyiv at a time when leaders from his own party, the Social Democratic Party of Germany (SPD), are suggesting that this is not the time. They would rather freeze Berlin's aid to Kyiv. His coalition partner and Foreign Minister, Annalena Baerbock of the Green party, knows and understands Scholz's consequential position. She has gone on the offensive to account for a U.N. report on Russian war crimes in Ukraine, highlighting that Berlin's role should not be to freeze but to aid Ukraine. Baerbock, however, is in a difficult position as her Green party is now widely seen as a drag on Scholz's government, with one poll giving the Greens a lackluster 19 percent approval rating.

Europe's Big-3; Chancellor Scholz, French President Emmanuel Macron, and Polish Prime Minister Donald Tusk, have pledged to supply Ukraine with more weapons. All three are in agreement that freezing the war would only help Putin. It would also mean that the Russian President gets to keep whatever he's occupied in Ukraine's east, and the millions of Ukrainians and children that are in the occupied territory will be treated in less than humane conditions as part of the Russian occupation.

The question remains, in this war, what does a win for Ukraine look like? Will the Russians pull out as they had in 1996 after a two-year bloody Chechen War of Independence? It is highly unlikely. Like

Ukraine, Chechnya had a long history of resistance against Russian rule, including a brief period of independence following the collapse of the Russian Empire. Like Ukraine, during the Soviet era, Chechnya was subjected to policies of forced collectivization and repression. After the disbanding of the Soviet Union in 1991, Chechnya declared independence from Russia under the leadership of President Dzhokhar Dudayev, sparking tensions with the newly formed Russian Federation. In December 1994, Russian forces, under the leadership of President Boris Yeltsin, launched a military intervention in Chechnya, aiming to restore Russian control over the breakaway region. The stated reasons for the intervention included concerns about Chechen separatism, lawlessness, and the rise of Islamic extremism. Like the war in Ukraine, the war in Chechnya also resulted in a significant humanitarian crisis, with widespread civilian casualties, displacement, and destruction of Chechen infrastructure. In August 1996, after nearly two years of fighting and mounting casualties, Russian and Chechen representatives signed the Khasavyurt Accord, which formally ended hostilities and established a ceasefire. Under the terms of the ceasefire agreement, Russian forces were sent home in buses from Chechnya. It was a humiliation that Putin responded with an iron fist. Under Putin's orders, Russian forces re-entered Chechnya in September 1999.

Putin's response came after a series of bombings in Moscow and other targeted residential buildings, resulting in significant casualties, collectively killing nearly 300 people and injuring over a thousand others.

While the Russian government blamed Chechen militants for the bombings, there have been controversies and allegations of involvement by elements within the Russian FSB. Some journalists believed it was a ploy to invade Chechnya and finish off what Russia began in 1994.

The Second Chechen War was characterized by intense fighting, human rights abuses, and widespread civilian casualties. The war officially ended in 2009 when Russia declared victory, but low-level insurgency and violence have persisted in the region since then. Chechnya remains a troubled region with ongoing tensions between the Russian government and various insurgent groups. It is possible that Ukraine very well may look like Chechnya unless Europe and the United States really harden their long-term support.

That kind of sustained assistance for Ukraine comes from Latvia, Lithuania, and Estonia, the NATO member states closest to the conflict. The problem is that the Russian advance is ongoing even when the American and European aid packages are taking their time to have an effect. There are reasons beyond moral and sovereign arguments why Europe and the United States should not give up on Ukraine. Before the 24 February 2022 Russian invasions of Ukraine, Europe was politicized with Ukraine, particularly in the context of Ukraine's aspirations for closer ties with the European Union (EU). It stemmed from Ukraine's desire for closer integration with the EU through initiatives like the Association Agreement. The possibility of EU membership stirred political debates within Europe. This was especially evident during the Euromaidan protests in Ukraine in 2013-2014, where Ukrainians demonstrated in favor of closer ties with Europe and the EU.

Ukraine's geopolitical position between Russia and the European Union made it a focal point for discussions about European security and stability. The tug-of-war between Russia and the West over influence in Ukraine heightened tensions, and Ukraine's role as a transit country for Russian natural gas exports to Europe, also brought it into European political discussions. The focus was particularly regarding energy security and diversification of energy sources to reduce dependence on Russian supply lines. Yet Europe also had suspicions about Ukraine in terms of human rights and democracy. Concerns about such categories, added to corruption, were subjects of keeping Ukraine out, as the country did not conform to European transparency values and economic norms. However, in 2024, Europe finds itself having to find a political settlement.

In NATO's Article 4, Consultation Mechanism, states: "The Parties will consult together whenever, in the opinion of any of them, the territorial integrity, political independence, or security of any of the Parties is threatened." While Article 4 does not directly mandate the defense of non-NATO members (like Ukraine), it provides a mechanism for NATO members to consult and discuss any perceived threats, including those that may affect the security environment beyond NATO's immediate borders. Depending on the situation, Article 4 consultations can lead to a range of NATO actions, including diplomatic measures, strategic adjustments, or military responses.

Although the NATO Treaty does not explicitly mandate the defense of non-NATO members, NATO has engaged in various activities that extend its security umbrella to non-member states through partnerships, cooperative programs, and specific missions authorized by the North Atlantic Council (NAC), NATO's principal political decision-making body. The Partnership for Peace (PfP) is a program of practical bilateral cooperation between individual Euro-Atlantic partner countries and NATO. Many non-NATO countries participate in PfP to enhance their defense capabilities and cooperation with NATO. The alliance has engaged in military operations beyond its borders that indirectly contribute to the defense of non-NATO members. For instance, NATO's involvement in Afghanistan under the International Security Assistance Force (ISAF) was based on a U.N. mandate to help stabilize the country and combat terrorism. Since the 2014 Russian annexation of Crimea and the ongoing conflict in Ukraine's east, NATO has significantly increased its support to Ukraine through military training, capacity-building programs, and political support, even though Ukraine is not a NATO member.

What is painfully visible in Brussels is though Ukraine is slowly becoming part of the European club, Europeans are increasingly uncomfortable about Ukrine. The EU looks to keep a very hushed tone in admitting new members and though Ukraine has jumped the line over several other states, European leaders are more comfortable in writing checks than solidifying their promises to Kyiv.

Brussels has always kept quiet on EU enlargement, and with a June 2024 European election looming, it is incredibly sensitive on how it handles Ukraine as well as hopes that an extreme pro-Russian right-wing coalition does not find a space in Brussels.

European Commission President Ursula von der Leyen, who is running for a second term, has promised to get the bloc ready for Ukraine. In her State of the Union speech in 2023 September, von der Leyen said "It is time for Europe to once again think big and write our own destiny."

One of the first tasks for the newly elected Members of the European Parliament (MEPs) will be to elect the President of the European Commission. The process begins with the European Council, composed of the EU's 27 heads of state, who will consider the election results before nominating a candidate. This nominee must then be approved by more than 50% of MEPs.

The political dynamics within the EU often involve the use of the "lead candidates" system, known as *Spitzenkandidaten* in German. This system, employed in the 2014 elections, involves each political group proposing a candidate for the Commission Presidency prior to the elections. The group that secures the most seats then gains the mandate to select the Commission President. However, this process is not binding. In the 2019 elections, the EU's national leaders opted for Ursula von der Leyen despite her not being a *Spitzenkandidat*, indicating that they might bypass this system again.

The political composition of the new European Parliament will significantly influence the selection of the Commission President. If right-wing and far-right parties make substantial gains, as expected, it could lead to a shift in the selection process and the policy direction of the Commission. A Parliament leaning towards nationalism and conservatism might prioritize different criteria for the Presidency, focusing on a candidate who aligns more closely with their political agendas.

For Ukraine, the election of the European Commission President is particularly consequential. The President sets the Commission's agenda and can steer EU policy on critical issues, including foreign policy and support for Ukraine. Ursula von der Leyen has been a strong advocate for Ukraine, supporting financial and military aid, amidst the ongoing conflict. Her re-election could ensure continuity in this support. Conversely, a new President with a different political alignment might alter the EU's stance on Ukraine, potentially reducing the level of assistance or shifting the focus towards other priorities.

The political groupings within the European Parliament and their alliances will be crucial in all decision-making process. If the center-right European People's Party (EPP) remains dominant but has to seek new allies due to a weakened center-left, the resulting coalitions will influence the policy direction significantly. Right-wing groups like the European Conservatives and Reformists (ECR) and Identity and Democracy (ID) could leverage their increased presence to push for a candidate who reflects their views on issues such as immigration, national sovereignty, and EU integration.

Forty-four million Ukrainians populate the largest landmass the EU would absorb in the European Parliament and the Council of the

EU. What Ukrainians make up in the landmass, won't make up in economic contributions. Ukraine would be the poorest new member of the EU. It is a status added with another attribute of "war-torn" that will cause Brussels anxiety. The conditions and criteria for EU membership, which effectively preclude war-torn countries from being considered, are outlined in the Treaty on European Union (TEU) and further elaborated in the Copenhagen criteria.

Article 49 of the Treaty on TEU sets out the basic conditions for a country to apply for EU membership: "Any European State which respects the values referred to in Article 2 and is committed to promoting them may apply to become a member of the Union. The European Parliament and national Parliaments shall be notified of this application. The applicant State shall address its application to the Council, which shall act unanimously after consulting the Commission and after receiving the consent of the European Parliament, which shall act by a majority of its component members."

While neither the TEU nor the Copenhagen criteria explicitly state that a war-torn country cannot apply for EU membership, the criteria implicitly exclude such countries because of the following: A war-torn country is unlikely to have the stable institutions required to guarantee democracy, the rule of law, and human rights. Ongoing conflict would severely undermine the functioning of a market economy and the country's capacity to cope with competitive pressures within the EU. A country in the midst of conflict would struggle to demonstrate the administrative and institutional capacity necessary to meet the obligations of EU membership.

Ukraine's status as the poorest admitted member will also have tensions inside the EU. Already, richer European states are frustrated with an extension of funding to poorer regions of Europe, something which has begun since the 2008-09 financial crisis and continues to linger. In some estimates, absorbing Ukraine would cost Europe €186 billion over the course of five to seven years. That would also include passing several economic and judicial tests on the course to EU membership. This is still possible if Germany and the United States nudged the EU to accept Ukraine.

Bulgaria, for instance, is often considered one of the poorest countries in the European Union in terms of GDP per capita. While it has made progress since joining the EU, Sofia still faces significant economic challenges, including high levels of poverty and unemployment, particularly in rural areas and among certain demographic groups. It was part of the fifth EU enlargement in 2007. However, for Bulgaria and Romania, joining the most coveted club in Europe was anything but a smooth transition. Both Bulgaria and Romania had to wait a strenuous three years before they could attain the status of EU membership. Concerns related to organized crime, corruption, and a beleaguered criminal justice system had Brussels slowing their motion of acceptance. Further complaints of illegal firearms, unsuccessful prosecutions, human trafficking, drug smuggling, money laundering, counterfeiting of goods, and currency manipulation, remained part of the EU concerns.

Bulgaria had to prove the complete independence of its judicial system and provide evidence of its decline in high-level corruption. The country had received prior warnings about possible penalties ranging from its planes being banned from EU airspace to a halt of its goods flowing across Europe. Both Bulgaria and Romania were also part of the beginning era of EU absorption fatigue, where some EU member states could not contribute amicably to the EU budget. There was already talk of how EU institutions are not committed to enlargement but rather kick out the problem children within.

Greece was a prime example. Athens became a significant concern for the EU in the wake of the 2008-09 financial crisis. Its economic woes were primarily characterized by unsustainable levels of public debt, a large budget deficit, and a lack of competitiveness in its economy. It was part of years of accumulation of high levels of public debt relative to its GDP, as it became unsustainable. The true extent of Greece's debt was revealed in 2009 when the newly elected government of Prime Minister George Papandreou revised the country's deficit figures upwards, triggering concerns among investors and financial markets. Greece was running a large budget deficit, which, coupled with its high debt levels, raised doubts about the country's ability to service its debt obligations. It led to a loss of investor confidence and rising borrowing costs for the Greek government. Its economy was struggling with low productivity, high unemployment, and a lack of competitiveness, particularly in sectors like manufacturing and services. Structural weaknesses in the Greek economy had been masked by easy access to credit prior to the financial crisis. Greek banks were heavily exposed to Greek government bonds, exacerbating concerns about the stability of the banking sector as the government's financial situation deteriorated. Concerns about Greece's debt crisis spreading to other Eurozone countries, particularly those with similar economic vulnerabilities such as Portugal, Ireland, Italy, and Spain (known as the "PIIGS," including Greece), heightened anxieties within the EU and financial markets. The Greece debt crisis led to a series of financial rescue packages orchestrated by the EU, the European Central Bank (ECB), and the International Monetary Fund (IMF), collectively known as the "Troika." The bailout programs aimed to stabilize Greece's finances, implement austerity measures, and enact structural reforms to improve the country's economic competitiveness. However, the austerity measures imposed as part of the bailout conditions led to social unrest and political turmoil. Greece would see six elections in the next fifteen years. The crisis also strained relations among EU member states, particularly between Greece and Germany, leading to debates about fiscal discipline, solidarity, and the future of European integration. The episode underscored the need for stronger fiscal coordination and economic governance within the Eurozone and prompted Brussels to think more forcefully about either keeping or kicking out financially irresponsible members.

After the 2008-09 financial crisis, Europe saw the rise of autocratic leaders. Non-EU member states like Serbia and its President Aleksandar Vučić along with Milorad Dodik, the president of Republika Srpska, the Serbian federal entity in Bosnia and Herzegovina, refused EU sanctions against Russia. At the same time, both would love to see the expulsion of peacekeeping troops from the European Union Force (EUFOR) from their respective regions. EUFOR's primary mission is in Bosnia and Herzegovina, where it supports the implementation of the Dayton Peace Agreement. Conducted by world powers, the peace agreement signed on 21 November 1995 brought an end to the three-year Bosnian war and established the framework for peace. EUFOR has also been involved in Kosovo, primarily in supporting the Kosovo Security Force (KSF) and maintaining peace. Serbia has an unresolved issue with the status of Kosovo, which declared independence from Serbia in 2008. Belgrade does not recognize its independence.

Russia views EUFOR as a better alternative than NATO, and is reluctant to assist in ending their mission in the region. EU leaders too are looking at states like Serbia and NATO members like Albania, Montenegro, and North Macedonia that can wait, perhaps even a considerable period, until the situation in Ukraine is resolved and EU ascension talks resume. The difficulty with that would be Brussels is prolonging the inevitable. New EU member states will have to pay up and its questionable if they will see the benefits in the short term. This could play into a clash between Brussels and the local political landscape. Its not totally inconceivable that when it comes to EU admission, Ukraine and its other ally Moldova will find itself in a similar fate. Like Greece, Romania and Bulgaria, both Ukraine and Moldova have similar problems. However, the EU is powerless when it comes to police-ing its member states to be true to their European way of order.

The challenge with problem children lies not only in the limits of enforceability but also in the difficulty of establishing clear, consistent rules and consequences within an existing set of expectations. Monitoring and enforcing these against past behavior is very difficult. Similarly, while the goal of aligning new EU member states with the economic and judicial standards of current members is commendable, it is fraught with potential conflicts with Brussels and other EU institutions.

Ukraine has endured more than a decade of wasted time in the EU negotiations process, and very little came out of it. Germany would be willing to actually open that question and may get the EU member states to agree on it, but Berlin has concerns of its own. When Russia invaded and annexed Crimea in March 2014, the reaction of the West was weak. Some European states and even Germany actually increased their consumption of Russian gas. Furthermore, it took almost a year to put together the Western-backed sanctions on Russia to take effect. From then on, Putin flexed his muscles in Syria and Libya. Ukraine became paralyzed and resorted to some European but mostly American aid.

Giving Ukraine an actual NATO collective defense commitment would benefit Europe, but the greater nervousness centers around Russia. It does not help that some NATO member states, regardless of their relationship with Russia, may be skeptical about how much

NATO commits itself to Ukraine, which can be interpreted as NATO expansion. The feasibility of defending a new member and the potential strain on NATO's resources would weigh higher than Ukraine's accession. Already, European politics is impacted by the situation in Ukraine. Political parties with isolationist tendencies, pro-Russia sentiments, or concerns about the implications of NATO expansion for their country's security and resources are opposing Ukraine's accession. The liabilities for NATO members; Bulgaria, Hungary, and Slovenia, all of which have favorable relationships with the Kremlin, do fall into a similar category.

NATO operates on the principle of consensus, meaning that all member states must agree on significant decisions, including the admission of new members. Disagreements or divergent opinions among NATO member states could hinder progress towards future memberships. This would require debate within NATO as its members are encouraged to seek peaceful resolution of disputes and conflicts through diplomatic means. Article 5 recognizes the possibility of using armed force to defend, not attack the aggressor, or to restore peace and security. NATO member states are expected to consult and coordinate with each other in the event of a crisis or armed attack. Decisions regarding the implementation of Article 5, including the nature and scope of the collective response, are made collectively by the North Atlantic Council, NATO's principal political decision-making body.

While a NATO security guarantee could serve as a deterrence, for Ukraine, it would mean that at least one member of the 32-member alliance would have to come to its defense. One NATO member state can respond, but only after attacked. Poland meets those requirements, although President Emmanuel Macron of France, who operates with a weak minority government, has hinted his forces could take that role.

In the last two decades, French troops have mostly taken part in peacekeeping missions in Afghanistan, Mali, the Central African Republic, Iraq, and Syria. Approximately 300,000 French soldiers have limited operational experience, and their capabilities and tactics in lethal warfare remain to be seen on the battlefield. The French have not won on its own merit since the recent 2013 Operation Serval in Mali. The campaign can hardly indicate French superiority in warfare against a ragged group of terrorists. It falls in a similar category to a previous French victory in May 1978 in the Shaba II conflict in the mineral-rich Katanga province in Zaire (now the Democratic Republic of the Congo) against also a rebel group known as the Front for the National Liberation of the Congo (FLNC).

The French triumph over rebel and terrorist groups may be a source of pride in Paris, but it would also explain why the French President may have indicated that his forces should be part of a coalition rather than go alone. Putin responded forcefully, warning of a nuclear war. The French President then signed a bilateral security deal with Ukraine, a move which changed his stance from a snitch in 2022, when he offered the Russian President security guarantees and continued to buy Russian oil, even after the war began, to now a nervous Hawk in 2024.

Macron's change in tone has come after some difficult turns. On 14 May 2017, when Macron first became President, he had come to view NATO in not-so-favorable terms. He believed the alliance was too dependent on the United States. Like his predecessors, Chirac, Sarkozy, and Hollande, he was very much pro-Russia. Having served as an Inspector at the Finance Ministry's Inspection générale des Finances (IGF), Macron was fully aware of French economic dependence on Russia. Like many other European countries, Paris needs Moscow for its energy imports, particularly natural gas. France, in addition, also had ties in agriculture, aerospace, and technology. Natural gas particularly constituted a significant portion of the economic relationship, and that is where the political problems began for Macron.

To avoid conflict with his European counterparts over Russia, Macron instead focused his foreign policy largely on the Middle East. He inherited NATO's vague priorities in the Syrian civil war, the turmoil in Libya, the crisis in Yemen, the challenges posed by ISIS, and Iran's growing influence. Macron sought "strategic autonomy" against what he described as a "brain-dead" NATO. However, it was NATO's influence that ultimately shaped the French President's stance.

President Donald Trump's decision to withdraw U.S. troops from northeastern Syria in October 2019, effectively paved the way for Turkey's military operation against the Kurdish-led People's Protection Units (YPG). Rojava, the center of the YPG administration and a semi-autonomous Kurdish-led region in northeastern Syria, navigated complex relationships with the Bashar Al-Assad government, opposition Syrian groups, and neighboring countries. The YPG first came under attack from Turkish forces in 2016 as part of Ankara's military operations in northern Syria, particularly in areas where the YPG was active. Turkey considers the YPG as an extension of the PKK (Kurdistan Workers' Party), which it views as a terrorist organization. As a result, Turkey has conducted multiple military operations targeting YPG-held areas along its southern border with Syria. The first major operation was "Operation Euphrates Shield," launched in August 2016, followed by subsequent operations such as "Operation Olive Branch" in 2018 and "Operation Peace Spring" in 2019. These operations aimed to push back YPG forces from the border region and establish a buffer zone controlled by Turkish-backed forces.

At the same time, there were disputes between Greece and Turkey, two NATO members, over gas fields in the Mediterranean as part of its Exclusive Economic Zone (EEZ). Both claimed rights to explore and exploit natural resources, including oil and gas, within their respective maritime zones. The main point of contention lay in the delineation of maritime boundaries, particularly in areas where the two countries' EEZs overlapped. Greece argued that its islands, particularly those in the Aegean Sea, are entitled to their own EEZs in accordance with the United Nations Convention on the Law of the Sea (UNCLOS). Turkey contested this interpretation, claiming that Greece unfairly limits its own maritime territory and ignores the principle of equitable delimitation. Previously, the discovery of significant gas reserves in the eastern Mediterranean had led to increased competition for exploration and drilling rights, with Turkey conducting its own exploration activities in disputed waters, often leading to tensions with Greece and Cyprus. It also led to disputes over claimed rights. Turkey's deployment of seismic survey vessels escorted by warships into contested waters, as well as Greece's military response, heightened tensions and raised concerns about a potential conflict. Macron backed Greece and as a result, found himself confronting Turkey in Syria.

France has historically maintained a significant interest in Syria due to historical ties and its own economic interests as part of its sphere of influence. Since the Crusades, with many French nobles, knights, and soldiers participating in various campaigns in the Levant, including Tripoli and the Principality of Antioch, which encompassed parts of present-day Syria, the French have kept a close watch in the region. The present Alawaite government owes its own ascendence to the French after the end of World War I.

"Nous revoilà, mes enfants!" which translates to "Here we are again, my children!" evoking the historical connection between France and Syria, recalling the presence of French Crusaders in the region during medieval times by General Henri Gouraud, who was appointed High Commissioner of the Levant (including modern-day Syria and Lebanon) by the French government after World War I. He pursued a policy of divide and rule in Syria and cultivated alliances with minority groups, especially the Alawites, who were concentrated in the mountainous regions to break the backs of the majority Sunni landowning class. He granted positions of authority and influence to Alawite leaders, thereby fostering a degree of loyalty to his French administration. An approach that empowered the Alawites politically and militarily, laying the groundwork for their political rise in the 20th century.

France, however, had grown distant from Syria. No French head of state had met President Bashar Al-Assad since President Jacques Chirac in 2001, when Assad visited France. Macron attended a summit in Istanbul hosted by President Recep Erdoğan on the Syrian civil war. He was joined along with then German Chancellor Angela Merkel and Russian President Putin. On 27 October 2018, the summit provided a reality that was evident. The Kremlin had more influence over Damascus than any others who were present. Having understood the situation in Syria, it is possible that Macron wanted to find a way to work with Russia in the post-Syrian civil war era.

After meeting with Putin in August 2019, at a joint press conference, Macron said, "Russia is very profoundly European" and that "Russia fully belongs within a Europe of values." A week later, after hosting the annual G7 summit in Biarritz, Macron argued that "Pushing Russia from Europe is a profound strategic error," and that the stability of Europe was in jeopardy.

When Russia invaded Ukraine on 24 February 2022, it was a massive strategic embarrassment for Macron. It made a mockery of his reconciliation efforts with Putin, reinvigorated NATO, and reminded those on the sidelines why Turkey is such a vital strategic partner. Ankara controlled the Bosporus and Dardanelles Straits in the Black Sea, providing a crucial seat at the negotiating table between Ukraine and Russia. When the war began, France became one of Ukraine's staunchest supporters. It provided significant military and economic aid, but Macron insisted that Russia should be invited for diplomatic talks for peace.

Macron's tone began to change in May 2023. He delivered a speech in Bratislava, expressing regret for misunderstanding the warnings about Putin, especially given his previous signing of security guarantees with the Russian President. Macron now shifted to hear the voices of other NATO members, believing they should have been heard but never had.

This was not only a change in shift for the French President but a significant tilt in French foreign policy. Nearly two decades back, it was French President Jacque Chirac who said the same thing to shut the voices of those Europeans who supported America's invasion of Iraq, calling them "reckless" and "infantile."

In March 2024, France signed an agreement with Armenia, a Russian ally, to foster a military deal. The French President did the same with Moldova. The government in Chișinău was nervous about its breakaway region of Transnistria, believed to be Russia's next target, and welcomed the French initiative.

Macron, like other pro-Ukraine European leaders, believes that Ukraine will achieve its strategic autonomy away from Russia's economic web, and much of that depends on the outcome of the June 2024 European parliamentary elections and the November 2024 American elections. Europe will have to decide whether to cede Ukraine to Russia or fill the gap left by America. It looks like the French President can achieve this with his key German ally, Olaf Scholz. However, he only has till 2027 to make a success as he nears the end of his term.

France's actual support for Ukraine has been pretty scanty. Macron's recent bilateral security agreement with Kyiv promises military assistance of up to €3 billion. It is less than 10% of what Washington can provide but six times more than the Germans. It is a perfect example of in times of war, European leaders promise more than what they can deliver.

As Europe's leaders fall short, Ukraine is using technological warfare to inflict lethal damage against the Russian advance, thanks largely to the Americans. During the second week of March 2024, it was announced that the American military was rushing $300 million worth of weapons to Ukraine. It comes at a difficult time for the army as it replenishes all the reserve weapons it has pulled from its stocks to help Ukraine. The transaction is part of a presidential drawdown authority (PDA), a transaction granted to the American President to provide certain types of military equipment, services, and training to foreign countries or international organizations. The authority allows the President to transfer defense articles, services, and funds from the U.S. Department of Defense to foreign recipients under specified conditions and limitations. It is only 5% of what was promised to Ukraine and a one-time check, but it has come after Polish leaders pleaded with the Biden administration to assist Ukraine at a critical moment against a vastly better-supplied Russian army.

The Kremlin has given the Russian army significant incentives and supplies, and that is showing a remarkable capacity for the Russian forces to regenerate themselves at a pace Western military leaders and experts had not anticipated. The downside is that the Kremlin is churning out quantity, not quality. The Russian numbers have increased, but the capability to take large areas without the assistance of pro-Russian militias in Ukraine remains in doubt.

The shortcomings also include fighters who are ill-trained, compared to those from 2022. There are losses in tanks, armoured vehicles, airplanes, helicopters and equipment. During most attacks on Ukrainian areas, Russian forces have rebuilt the older types of armoured vehicles. They are not exactly top quality. It is a result of Western-backed sanctions which impacted the shortage of equipment.

As Russian forces make gains in the east, the Kremlin is adding the resurgence of a previously old strategy. Fill Europe with fake news and disinformation, and shore up right-wing and fascist forces enough to the point that they make significant gains in elections, like the June 2024 European parliamentary elections, to derail political support to Ukraine. Militarily, the approach is to flood it with more pro-Russian mercenaries than Russian soldiers and use the aggregate manpower to flush out Ukrainian forces through overwhelming artillery production and older tanks.

Since the 2023 summer, the Russian military has regrouped, reorganized, and restrategized. Military units created training regiments along Ukraine's northeastern border and in occupied areas. Russian units have become more standardized and much less of a private army setup. It is in a state of an almost half a million-man-powered army. These Russian forces conduct small raids and small operations, usually concentrating on towns, villages, and smaller cities. Depending on size and strategic importance, the Kremlin's aim is to inflict lethal damage on Ukraine's forces.

Nearly 33% of the Russian army is now concentrating its energy in Ukraine. Putin looks confident as he will be well supplied in arms and manpower well on to the end of 2025. The Kremlin will be spending approximately 6% to 7% of their GDP in defense from here on.

Despite sanctions, the Kremlin is receiving outside help. Chinese support for Russia has enabled the Kremlin in ways it previously would not have conducted itself. Beijing has played a constructive role in its ambiguous "peace plan" and has consistently blamed NATO and the West for provoking Russia into launching the attack on Ukraine. China has refrained from calling the conflict "a war." It is of a similar mindset to Russia's, on taking back Taiwan.

Previously, China may have assessed that the war would be quick and had little reservations, but two years later, Beijing has set limits on how it will support Russia. China's main insurance is Putin's oil and gas infrastructure, which it needs to boost its own economy.

China needs Russia, particularly to set the agenda against United States and the European Union. Similarly, the Kremlin needs China much more to counter the American hegemony and to assert its own influence on the global stage. Both China and Russia view the United States and its European allies as their primary geopolitical rivals and share a common interest in countering their influence and preserving their own sovereignty and security. China and Russia often coordinate their actions and positions in international forums to push back against Western initiatives perceived as detrimental to their interests. It is the deep economic ties through trade, investment, energy cooperation, and infrastructure projects such as the Belt and Road Initiative, which is a Chinese economic lifeline against Western interventions. However, the China-Russia partnership has limits.

Beijing hasn't signed an agreement to build the Power of Siberia II gas pipeline or supply lethal weapons to Russia. It hasn't violated Western-backed sanctions but it has provided intelligence to Russia. At the the same time there are suspicions between the two. Russia is wary of China's growing influence in Central Asia and the Russian Far East, while China is cautious of Russia's assertiveness in Eastern Europe and the Arctic.

After the Ukraine war began, China took a different tone from Russia, taking a different direction from its previous state of rivalry against the Kremlin. China's exports to Russia grew by 67.2 percent in the first half of 2023, consisting of electrical machinery, telecommunications equipment, industrial machinery, and mechanical appliances. It also included iron and steel products, aluminum, copper, and other metal goods. In addition, China exports automobiles, motorcycles, and automotive parts to Russia, catering to the country's growing demand for transportation.

Beijing sees the Kremlin as a substitute for the Western automakers that have slowed operations in Asia. On the other hand, the Kremlin needs Beijing for its natural gas and other markets to flow into Asia and other vendor networks, to sell to the same Europe it cannot sell due to sanctions.

In March 2023, China, Russia, and Iran launched joint military exercises in the Gulf of Oman, a gesture of Beijing's efforts to expand its influence in the Middle East. Three months later, the Chinese and Russian military had their sixth joint air strategic patrol in the airspace of the Sea of Japan and the East China Sea.

When Chinese and Russian aircraft entered the southern and eastern parts of the South Korean air defense identification zone, Korean fighter jets went after four Russian and four Chinese military aircrafts. Japan responded similarly. The joint exercises are seen as particularly provocative. There is a feeling that China has ramped up military aid to both the Russian military and its intelligence services as it conducted joint military exercises and provided the use of M-17 military helicopters, jamming technology for military vehicles, parts for fighter jets and components for defense systems like the S-400 Surface-to-Air Missile System. Iran too, has assisted Russia through its Shahed 136s, the Mojaher 6 drones, and plans to build a drone factory in Yelabuga, in Kazan.

As the Russian forces are equipping themselves from outside

parties and third parties, its numbers will only continue growing, and so too will its missile production. What that means is Ukraine's forces will not only have to be on the defensive mode, but also dig defensive fortifications. This would include anti-tank ditches as it conducts offensive operations elsewhere.

Ukraine targeted a drone production plant and an oil refinery in the cities of Yoba and Nish, nearly 746 miles from the Ukrainian border. The Ukrainian military has multiple types of long-range kamikaze drones. On 3 May 2023, there was an incident when the Kremlin came under a drone attack. Russia does have an extensive air defense system, and it does have electronic warfare defenses, but its efficiency was absent when the Ukrainians attacked. The Russian radio electronic intelligence has radars, but the defense is not absolute, and there appear to be key Russian security gaps. It is part of a Ukrainian maneuver where its forces can map out drone flights along major routes away from large cities, along forests and rural areas where its drones would be least visible.

Security has not hampered Russia's economic trajectory, although time will tell. While Western-backed sanctions have created dents in the economy, targetting export controls would have been a powerful maneuver to halt the Kremlin's access to high-tech products from elsewhere. The Kremlin has adjusted its supply chains and continues to have access to military inputs in significant volumes, and continues to rely significantly on foreign components for its military production.

Loopholes in export controls in unsanctioned products, misclassified items, and unsanctioned recipients, assisted Russia through third-country intermediaries. Unmonitored transit routes deliberately bypassed compliance. It left the Russian coffers open for profits. The failure of Western institutions to close these loopholes has led to the deaths of Ukrainians.

The roots of the maturing of these loopholes go back to the disbanding of the Soviet Union in 1991. Economic upheavals during the transition from a centrally planned economy to a market orientation, provided Russian traders with an understanding of the financial climate and conditions. They sought opportunities that could open their doors in the post-Soviet era. It was under President Boris Yeltsin that Russia embarked on a program of privatization and economic liberalization where State-owned enterprises were privatized and price controls were lifted. It was the era of transactions and transitions, marred by corruption, asset stripping, and economic instability, which led to a significant decline in living standards for many Russians.

While nearly all of Russia was struggling financially and finding an identity in the post-Soviet era, Russian Oligarchs close to Yeltsin found ways to investments and entrepreneurship, contributing to the growth of a number of industries, including energy, telecommunications, finance, and manufacturing, which only later helped stimulate economic growth.

Russia is one of the world's largest producers of oil, natural gas, metals, minerals, and other natural resources. The country's vast resource wealth has played a crucial role in the global demand for energy and commodities, which surged in the early 2000s, giving Putin the economic boost he needed to rebuild his battered state. High oil and gas prices during this period provided a substantial boost to Russia's export revenues and government coffers. It was a relief from the 1998 Russian financial crisis; caused by the Yeltsin government's wreckless implemented measures to stabilize the economy, through tighter monetary policy, and banking modifications. The reforms from the 1998 financial crisis helped restore some confidence and laid the groundwork for more stable growth in subsequent years.

Putin's rise to the Russian Presidency on 7 May 2000 brought a period of relative political stability. He pursued policies aimed at consolidating state control over key sectors of the economy, including energy, while also implementing measures to improve the business climate and attract foreign investment. Russia benefited from favorable global economic trends in the early to mid-2000s, including robust demand from emerging markets, particularly China, and a period of relatively high global economic growth. These factors contributed to Russia's export-driven economic expansion during this period.

In 2004, Russia took steps to reduce its external debt and modernize its economy. The government paid off its Soviet-era debts ahead of schedule, bolstering investor confidence and reducing the country's vulnerability to external shocks, which could have taken the country back to the economic problems of the 1970s.

Under then General Secretary of the Communist Party Leonid

Brezhnev, the Soviet Union was stagnating, but it exploded in economic upswing in 1978. Brezhnev's "Economic Stagnation" may have been averted had the Soviet Union not invaded Afghanistan on 24 December 1979. Economically, the war was a disaster; the chief casualty beyond the 15,000 Russian lives was the Soviet coffers. While exact figures are hard to determine, varying estimates and the secrecy of Soviet military expenditures, it is generally accepted that the war cost approximately 8.2 billion rubles annually at its peak. The total cost of the war over the entire decade has been estimated at around $40-$50 billion in 1980s estimates.

Like Brezhnev, Putin's Russia was economically booming due to high oil and gas prices. This is when he found the confidence to invade Georgia in the summer of 2008. In 2014, a similar occurrence led to the invasion and annexation of Crimea. In September 2015, Russia intervened in Syria. The evidence of a period of economic upswing often led to Putin comfortably waging wars.

When it came to Ukraine, while it was initially believed that the Russian economy would be badly hit, and it was, since 2023, the country has seen remarkable economic growth. The Russian economy outperformed both the United States and Europe, increasing in size by 3.6% from a 1.2% decline in GDP in 2022, even with powerful Western-backed economic sanctions in place and cut off from major global markets. However, the Russian economic growth appears to have been driven mostly by ramped-up Kremlin spending on the military. Whether the war could withstand economic growth is difficult to assess, but it will have downturns.

In a war economy, resources such as capital, labor, and materials are often diverted from the private sector to public categories. Russia has prioritized civilian sectors to support military operations which potentially can lead to inefficiencies and deficits in resource allocation, hindering economic productivity and growth in civilian industries in the years to come.

Increased military spending can lead to large government budget deficits as Russia borrows to finance war-related expenditures, which can result in higher levels of public debt, which may also require austerity measures or higher taxes in the future. The Russian economy can potentially endure constrainment in long-term economic growth. Pressures on prices, leading to inflation, would erode the purchasing power of the average Russian, reducing real incomes and standards of living for households, especially those on fixed incomes or with limited access to resources.

Industries that are deemed non-essential for the war effort may suffer and a lack of subsidies can lead to large unemployment, bankruptcies, and a decline in output in non-war economy sectors.

Military activities, including weapon production, deployment, and warfare itself, can have significant environmental consequences, such as pollution, deforestation, and habitat destruction. These impacts can degrade Russian ecosystems, harm biodiversity, and undermine the long-term sustainability of natural resources, with economic implications for agriculture, tourism, and even expand problems related to climate change.

The Russian economy is expected to continue growing in 2024, though at a diminished pace. The Russian government forecasts a 2.3% increase in GDP, below the 2.6% forecast released by the International Monetary Fund (IMF). The Kremlin has increased tax revenues, drawing down the national wealth fund, and has become increasingly cautious in borrowing. Even under a state of caution, the Russian government deficit is historically high in 2024, at nearly 10% of the overall budget.

One side effect is the high inflation. In 2023, inflation stood at 7.4%, impressively down from 11.9% in 2022. To prevent inflation from getting out of control, the Russian central bank raised interest rates to approximately 16%. For Russians living in the cities, the impact of sanctions is hardly felt. Inflation is high, but rising prices have been met with higher pay for workers because unemployment is near historic lows. Western products have been replaced by Chinese, Iranian, and domestic products. The Kremlin has put in place economic maneuvers to bypass Western-backed sanctions. In rural areas, there are shortages of supplies, which is a complete reverse of circumstances when it comes to major cities. It is working in 2024, but nervousness remains for the future.

For businesses linked to the Kremlin, the intermediaries that fund the Kremlin's war chest, profits have poured into their coffers. Crude oil tankers have engaged in opaque and secretive transfers and transactions. Many are under Western-backed sanctions, but the Black Sea coast provides the transfer of Russian crude oil from big tankers to smaller ones, as a means of bypassing sanctions. Transfers of trade transactions of billions in capital from millions of barrels of crude oil have become increasingly profitable. Where such barrels end up is anyone's guess, and it doesn't matter as long as it brings revenue to the Kremlin.

These transactions and transfers are purposefully conducted in the middle of the ocean. The larger tankers are owned by a large company that buys in volumes where transactions are heavily connected to black money. The capital is not only for Russian dealers but also their allied handlers. Smaller accounts benefit Venezuela, Iran, and other countries within the Western-backed sanctions network. The smaller tankers are often owned by sanctioned individuals, many with links to the Kremlin.

These businesses have survived the Putin purges since the Ukraine war began. Since 2022, more than 50 businessmen with links to the Russian oil and gas industries have either disappeared or been found dead under unfamiliar circumstances, as part of what was called part two of the "sudden oligarch death syndrome." It is a phrase that went back to 2014 and 2017 when several Russian oligarchs perished.

In January 2022, the first to die was 60-year-old Leonid Shulman, transport chief for Russian energy giant Gazprom. He was found dead with a suicide note in the bathroom of his country house in the Leningrad Oblast. Alexander Tyulakov, another Gazprom executive, was also found dead in the garage of his St. Petersburg home in February of the same year.

Those who have survived the "sudden oligarch death syndrome," have amassed profits connected to the Russian crude. It is an unsanctioned category, and ship-to-ship transfers are often common and legal. However, there is a feeling that smaller crude oil tankers, as they ship to big tankers, that those vessels are going to ports where the original place of purchase is easily blurred. It is enough to transfer to another carrier that sells in non-sanctioned countries. This is a Kremlin ploy to evade sanctions, which complicate matters for the authorities, and they often look the other way. It does not affect global prices as most attention is directed to oil from the Middle East and not Russia. However, selling to non-sanctioned countries through transfers also means that the non-sanctioned countries refine the oil.

Russian oil products are still flowing into Europe through these channels and refineries. Substantial capital has been raised through such transactions, and the Kremlin, through its arm Rosneft, the state oil company, is the beneficiary.

For oil traders, the temptation for large commissions under this kind of climate is all too tempting. Profits ranging from $20-$50 million within a matter of six months are hardly something traders can avoid. They dream of such circumstances, and without much regulation to tie their hands, it is a booming, profitable route.

The Western-backed sanctions were meant to dent oil and gas revenues and halt the payment for the "special military operation" in Ukraine. Instead, it has only made the Kremlin richer than before.

Western-backed sanctions typically target new investments and transactions rather than existing ones. Russia had long-standing contracts with foreign companies for the extraction and sale of oil and gas. These contracts continued to generate revenue even after the Western-backed sanctions were imposed.

Opportunities in the black market and illicit trade thrived under the climate of sanctions. Despite restrictions, the Kremlin found ways to sell their oil and gas through clandestine channels. By circumventing sanctions through third-party intermediaries and using their underground economy (which dates back to the Soviet-era) they generated significant revenues. In some cases, intermediaries engaged in non-monetary transactions to bypass financial restrictions, exchanging oil and gas for goods and services.

Russia sold a portion of their oil and gas domestically, providing revenue to the government despite international restrictions on exports. Smuggling and evasion were already a common practice even before the war in Ukraine began. Russia covertly generated revenues through outside international oversight and alternative trading partners. These channels were willing to engage in barter trade deals that circumvent the restrictions imposed by Western-backed sanctions. These arrangements allowed the Kremlin to continue exporting oil and gas in exchange for Western goods or services.

One country that found itself in the middle between the United States and Russia was India. Privately, most Indian lawmakers were against the Russian invasion of Ukraine, but in public they showed their solidarity with Moscow due to its long historical Soviet-era relationship.

The Soviet Union recognized the state of India in April 1947, even before its independence from British rule on 15 August 1947. In 1949, when the United States declined Prime Minister Jawaharlal Nehru's request for food aid, the Soviet Union stepped in. By 1951, a delivery of 100,000 tonnes of wheat was exchanged for the export of traditional Indian commodities. That same year, the Soviet Union vetoed the Kashmir resolution at the U.N. in favor of Nehru's government. It was the first of many Soviet-backed vetoes in defense of India.

Two years before his death in 1953, Stalin famously told Sarvepalli Radhakrishnan, the Indian Ambassador to the Soviet Union and the future second President of India, "Both you and Mr. Nehru are persons whom we do not consider our enemies. This will continue to be our policy, and you can count on our help." It was a significant turning point, as for years, Stalin was suspicious of British-educated Indian leaders and believed them to be British proxies.

At the invitation of Soviet Premier Nikolai Bulganin and Soviet Communist Party General Secretary Nikita Khrushchev, Nehru visited the Soviet Union in June 1955. The Socialist Nehru visited Ukraine and Turkmenistan, greeted by bouquets of roses from huge crowds. Nehru won the hearts of the Politburo, and his visit laid the foundations of India-Soviet relations that have lasted to this day.

From then on, Soviet Union became a major supplier of arms and military equipment to India. In the 1962 Sino-Indian War, New Delhi was backed by Moscow. Today, among senior Indian politicians, there remains a high degree of nostalgia for the Kremlin. It is rooted in events when the Nixon administration partnered with Mao's communists to take on India. The two powers backed India's arch-rival Pakistan during the 1971 India-Pakistan war. It resulted in Soviet-backed India's victory, liberating East Pakistan to what would become the independence of the modern state of Bangladesh. For a younger generation of Indian leaders, Russia is a significant ally against another rival, China.

India has a large trade deficit that favors China. The two countries failed to resolve their border dispute, and Indian media outlets have repeatedly reported Chinese military incursions into Indian territory. In early 2018, the Chinese and Indian forces engaged in a standoff at the Doklam plateau along the disputed Bhutan-China border. Since the summer of 2020, armed standoffs and skirmishes at multiple locations along the entire Sino-Indian border have escalated. It is a dangerous standoff, unseen since the 1962 Sino-Indian War.

After Europe and the United States imposed sanctions on Russia, India provided options for Putin. It is no secret that India will continue its long-standing economic and military relationship with Russia, as well as balance its relationship with the United States.

The Indian relationship with the United States has come under strain after allegations by American and Canadian intelligence networks of Indian state-sponsored killings on their soil. On September 2023, Canadian Prime Minister Justin Trudeau spoke of "credible allegations" involving India in the killing of 45-year-old Hardeep Singh Nijjar, a Sikh separatist in British Columbia. India denied any role.

In November 2023, a similar incident occurred in New York. Nikhil Gupta, believed to be an Indian spy, was accused of trying to hire a hitman for $100,000 in cash to kill a Sikh separatist named Gurpatwant Singh Pannun. He holds both American and Canadian citizenship and is the general counsel for Sikhs for Justice, an organization that advocates an independent Sikh state called Khalistan. New Delhi is very sensitive to the prospect of a new independent state, which historically concentrated areas in India's Punjab state for a Sikh homeland. A lot of the Indian reaction that we see today is rooted in the trauma of the 1947 partition, which looms large in the corridors of Indian policymakers. The creation of the state of Pakistan from lands that previously belonged to India is not just the after-effects of British colonial rule but the present reality of a rival nuclear power next door. Pakistan, born out of the demands of the minority Indian Muslims, need not be repeated more than 75 years later in the form of the creation of Khalistan.

Proponents of Khalistan, like those of Pakistan, argue that Sikhs have faced discrimination and marginalization within India and seek self-determination and autonomy in a separate Sikh-majority state. It is a contentious and deeply polarizing issue within India, with many opposing views both within the Sikh community and among the broader Indian population. President Biden raised the issue during Prime Minister Narendra Modi's visit to Washington on June 2023, but with little to no resolution.

India maintains its independent options for its own foreign relations while renewing its long-standing commitment to strategic non-alignments within its foreign policy. Among a younger generation of politicians in New Delhi, there remains a degree of sympathy for Putin's narrative against NATO expansion. It is a similar experience in India's own province of Kashmir. China and Pakistan, India's two main rivals, have their pieces of the province, Aksai Chin (China) and Azad Jammu and Kashmir (Pakistan), bordering India. Kashmir is the catalyst that has produced three India-Pakistan wars and one war with China. Like Russia, India sees forces approaching closer to their periphery, looking further to disrupt its economic priorities and shifting its attention over to a military response. However, most analysts believe that the economic priority is central to Prime Minister Modi's legacy as he and his Bharatiya Janata Party (BJP) look to win their third consecutive general election in 2024.

After two years of war in Ukraine, India has benefitted from discounted Russian crude oil, a whopping 20% discount, and a ten-fold increase from pre-war consumption of crude oil imports. It has certainly benefited the Kremlin in helping to control crude prices. When the war began, there was a risk of oil prices shooting upwards. Under the present climate, Indian companies benefited from the export of refined Russian oil products, many of which they sold to Western markets.

India's position to vote or abstain in favor of Moscow in the United Nations has remained unchanged. New Delhi is protecting what it believes is its own national interest. The EU and the United States have had no choice but to tolerate India's position, recognizing as they do so, businesses in energy-hungry India cannot afford to isolate the convenient options of Russian oil which is crucial to India's economic ascendance. The Indian contribution, particularly, has assisted Russian imports of oil by 33 times.

New Delhi played a similar role with other countries in Asia, Africa, and Latin America, who declined to enforce Western backed sanctions on Russia, giving the Kremlin a lifeline. Western sanctions in reality created a network between a pro-West and pro-Russia sphere. It also developed trading patterns in ways that might outlast the conflict.

For instance, one of the most enduring effects of the Napoleonic Wars (1803-1815) was on trading patterns. The outcome produced an upward trend of British economic power. The British Royal Navy's blockade of French ports and its control of maritime trade routes severely constrained France's ability to engage in international trade. Meanwhile, Britain expanded its colonial holdings and trade networks, becoming the dominant maritime trading power of the 19th century.

Britain forged closer economic ties with its colonies and trading partners outside of Europe, while European countries sought to diversify their trade relationships and reduce dependence on traditional trading routes. Furthermore, the conflicts set the stage for the subsequent Industrial Revolution in Britain, as the demand for goods and materials to support the war effort spurred technological innovation and industrialization. The transformation had long-lasting effects on global trade patterns, as Britain became the world's leading industrial power and exporter of manufactured goods.

There are some similarities between the Napoleonic wars and the after-effects of the war in Ukraine. The Russian "special military operation" is a tectonic shift from a world in pre-2022 to a post-2022 era. Two years into the conflict, there is increased volatility in oil prices, food shortages, and supply chain issues. Those who are beholden to Russia and those who condemn it have become two large factional parts of the world. It is unlike any other global dynamic witnessed since the 19th century. It is now an era of a clash of Western-backed sanctioned countries versus pro-Western states. The chief difference is their use of the U.S. dollar. The United States Department of Treasury closely monitors any potential threats or challenges to the status of the U.S. dollar. It also includes the ability to borrow in its own currency, lower borrowing costs, and enhanced influence over global financial markets. There is no doubt that there have been numerous forecasts of the threat of dethroning of the U.S. dollar as the world's reserve currency. The American threat and the economic relationship between India and Russia are interconnected. Recently, India and Russia have sought to strengthen their economic ties through initiatives such as the International North-South Transport Corridor, which aims to facilitate trade and transport between South Asia, Central Asia, and Europe. During the first year of the Ukraine war, American diplomats made strenuous efforts to convince New Delhi to condemn Russian actions. At the very least, Washington petitioned to limit India's long-standing political and trading relationship with Russia. The Kremlin's refusal to use the U.S. dollar in its transactions with India and replacing it with the "ruble-rupee" setup allows for bypassing American financial controls and sanctions, thereby strengthening the Russian ruble.

The more Russia sells its oil and natural gas through exports, the more it increases the ruble's exchange rate, which will also mean huge increases in Indian products in the Russian market. India is a global hub for information technology services and software development, with a large pool of skilled professionals and technology companies. Russia may seek outsourcing services, software solutions, and expertise from Indian I.T. firms to support its own technological needs and development initiatives. India is also known for its pharmaceutical industry, which produces a wide range of generic medicines and vaccines at competitive prices. Russia, like many other countries, may import pharmaceutical products from India to meet its healthcare needs.

The Russian policy to abandon the U.S. dollar to trade in every area, in an alternative currency in BRICS trading bloc, (Brazil, Russia, India, China, and South Africa) is already showing results.

Another alternative is conducting transactions in an existing and stable currency and minted by a non-sanctioning country to bypass Western sanctions. The Indian rupee and the South African rand fit the bill. However, the Chinese yuan was the only one actively seeking an international role and had the leverage to do exactly what the Kremlin needs.

In February 2022, Beijing relaxed its yuan controls. It avoided an outright grant to the Kremlin by giving them more yuan than the depreciated Russian rubles. Since Russia's currency was weak to the yuan, it received less of its own currency for the funds received, giving Beijing the advantage to not subsidize Russia's war. As a result, it became expensive for Russia to buy Chinese goods and China had the upper hand in determining prices for its imports and drive down Russian export prices.

In response, the Kremlin then began a fiscal policy of converting its reserves into yuan and creating transaction channels for a joint ruble-yuan setup. The success of the ruble-yuan setup had Russian economists report a conversion of 60% in the National Wealth Fund.

Since the beginning of the war, the transactional trade in the ruble-yuan has gone up 80 times. However, this kind of arrangement will lead to transactional dependence, with the Russian ruble being dependent on the yuan.

Beijing's detailed and hawkish controls of the ruble-yuan exchange rate will create future risks for the Kremlin in terms of trade balance. This is particularly a problem for the Kremlin if the Russian Central Bank is unable to sell Chinese bonds. If Beijing controls it so tightly, in the future, the Kremlin will find it impossible to liquidate the yuan-denominated assets.

The Ukraine war has made Russia a "yuan" dependent economy. The steps have helped the Kremlin bypass Western sanctions, but they have also created a huge set of other problems. As long as Western sanctions remain, Beijing owns the economic veins of the Kremlin.

Under such circumstances, the Kremlin does have a few options. Since 2014, Russian gold holdings have tripled, worth approximately $140 billion, and out of the reach of Western-backed sanctions. Russia is also the second largest gold producer in the world, but it sells its gold at a price nearly 30% less than that of China. There is a fear that Russian gold to China will be sold at even cheaper rates because Western-backed sanctions have halted the purchase of Russian gold for its retailers, which only means that the Kremlin would have to rely on its network of intermediaries, including Belarus, Cote d'Ivoire (Ivory Coast), Cuba, Iran, Myanmar, North Korea, and Venezuela, to do what it can't. When it is short on cash, its network will not give it a lifeline compared to the traditional and economically well-to-do markets of America and Europe; therefore, the problems for the Kremlin will still continue.

The Kremlin has not come close to feeling a financial pinch nor bankruptcy as its energy sales have continued to thrive. The issue is that Russian gold cannot be used as collateral for loans or "swaps," which provide the sale of transactions without physically moving the gold. There are countries that can afford to fall on the bad graces of Europe and the United States when they risk buying Russian gold. This is where the Kremlin will find a lifeline.

China and India can help with loaning cash to the Kremlin, which would only mean the buyers would not know that it is Russian gold. It is a practice that can work. In 2012, Iran sold natural gas to Turkey in exchange for gold, which was then sold for cash in Dubai. Tehran could do the same for the Kremlin. For China, Russian gold is central to the process of increasing its yuan reserves and dethroning the U.S. dollar as the world's reserve currency, so the competition and demand for Russian gold are still present.

To dethrone the U.S. dollar is almost a Chinese fantasy. Not only does it take volumes of transactions, but it is also very expensive. The only reason consumers use the U.S. dollar is because of its stability, liquidity, and confidence among both sides of the transaction parties. Even with the inclusion of BRIC nations, Russia and China will not be able to undermine the U.S. dollar. The only thing that can cause harm to the U.S. dollar is the internally divided political landscape within the United States. However, even then, the yuan has not done its time nor has the kind of confidence as the U.S. dollar does among consumers.

For instance, the term "petrodollar" refers to the practice of pricing oil in U.S. dollars. Since the 1970s, most global oil transactions have been conducted in U.S. dollars. This system was solidified after the U.S. negotiated agreements with major oil-producing countries, notably Saudi Arabia, to price their oil exclusively in U.S. dollars in exchange for military and economic support. The petrodollar system reinforces the global demand for the U.S. dollar, as countries need dollars to purchase oil, contributing to the dollar's status as the world's primary reserve currency. When oil prices rise, oil-importing countries need more U.S. dollars to buy the same amount of oil, which can increase the demand for dollars and strengthen the currency. Iran produces approximately 3 million barrels of oil per day (*Source*: Nikkei Asia). The money from these Iranian fuel barrels is also assisting rogue groups like Hezbollah, Hamas, the Houthis, and Iraqi militias, which also stem through Tehran's crude oil coffers. Russia produces 9.6 million barrels of crude oil per day (*Source*: PBS). Their barrels begin their journey from Siberia to India's Jamnagar Manufacturing Division (JMD), at Motikhavdi Village, in the Indian state of Gujarat. Before February 2022, this location did not process any Russian crude, but today it is more than 30% and blended with others in gasoline, diesel, and other products that is purchased by American and European companies. After February 2022, other countries found a refining ambiguity and used it. They began buying oil legally, refined it, and then sold it to American and European companies like B.P., Sunoco, and Shell.

Russia is the third-largest producer of oil worldwide, accounting for over 12 percent of global crude oil production (*Source*: Statista). If the U.S. were to shut off all purchases of all oil originating from Russia, the reality of expensive and unaffordable prices in petrol stations would affect all Americans. Substantial amounts of fuel, worth millions, are derived from Russian crude, continue to end up in American gas tanks. Hundreds of thousands of barrels of fuel arrive at American ports, yet it is not widely known that a portion of this fuel is partially sourced from Russian crude oil. This dynamic creates a significant contradiction: while the United States provides aid to Ukraine, it simultaneously funnels money into Putin's coffers, inadvertently financing actions in murdering Ukrainians.

Chapter 3

A PRICE OF CONSEQUENCES

The Soviet Union's accumulation of massive public debt can be attributed to a confluence of factors, both domestic and international priorities. Internally, economic mismanagement played a pivotal role. The centralized planning system led to inefficiencies, waste, and a lack of innovation. The Soviet system, which prioritized heavy industry over consumer goods, resulted in chronic shortages and a declining standard of living for Soviet citizens. Military spending further exacerbated the economic strains. The arms race with the United States during the Cold War required substantial financial resources, diverting funds from essential domestic needs. It was compounded by the protracted ten-years war in Afghanistan. The war which began in 1979 not only demanded significant financial outlays for military operations but also resulted in a high human cost, with substantial casualties and the long-term economic impacts. Externally, the Soviet Union faced mounting pressures in Europe and the Middle East. The geopolitical strategy to maintain influence in Eastern Europe required economic and military support for allied regimes, which also strained the Soviet budget. Additionally, fluctuating oil prices and the economic sanctions imposed by Western nations further limited the Soviet Union's financial flexibility. The economic difficulties were exacerbated by the legacy of Brezhnev's "Economic Stagnation." This period, which spanned from 1973 to the early 1980s, was marked by a slowdown in economic growth, declining productivity, and technological lag. The stagnation entrenched structural inefficiencies and left the Soviet economy ill-prepared to adapt to global economic changes.

One notable example, the central planners in the Soviet Union made decisions based on political considerations rather than economic rationality in the pursuit of ambitious industrialization goals, particularly in heavy industry.

Under Brezhnev, the Soviet Union set pioneering targets for industrial production, especially in sectors like steel, machinery, and heavy manufacturing. These targets were often driven by political imperatives, such as showcasing the achievements of socialism, projecting military power, and maintaining political control rather than economic necessity.

Central planners prioritized meeting these production targets at all costs, often disregarding economic constraints and practical considerations. As a result, resources were allocated inefficiently, and industrial projects were sometimes undertaken without proper feasibility studies. A key facet of this approach was the construction of large-scale industrial complexes, such as steel mills, chemical plants, and machinery factories, in remote or economically unsuitable locations. These projects were often undertaken for political reasons, such as fulfilling regional development quotas or bolstering the prestige of local party officials, rather than based on economic viability or market demand. The emphasis on heavy industry and the neglect of consumer goods production also contributed to imbalances in the Soviet economy, leading to shortages of consumer goods, low-quality products, and inadequacies in resource allocation, which led to massive public debt.

After the disbanding of the Soviet Union in December 1991, the successor state, the Russian Federation, inherited all Soviet public debt. The new state became the world's second-largest producer of natural gas, behind the United States, and has the world's largest gas reserves. It is also the world's largest gas exporter. President Putin made it a top priority as part of his foreign policy with Europe as a way to pay off Soviet-era public debt.

The gas exports provided the Kremlin with a substantial source of revenue, capitalizing on its abundant gas reserves to generate income. The revenue helped to stabilize the Russian economy after the

Yeltsin era and allowed the Russian government to invest in infrastructure, social programs, and other areas crucial for economic recovery. It also enabled Russia to earn foreign currency, which was crucial for stabilizing the country's external accounts. It was a welcome relief after a decade of severe balance of payment problems.

From 2004 onwards, gas exports helped alleviate economic issues by providing a steady inflow of foreign exchange, which stabilized the Russian ruble and improved the country's ability to service its external debt. Exports facilitated investments in the modernization of Russia's energy sector. The modernization not only increased the efficiency of gas production and transportation but also enhanced Russia's overall economic competitiveness. Investment in infrastructure also created jobs and stimulated economic growth in related industries. The profits from exports helped Putin significantly in geopolitical leverage, especially in Europe, where Russia supplies a substantial portion of gas. The influence allowed Russia to negotiate favorable terms for its gas exports, as well as to exert political pressure when needed.

In 2006, by leveraging its gas reserves, Russia strengthened its position as a major player in global energy markets, which contributed to its international standing and influence.

European leaders realized that there was no truly reliable alternative to Russia as an energy partner. The German government, in particular, continued its reliance on Russian energy. Arrangements were made to determine which fields had access to which pipelines. Gazprom, the Russian state-owned multinational energy corporation, set the prices and the conditions, and without it, Nordstream, which became operational in 2011, consisting of two parallel lines running from Vyborg in Russia to Lubmin in Germany, would not be what it is today. The gas pipeline system also transports Russian natural gas to Europe. It consists of two parallel pipelines, Nordstream 1 and Nordstream 2, which run across the Baltic Sea.

Nordstream AG, a subsidiary of the Russian state-owned energy company Gazprom, owns and operates the Nordstream pipelines. Gazprom holds the majority stake, while European energy companies, including E.ON, Wintershall, ENGIE, OMV, and Shell, hold minority shares. It had a significant geopolitical set of implications for Europe's energy landscape.

Proponents argue that it enhanced energy security by providing a direct and reliable route for Russian gas supplies to reach European markets, diversifying supply routes, and reducing dependence on transit countries prone to political tensions. However, critics raise concerns about Nordstream's potential to increase European reliance on Russian gas, undermining Ukraine's transit role and weakening Europe's negotiating position with Russia.

Nordstream has faced criticism from environmental groups regarding its potential impact on the Baltic Sea ecosystem. Additionally, the project has economic implications for European energy markets, affecting gas transit fees for countries along traditional transit routes and potentially influencing gas price dynamics in Europe. By 2019, there were signs that Western Europe especially needed Nordstream as an opioid. Take Nordstream away, and Western Europe would have withdrawal symptoms. Putin realized the realities much earlier and was convinced that, in invading and annexing Crimea in 2014, he would not endure any consequences from his European counterparts. He was right, as the prospects of Nordstream 2 were not halted. Even when Western-backed sanctions came after Russia annexed Crimea, it had little consequence. Russia still hosted the 2014 Winter Olympics, and it went on to host the 2018 FIFA World Cup without any boycotts. Putin may have been emboldened to go to war against Ukraine in February 2022 since he realized the only thing that would come his way was only more Western-backed sanctions.

The first significant instance of Russia leveraging its political influence in Europe occurred in January 2006, when the Kremlin cut gas distribution to Ukraine. The action was taken amid a contentious dispute between Russia's state-owned gas company, Gazprom, and Ukraine's state energy company, Naftogaz. It was centered around gas prices and outstanding debts. At the heart of the crisis were disagreements over the appropriate price Ukraine should pay for Russian natural gas. Gazprom sought to increase the price to reflect market levels, arguing that the subsidized rates were unsustainable. In contrast, Ukraine contended for a lower price, citing its historical ties as a former Soviet republic and the economic hardships it faced.

As negotiations faltered and Gazprom's deadline for payment lapsed, Russia proceeded to cut off gas supplies to Ukraine. The disruption had significant implications for Europe. Given that Ukraine served as a crucial transit route for Russian gas to Europe, the reduction in gas flow affected several European countries, starkly illustrating Europe's vulnerability to disruptions in Russian gas supplies. The event marked a pivotal moment for European countries, revealing the potential consequences of their dependence on Russian energy resources and highlighting the geopolitical leverage that Russia could exert through its energy exports. While the gas cutoff lasted for a few days before a compromise was reached and later resumed, the incident highlighted the vulnerability of Europe's energy supply to disputes between Russia and Ukraine, leading to concerns about energy security and the need for diversification of energy sources and transit routes.

Subsequent gas disputes between Russia and Ukraine continued in 2009, 2014, and 2015, each resulting in temporary disruptions to gas supplies to Ukraine and to Europe.

Gazprom has been exploiting its European neighbors for decades and furthering Putin's political agenda. French President Jacques Chirac, German Chancellor Gerhard Schröder, British Prime Minister Tony Blair and Italian Prime Minister Silvio Berlusconi, were content with Russia not connecting Nordstream 1. All were fine with removing the transit flow from Ukraine and diverting the pipeline into different routes.

The German Chancellor in particular pursued a strenuous lobbying campaign of the pipeline where Germany not Ukraine, would be the transit point of Russian gas supplied to Europe. He began his campaign during the last days of his Chancellorship during November 2005. However, other developments nearly derailed his plans. After leaving public life Schröder was appointed chairman of the board of Nordstream AG, and Rosneft. In May 2022 he resigned.

Nordstream was not the only Russian ploy. The Kremlin's broader strategy of using its energy resources to bolster its geopolitical power, ensure the stability and security of its natural gas exports, also had another avenue in the Caucasus.

The Mozdok–Tbilisi pipeline, also known as the North Caucasus–Transcaucasia pipeline, is a natural gas pipeline that runs from the Mozdok area in the North Caucasus region of Russia to Tbilisi, the capital of Georgia. The pipeline plays a significant role in supplying natural gas to Georgia, which relies heavily on imports to meet its energy needs. It serves as an essential link in Georgia's energy infrastructure, providing a reliable source of natural gas for residential, commercial, and industrial use. The pipeline is part of a broader network of pipelines that transport Russian natural gas to various countries in the Caucasus and beyond. It connects to the South Caucasus Pipeline (SCP), which extends from Azerbaijan through Georgia to Turkey and ultimately to Europe via the Trans Anatolian Natural Gas Pipeline (TANAP) and the Trans Adriatic Pipeline (TAP). The pipeline system plays a crucial role in diversifying energy routes and enhancing energy security in the region. It also has geopolitical significance, as it allows for the transportation of natural gas from the Caspian Sea region to European markets, reducing dependence on traditional transit routes through Ukraine.

On 22 January 2006, there were two explosions at the North Ossetia site of the Mozdok–Tbilisi pipeline. The Western-backed President Mikheil Saakashvili's government claimed Russia was sabotaging the surrender of pipelines to Gazprom. Saakashvili's government had previously refused to sell its own pipelines to Russia. In eight days, gas supplies resumed, but the reasons for the explosions and the chief culprits were never found. The Kremlin blamed Chechen and Islamist terror groups. Shortly after, President Saakashvili wrote an opinion piece in *The Washington Times*, cautioning the West's dependence on Russian energy. He petitioned in favor of Georgian oil and gas as a viable alternative. It was the moment when Putin had begun the clock to end Saakashvili's reign.

The Columbia University law school-educated Saakashvili, rose to power in Georgia following the peaceful Rose Revolution in 2003, which ousted the government of Eduard Shevardnadze, the former Soviet Foreign Minister of Secretary Mikhail Gorbachev.

Putin first met Saakashvili on February 2004 in Moscow, a month after the Georgian presidential election. From the beginning, Putin was irritated by Georgia's pro-West President, who harbored aspirations for closer ties with the West, including his desire to join NATO and the European Union (EU). In addition, Putin was particularly sensitive on Saakashvili's take on the breakaway regions of South Ossetia and Abkhazia.

Saakashvili wanted to assert Georgian control over the breakaway regions, which had de facto independence backed by Russia. South

Ossetia and Abkhazia, had declared independence from Georgia in the early 1990s, leading to unresolved separatist conflicts. Saakashvili did not give in to their demands. He found confidence when NATO issued a declaration for membership to Georgia and Ukraine during the April 2008 Bucharest Summit. However, no specific timeline or roadmap for accession was announced, leading to ambiguity regarding the exact timing of Georgia's membership.

Georgia, as a NATO member, would constitute a direct threat to Russia's security. It would further encircle Russia, potentially limiting Russia's strategic depth and increasing its vulnerability to Western military capabilities. Most importantly, it would also diminish Russia's influence in the South Caucasus region. Russia has historically considered the Caucasus as within its sphere of influence, but NATO's presence could escalate tensions and increase the risk of conflict between Russia and NATO forces.

For Europe, Georgia's NATO membership would strengthen the alliance's eastern flank, extending NATO's security umbrella further into the Caucasus region and would contribute to enhancing overall security in Europe, particularly in the face of potential terror threats in the region. It would also halt interference from Russia, contributing to regional stability particularly on economic growth, especially for those like Georgia.

Stalin's place of birth Georgia is a strategic location in the South Caucasus region which makes it a critical transit route for energy resources, including oil and natural gas pipelines. NATO membership for Georgia would help safeguard energy transit routes and contribute to energy security in Europe by diversifying energy sources and reducing dependence on Russian energy supplies.

European trade relations with Russia could deteriorate under such realities, but the Georgian President did not mind. Despite differences between the two capitals, trade in natural gas has generally continued, albeit subject to fluctuations and occasional disputes over pricing and terms of supply.

When NATO issued a declaration for membership to Georgia and Ukraine during the April 2008 Bucharest Summit, it was evident Russia would likely respond soon with economic sanctions or cancellation of trade, which appeared to be on the horizon, but a military showdown was far from anticipated in Tbilisi.

On 7 August 2008, Georgia launched a military operation to regain control over South Ossetia, which it viewed as part of its sovereign territory, beginning the first steps of the five-day war. The conflict escalated rapidly, with heavy fighting occurring in South Ossetia and other parts of Georgia. Russian forces launched a large-scale military operation, conducting airstrikes, artillery bombardments, and ground offensives against Georgian targets. Georgian forces initially offered resistance but were quickly overwhelmed by the superior firepower and Russian fighter jets. Georgia endured significant damage to their infrastructure and the war ended on 12 August 2008, with a ceasefire agreement brokered by French President Nicolas Sarkozy, who was acting on behalf of the EU. Russian and Georgian forces were to withdraw to their respective positions, and international monitors were deployed to oversee the ceasefire. The aftermath of the war had significant geopolitical implications. Russia recognized the independence of South Ossetia and Abkhazia, leading to heightened tensions between Russia and the West. The conflict also strained relations between Russia and Georgia, with the two countries remaining in a state of diplomatic deadlock and mutual mistrust. The episode remains a contentious and unresolved issue, with the status of South Ossetia and Abkhazia remaining a source of conflict and instability in the region.

Geographically, the two regions served as a buffer zone for Russia, and by maintaining influence in these breakaway regions, the Kremlin exerted control over Georgia's internal affairs and limited Tblisi's ability to integrate fully into Western institutions like NATO and the EU. South Ossetia hosts several Russian military bases and installations, which provide Russia with a strategic foothold in the region. These military assets allow the Kremlin to project power beyond its borders and respond quickly to potential security threats in the South Caucasus. Additionally, the presence of Russian troops in South Ossetia acts as a deterrent against potential military aggression from Georgia or other neighboring countries. Maintaining a presence also allows Russia to safeguard its economic and strategic interests in the region, including energy transit routes and transportation corridors. Many residents of South Ossetia identify closely with Russian culture and see Russian troops as protectors of the interests of South Ossetians, which helps legitimize the Kremlin's involvement in the region.

Abkhazia's Taman Bay provided Russia access to the Black Sea. It is a critical waterway for trade, commerce, and military operations. Abkhazia is known for its natural resources, including agricultural land, minerals, and potentially offshore oil and gas reserves. Control over Abkhazia provided Russia with access to these resources, which can contribute to its economic development and energy security to safeguard its economic and strategic interests in the Black Sea region, including access to ports and maritime routes. Another useful asset is Abkhazia's Tuzla Spit, a narrow stretch of land in the Kerch Strait, which separates the Black Sea from the Sea of Azov and serves as a focal point between Russia and Ukraine. Control over the area is crucial for both Russia and Ukraine as it impacts naval and commercial shipping routes. The spit itself is part of a larger region that includes the Kerch Peninsula and the island of Tuzla, which became particularly contentious following the disbanding of the Soviet Union in 1991.

The Tuzla Spit was originally part of Soviet Russia but was administratively transferred to the Ukrainian Soviet Socialist Republic (Ukraine SSR) in 1954 by Khrushchev. The administrative boundary became a point of contention in August 1991. Since then and in 2003, tensions escalated when Russia began constructing a dam towards Tuzla Island, which Ukraine perceived as an attempt to alter the maritime boundary and assert control over the Kerch Strait.

For Putin, there was also another problem. The Baku-Tbilisi-Ceyhan (BTC) pipeline is a major oil pipeline that runs from the Azeri-Chirag-Guneshli oil field in the Caspian Sea off the coast of Azerbaijan to the Mediterranean port of Ceyhan in Turkey. The pipeline would give Tbilisi a lifeline, but in due time, could also find its way to connect Ukraine and threaten Gazprom's control of Kyiv and the capitals of Europe. The BTC also pulled Washington closer into what looked like the Russian-Iran space. The very aim of the 1,099-mile pipeline was to transport crude oil from the Caspian Sea to international markets, bypassing Russia and providing an alternative route for exporting a million barrels of oil from the landlocked Caspian region. It allowed oil-producing countries in the Caspian Sea, particularly Azerbaijan, to diversify their export routes and reduce dependence on traditional transit countries, especially Russia. The BTC pipeline became operational in 2006. The project was a collaborative effort between several international oil companies, including B.P. (British Petroleum).

Starting from Shah Deniz, in the oil-rich Azerbaijan area, to Ceylan in Turkey, provided access to diversified energy supplies and reduced reliance on Russian-controlled pipelines. The BTC passed through politically unstable regions in parts of Georgia, where there have been occasional security incidents. Additionally, the pipeline has been the target of terrorist attacks in the past, highlighting the security risks associated with energy infrastructure projects in a volatile region. Putin would bypass Saakashvili and create a strategic engagement with Georgia's neighbor Azerbaijan. While Baku sought to diversify its energy export routes and reduce dependence on the Kremlin, it still maintains energy cooperation with Russia.

The Azerbaijan President Ilham Aliyev, the heir of Azerbaijan's third President Heydar Aliyev, the influential First Deputy Premier of Mikhail Gorbachev, came from similar KGB stock as the Russian President. Both were groomed in key Soviet institutions of Moscow State University and the KGB, which shaped their world views about adversaries, friends, and the West. Both have an affiliation to their version of Soviet history. In his speeches, Aliyev calls the Armenian Nagorno-Karabakh "Western Azerbaijan" and, similarly, the Iranian province of Azerbaijan "Southern Azerbaijan." It is a sign of things to come, but like Putin, has powerful rivals to stop his expansionst conquest for a "Greater Azerbaijan."

The most severe confrontation Aliyev endured during his time in office was in September 2023, marking the largest attack by Azerbaijan on Armenia in the history of their conflict, resulting in casualties on both sides. Armenia and Azerbaijan have already fought two wars over Karabakh in the three decades since the Soviet Union disbanded. The most sensitive issue is the status of the 120,000 ethnic Armenians in Karabakh backed by Yerevan. Azerbaijan accuses Armenia of fuelling separatism in the area.

Nagorno-Karabakh is believed to have significant economic resources, including fertile agricultural land, mineral deposits, and potential hydrocarbon reserves. Control of the area will provide Armenia or Azerbaijan with significant revenues for its coffers.

There is a feeling that under the watchful eye of Yerevan's allies in the Kremlin and Tehran, Aliyev will not be able to control the entire Nagorno-Karabakh area. His country is in a stalemate war, resulting in a prolonged period of deadlock.

The issue of Nagorno-Karabakh is rooted in the Treaty of Turkmenchay. A treaty signed in 1828 between the Russian Empire and Qajar Persia, primarily delineated the border between Russia and Persia. It had significant implications for the modern state of Azerbaijan, particularly its territorial integrity and security.

Following the end of the 1826 Russia-Persian War, which ended in a decisive victory for Russia, Qajar Persia ceded several territories to Russia. It included parts of present-day Azerbaijan such as the Khanates of Erivan (Yerevan) and Nakhchivan (Azerbaijan), establishing a new Russia-Persian border along the Aras River. It led to Azerbaijan's inclusion within the Russian Empire, which later became part of the Soviet Union.

The modern state of Turkey upholds the Treaty of Turkmenchay as a historical reference point to emphasize Azerbaijan's historical and cultural ties with Turkey. Ankara supports Azerbaijan's territorial integrity and sovereignty. While the treaty itself does not contain provisions for the Turkish defense of Azerbaijan, Turkey's commitment to upholding the treaty underscores its broader diplomatic and strategic alignment with Azerbaijan. Furthermore, Turkey's support extends beyond the Treaty of Turkmenchay and is rooted in shared cultural, ethnic, and linguistic ties between the two countries. Ankara has historically been a vocal advocate for Azerbaijan, particularly in the context of the Nagorno-Karabakh conflict with Armenia, and has provided diplomatic, economic, and military assistance to Azerbaijan.

It is a similar tone to Turkey's intervention in the Syrian civil war, where Turkish forces entered the conflict, hoping to dethrone the Alawite regime of President Bashar Al-Assad in Damascus. In August 2016, Turkey launched Operation Euphrates Shield along with allied Syrian opposition groups. The primary objective was to clear the border region between Turkey and Syria of both ISIS militants and Kurdish militia groups, particularly the People's Protection Units (YPG), which Turkey views as an extension of the Kurdistan Workers' Party (PKK), a designated terrorist organization. Turkey wanted to establish a buffer zone along the Turkey-Syria border and prevent the YPG from gaining further territory.

Against the Turkish forces, Damascus could not retaliate against a

NATO member. If it did shoot down a Turkish fighter jet, it would incur the wrath of Article 5 of the NATO charter, whereby a collective declaration of war would not only ensure Ankara's success but also the absolute demise of the Bashar Al-Assad regime. For nearly four years, Syrian forces had to orient a defensive posture until September 2015, when the Russians entered the Syrian civil war.

The same Europe that provided the backing of Turkey would endure the real consequences of Turkey's adventure in Syria. The arrival of Syrian refugees in Europe began to gain significant attention and visibility in the summer and fall of 2015, although individual Syrian refugees had been arriving in European countries prior to that year. Thousands of refugees, fleeing violence, persecution, and humanitarian crises in Syria and other conflict-affected countries in Afghanistan, Iraq, Libya, and other African states, embarked on perilous journeys to seek safety and asylum in Europe. Harrowing tales of dangerous journeys, often by sea, to reach in search of safety, protection, and better opportunities made the headlines all over the world. The images of overcrowded boats crossing the Mediterranean Sea, dangerous land routes, and refugee camps overwhelmed by the sheer number of arrivals captured global attention and sparked a humanitarian crisis in Europe. The emergency prompted responses from European governments, international organizations, and civil society, leading to debates over refugee policies, border controls, and burden-sharing arrangements within the EU. The arrival of Syrian refugees in Europe marked one of the largest refugee movements in recent history and had profound social, political, and humanitarian implications for Europe.

There is a feeling that Putin miscalculated what he hoped one of his aims in Syria would be. He thought Europe would actually be grateful to him for doing what Turkey's Erdoğan wouldn't do, which was to stop the flow of millions of refugees coming into Europe. If Russian troops could stabilize Syria, make it secure, Europe could send large numbers of Syrian migrants back, or so he thought, as leverage for a "slap on the wrist" for his annexation of Crimea.

Putin's advisors, including his foreign minister Sergey Lavrov, were surprised during a 2016 February U.N. session of the European reaction. There was no expressive European gratitude for Russia or Putin. The Syrian civil war continued with a sectarian nature. It pitted

Iran and Russia-backed Alawites and their allies Hezbollah against moderate rebel groups, Islamist factions, and jihadist organizations such as Hayat Tahrir al-Sham (formerly known as al-Nusra Front) and the Islamic State of Iraq and Syria (ISIS). Kurdish militias, primarily the People's Protection Units (YPG) backed by the United States, Britain, and France, carved out the richest Syrian land with their capital in Rojava. Saudi Arabia, Qatar, and the United Arab Emirates (UAE) supported opposition groups, as well as Israel, which has conducted airstrikes against Iranian, Hezbollah, and Syrian government targets.

In October 2019, an understanding was reached on the battleground facilitated by the Russian leadership, that Israeli and Turkish jets would not harm Russian fighter jets. Previously, Turkey shot down two Russian Sukhoi Su-24 fighter planes on 24 November 2015. The incident occurred near the Syria-Turkey border. Ankara claimed that the jets violated its airspace and were warned multiple times before being shot down by Turkish F-16 fighters. One of the Russian pilots was killed, while the other was rescued. The incident significantly escalated tensions between Russia and Turkey. The Kremlin imposed economic sanctions on Turkey as it also accused Ankara of supporting terrorist groups in Syria. It took the 24 February 2022 Russian invasion of Ukraine for relations to normalize between Ankara and Moscow.

In 2024, all situations suit Putin perfectly well. A preoccupied Azerbaijan in its war with Armenia, a Georgia with separatists in the north, and Turkey busy with the Syrian civil war, will create enough petty problems for BTC and keep Gazprom safe to sell gas via third-party subsidiaries to Europe uninterrupted. What also suits Putin is the firm European divide at the forefront of Nordstream. Germany did not consult Poland or the Eastern Europeans as it received a direct supply of natural gas. The pipeline enhances Germany's energy security by providing an additional route for gas imports, diversifying its energy sources. However, traditional gas transit routes in Ukraine, Belarus, and Poland may see a reduction in transit fees and leverage as a result of Nordstream bypassing them. The former German Chancellor Angela Merkel believed that the Russian-German arrangement in the Nordstream was purely an economic suitability. However, Berlin defied Brussels and also Paris, the Scandinavian countries, Warsaw, the Baltic states, and Washington, to act in its own interest.

Nordstream ultimately made the departure from the traditional stand of post-World War II Germany. Merkel's Germany decided to go at it alone against a host of oppositions. The example of Nordstream shows how Germany is departing from its traditional stance of consulting Britain, France, and the United States. Dangerously, it was also a green light for Putin to use pipelines to use Germany to conform to his demands in Europe and in Ukraine.

The Minsk peace process was a mere set of carrots provided by Merkel's Germany to say sorry to Ukraine over its conduct during the Russian annexation of Crimea. Merkel's successor, Chancellor Olaf Scholz inherited Ukraine's distrust, and then the 2022 war came when he had to make amends. Zelenskyy's regime showed positive signs of taking on the Russian forces, as it looked like the reward would be entry to the EU, but on 26 September 2022, the fate of Nordstream took a disasterous turn. Underwater explosions affected the two Nordstream natural gas pipelines, only a few weeks before Ukraine's second war anniversary. *Reuters* noted that Swedish seismologists registered the damages of three out of four lines of the Nordstream system, sending plumes of methane into the atmosphere. Sweden did confirm it was a deliberate act but failed to cite the main culprit. German investigators reported to the U.N. that trained divers may have attached explosives to the pipelines.

What came to light on 27 September 2022 in the German magazine *DER SPIEGEL*, that CIA only a few months back had warned its contacts in Germany, about possible attacks on Baltic Sea pipelines. The intelligence report was based on information provided by a source in Ukraine, and CIA shared it with Germany and other European countries.

Nordstream was the making of Germany's former Chancellor Angela Merkel, who revealed in 2022 her disagreement with Ukraine's prospects of joining NATO at the 2008 Bucharest summit. Her role in the Minsk Agreements, where Ukraine was pressured into concessions after Crimea was annexed and eastern Ukraine was almost ceded to the Russians, was not something she appeared to regret. She said that her "heart always beats for Ukraine." But had she not blocked Ukraine's admission, there is no doubt that Putin would have had to pick between two conflicts in 2008, and he would have surely chosen Ukraine over Georgia.

Even today, Georgia has not escaped the eye of the Russian President. From 2023 onwards, Georgia saw widespread street demonstrations against the proposed "Law on Transparency of Foreign Influence," which would require Non-Government Organizations (NGOs) receiving over 20% of their funding from abroad to register as foreign agents. Critics, including the EU and Western countries, argue the bill would stifle democracy and press freedom. Supporters claim it promotes transparency and protects national sovereignty from harmful foreign influences.

The President of Georgia Salome Zourabichvili, who became alienated from her own government, after the beginning of the 2023 Georgian protests and barely survived an impeachment, vetoed the bill. The Georgian parliament led by the Georgian Dream political party, bypassed her and passed the law.

The law, likening to the Russian foreign agent law has produced suspicions of a Kremlin hand. It is like the Russian law enacted in 2012, which requires organizations that receive foreign funding and engage in "political activity" to register as "foreign agents." The law specifically mandates foreign organizations must label their publications with a "foreign agent" disclaimer and undergo additional scrutiny and reporting requirements. It has been criticized for being vague and broad, allowing the Kremlin to target and suppress NGOs, independent media, and activists, thereby restricting freedom of speech and civil society activities. The term "foreign agent" in Russia carries strong negative connotations, reminiscent of Cold War-era espionage accusations.

In Georgia, there are widespread speculations that the 68-year-old Oligarch Bidzina Ivanishvili, the founder of the ruling Georgian Dream political party, is pulling the strings behind the scenes. He made his personal fortunes in Russia during his close association with former President Yeltsin in the mid-1990s, and while precise figures are not publicly available, estimates suggest that Ivanishvili's business empire could account for a significant portion of Georgia's GDP. Some analysts estimate his direct and indirect influence to be around 5-10% of the national economy. As Prime Minister (2012-2013) and as an influential political figure afterward, Ivanishvili has often tried to balance Georgia's pro-Western aspirations with a pragmatic approach toward Russia. He pursued a policy of "normalization" with the

Kremlin, trying to reduce tensions from the era of President Mikheil Saakashvili's reign and restore economic relations without compromising Georgia's sovereignty and territorial integrity, especially concerning the Russian-occupied regions of Abkhazia and South Ossetia. However, accusations of pro-Russian sentiments plagued his reputation, facing allegations from political opponents of being too conciliatory towards Russia. Critics argue that his policies might undermine Georgia's sovereignty and its aspirations for European integration. Even after officially stepping down from political office in 2013, Ivanishvili continued to influence the Georgian Dream party and Georgian politics. He is often scrutinized for perceived pro-Russian leanings, a significant problem given Georgia's ongoing aspirations to join NATO and the EU. The very fact his own party passed the "Law on Transparency of Foreign Influence" will shatter Georgia's European future, which also gives enough indications that Ivanishvili's balancing act has tilted to favoring Putin's preferences over Georgians. The only body that can now restore some level of a peaceful transition from protest to peace is Georgia's security services. Its Chief, Grigol Liluashvili is a long-time Ivanishvili associate. Western powers can only hope he does not make the mistake of a brutal clampdown, but he will stop the opposition from their momentum on the streets and could very well influence the Georgian elections in October 2024, but he too will feel the Kremlin frustrations and pressure. The repercussions will be felt by Georgia's youth, just like in 2008, along with Ukraine, wanted their future with the West and not Russia.

When it came to Ukraine, 2008 is an important year to analyze the country was riddled with corruption, Ukraine's oligarchs, not Kyiv, had real authority over state affairs and as former Chancellor Merkel stated…"What would have happened if, in 2014, no one had cared and Putin had simply continued?" She added: "Those seven years [from 2014 until the build-up of Russian forces in 2021] were very, very important for the development of Ukraine." During those seven years, Canada, the United States, and some European countries provided military advisors to Ukraine to strengthen its military capacity to firm up its eastern line against Russian proxies in Donetsk and Luhansk. However, Merkel spoke candidly about how she understood Putin and the danger that was to come to Europe's door. She claimed

Washington's main obstacle was not Brussels but Berlin's failure to arm Ukraine. The episode can be interpreted as Merkel's government doing the bidding on behalf of Putin.

In 2015, Merkel declared that Germany would not supply Ukraine with weapons, a stance supported by several European allies. This decision reflected broader European hesitations about Ukraine's alignment with NATO, reminiscent of the 2008 sentiments shared by leaders such as French President Nicolas Sarkozy. At that time, the prevailing view was that Ukraine did not meet the necessary "political conditions" for NATO membership, though this justification likely masked deeper concerns about Ukraine's economic and geopolitical stability, but also strong Russian reservations.

A significant factor influencing Germany's cautious approach was its economic entanglement with Russia, particularly in the energy sector. Germany's reliance on Russian gas, which began escalating before Merkel's tenure, surged dramatically from 2008 onwards, culminating in a dependency where Russian imports accounted for up to 65 percent of Germany's gas needs by 2022. This dependency was exemplified by the Nordstream 2 pipeline project, a $12 billion initiative that was only halted following Russia's invasion of Ukraine. Despite recognizing the geopolitical risks posed by Putin's regime, Merkel's government continued to prioritize Russian gas within its energy strategy, inadvertently enhancing Russia's leverage over Germany and Europe.

When General Philip Breedlove, then NATO's supreme commander in Europe, proposed arming Ukraine, Merkel's cabinet dismissed the idea as "dangerous propaganda." The reaction underscores a broader strategic ambivalence within Merkel's government, which acknowledged the threats posed by Putin's aggressive policies but refrained from taking decisive countermeasures. Merkel perceived Putin's expansionist ambitions and paranoia as erratic and inherently unstable, viewing them as challenges that could be managed temporarily but not decisively confronted by military responses. Consequently, her government's policies were characterized by a blend of cautious engagement and strategic dependency, which ultimately constrained Germany's and Europe's ability to effectively counter Russian aggression.

This is at odds with the reality now. The Russian President

continues his assault on Ukrainians and is looking to entrench the Baltics and Poland. Merkel called Russia's invasion of Ukraine "a great tragedy," but like all tragedies that stem from friends, not enemies, it is almost a euphemism to avoid blame.

Merkel's "soft stand" allowed Putin to strengthen not only Russia's economic links with Germany but also with powerful companies in Europe. Nordstream was a German addiction that was too good and too great to pass. There is a feeling that the German Chancellor was backed by big businesses to press on with her backing for the gas pipeline, despite opposition from the United States. Germany became, for the Kremlin, an economic tool where Putin could do as he pleased. This had a remarkable resemblance to East Germany's relationship with the Soviet Union. After nearly 33 years since the disbanding of the Soviet Union and in an era of an economically integrated Europe, Merkel's Germany oddly resembles the foreign policy of East Germany (GDR), a close alignment and subordination to Soviet interests. Most particularly, East Germany's economy was closely tied to the Soviet Union through the Council for Mutual Economic Assistance (Comecon). The GDR relied on Soviet resources, especially energy supplies, and followed economic policies that aligned with Soviet plans. Most catastrophically, the GDR's foreign policy was coordinated with and often directed by Moscow in opposition to NATO and Western influence, something today which peculiarly looks unchanged.

The Soviet era produced political lessons for future European leaders, particularly those from the Eastern Bloc. The lasting effects of Soviet-era policies on their future post-Soviet political outlooks and policies were meant to be a tonic to the future of Europe. During their youth, many European leaders experienced first hand the dominance and influence of the Soviet Union over their nations, which shaped their perspectives on international relations, security, and energy.

Miloš Zeman, the President of the Czech Republic since 2013, grew up in Soviet-controlled Czechoslovakia and was a member of the Czechoslovak Communist Party, serving in various government positions before becoming a prominent politician in the post-communist era in the Czech Republic. Donald Tusk, the Prime Minister of Poland and former President of the European Council (2014-2019), grew up in Communist Poland. He was active in the anti-communist opposition movement and played a role in Poland's transition to democracy after the disbanding of the Soviet Union. Viktor Orbán, the Prime Minister of Hungary since 2010, came of age in Communist Hungary and was involved in anti-communist activism as a young man. He was a prominent member of the Alliance of Young Democrats (Fidesz), which played a key role in Hungary's transition to democracy. However, he had an odd political awakening and diverted to an autocratic path.

Merkel's upbringing in East Germany (GDR), under Soviet influence, profoundly shaped her geopolitical outlook and approach to international relations, particularly with Russia. Growing up in a divided Germany, Merkel experienced firsthand the realities of life in a state closely monitored by the Stasi, the East German secret police. A unique perspective provided her with a deep understanding of both the oppressive mechanisms of the Soviet system and the broader implications of living under a regime heavily influenced by Moscow. Unlike many Western leaders whose perceptions of the Soviet Union were shaped from a distance, Merkel's lived experience offered her a more intimate understanding of Soviet-style governance and its impact on daily life. This background likely contributed to her cautious and pragmatic approach to dealing with Putin, characterized by an understanding, allowing her to anticipate Russia's strategic moves and motivations more accurately, leading to a diplomatic approach, not a military one, that balanced the need for dialogue with the necessity of maintaining a strong stance on issues such as Ukraine, energy security, and peace in Europe. As Olaf Scholz faces the complex challenge of inheriting Merkel's past policies amidst a more volatile geopolitical environment, he must navigate a price of consequences of engaging with Putin. In this context, Scholz's commitment to supporting Ukraine at any price becomes a pivotal element of his strategy, reflecting a shift towards a more assertive stance in safeguarding European security.

Chapter 4

A DEPENDENT ALLIANCE

On 4 April 2024, NATO celebrated its 75th anniversary. The North Atlantic Treaty Organization is an intergovernmental military alliance between 32 countries. It was established in 1949, with 12 nations and its primary purpose was to guarantee the security of its members through political and military means. The core principle is collective defense, directed in its Article 5, meaning an attack against one member is considered an attack against all members, and all members will respond accordingly. The 24 February 2022 Russian invasion of Ukraine has given credence to what NATO, as an alliance, is really not.

After World War II, the expansion of Soviet influence in Eastern Europe, particularly the establishment of communist regimes in Poland, Czechoslovakia, Hungary, and Romania, raised concerns among Western European nations and the United States about Soviet intentions. The outbreak of the Cold War between the Western powers, led by the United States, and the Eastern Bloc, led by the Soviet Union, heightened fears of potential military aggression and confrontation. The 1948 Berlin Blockade and the Soviet-backed coup during the same year in Czechoslovakia, were among the events that underscored the need for a collective defense mechanism. War-battered France and West Germany sought security guarantees and believed that a collective defense alliance would deter aggression and provide a framework for mutual assistance in the event of a Soviet attack. The

United States led by example in guaranteeing security to the beleaguered Western Europeans.

NATO leaders in the last 75 years would like to compare their standing better than the stability to the period known as the "Long Peace," referring to the relatively non-large scale wars that followed the end of the Napoleonic Wars in 1815 and lasted until the outbreak of World War I in 1914.

The so-called "Long Peace" was characterized by a series of smaller conflicts and political tensions that were often masked by other quarrels. In 1821, Greece fought for independence from the Ottoman Empire with support from European powers, including Britain, France, and Russia. In 1828 and again in 1877, the Russians and the Ottomans fought over territorial disputes in Eastern Europe and the Caucasus. In 1830, Belgium revolted against Dutch rule and declared independence, leading to the Belgian War of Independence. In 1848, Italy underwent a process of reunification involving numerous conflicts, including the first Italian War of Independence (1848-1849), the second Italian War of Independence (1859), and the third Italian War of Independence (1866). In 1853, the Crimean Peninsula came under conflict involving Russia on one side and an alliance of France, Britain, the Ottomans, and Sardinia on the other. In 1848, the Schleswig Wars centered on the duchies of Schleswig and Holstein, involving Denmark, Prussia, and Austria. It ignited again in 1864 after a decade of normalization. The main conflict that would mark as a ticking time bomb for Europe came in the 1870 Franco-Prussian War. The outcome shaped the geopolitical landscape of Europe and contributed to the larger European tensions in the 20th century.

In 1871 following Prussia's victory over France, the southern German states, previously allied with Austria, joined the North German Confederation under Prussian leadership. This outcome led to the proclamation of the German Empire with Wilhelm I of Prussia as Kaiser. The creation of a powerful, unified German state altered the balance of power in Europe and posed a challenge to the established order dominated by Austria, Britain, and France. The defeat of France in the 1870 Franco-Prussian war left deep scars and a sense of resentment within French society. France lost the provinces of Alsace and Lorraine to Germany, which became a source of bitterness and desire for revenge. The quest to regain lost territory and restore French prestige fueled a sense of rivalry and hostility for the coming decades.

After 1871, European powers began to form alliances to deter potential aggression. France sought allies to counter the growing strength of Germany, leading to the formation of the Triple Entente between France, Russia, and Britain. Meanwhile, Germany forged alliances with Austria-Hungary and Italy, forming the Triple Alliance. These alliance systems created a delicate balance of power in Europe, but also increased the risk of conflict.

There was a broader trend of militarism and an arms race, with European states investing heavily in military technology and expanding their army and navy in preparation for potential conflicts. The rivalry between France and Germany, combined with the alliance systems, intensified this arms race and heightened tensions across Europe.

Deterrence looked to dim tensions between European powers to maintain a balance of power and prevent potential conflicts from escalating into a full-scale war. Diplomatic efforts played a crucial role in resolving disputes and managing tensions. European states engaged in complex diplomatic maneuvers, negotiations, and alliances to maintain a delicate balance of power and prevent any single nation from becoming too dominant.

The steps to combat the French-German rivalry, Europe's two great powers from the conclusion of World War I, did not work to alleviate the problems of Europe and, in fact, only a few years later, produced the rise of totalitarian and fascist forces.

For Ukraine's policymakers, these events should play a part in how much trust they have for NATO and their member-states. More importantly, realize that historic underlying tensions will forever influence Europe's policy makers. That the historic rivalry of Europe's great powers serves as warnings about deep and heated tensions, the illusion of stability, and the potential for conflict escalation dangerously from within will make Europe and difficult partner in a time of war.

Europe's "Long Peace" was severely fragile and dependent on the cooperation of major powers, which could easily unravel, as seen in the lead-up to World War I. It is quite visible that seemingly stable political arrangements were deceptive and would collapse under pressure. This is something Zelenskyy's government has calculated in their set of emergency measures as the so-called "Long Peace" provided the wars they were not fighting in Europe to fight elsewhere.

As the great rivalry between Britain and France materialized in America, Carribean and India, so too did the rise of Russia during the same period. The Napoleonic Wars, particularly the 1812 French invasion of Russia, contributed to Napoleon's defeat. Russia showcased its military strength, strategic importance and how useful its blessed cold weather could be its best defense against Europe. The event significantly enhanced Russia's prestige and influence in European affairs during the 19th century.

Today, Ukraine is serving as a critical venue for conflict between the West and Russia, embodying the 21st-century ideological struggle between freedom and authoritarianism. It is a proxy battleground where Ukraine, with the help of the West, is taking on Russia as Putin exerts his expansionist objectives.

Europe, even with NATO, saw conflicts. The most prominent example was in 1969, in Northern Ireland. It is a time when sectarian conflicts between Irish nationalists and unionists involving paramilitary groups and British security forces, which came to be known; "The Troubles." The leadership within NATO convienienty found a way to stay out of it. Since NATO's primary focus during the Cold War was on collective defense against the Soviet Union and its allies, Northern Ireland was seen as a British domestic issue.

The excuse to stay out of conflict continued even after the disbanding of the Soviet Union, when conflicts surged in Europe. In 1991, the breakup of Yugoslavia, led to the Croatian War of Independence, the Bosnian War, and the Kosovo War. In 1992, conflict between Moldova and the breakaway region of Transnistria soon took hold, and the threat of the stalemate war continues to this day. NATO's success in European security is largely attributed to the leadership of the United States. The reality is Europe's 29 armies in the 21st century just can't handle military operations on their own.

After the disbanding of the Soviet Union in December 1991, NATO became another version of a U.N. peacekeeping set of units while letting the United States take the lead. The alliance was taking a nearly three-decade-long holiday until February 2022, when

Russia invaded Ukraine.

NATO's Supreme Allied Powers headquarters in Brussels is home to one of the most well-protected buildings in the world. It serves as the alliance's political and administrative hub. The headquarters complex is located in the Evere municipality and houses various NATO offices, agencies, and decision-making bodies. The alliance credits itself as the world's largest defense that provides security for more than a population of 1 billion.

NATO's Command and Control (C2) structure is a framework that coordinates military operations and activities among member states to ensure effective command, control, and communication in both peacetime and during times of crisis. The C2 structure enables NATO to plan, execute, and manage military operations in accordance with its mission of collective defense and crisis management. It includes strategic-level commands responsible for overall direction, planning, and coordination of military operations.

Supreme Headquarters Allied Powers Europe (SHAPE) is located in Mons, Belgium. SHAPE is NATO's strategic headquarters, which is responsible for planning and executing military operations in the Euro-Atlantic area. It monitors the operational readiness and deployment of NATO forces. It also coordinates with national military authorities of member states. Allied Command Transformation (ACT) is headquartered in Norfolk, Virginia. ACT is responsible for transforming and developing NATO's military capabilities, doctrine, and interoperability. It conducts research, testing, and training, to enhance the effectiveness and readiness of NATO forces. The Operational Command, NATO's C2 structure, also includes operational-level commands responsible for conducting military operations in specific regions. These operational commands include Joint Force Commands (JFCs) located in strategic regions around the world, including JFC Brunssum (Netherlands), JFC Naples (Italy), and JFC Norfolk (U.S.). These commands are responsible for planning and executing military operations, conducting exercises, and ensuring readiness within their respective areas of responsibility. Component Commands are subordinate to the Joint Force Commands and focus on specific military functions, such as air, land, maritime, or special operations, providing operational-level command and control of assigned forces and assets. Member states provide forces, capabilities, and personnel to support NATO's missions and operations, which are integrated into NATO's overall command and control framework. Communication and Information Systems is also a NATO's C2 structure, which relies on advanced communication and information systems to facilitate rapid and secure exchange of information among headquarters, commands, and deployed forces. These systems enable real-time situational awareness, decision-making, and coordination of military activities.

The present organization setup is a stark contrast to the days of NATO's founding in 1949. When the alliance was founded, it had no military structure and no command center. It was really a symbolic American promise to its 11 other allies (Britain, Belgium, Canada, Denmark, France, Iceland, Italy, Luxembourg, Netherlands, Norway, and Portugal). The alliance was created as part of an American vision against a Soviet threat. The danger looked like a sure thing after the Soviets successfully tested their first atomic bomb in August 1949. The United States no longer had a monopoly on nuclear weapons. It was the start of nearly a half-a-century-long arms race and the Cold War.

Some European historians, with evidence from Soviet policies, strategies, and foreign policy, highlighted that militarily, the Soviets were never really a threat to Western Europe and that they were too busy consolidating their hold within the Iron Curtain. Marxist historians viewed the Soviet Union more sympathetically and often interpreted Soviet actions as defensive responses to Western imperialism and capitalism. During period of the 1970 detente, there were European historians who advocated for improved relations and cooperation between the Western powers and the Soviet Union. They argued that dialogue, diplomacy, and arms control agreements could reduce tensions and mitigate the perceived threat of an American and Soviet nuclear war.

Revisionist historians challenged conventional interpretations of the Cold War and questioned the belief of a monolithic Soviet threat to Western Europe. They emphasized factors such as misunderstandings, miscalculations, and the role of domestic politics in shaping Cold War dynamics, arguing that the Soviet Union's intentions and capabilities were often exaggerated.

The Vietnam war can be loosely depicted as the 20th century version of what we see in Ukraine today. While the three-decades long conflict was a hangover from the 85-year French occupation dating back to 1870, the war was primarily fought between Communist North Vietnam and its allies, including the Soviet Union and China, against South Vietnam and its principal ally, the United States.

The United States would go on to lose more than 58,000 of its own, but justified its involvement by invoking the "domino theory." It was the means by which one country in Asia would fall to Communism, followed by neighboring countries in the form of dominos. Vietnam's location too, was a key strategic importance. It is situated at the crossroads of Southeast Asia, bordered by China to the north and Laos and Cambodia to the West, with significant maritime routes that provide access to vital shipping lanes connecting the Indian Ocean to the Pacific, making Vietnam strategically significant. Since President Truman, successive American Presidents till President Ford, believed the fall of Vietnam would also mean the entire region falling to Communism.

The theory painted the Soviet Union and its allies as orchestrating a global Communist expansion, leading to fears of Soviet domination in regions beyond Europe. The Vietnam War was viewed by many in the West as a proxy conflict between the United States and the Soviet Union, serving as a battleground in the larger Cold War struggle for influence. While the Soviet Union provided military aid and support to North Vietnam, its role in the conflict was often exaggerated by Western policymakers and media. In response, the United States increased its military spending and commitment of troops to North Vietnam, while the Soviet Union expanded its support for Communist movements worldwide. This escalation of military activity contributed to perceptions of a looming Soviet threat and the need for increased vigilance and preparedness in the form of a struggle between the forces of democracy (represented by the United States) and the forces of Communism and Totalitarianism (represented by the Soviet Union and its allies).

While NATO was the chief instrument of such rivalry, there is another argument that attests to the need for the creation of such a grand alliance. NATO was the answer to the battle within America against right-wing movements.

Since the end of World War II and well into 1955, the United States saw the emergence and growth of various right-wing activities, organizations, and ideologies. These movements often espoused conservative, nationalist, and anti-communist views. Both the Truman and Eisenhower administrations believed that the Soviets would militarily take advantage at a time when American democracy was divided, but if NATO could hold them off, America's politicians could take on the problems at home.

One example was the John Birch Society. It was founded in 1958 by the candy businessman magnate Robert W. Welch Jr., and the right-wing organization promoted anti-Communism, limited government, and traditional American values. It opposed what it perceived as Communist infiltration in the United States and advocated for a staunchly conservative agenda.

Another was the American Nazi Party. It was led by George Lincoln Rockwell, a veteran of World War II and the Korean War. His organization continued to exist and still does to this day, although its influence waned in the post-war era. It espoused white supremacist, anti-Semitic, and fascist ideologies, seeking to promote a racially homogeneous America.

Other groups too, while different had similar right-wing views. The Christian Nationalist Crusade had a similar stance. It was founded by clergyman Gerald L.K. Smith in 1947, and it was a right-wing organization that combined Christian fundamentalism with nationalist and anti-Communist sentiments. It opposed what it saw as the secularization of American society and advocated for conservative social policies.

Various anti-Communist organizations and movements emerged during this time, including the American Legion, the National Association of Manufacturers, and the Crusade for Freedom. These groups mobilized public opinion against Communism and supported measures to contain its spread domestically and internationally.

In the South, the states' rights movement gained prominence, particularly in opposition to federal desegregation efforts and civil rights initiatives in the 1950s. Politicians such as Strom Thurmond of South Carolina and organizations like the States' Rights Democratic Party (Dixiecrats) advocated for maintaining segregation and preserving states' rights against federal intervention.

Within the U.S. Senate, Wisconsin Senator Joseph McCarthy's anti-Communist crusade fueled a broader climate of fear and suspicion regarding communist infiltration in American society. McCarthy and his supporters accused numerous individuals of being Communist sympathizers, leading to widespread investigations, blacklistings, and political purges, including members of several past Presidential administrations.

In 1948, Whittaker Chambers, a former Communist turned anti-Communist, testified before the House Un-American Activities Committee (HUAC) that the Baltimore-born Alger Hiss, a former official from the Roosevelt administration and a graduate of Johns Hopkins and Harvard Law, who was then serving as a high-ranking official in the State Department, had been a member of a Communist cell in the 1930s. Chambers alleged that Hiss had passed classified documents to him for transmission to the Soviet Union.

The accusations against Hiss sparked a series of investigations by federal agencies and congressional committees, including the Federal Bureau of Investigations (FBI) and the House Un-American Activities (HUAC), led by California Congressman Richard Nixon (future Senator, Vice-President and President) and South Dakota Congressman Karl Mundt. Hiss vehemently denied the allegations, asserting that he was a victim of mistaken identity and political persecution. However, the investigations continued. Hiss was eventually indicted on charges of perjury for denying under oath that he had passed classified documents to Chambers. His first trial in 1949 ended in a hung jury, but he was convicted in a second trial in 1950. The case against Hiss became a cause célèbre, dividing public opinion and igniting debates about the extent of Communist infiltration in the U.S. government. It had far-reaching political implications, contributing to the rise of McCarthyism and the broader anti-Communist hysteria in the United States. McCarthy and his allies portrayed the Hiss case as evidence of Communist subversion within the highest levels of the U.S. government, using it to justify their crusade against alleged Communist sympathizers.

After convicted in a second trial in 1950, Hiss was sentenced to five years' imprisonment but served three years and eight months in Lewisburg Federal Prison in Union County, Pennsylvania. While in prison, he actively worked as a tutor to fellow inmates. After his release, and among the books he wrote, particularly the 1988 publication of *Recollections of a Life*, where he maintained his innocence and claimed the typewritten documents traced to his typewriter had been forged. He died on 15 November 1996.

The Hiss case remains controversial and subject to historical debate, intertwined with perceptions of the time. As security and anti-Communist hysteria plagued the United States, beyond the end of McCarthyism (his death in 2 May 1957), when it became evident that many of Senator McCarthy's accusations were baseless and that he had little substantial evidence. NATO gave a lifeline to democratic governments in Europe, that could tell their constituents that with global security came domestic economic stability. However, that was not entirely the case.

Despite the West encountering challenging but manageable domestic discontent, NATO was not immune to cracks within the alliance. It is something that still resonates today and one which Ukrainians are particularly sensitive to, as the fallout will affect them most dangerously.

From the birth of the alliance, one of the main tensions within NATO was the debate over the rearmament and integration of West Germany into the alliance's military structure. Following World War II, West Germany (FDR) was initially excluded from NATO due to concerns about its past aggression and its potential for rearmament. However, as the Cold War intensified, there was increasing pressure within the alliance to integrate West Germany. It raised several tensions and debates within NATO. All members of the alliance, particularly France, were wary of the prospect of West Germany rearming. Memories of World War I and II, and even the 1870 Franco-Prussian war, were still fresh, and there were concerns about a resurgent West Germany and the potential for it to destabilize Europe. The United States ended the debate. The Americans, at their peak, had approximately 250,000 to 300,000 troops stationed in West Germany in 1952.

NATO today is a key Ukraine backer, and Poland resembles West Germany the most, since it borders Ukraine. Then West Germany was at the frontline of the Cold War, bordering the Soviet-backed Warsaw Pact countries. Today, Poland is a frontline NATO state that also borders Russia and Belarus. Its geographic location makes it a critical buffer and a strategic point of defense for NATO against potential Russian aggression. Poland also hosts a significant number of NATO troops and has been a central part of NATO's Enhanced Forward Presence initiative. It mirrors the role then West Germany played as a base for NATO forces, particularly for American troops, during the Cold War. Tensions within NATO did escalate to conflict. On 18 February 1952 Greece and Turkey became members of NATO. In 1955, the Cyprus conflict showcased a battle between two of NATO's own. Greece and Turkey came to the aid of their fellow Greek and Turkish Cypriot communities on the island. Tensions further escalated in 1974, when a coup d'état backed by the Greek military junta took place in Cyprus, leading to Turkey's military intervention in response. It resulted in the de facto partition of Cyprus into the internationally recognized Republic of Cyprus in the South and the self-declared Turkish Republic of Northern Cyprus in the North.

Further strains followed within the alliance. France's withdrawal from the NATO-integrated military structure in 1966, under President De Gaulle, created some tensions with West Germany. De Gaulle's vision of an independent French defense policy, including the development of a French nuclear deterrent, diverged from West Germany's reliance on the NATO alliance for security. France returned to full participation in NATO's integrated military structure in 2009.

NATO's Article 3 outlines the commitment of member states to maintain and develop their individual and collective capacity to resist armed attack. It is divided into criteria of Collective Defense, Right to Self-Defense, Mutual Assistance and Security. Article 3 emphasized the importance of military readiness and defense preparedness among member countries.

"The Parties agree that an armed attack against one or more of them in Europe or North America shall be considered an attack against them all, and consequently, they agree that, if such an armed attack occurs, each of them, in exercise of the right of individual or collective self-defense recognized by Article 51 of the Charter of the United Nations, will assist the Party or Parties so attacked by taking forthwith, individually and in concert with the other Parties, such action as it deems necessary, including the use of armed force, to restore and maintain the security of the North Atlantic area." In 2024, the realities differ sharply to the pre-existing design of the alliance.

Britain has undergone several rounds of defense cuts and

restructuring since 2011, resulting in reductions to its land forces. In 2010, the British government conducted the Strategic Defense and Security Review (SDSR), which outlined significant defense cuts and restructuring measures in response to budgetary constraints and changing security priorities. The SDSR resulted in reductions to the size and capabilities of the British Army, including cuts to personnel, equipment, and infrastructure. In 2012, the British Army announced its 2020 plan, which aimed to restructure and modernize the army to meet evolving security challenges. As part of the plan, the army underwent a significant reduction in size, with the goal of reducing the number of regular army personnel from around 102,000 in 2010 to approximately 82,000 by 2020.

Like Britain, nuclear-reliant France has faced budgetary constraints too, and the need for defense reforms in response to changing security environments and fiscal pressures. Defense spending priorities have shifted, leading to adjustments in force structure and capabilities. It has focused on modernizing its armed forces, including the Army, to enhance effectiveness and readiness while optimizing resources. It has involved streamlining structures, improving interoperability, and investing in advanced capabilities. France sees NATO, the European Union (EU), and European coalitions of like-minded partners as part of a broader aim to mend its deficits and use its influence in the force structure decision-making and operational bodies.

France's past rival Germany does have land forces but its no where near to capability levels of fighting a war, let alone winning it. For the German army, the "Bundeswehr," modernization has been slow, a military industrial complex is not in parity with others and there are financial sensitivities around re-awakening the past behaviors in fear of preserving a very delicate model of democracy.

The German army needs €300 billion to modernize, and then there are personnel and recruitment issues. Many Germans, under the Federal Vacation Act (Bundesurlaubsgesetz), enjoy an entitlement to a minimum of 24 working days of paid vacation per year, based on a six-day work week. For employees working a five-day work week, this translates to a minimum of 20 vacation days per year. During wartime, the Bundeswehr would find it extremely difficult to provide that to its servicemen. It is no secret that application numbers have progressively been on the decline for decades. The Bundeswehr enjoys a very qualified officer class, but that is where it ends. The much-needed lower ranks that often do the heavy lifting are scarce, and this poses huge issues when it comes to combat readiness.

For Ukrainians, these attributes provide several reasons to be cautious about Western European leaders and the leadership in NATO, as historical experiences, geopolitical dynamics, and differing threat perceptions all contribute to a sense of wariness.

As Britain, France, and Germany struggle, there are additional problems within the NATO structure. The alliance of 32 member-states also means 29 additional layers of bureaucracy in deployment, logistics, and decision-making. It is like taking military supplies from Copenhagen to Lublin, only to be checked and approved at several checkpoints, which further causes delays, something during a critical time will contribute to dangerous circumstances for Ukrainians.

The pressing problem stands among European federal and regional governments, many of whom are in coalition and some who do not wish for the success of the alliance. They are beholden to pro-Russian electorates, yet these coalitions remain crucial to NATO. A reality which Kyiv has no choice but to live with.

Bavaria, one of the 16 federal states (Bundesländer) of Germany and located in the southeast, is the largest state by land area and the second-most populous after North Rhine-Westphalia. The state has the key German transport route for aid to Ukraine, traveling to Lithuania. Tanks are transported by train since peacetime bridges cannot bear the weight of such heavy military equipment. The German railways offer NATO a 33% better option for deployment compared to land, air, and sea, but delays are common. This comes at a time when Russia fires 50,000 artillery rounds on average/per day. For Ukraine to measure to that level, it would take German ammunition to fit Dutch barrels, distributed to Polish depots, and then mascarade into Ukraine for use. This is also not helped by a shortage of fuel.

Bavaria, like the rest of Germany, has a well-established tradition of workers' unions (Gewerkschaften). These unions play a significant role in representing the interests of workers, negotiating collective bargaining agreements, and advocating for better working conditions and wages. The largest and most influential labor union in Germany is the German Confederation of Trade Unions (Deutscher Gewerkschaftsbund, also known as DGB), which represents workers across various industries. The DGB is an umbrella organization comprising several individual unions, each representing specific sectors or occupational groups. In addition to the DGB-affiliated unions, independent unions, and professional associations, represent workers in Bavaria. These include unions representing specific industries such as manufacturing, automotive, healthcare, education, and public services. One of the key factors of delays in railway transport is rail strikes that have roots in these unions.

Bavaria is where Chancellor Olaf Scholz's Social Democratic (SPD) rivals; the center-right Christian Social Union (CSU), who are in a ruling coalition government with Free Voters (FW). The Chancellor will find it extremely difficult if and when the time comes to speed things up in Ukraine, as he is at the mercy of the CSU-FW leadership.

Much like Scholz's limitations, NATO too, has its hands tied. Article 5 of the NATO charter, which speaks to an armed attack on one as an attack on all, is surprisingly NOT a designed trigger on all 32 member states. There is a strong emphasis on consultations among all 32 NATO members. All have to officially accept at the federal government level and then have their respective parliaments approve their military to join the alliance as it responds to the attack of a fellow member. It will not be a quick process if an attack does take place. Some members may be expedient, but others may find themselves delayed.

For instance, on 24 March 2024, the Polish government demanded an explanation from Moscow after one of its missiles strayed briefly into Polish airspace. NATO knew fully well that it was the third missile attack directed at Ukraine, but it fell into Polish territory. In response, the Polish government cited a violation of their airspace and activated their F-16 fighter jets. Polish Defense Minister Władysław Kosiniak-Kamysz believed it was a targeted strike on Poland. The incident has a few important implications for NATO. There is no doubt the Baltic states would have a different take on the matter, but to the larger alliance, the Russian "accidental" strike in Poland means that the Ukraine war isn't limited to a missile crossing into a neighbor's border. Poland is not directly arming Ukraine in strict military terms. True that it is allowing the use of its territory for military supplies to reach Ukraine and participating in Western-backed sanctions on

Russia, but it is not at war with Russia. The Kremlin interprets this differently. NATO member Poland may not be directly arming Ukraine, but Russia is at war with NATO. Like Vietnam, Ukraine is viewed by the Kremlin as a proxy conflict between Russia and the United States and its allies, with Ukraine serving as a battleground in an indirect war against the West.

For NATO, the 24 March incident was not significant enough for a collective suicidal military response. European analysts were quick to point out that the NATO treaty "doesn't force" members to commit to the alliance response. In other words, Poland may want to respond to the Russian attack, but NATO does not want to. It goes to show how NATO's eastern border has become so sensitive that such incidents can spark a potential military conflict. True that NATO leadership is heavily invested in not allowing a fellow member to widen the Ukraine war, but here is where another sign of troubles can materialize; a clash between NATO leadership and the leaders of their member states. If that happens, Russia will achieve one crucial aim, the breakup of the alliance at a time of war.

The last time Poland decisively defeated Russia in a war was in August 1920, in the aftermath of World War I and the Russian Revolution. Both Poland and the Soviets sought to expand their territories and influence in Eastern Europe. The conflict was marked by several significant battles and campaigns, including the Battle of Warsaw in August 1920, often referred to as the "Miracle on the Vistula," where Polish forces decisively defeated the Red Army. The victory at the Battle of Warsaw halted the Soviet advance into Central Europe and forced the Soviet leadership to reconsider their military strategy. In the aftermath of the battle, both sides engaged in negotiations, leading to the signing of the Peace of Riga on March 1921. The peace established the eastern border between Poland and Soviet Russia along the Curzon Line, which granted Poland significant territorial gains at the expense of the Soviets.

More than a century later, Russia has one of the largest militaries in the world, with substantial manpower and reserves. Poland's armed forces, in contrast and unlike its NATO counterparts, have been modernizing and expanding in recent years. The war in Ukraine is slowly inching into Poland, reminding Berlin, London, Paris and Washington, how sensitive the Ukraine war is becoming to pull NATO into a conflict with Russia.

Under Article 5, what if one or more members refuse to fight Russia? Hungary, a NATO member and an ally of Russia, disagrees with Poland over a range of issues. Budapest wants to curtail the EU's response to migration issues. The two Visegrád allies have huge differences, and that will also fester in how they respond to the war in Ukraine. Prime Minister Victor Orbán's stand is so dangerous for the alliance that NATO Secretary General Jens Stoltenberg had to compromise by signing a June 2024 letter, confirming that he would maintain a pledge to permit Hungary to opt out of supporting Ukraine at NATO. The controversial move is a ticking time bomb that can erode the consensus rule at NATO. A no-vote from the 13th largest European military-Hungary with 41,600 active troops, would be a huge blow to the alliance. It would also create volatility within NATO's soft power in terms of community, solidarity, and unity.

75 years may have brought 29 European leaders together in one room, but old scars still remain from as far back as the Napoleonic Wars in 1815. Article 5 is really the making of the United States in the event then-West Germany was to be attacked by the Soviet Union. After Germany's reunification and integration of former Iron Curtain states into the NATO fold, Article 5 became a weak order of unity to enforce.

Just as those in the alliance can be part of a no-vote, others too, are free to decide whether to stand by an ally. For instance, if Poland was attacked by Russia, Bulgaria and Slovenia could very well be part of a Hungary led no-vote, but for the yes-vote members, their response could very well mean anything but a military confrontation.

Article 5 does not state specifically a military response. The only soft guarantee is that the United States, the largest military in the alliance, will back whichever NATO member is under attack.

The first Chancellor of post-World War II West Germany, Konrad Adenauer may have comprehended this labyrinth better than most, even among those in the modern era. The Cologne-trained lawyer wanted a greater guarantee than Article 5 for the future of his new West Germany. He petitioned for American soldiers, along with British and Canadians, to be stationed on his home soil. By doing so, Adenauer made leaders from London, Ottowa, and Washington complicit in the safety of their armies directly with West

Germans. Adenauer's West German defense, a NATO eastern border, in reality, meant the protection of Adenauer's own government. The Zelenskyy government may draw lessons from this period.

The stationing of American troops under NATO protection of a country that caused two World Wars was not popular in public opinion, even among Adenauer's cabinet and his electorate. West Germany faced severe devastation and hardship in the aftermath of World War II, with widespread destruction of cities, infrastructure, and industries. Berlin, Hamburg, Frankfurt, Essen, Dusseldorf, Stuttgart, and even Adenauer's home city, Cologne, a major industrial and cultural center, suffered extensive damage from Allied bombing raids, including the devastating Operation Millennium in May 1942. The episode was a significant military operation orchestrated by the Royal Air Force (RAF) Bomber Command, marking a pivotal point in the strategic bombing campaign against Nazi Germany, as it aimed to demonstrate the RAF's capability to deliver a massive bombing raid.

The presence of NATO troops served as a constant reminder of the war's consequences and the loss of life and resources to West Germans. In due time, it shaped their anti-war sentiments. It was a stark reminder of the horrors of World War II and the subsequent occupation that followed. Many West Germans resented the loss of sovereignty and perceived the occupation as humiliating and intrusive. The post-war period witnessed mass displacement and dislocation of millions of Germans expelled from former German territories in Eastern Europe and forced to resettle in the truncated German state. Measures aimed at de-Nazification, de-militarization, and democratization were present in West Germany, but it's debatable how far they were successful in East Germany. While some West Germans welcomed these efforts as necessary for rebuilding a democratic and peaceful society, others perceived them as intrusive and heavy-handed. In the post-reunification era, while some attitudes have changed, German militarism still remains a taboo subject.

Today, Germans are more than happy in their intellectual, political, and economic prosperities. However, with it has come a very isolationist political attitude. A majority of Germans are distant from the realities of the Baltic states and the denizens of southeast Poland, where the effects of the Ukraine war are felt the most. The majority of the German attitude is to let other European countries worry about Ukraine, as it has nothing to do with Germany. It is also a similar attitude shared by a large section of the American population. Such attitudes are the root of the disconnect between how much the effects of the war could spread.

For instance, the German electorate has huge reservations over their feelings about their country's economic, military, and political backing of Ukraine. These reservations have already placed Scholz's key coalition ally, the Green Party in a very difficult position. It is very possible the Greens will not find electoral success in the next German federal elections, expected by September 2025. Such realities have not halted Scholz, although differences in his cabinet are growing.

A 5,000-man German brigade is due to be permanently stationed in Lithuania and operational by 2027. The consequences of such a move will be felt in Ukraine and in Scholz's Social Democratic Party's (SPD) prospects in the next German federal elections.

The stationing of a NATO-member brigade is a violation of the NATO-Russia Founding Act on Mutual Relations, Cooperation, and Security. Signed on 27 May 1997 in Paris, the agreement now looks to be a relic of the past. Putin's Kremlin is immeasurably different from Yeltsin's, which agreed to make such a concession with the West. The document between NATO and Russia aimed at fostering cooperation and building trust in the post-Cold War era to redefine the relationship and establish a framework for cooperation based on shared security interests, outlining principles, including respect for sovereignty, territorial integrity, and the inviolability of borders; refraining from the threat or use of force against each other; and resolving disputes through peaceful means including crisis management, arms control, nonproliferation, and counter-terrorism. The agreement also established mechanisms for regular consultation and cooperation between NATO and Russia, including the establishment of a NATO-Russia Permanent Joint Council (PJC) to facilitate dialogue and cooperation at various levels. More importantly, it clarified that NATO's enlargement did not constitute a threat to Russia's security or undermine the security of other states, and that NATO and Russia would work to build a stable, peaceful, and undivided Europe. Today Russia has no intention in honoring such an agreement.

After the Russian annexation of Crimea in 2014, NATO did show restraint in deploying new troops and heavy weapons to its east and avoid violating the provisions of the NATO-Russia Founding Act, but there was another problem on the Russian side. The Kremlin stationed un-warned nuclear-capable missile systems in Kaliningrad. It is a city separated from the rest of Russia bordering Lithuania and Belarus. The area is heavily militarized. It has maritime borders with Poland and Lithuania and is strategically located on the Baltic Sea. It is of significant military importance for Russia as it houses the headquarters of the Russian Baltic Fleet and nuclear-capable missile systems.

The Iskander-M Tactical Ballistic Missile System is one of the most notable missile systems deployed. It is a short-range, mobile ballistic missile system capable of carrying conventional or nuclear warheads. It has a range of up to approximately 310 miles and is designed to target a variety of ground-based and naval targets with high precision. The Bastion-P is another system, but most specifically a mobile coastal defense missile system category equipped with supersonic anti-ship cruise missiles, such as the P-800 Oniks (NATO reporting name: SS-N-26 Strobile). The Bastion-P system provides anti-ship and land-attack capabilities and can be armed with conventional or nuclear warheads. Another is the S-400 Surface-to-Air Missile System. While primarily an air defense system, the S-400 has the capability to engage targets at extended ranges, including ballistic missiles. It is capable of intercepting and destroying a wide range of aerial threats, including aircraft, drones, and ballistic missiles.

Kaliningrad is also equipped with other air defense systems, including the S-300 surface-to-air missile system and various short-range air defense systems, providing layered defense against airborne threats. The deployment of these missile systems has raised concerns among NATO member states, especially Poland and Lithuania, about their potential to threaten neighboring countries and complicate regional security dynamics. The presence of advanced missile systems in Kaliningrad underscores Russia's strategic interests in the Baltic region and its commitment to enhancing its military capabilities along its western borders.

Putin has frequently blamed NATO for moving further East and for violating its agreement with the Soviet Union and its successor state, Russia. NATO, in his view, has further violated the agreement to place a NATO military installation so close to Russia's western border. There are ongoing disagreements about who violated the agreement first, between the Kremlin and NATO, with accusations of broken promises from both sides. What cannot be ignored is the specific timing of the first deployment of ballistic missiles in Kaliningrad. The date is not publicly disclosed, as Russian military movements and deployments are often kept confidential for strategic reasons. However, reports and analysis suggest that Russia has periodically deployed various missile systems, including ballistic missiles in Kaliningrad, as part of its military posture and strategic deterrence without any aggression coming from the West. These deployments have occurred at different times in response to no threats or as part of NATO's defensive military exercises.

One notable deployment occurred in 2016 when Russia deployed Iskander-M ballistic missile systems to Kaliningrad as part of military exercises. The deployment was widely interpreted as a response to NATO's military presence in Eastern Europe. Bear in mind that the deployment also occurred against the backdrop of the Russian-led annexation of Crimea and support for separatist rebels in eastern Ukraine. The Kremlin has consistently maintained the narrative that NATO deployments are perceived as threats. NATO military exercises mean demonstrations of force. However, it is Russia that is deploying ballistic missiles and is using force in Ukraine.

The Russian war momentum had begun as far back as 1999 when the geopolitical focus had notably shifted. The emergence of Islamic terrorism as a primary security threat became a central concern for the Kremlin. It was exacerbated by conflicts in Chechnya, where Russia faced a violent separatist movement. The Kremlin perceived Islamic terrorism as deeply intertwined with the Chechen insurgency, framing it as part of a broader struggle against extremism emanating from the region. The reorientation towards combating Islamic terrorism marked a significant change in Russia's security priorities. The September 11 attacks in the United States further solidified this shift, aligning Russia's stance more closely with Western nations in the fight against global terrorism. However, the underlying tensions regarding NATO's expansion and the broader post-Cold War order continued to influence Russia's foreign policy outlook.

The September 11 attacks produced an outcome where Article 5 was petitioned within NATO for the first time. After 9/11, there was a sense that the United States would expect further attacks. On 12

September 2001, a meeting was convened, which triggered NATO's invocation of Article 5. Robert Nicholas Burns, the United States Ambassador to NATO, outlined the events, and the NATO Secretary General George Robertson developed a consensus among members who were standing in solidarity with the United States.

Among NATO members, the discussion centered around the fact that if it was determined that the attack on the United States was directed from abroad, it should be regarded as an action covered by Article 5. Only after a few days, and without debate, and at the behest of the United States, all other 14 NATO countries at the time joined the coalition of 70 countries in the 2001 invasion of Afghanistan, also known as Operation Enduring Freedom.

The same NATO that is aiding Ukraine today was helped by Putin's Russian forces into the same Afghanistan where almost two decades prior, an estimated 3,000 Ukrainians who were part of the Soviet military lost their lives. For Ukraine, Afghanistan provides a crucial lesson. Within the best of intentions, the ally that backs you economically and militarily in a war, after some time, will lose interest. The circumstances will lead to a so-called "honorable exit," followed by abandonment. Although abandonment appears to be the norm.

For instance, when aid did not arrive in Kyiv for nearly six months, Ukraine nervously came close to abandonment from its chief ally, the United States. While Ukraine has not attained the abandonment status for much of 2024, it looked like it would, given the dynamics in Washington.

During the Soviet war in Afghanistan, Operation Cyclone, the longest and most expensive covert CIA work was undertaken. The aim was to provide military and financial aid to Afghan insurgents fighting against the Soviet Army and Soviet-backed Democratic Republic of Afghanistan. The initial American aid was relatively modest and aimed at providing support to the mujahedeen fighters who were resisting the pro-Soviet Afghan government. After the Soviet invasion, the U.S. support for the mujahedeen significantly increased, with substantial financial, military, and logistical support, which provided to help them combat Soviet forces. The American support continued throughout the 1980s and played a crucial role in the Soviet Union's eventual withdrawal from Afghanistan in 1989. However, after the war ended, the Americans threw their allies to the wolves. Washington lost interest, and the Soviets were on the cusp of disbanding. Only the most sadistic factions survived to rule Afghanistan afterward. Lawless warlords savaged and terrorized Afghans until the Taliban took over. Some of the groups and individuals supported during Operation Cyclone later became part of the Taliban and other extremist organizations, which contributed to the complex geopolitical landscape leading to the events of 9/11 and the subsequent America's War on Terror.

In 2001, Putin's forces provided logistical support, intelligence sharing, and access to its airspace for U.S. military operations, in the hope that Washington would not object to its raids in Chechnya. The FSB went so far as to provide assistance in intelligence gathering and sharing information on the Taliban and al-Qaeda forces in Afghanistan. Putin prioritized the so-called Northern Transport Corridor which worked well for several years in aiding NATO. Also known as the Northern Distribution Network (NDN), it was a network of routes used to transport supplies to NATO forces during military operations in Afghanistan. In 2010, when the relationship oscillated between cooperation and confrontation between the United States and Pakistan, the NDN proved to be more than a useful American and NATO option, as it bypassed Pakistan and became an essential path for supply and transport lines.

Persuaded by Putin, former Soviet states like Kazakhstan, Uzbekistan, Tajikistan, and Kyrgyzstan, made the NDN a safe corridor. They facilitated the movement of goods through their territories via roads, railways, and air routes. Russia, in particular, played a significant role by allowing goods to be transported through its own territory.

In 2003, NATO assumed command of the International Security Assistance Force (ISAF) in Afghanistan as American forces prioritized Iraq, marking its first major operation outside of Europe. ISAF's mission was to assist the Afghan government in maintaining security and stability, combating insurgent groups like the Taliban, and supporting reconstruction efforts. Over the years, NATO's role in Afghanistan expanded, with member states contributing troops, equipment, and financial resources to support the mission. At its peak, NATO forces were one of the largest multinational military operations in history, and its mission in Afghanistan faced numerous challenges, including a resilient insurgency, corruption within the Afghan government, and difficulties in building effective Afghan security forces.

Like the United States, NATO forces suffered significant casualties, with thousands of soldiers killed or wounded in action. At the end of NATO's combat mission in Afghanistan in 2014, approximately 3,500 NATO soldiers had died during the conflict. This number includes troops from the United States and other NATO member countries involved in ISAF and later in the Resolute Support Mission.

In 2011, NATO and Afghan authorities agreed on a transition process that aimed to gradually transfer security responsibilities from NATO forces to Afghan security forces. The process involved the gradual withdrawal of NATO combat troops and the development of Afghan security forces to assume greater responsibility for security. The Resolute Support Mission focused on training, advising, and assisting Afghan security forces. While the combat mission officially ended, NATO continued to maintain a presence in Afghanistan to support Afghan security forces and institutions. In April 2021, NATO announced its decision to begin withdrawing troops from Afghanistan.

There is no doubt that some generals in the Ukrainian armed forces are acutely aware of NATO's limitations, especially considering the alliance's mixed record in Afghanistan. The twenty years in Afghanistan highlighted a critical lesson: military power alone is insufficient to resolve complex political problems. Despite the substantial military efforts and resources committed, the absence of a coherent and unified political strategy, coupled with the failure to address fundamental underlying issues, ultimately led to NATO's inability to achieve a lasting solution in Afghanistan.

The NATO experience underscores that military intervention, while necessary, cannot substitute for the intricate work of political stabilization and governance. In Afghanistan, the inability to establish a stable and inclusive political framework, address corruption, and win the hearts and minds of the local population proved to be a set of significant shortcomings. It serves as an important reminder to Ukraine's leadership of the crucial alignment and balance between military and political strategies.

For Ukraine, understanding that while NATO's military support can provide essential defensive and strategic advantages, it is not a panacea. Ukraine's leaders must recognize that the effectiveness of any military intervention by NATO will be inherently limited if not accompanied by robust political solutions from Kyiv.

What was evident on the ground in Afghanistan was other non-NATO countries were playing a much more important role. Countries like India provided limited security but also provided aid and were incredibly dedicated to the reconstruction of Afghanistan. NATO, in contrast, was unable to halt the growth of the poppy crop, and while it could have stopped convoys, arresting the big drug smugglers and traffickers whom all locals knew, NATO forces looked the other way, as it did not want an all-out confrontation. NATO did gather limited intelligence, but it did not act on what was visibly in front of them, which was an insurgency developing, funded by numerous sources ranging from corruption and the poppy crop proceeds. NATO had helicopters and other equipment at their disposal, but simply could not effectively further improvements in any major areas of Afghanistan. In reality, NATO was a police force with civilian tasks. It was rebuilding the nation in education, healthcare, and civil infrastructure projects, and that too with very limited success.

There are reports of NATO forces not engaging in combat operations at night. Some of that is true, but it has a wider explanation. The Taliban insurgency often exploited the cover of darkness to conduct ambushes, attacks, and other operations against NATO. It led to the perception that NATO forces were less active or effective at night. NATO forces did conduct raids at night, but there were logistical challenges associated with operating in Afghanistan's rugged mountainous terrains and remote regions. These challenges affected the frequency and intensity of nighttime operations. There was also a political angle to NATO's less-than-fruitful results.

The Taliban had staged a propaganda campaign of kidnapping of European journalists. In March 2007, Daniele Mastrogiacomo, an Italian journalist working for *La Repubblica*, was kidnapped by the Taliban in Helmand Province along with his interpreter, Ajmal Naqshbandi, and their driver, Sayed Agha. The kidnapping occurred during a period of intense conflict in Afghanistan, with the Taliban insurgency gaining momentum in several regions of the country and drawing international attention to the security situation in Afghanistan.

In Italy, the incident shook the very fragile Prime Minister Romano Prodi's government. Within NATO, Italy ranks 6th, behind Germany, with approximately 175,000 active troops. It was part of the ISAF mission. After negotiations between Italian authorities and the Taliban, Mastrogiacomo was released in exchange for the release of Taliban prisoners held by the Afghan government. Tragically, however, his interpreter, Ajmal Naqshbandi, was executed by the Taliban during the negotiations despite pleas for his release.

In Italy, Prime Minister Romano Prodi's government fell by 2008, but it was the beginning of NATO pulling back its engagement in Afghanistan.

The interconnected nature of NATO's military operations and European political decisions highlights several critical issues that are relevant for understanding the potential vulnerabilities in the relationship between military actions and political decisions within NATO. Governments often face intense scrutiny from their citizens and media, which can influence their stance on military engagements. Ukrainian leaders should be aware that public sentiment can significantly impact political decisions related to NATO operations. Each NATO member state has varying priorities and approaches based on their national interests. Some will choose to negotiate and undermine the broader mission, while others will continue with the NATO line. Ukrainian leaders have already recognized that national interests and strategies can sometimes diverge, affecting alliance cohesion and operational effectiveness. The perception that one member state's actions might compromise the collective mission can lead to mistrust, and disunity is no longer uncommon, but NATO has to address it.

Ukraine has stood in the way of Russia, but their real fear is if Europe or the United States at some point refuse to support them. This was quite evident in the six months when Ukraine did not receive economic and military aid. If the $61 billion had not been authorized by the U.S. Congress, no doubt Ukraine would be significantly weaker, if not collapse.

2003 was an important year for Ukrainians to comprehend their allies more than their attackers. That year, Afghanistan had become an American leftover that got dumped onto NATO as the George W. Bush administration focused on invading Iraq. This is the catalyst that broke the Russia-West cooperation. The Soviet Union may have sold its client to the West, but that was not the case with Putin.

During the 1990 Gulf War, among the $6 billion in loan commitments from nine countries, of which $1.5 billion was allocated to the Soviet Union as part of a package to not side with Saddam's Iraq by Saudi Arabia. Kuwait also matched the Saudi pledge to the Soviets, and the United Arab Emirates (UAE) provided another $1 billion for a total commitment to Moscow of $4 billion in loan guarantees and grants. Gorbachev's government accepted the Saudi offer and did not take any military action to defend its ally, Iraq.

Under Putin, however, Russia had economic interests in Iraq, particularly in the oil and energy sectors. Russian companies along with the French had contracts for oil exploration, production, and infrastructure projects with Saddam's government since 2000. For Putin, it was unacceptable that the United States was getting in his way.

Several countries at the United Nations expressed opposition to the American and British-led 2003 invasion of Iraq. The road to war lacked explicit authorization from the United Nations Security Council. Among the countries that vocally opposed the invasion was France. President Chirac's government was one of the most prominent opponents of the invasion as it threatened to use its veto power as a permanent member of the United Nations Security Council to block any resolution authorizing military action against Iraq. Germany also strongly opposed the invasion, with Chancellor Gerhard Schröder's government taking an anti-war stance. Together, both abstained from voting on United Nations Security Council Resolution 1441, which demanded Iraq's disarmament but stopped short of explicitly authorizing military action. China expressed reservations about the invasion and emphasized the importance of resolving the Iraq crisis through peaceful means and through the United Nations.

Putin opposed the invasion. During his speech at the United Nations Security Council on 5 February 2003, encapsulated Russia's concerns. Putin said, "War is always a reflection of a failure of politics. The use of force can only be considered as the very last resort."

Several other countries, including Canada, Mexico, and Brazil, also opposed the invasion and expressed skepticism about the evidence presented to justify military action against Iraq.

President George W. Bush's administration neither got consent from the U.N., nor in Putin's view, planned for the morning after the invasion. Iraq became the starting gun when Putin parted his way with the West.

In the four years between the American invasion of Iraq and Putin's Munich speech in February 2007, several episodes occurred that had the Kremlin think twice about whether it should wait, tolerate, or do nothing, as it saw American actions in Iraq, also affecting its key ally Syria.

The Bashar Al-Assad government was concerned about the potential for American military action against Syria to spill over from Iraq. Damascus found itself surrounded by American military forces in Iraq to its east, along with American military bases in Turkey and Jordan, with its arch-enemy Israel to the south. The American presence in Iraq shifted the regional dynamics and increased Syria's sense of vulnerability. The George W. Bush administration's rhetoric of promoting democracy and regime change in the Middle East, exemplified by the invasion of Iraq, contributed to international pressure on the Assad government to liberalize and democratize. However, rather than leading to significant political reforms, Assad's response was to crack down on dissent and tighten his grip on power.

The United States accused Syria of supporting insurgents and terrorists in Iraq and Lebanon. The invasion of Iraq provided the United States with a justification for increased pressure on Syria to change its behavior and distance itself from groups and activities deemed destabilizing in the region. In Putin's view, if the United States could destabilize the Middle East, why couldn't Russia do the same in Europe?

Iraq, after Saddam's overthrow, produced increased instability for its neighbors, especially Syria, exacerbating existing challenges such as refugee flows, sectarian tensions, and the rise of extremist groups.

What incensed Putin the most was on 20 January 2007, when the George W. Bush administration announced their intention to build a missile defense site in Poland, which would host interceptors designed to counter potential missile threats from Iran. Once finalized, the Aegis Ashore Missile Defense System (AAMDS) in Poland will be fully integrated into the U.S. Ballistic Missile Defense System. Aegis was ready to operate under a NATO command and control structure.

The official transfer to NATO is scheduled to occur in the spring to summer of 2024. By October of 2007, the United States signed a similar agreement with the Czech Republic and later with a new NATO member, Romania. The Americans were going to install a radar system as part of the missile defense shield. For Putin, it was a direct threat to Russia's security.

The United States had reached an agreement to place ground-based mid-course interceptors that would provide Europe with protection from short and intermediate-range missile attacks. Previously, there were concerns over a similar European type ground-based interceptors. Due to their poor performance in subsequent tests, prompted European officials to look to the United States. Washington already had a system that could do the job. Named Zeus, the Navy's Aegis combat system was developed for Fleet Air Defense and had performed exceptionally well in several rounds of tests. The versatility of the ship-based system was further demonstrated when it successfully intercepted and destroyed a non-functioning spy satellite. In Romania, the Americans placed a battery of SM-3 anti-ballistic missiles manned by a crew of U.S. Navy personnel and civilian technicians. The facility became operational in May of 2016. In the future, the U.S. Navy will have weapons operating hundreds of miles from the sea and will be able to direct attacks from former Iron Curtain states. The effectiveness of Aegis led to the development of its part of the ballistic missile shield to defend NATO member states. In response, Russia has conducted military exercises near its western borders, with Belarus, as a show of force and to demonstrate its military capabilities.

In addition, Russian officials have lodged diplomatic protests against NATO's deployment of missile defense systems and also invested in developing and deploying its own missile defense systems and advanced missile technologies, which it sees as necessary to counterbalance NATO's capabilities. Ultimately, Putin concluded, as events unfolded in areas close to the Russian border, that NATO was not doing this alone; the alliance was principally an arm of the United States.

The American President is the most important individual in the alliance. NATO without America is a pacifist humanitarian defensive peace keeping force. The United States plays an extremely important leadership and logistics role in NATO, providing lead, leverage, and life to the alliance. Without the U.S., NATO is not an alliance.

In July 2018, NATO Secretary General Jens Stoltenberg and U.S. President Donald Trump clashed on camera at a NATO Summit in Brussels. Differences over Germany paying only a little over 1% of their GDP in defense, whereas the United States paying upwards of 4.2%, was at the root of the tensions. The American President was angry at countries like Germany that contribute less to defense and then make pipeline deals with Russia. He uttered that as Americans pay for their defense, billions are going into the coffers of Russia. The Dutch Prime Minister Mark Rutte calmed the situation when he suggested that the American President could take the credit for the next round of NATO increases in military spending. The move comforted Trump, but the real architect behind the increase in NATO military spending was not Rutte, but President Barack Obama.

The Obama administration emphasized the growing security threats facing the NATO alliance, such as the resurgence of Russian aggression in the annexation of Crimea in 2014, instability in the Middle East, and the rise of terrorist groups like ISIS. By framing increased defense spending as a necessary response to these shared threats, the Obama administration underscored the importance of a robust collective defense. The American President used his diplomatic channels to engage directly with NATO leaders, advocating for increased defense budgets during bilateral meetings and NATO summits. He consistently conveyed that all member states should meet the agreed-upon target of spending at least 2% of their GDP on defense. For instance, at the 2014 NATO Summit in Wales, he reiterated the need for greater defense investment and secured a commitment from member states to aim for the 2% GDP target within a decade. Recognizing that economic factors influenced defense budgets, Obama often linked defense spending to economic stability and growth. He argued that strong defense capabilities would help maintain global stability, which in turn would support economic prosperity. The Obama administration committed to maintaining robust U.S. defense spending, demonstrating that the U.S. was willing to shoulder its share of the burden. This approach aimed to encourage other NATO members to follow suit, setting a standard for allied contributions. The American President worked closely with key European leaders to build consensus and strengthen collective resolve, fostering strong relationships with leaders like then-German Chancellor Angela Merkel and then-British Prime Minister David Cameron, leveraging these alliances to promote the defense spending agenda.

President Obama argued that a more equitable distribution of defense responsibilities would enhance the overall strength and unity of the alliance.

Trump's tone and take were very different from his predecessor. During the 2024 Presidential campaign trail, the former President has encouraged Russia to do "whatever the hell" they want. The message made NATO members considerably nervous. The idea of a potential Russia-NATO war has become a major talking point in European security circles. It is a cause for concern if former President Trump returns to the Presidency after the November 2024 elections. Not only would the European Union (EU) and NATO have to readjust to suit their cross-Atlantic conditions if they wanted an amicable relationship with the American President, but they would also have to slow the possible end of aid to Ukraine. This is a reality that especially the Baltic states, which share borders with Russia, would be unwilling to concede. The United States needs NATO diplomatically just as much as NATO needs the United States militarily.

NATO facilitates military cooperation and interoperability among its members through joint military exercises, training programs, and sharing of intelligence. The alliance enhances the United States' ability to work closely with European allies and others, partnering on common security challenges. The NATO military cooperation often extends to diplomatic efforts, as coordinated military action can be a component of broader diplomatic and political realities and results. These strategies have also played a key role in crisis management and conflict resolution, as well as stabilizing regions of strategic importance. NATO-led missions and operations, such as peacekeeping missions in the Balkans and counter-piracy operations off the coast of Somalia, demonstrate the alliance's diplomatic engagement in addressing global security challenges.

The alliance serves as a forum for diplomatic dialogue and cooperation with non-member states, international organizations, and other stakeholders. Through partnerships with countries around the world, NATO contributes to the diplomatic efforts to promote stability, security, and cooperation in various regions. These partnerships enable the United States to engage with countries beyond NATO's borders and advance its diplomatic objectives.

The American leadership is essential for maintaining unity and consensus among NATO member states. American participation in shaping alliance policies, priorities and responding decisively to security challenges remains a key to NATO's success. American forces are the largest and most technologically advanced military within NATO. Its military capabilities, including airpower, naval forces, ground troops, and advanced weaponry, contribute significantly to NATO's overall military strength. Its advanced capabilities enhance NATO's ability to deter potential adversaries and respond effectively to security threats. The United States also provides NATO with access to strategic assets, such as intelligence, surveillance, and reconnaissance capabilities, as well as logistics and transportation infrastructure. These assets are essential for NATO's operations, enabling the alliance to respond to emerging threats. American military personnel play a crucial role in NATO's command and control structure, including the Supreme Allied Commander Europe (SACEUR) and various subordinate commands. U.S. military personnel hold key leadership positions within NATO's command structure, providing strategic direction and coordination for alliance operations and missions.

The United States' global military presence and power projection capabilities contribute to NATO's ability to project force beyond the Euro-Atlantic area. U.S. military bases and facilities around the world serve as logistical hubs and staging areas for NATO operations, allowing the alliance to deploy forces quickly and effectively in various regions.

The United States is also the largest financial contributor to NATO's common-funded budgets, which supports alliance activities and infrastructure. U.S. financial contributions help sustain NATO's operations, exercises, and initiatives, ensuring the alliance's operational readiness and effectiveness. An American withdrawal from NATO, will spark an internal civil conflict within Europe. Each European country will then beg for a bilateral treaty with the United States. France, Germany and Poland will find themselves in a very complicated set of alliances, similar to 19th century Europe.

Withdrawal of a member state is permitted in NATO Article 13, which states that any member state can leave NATO if they provide a denunciation to the U.S. government, with a withdrawal period of one year. In effect, the country only has to contact the U.S. government and say that it wants to leave NATO, and the U.S. will distribute the notice to other members and wait for a year before ratifying it. How will such measures playout if the U.S. itself wants out is a worrying factor. The most dangerous risk isn't American withdrawal from the alliance, but rather what happens to Europe without America. An American withdrawal would also mean Congress would have to sign-off on it, not their President, but that can happen under a Republican-majority Congress. However, some factions even in the Republican party would concede to the realities of the 21st century. These certainties include Japan arming again, so are the Saudis, the Iranians, and others.

Putin's key partner, China, is treading a fine line from becoming a threat to the West. The Chinese armed forces will be comparable to the American forces by 2035 and will have several capabilities that they do not have now. Beijing has built massive military bases on pockets of the South China Sea to service its large fleets. This is happening for one crucial reason: Xi Jinping wants beyond parity with the West.

China maybe a mixed set of worries for American allies in Asia, but Ukraine is becoming a long headache for Europe. NATO members have to come to terms with the idea that the United States may simply decide its lucrative economic priorities lay in Asia more than in conflict-ridden Europe, which would mean pacifist Europe might have to build back the 19th and 20th-century military industrial complex that once was part of their identity. If that does happen, there is no way Europe would have a centralized army in NATO. The alliance would become a set of loose factions operating with different allegiances, dangerously, some that may also forge an alliance with Russia. However, suppose that did not happen. Suppose NATO stayed intact even after an American withdrawal; the present problems will still remain, and the alliance will still struggle to take on large missions on its own.

Two years into the war, Ukrainian forces have become significantly more adept at executing mid-level and potentially larger military missions, leveraging their extensive battlefield experience. Ukraine at any price, would want to be integrated into NATO. It comes at a difficult time when the potential loss of a substantial number of American troops within the alliance, predictably after the results of the 2024 November American elections. Ukraine has developed an army capable of performing operations that European forces might find difficult. Nevertheless, this point may be rendered moot as NATO members continue to hold the belief that they are not directly at war with Russia, but Russia is actually at war with them.

Chapter 5

UKRAINE'S KEY ALLIES

Russia has historically been sensitive to any country meddling in its borders since traditionally, it sought to maintain pro-Russia states along its borders to provide a strategic depth. This concept was especially important given Russia's historical view of neighboring countries, as part of its sphere of influence and Ukraine was crucially part of this preference. Any attempt to influence, for the Kremlin is perceived as an encroachment on its traditional sphere of control. So sensitive is the Russian stance that in March 2024, a Russian missile nearly killed the Greek Prime Minister Kyriakos Mitsotakis while he was visiting Odessa. The episode sparked another round of anxious verbal battles about the potential triggering of NATO's Article 5. The awful truth however is NATO commanders don't want to be drawn into a war with Russia, and supporting Ukraine politically is becoming a liability for some European leaders. But two years into the war, the Kremlin is responding, going so far to break the wills of Ukraine's key allies.

One recent incident highlights the depth of how much Russia is willing to go to achieve its aims. The recent wiretapping affair surrounding a conversation between German Air Force officials speaking in detail for 38 minutes about delivering missiles to Ukraine speaks to some core sensitivities between Germany and Russia. The conversation also included how Ukraine could use Taurus, a German-Swedish-made air-launched cruise missile developed by

Taurus Systems GmbH in what was discussed in the Taurus KEPD 350 (Kinetic Energy Penetrator Destroyer). It is a long-range, precision-guided cruise missile primarily designed for attacking heavily defended targets such as bunkers, air defense systems, and other high-value targets, carried by fighter aircraft like the Eurofighter Typhoon and the Panavia Tornado.

The wiretapping incident exposed how, with minimum effort and maximum damage, the Russian intelligence—the FSB penetrated Ukraine's second most important economic and military supporter. It is a direct hybrid warfare on Germany and further attests that Berlin might become indirectly at war against the Kremlin.

The details of the Taurus missiles discussed are particularly sensitive. The Taurus has a range of approximately 311 miles, nearly double that of Britain and France's inventory delivered to Ukraine. Targets were also discussed, including the Kirch Strait bridge connecting Crimea with the Russian mainland. It is also a bridge Ukrainian forces have been trying to destroy for some time.

There are verifications that these discussions held by German Air Force officials were formal discussions but it was not held on an internally secured or classified network. Since it was in a WebEx platform, it was easily hackable for the FSB.

Chancellor Scholz wants a detailed internal investigation, but the damage may lead to more covert means of penetrating other sensitive and secure networks by the FSB.

Maria Zakharova, the spokeswoman for the Russian Ministry of Foreign Affairs, asserted that the Germans owe further explanations to the Kremlin. The recorded evidence was first brought to the media by the Russian state-backed TV network, RT (formerly Russia Today). Its Editor-in-Chief, Margarita Simonan, posted it on her social media accounts. She is a high-profile figure, and it does beg the question of how much the incident can tilt the German-Russian relationship into an all-out conflict.

For the last two decades, Ukraine has felt similar hybrid warfare. In 2000, then-Ukrainian President Leonid Kuchma was wiretapped talking about the killing of Georgiy Gongadze, the Georgian-born opposition journalist who was known for his critical reporting on Kuchma's government and corruption in Ukraine. Gongadze's decapitated body was found later after his disappearance. Recordings surfaced of Kuchma discussing harming Gongadze. These recordings led to widespread protests and international condemnation. Kuchma consistently denied involvement in Gongadze's murder, and the case remained unresolved for years. In 2005, the prosecutor-general of Ukraine asserted that Kuchma's former interior minister, Yuri Kravchenko, had ordered Gongadze's killing. Kravchenko allegedly committed suicide before he could stand trial. Despite suspicions and allegations, there hasn't been a conclusive legal determination of Kuchma's direct involvement in Gongadze's murder.

Gongadze died on 17 September 2000. It was around this time that President Putin was upset with Kuchma over what he saw as Ukraine moving away from Russia's economic orbit and becoming more independent. Putin badly needed Ukraine's consumers, who provided the single largest revenue from Russian goods. Under the setting of low oil and gas prices, he needed Ukrainians to buy their traditional purchases of Russian chemicals and fertilizers, which were used particularly in agriculture. Russian businesses supplied machinery, equipment, and vehicles to Ukraine, contributing to the country's industrial and transportation sectors. To lose Ukraine's 45 million population to Europe would mean losing a significant consumer base within Russia's Eurasian Economic Union (EAEU).

Kuchma had risen steadily as President from his position of Prime Minister. He had done a fantastic job on Ukraine's economy, turning it into a market economy after inheriting an aged Soviet infrastructure. His reforms included the privatization of state-owned enterprises, deregulation, and attempts to attract foreign investment along the same lines as Russian President Boris Yeltsin's economic playbook, but only successfully. Ukraine saw privatization, increased trade, and a more favorable business environment in transportation, energy, and telecommunications. Ukraine's agricultural sector saw some growth and modernization, with reforms aimed at privatization and land reform helping to increase agricultural productivity and export potential. However, like Yeltsin, Kuchma's economic recipe included establishing the Ukrainian oligarchs. As Ukraine saw economic success, many of Kuchma's oligarchs entered politics. Their economic interests were not limited to Ukraine. In Russia, their capital spanned into various sectors, including energy, metals, mining, banking, media, and real estate investments, benefiting from economic ties between

Ukraine and Russia.

Ukraine has historically been dependent on Russia for its energy supplies, particularly natural gas. Oligarchs involved in the energy sector, in the gas trade or energy distribution, had close business relationships with their Russian counterparts and sometimes Putin himself. The relationship between Ukrainian oligarchs and Russia did have conflicts of interest, especially as geopolitical tensions gathered momentum. They faced pressure to balance their business interests in Russia, particularly from Kuchma's successor, President Viktor Yushchenko.

Since 2014, amid heightened tensions between Ukraine and Russia, there have been instances of sanctions imposed on Ukrainian oligarchs with ties to the Kremlin. Kuchma's own son-in-law, Viktor Pinchuk, is one of them, who now lives in Russia in exile.

The involvement of Ukrainian oligarchs in intelligence services is marred by allegations suggesting connections between certain oligarchs and intelligence activities. One individual is businessman Pavel Fuks. He is known for his ventures in real estate and development sectors. Fuks has also been active in charitable activities, supporting initiatives in education, healthcare, and social welfare. He gained prominence in the 1990s during the period of economic transition in Ukraine and made a fortune in Russia. He came under sanctions imposed by Ukraine in 2021 and is also under criminal investigation for fraud and tax evasion. *The Guardian* has established that Fuks had the status to remain in Britain since 2017. The European Union (EU), United States, and Britain have not placed restrictions on Fuks (he is, however, not allowed to travel to the U.S.), allowing him to do his business as usual. As Putin's regime sought to put Ukraine under economic pressure after Russia's takeover of Crimea in February 2014, wealthy Ukrainians came under Kyiv's sanctions. Fuks was among the names on the 2018 list. Other oligarchs like Fuks, supported the Ukrainian Armed Forces and other defense units during the 2014 Russian invasion of Crimea. They also funded conscripted employees, utility workers, rescuers, military doctors, and representatives of the national media who work in the combat areas. By providing transport, drones, protective engineering structures, body armor, protective equipment, and medical assistance, it is certainly possible that the likes of Fuks and Pinchuk may have provided critical information to the FSB through such links.

The oligarch connection to intelligence services is a murky one, and recent events do show a blurred line connecting Ukraine's oligarchs to the FSB. It also means that the FSB looks to become more effective than its Western counterparts in Ukraine. The FSB operates within a complex political and legal framework, where issues of transparency, accountability, and the balance between security and civil liberties are perennial concerns. The agency's effectiveness is often weighed against broader considerations, especially in a global context where espionage and surveillance practices are increasingly scrutinized. For instance, in March 2018, two FSB operatives were discovered in Britain, trying to assassinate a Putin critic. It took a mere 24 hours for the Metropolitan Police Service (MPS) to discover who they were. The two poisoned were former Russian intelligence officer Sergei Skripal and his daughter Yulia in Salisbury. The two Russian operatives identified as suspects in this case were later revealed to be Alexander Petrov and Ruslan Boshirov, though these names are believed to be aliases. The poisoning involved the use of a nerve agent called Novichok, which is believed to have been applied to the front door handle of Sergei Skripal's residence. Both Sergei and Yulia Skripal survived the attack, but it resulted in a significant international diplomatic crisis. Britain accused Russia of being responsible for the poisoning, leading to the expulsion of Russian diplomats and the imposition of sanctions on Russia by Western governments. Russia denied involvement in the incident and dismissed the accusations as baseless.

A similar situation occurred in Berlin in the attempted assassination of a Chechen dissident named Zelimkhan Khangoshvili in August 2019. Khangoshvili, who had fought against Russian forces in Chechnya, was shot dead in a Berlin park by a man riding a bicycle. German authorities later identified the suspect as a Russian citizen named Vadim Krasikov, who had arrived from Moscow on a valid Russian passport under a different name. The German federal prosecutor's office stated that there was sufficient evidence to suggest that the killing was carried out on behalf of Russian state agencies. Russia denied any involvement in the assassination attempt, dismissing the accusations as unfounded.

Almost five years later, for Germany, it is a delicate time for a security leak. It is a major embarrassment for Berlin as it is careless at one of the most sensitive levels. German Defense officials are exposed as part of Russian hybrid warfare, which looks like a payback for the 2019 incident. The episode does reveal that the digital world is a magic carpet for the FSB. Ultimately, it steers social media attention to prioritize what has gone wrong versus what will be done. The Russian hybrid warfare looks to target the top backers of Ukraine, keep them busy with ludicrous fallouts to analyze, and take their eye away from the main priority of safeguarding future leaks.

The FSB has been very successful in placing topics that are not part of mainstream news. The tactic is simple. Target, expose and sow doubt. A successful result would mean advanced levels of echoes related to incidents in Western capitals, which may very well negatively affect security collaboration, sharing intelligence and military exercises that benefit Ukraine. Russian hybrid attacks on European infrastructure are not new, but they are getting more and more efficient.

This is not Germany's only problem. Even before the incident, within the German electorate and in Europe, there were significant doubts about its politicians. That doubt will now remain in the German discourse. For Ukraine, it is a serious problem as it sees the undermining of the trust and reliability it had in Germany. Furthermore, if this sort of incident has happened now, what if other information was leaked in the past that did not get exposure?

Previously, Germany has seen many of its military officers on trial for espionage. A recent 2023 December case parallels potential problems, especially as German forces work to aid Ukrainian troops. The December case involved an unsuspecting manager at Germany's foreign intelligence agency, B.N.D., selling highly classified material to Russia with an intermediary diamond dealer. Both Carsten Linke, a 53-year-old retired officer, and Arthur E., a 32-year-old, face charges of high treason. They are accused of providing information about Western intelligence related to accessing an encrypted messaging service used by the Russian-state-backed Wagner group. Both men claim to have helped a wealthy Russian by obtaining a German visa for him. In return, they got a stake in a mine in Africa. The matter, however, took a different turn when the Russian came back with demands for sensitive intelligence.

The New York Times has described the story as follows: "Mr. E., prosecutors say, made three trips from Germany to Russia in fall 2022. Meeting with operatives from the Russian agency, the FSB, at a restaurant and an apartment in Moscow, he is accused of bringing them material that was classified as "top secret" by German intelligence, part of which originated from partner agencies in other Western countries. The Russian agents, in return, gave him a list of 12 questions. During one dinner, they are said to have handed Mr. E. four envelopes, taped shut and containing hundreds of thousands of euros in cash." One was caught in Florida, the other in Germany.

Historically, Germans have often been sympathetic to Russia due to significant economic ties, including trade, investment, and energy cooperation. German companies have been motivated by economic interests in fostering positive relations with Russia to benefit from trade opportunities and access to natural resources. Germans were, to a certain point, blind towards Russia after the 2008-09 financial crisis, having to bail out several of its fellow European countries, with the majority of German attention was to the West, not to Europe's East.

Chancellor Olaf Scholz's Social Democratic Party (SDP) would never dream of going to war against Russia, but it is only a few steps away from doing so. Germany is aiding Ukraine to fight a war against Russia, but Russia is at war with the West, which also includes Germany.

As part of its hybrid warfare, Russia is exporting fear into Germany. It is influencing and persuading Germans that what is happening in Ukraine is a conduct of their own politicians and not Russia's. The key Russian target is the Chancellor's Socialist Democratic Party (SDP).

Trojan-infected election propaganda is in full swing in the June 2024 European elections. The upcoming European elections hold significant implications for the European Union's future, particularly concerning its policies on climate change, migration, and the extent of European integration. The political landscape has been shifting rightward, with right-wing and far-right parties gaining considerable ground across Europe. This trend suggests that the next European Parliament may lean more towards nationalism and stricter immigration controls, potentially impacting the EU's overall approach to these critical issues.

A stronger right-wing presence in the European parliament may result in more conservative stances on migration, favoring tighter borders and reduced immigration. It could also lead to more resistance against deeper EU integration, with a focus on national sovereignty over collective EU policies.

The European Parliament, based in Brussels and Strasbourg, plays a crucial role in shaping the laws that affect all EU citizens and in approving the annual budget, which in 2024 stands at €189 billion. The Parliament shares this legislative and budgetary power with the Council of the European Union, composed of national governments, thus making the outcome of the elections pivotal for future policy directions.

Additionally, the composition of the European Parliament influences the selection of the European Commission President, a role central to driving the EU's executive agenda. A shift towards right-wing dominance could steer the Commission towards more conservative policies, potentially slowing down progressive climate initiatives and emphasizing national over collective interests.

For Ukraine, these developments are particularly of concern. The EU's stance on supporting Ukraine amidst ongoing conflict, could be affected by the internal political dynamics. A right-leaning Parliament might prioritize national security and stricter border controls, possibly affecting the EU's willingness and capacity to support Ukraine comprehensively. Conversely, a more integrated EU with a focus on collective action might continue to provide robust support to Ukraine, reinforcing its strategic and humanitarian commitments.

There are fears that Putin could use disinformation to exert targeted influence and bring far-right-wing forces to power. For Europe's progressives, educating their electorate is not enough. Their message that their economies will continue to do well, as their governments support Ukraine, should be the main angle. They would have to use repeated slogans to foster that message. True, this is about security in the regional level but at a local level, this is important too.

NATO wants to include cyber and hybrid attacks in Article 5, but the alliance will struggle to prove where those attacks come from. Attacks of such kind are especially dangerous for the Baltic states. This is where the Ukrainian cyber defense can really assist Europe in its technical know-how of the Russian danger.

It took Ukraine six months to kick Russian TV channels out of the networks after the annexation of Crimea in February 2014. Ukraine went from having no knowledge to now leading that space to counter Russian cyber attacks. Today, Ukraine can help Europe in cyber warfare defense, a reality that was very different in 2014.

Germany, like Ukraine, has a large Russian-speaking population. They watch Russian television channels and the Kremlin propaganda that comes with it. In January 2016, reports emerged that a 13-year-old girl of Russian descent, identified as Lisa F., had been allegedly abducted and sexually assaulted by migrants in Berlin. Russian state media outlets, including Russia's state-owned Channel One television network, seized upon the incident, portraying it as evidence of the dangers posed by migrants in Germany. The coverage sparked protests organized by Russian-speaking communities in Germany.

However, German authorities later conducted an investigation and found no evidence to support the allegations of abduction and sexual assault. Instead, it was determined that Lisa F. had fabricated the story, and she later admitted to lying about the incident. The Lisa F. case drew attention to the spread of disinformation and propaganda, particularly by foreign state actors, to sow discord and undermine trust in Western institutions. It also highlighted the complexities of managing relations between Germany and Russia, especially amid heightened tensions over issues such as migration and geopolitics.

That same year, in the United States 2016 Presidential election, Russia leaked information from the Democratic Party servers to undermine the party's nominee, Hillary Clinton. It involved the hacking and subsequent release of emails from various Democratic Party organizations and individuals in the Democratic National Committee (D.N.C.) and high-profile figures within the Democratic Party. The leaked emails, which were published by WikiLeaks and other platforms, revealed internal communications, discussions, and strategies about campaign tactics, fundraising efforts, and sensitive political matters. The incident undoubtedly fueled controversy, speculation, and criticism. It was a broader Russian interference campaign aimed at influencing the outcome of the election and sowing discord within the U.S. political system. The real damaging exposure was the emails from D.N.C. officials, discussing ways to undermine the Vermont Senator Bernie Sanders' campaign during the Democratic primaries in favor of Hillary Clinton. The revelation fueled existing tensions between Sanders' supporters and the D.N.C. establishment. While the leaked emails did not reveal any illegal activity, they exacerbated existing divisions within the Democratic Party and contributed to the perception among some Sanders supporters that the primary process was rigged against him. The perception of unfairness further strained unity within the Democratic party and had implications when Clinton took on the Republican nominee, Donald Trump.

It is the same hybrid warfare happening again in Europe. The German military is already planning for an unlikely Russian invasion of Europe. Under such an assessment, Russia will begin the assault technologically, launching coordinated cyber attacks on the countries closest to its borders, specifically the Baltic states. The aim would be to incite political tension and then the rise of pro-Russian leaders.

One of Ukraine's staunchest supporters is Prime Minister Kaja Kallas of Estonia. Upon Russia's invasion of Ukraine, she invoked Article 4 of the NATO charter. It is the start of major NATO operations in situations of urgency, such as "territorial integrity, political independence or security of any of the parties threatened." Previously, it was used four times out of seven over Turkey's military adventures in Iraq and Syria against the Kurds. While Article 4 does not automatically trigger military action, it demonstrates NATO's commitment to collective defense and solidarity among member states in the face of perceived threats. In 2016, the Baltic States invoked Article 4 amid concerns about Russia's military activities in the region and perceived threats to their own security. NATO allies held consultations to address these concerns. Kallas is now on a Wanted list in Russia. Her crime is the removal of Soviet-era monuments in Estonia. She has been Prime Minister since January 2021 and has been taking the lead in petitioning Europe to invest more in defense and to engage tech sectors to aid the military effort in Ukraine. Her method of pooling bonds at the EU level rather than having individual European countries issue bonds is also a way to enhance the capabilities of European economies. She has the support of European Council President Charles Michel and is hoping to convince her European counterparts to do more. Most European countries don't have funds or raise capital outside their economies. Her vision is to do this task collectively at the EU level. Estonia has the most startups per capita and wants to boost the defense industry. The problem lies in private funds being closed to investments in defense, but Kallas's problems extend to the Kremlin, which is also trying to stop her from being a real candidate for the top jobs in Europe, including the Secretary General of NATO. While that position will very well go to a Western European (probably PM Mark Rutte of the Netherlands), she maintains a strong stance against Russia and is attuned to Russian propaganda in her own country. Like Ukraine, Putin says Estonia is not a real country. One angle to this is that the Russian President is laying the groundwork for the sizeable minority of the Russian-speaking population in Estonia to rise and throw the likes of Kallas out of power.

Estonia's Russian-speaking population has faced discrimination and challenges, particularly in the aftermath of the disbanding of the Soviet Union. Estonia declared its independence on 20 August 1991 (four days before Ukraine) and became the third (after Latvia and Lithuania) Soviet Republic to declare independence from Moscow. This was the first time the country regained independence since the 1920 Treaty of Tartu in the aftermath of World War I.

Estonia began 1992 with a set of new policies that was part of a breakaway from the Soviet model. One of them included restoring the Estonian language as the primary language of the state. It included requirements for proficiency in Estonian for citizenship and for access to certain government services. These language policies have been criticized for disproportionately affecting the Russian-speaking minority, many of whom are ethnic Russians. Estonia's citizenship policy has also been a source of controversy. Following independence, Estonia granted citizenship to those who were citizens before the 1940 Soviet annexation and their descendants, while others had to apply for citizenship through a naturalization process. It was criticized for being lengthy and difficult, leading to a significant number of stateless individuals, many who are Russian-speaking minorities who protested of their difficulties in accessing education and employment opportunities, particularly in sectors where proficiency in the Estonian language is required. Discrimination in hiring practices and limited availability of Russian-language education in some areas have been cited as barriers to integration and upward mobility. Furthermore, there have been challenges in achieving social integration between Estonia's Russian-speaking minority and the ethnic Estonian majority. Cultural and linguistic differences, as well as historical tensions, have contributed to social divisions and mistrust between communities. Members of the Russian-speaking minority feel marginalized in the political process, with limited representation in government and a perception of underrepresentation in decision-making bodies.

There are sizeable Russian-speaking minorities in all three Baltic states. They account for nearly 22% of the population, with the exception of Lithuania, which only has approximately 5% of Russian speakers. Deportation of such groups has not been a state priority in Estonia but is now in Latvia. The government in Riga wants its Russian-speaking population to pass a Latvian language test or face potential deportation. Around 1,200 Russians were identified for deportation at the end of 2023. However, Riga insisted that the deportation was caused by the non-renewal of residency permits and not the language tests. This is what Putin has been targeting to weaken Ukraine's diehard backers. The citizenship and language issue was something Russian propaganda had targeted back in 2004 in Ukraine. Highlighting discriminatory practices against Russian speakers in Ukraine's east and specifically pointing out to the inhabitants of the Donbas, was a key part of the strategy.

Like Georgia's former President Mikheil Saakashvili, Estonia's Prime Minister Kaja Kallas has fallen in the bad graces of Putin. Her crime is that she ordered the removal of Soviet-era statues of Lenin. Kallas saw the move as part of a campaign to stop domestic clashes against Estonia's Russian speakers. She did not want to expand on the historical Soviet wounds that were opened because of the war in Ukraine and instead, wanted Estonians to look to a pro-West future.

Estonia is a country with strategic and significant avenues for both military and economic objectives. The country gave the Soviet Union access to vital seaports in the Baltic Sea. Stalin aimed to enhance Soviet security, strengthen his Western defenses, and establish a foothold to counter potential threats from neighboring countries. He also wanted to use Estonia's valuable natural resources, including timber, oil, shale, and mineral deposits. These resources were important for the Soviet economy and industrial development, contributing to Stalin's desire to incorporate them into the Soviet Union's economic system. For Putin, Estonia serves as a transit route for Russian energy exports, particularly through its ports and pipelines.

There is a feeling that Estonia's pro-West political class believes that it's only a matter of time until the same tanks that are killing Ukrainians will descend upon their borders from the Russian city of Pskov. According to DGAP (German Council of Foreign Relations), conflict between Russia and NATO has been brewing for over two decades, and it's only a matter of time before Russia marches on beyond Ukraine. The report also states that Russia has long sought to restore its imperialistic model in Europe, aiming to take back all territories lost from the breakup of the Soviet Union.

The biggest contributor to NATO's hesitance to openly confront Russia is its frequent threats of using nuclear weapons. For example, one of the primary reasons NATO delayed sending F-15s to Ukraine was because the Russian Ministry of Defense claimed such a move was presenting a nuclear threat to Russia. The real excuse was that F-15s could theoretically carry and launch nuclear weapons, prompting Russia to respond. Ultimately, NATO called Putin's bluff and started sending old F-15 planes to Ukraine in late 2023, where they are currently being used for training purposes before being put into service later in 2024. However, even with bolstered weaponry and equipment through F-15s and advanced missiles, some reports suggest that this may not be enough for Ukraine. According to *Reuters*, Russia's planned military defense budget for 2024 is roughly $110 billion, a third of its total budget. This would put Russia above the U.S. in military spending for the year compared to its total GDP. While Russia has certainly taken a beating, with collective economic and military losses, the rise in the military budget indicates that Russia could feasibly conscript and train 280,000 soldiers each year. Even in a hypothetical scenario, Russia would have more soldiers than it had at the beginning of the February 2022 invasion. If the war expands to include NATO, the numbers won't change. Some conservative estimates suggest that the war against NATO would begin in six to ten years, giving Russians anywhere between 1.7 to 2.8 million troops to throw at the frontlines. Worryingly, new recruits will endure baptism by fire. They will serve in Ukraine first and gain valuable experience for the upcoming fight against NATO, which uses similar weapons and tactics.

Furthermore, Russia claims to have the capacity to build 100 tanks per year. While these are unlikely to be fully functional new tanks, and many are expected to be refurbished from Soviet-era pieces with modernization, Russia could assemble a monumental force to bear upon NATO's most vulnerable choking point, the Suwalki Gap.

Located in northeastern Poland and southeastern Lithuania, the Suwalki Gap is a narrow strip of land that serves as the only overland connection between the Baltic States and the rest of NATO territory. Strategically, it is a critical corridor because it separates the Russian exclave of Kaliningrad from Belarus. If Russia were to seize control of the Suwalki Gap, it could effectively cut off the Baltic States from the rest of NATO, isolating them and potentially hindering NATO's ability to respond to a crisis in the region. NATO has increased its presence and conducted military exercises around the Suwalki Gap, to demonstrate its commitment to the defense of the Baltic States and deter potential Russian aggression. Additionally, efforts have been made to improve infrastructure and mobility in the area to enhance NATO's ability to reinforce the Baltic States. However, the reality is that the Baltic states stand at the lower middle tier in terms of NATO troop numbers. Latvia, which contributes the highest troop numbers among the three, only has approximately 16,000 active soldiers to defend itself. The Baltic states would need an ally with an army of large numbers to counter the larger Russian army. If the United States withdraws from NATO, that burden will fall on Poland.

Warsaw has learned from its bitter experiences with the Soviet Union in the 20th century. It has adopted a more militant stance and re-established itself as one of the most conservative powers in Europe. If the Baltic states come under attack and some members of NATO opt not to respond to the Russian aggression, Poland would be most qualified to respond with its own military. Currently, the Polish army has approximately 165,000 active troops, 7th in troop contributions in NATO. It has a much more positive attitude toward defending its borders and has a territorial defense force set up in 2017, consisting of weekend soldiers who take occasional refresher lessons. While Poland has clashed with the rest of Europe politically, particularly in regard to how it handles migrant issues, the country is united in the efforts to bolster its military. Its budget for 2023 outlined that it would double its military spending to 5% of its Growth Domestic Product (GDP). As a result, Poland will likely become one of the best military equipped nations in Europe. It has signed a deal to receive 250 modern

Abrams tanks from the U.S. and it is on a path to modernizing its land forces. The U.S. is also sending 32 F-35 fighters to Poland, and it already has a stockpile of F-16s that it's not parting with any time soon (unlike the Netherlands and Denmark, which are sending theirs to Ukraine).

Prime Minister Donald Tusk's government has turned to South Korea for major equipment purchases, including 180 K2 Black Panther tanks, 200 K9 Thunder howitzers, 48 FA-50 light attack aircraft, and 218 K239 Chunmoo rocket launchers. The deal is expected to exceed over 1,000 tanks and 600 artillery pieces, giving Poland nearly unrivaled military power in Eastern Europe.

Some analysts suggest that Russia isn't putting a concerted effort into Ukraine, only using its Soviet-era weaponry to try and beat other Soviet-era weaponry fielded by Ukrainians. Should Russia decide to mount an offense against NATO, it would face an opponent like Poland, which uses modern weapons, armor, and aircraft.

In a potential war against Russia where NATO doesn't have U.S. backing, Germany would be its biggest funder, followed by Britain, France, and Italy. As long as Russia remains embroiled in a war with Ukraine, it's unlikely to start another war against Poland or Germany. Such a situation would spread Russia's forces too thin, but the Kremlin is known to make erratic decisions and could potentially do what it never intended. To avoid Russian aggression on one of its members, NATO has to continue to equip Ukraine with enough firepower to mount a longer defensive campaign to halt Russian advances. The alliance won't have enough time to bring sweeping changes to its military structure and equipment to counter Russia's offensives, which is why it needs Ukraine. In the end, NATO's success hinges on its leadership and competence, which would ally with a Ukrainian army that would rank just below Turkey and the United States in active troop contributions if embedded in NATO. The real question is whether the Kremlin can conduct another war against Ukraine's key allies as it also continues its war on Ukraine. To answer that, the Kremlin need not look further than the 1939 Molotov-Ribbentrop Pact, which at first brought success for Stalin and later became a path of consequences. The reality however, is Ukraine's allies are feeling the pinch of the war that is slowly approaching within its own borders in the form of Russian propaganda, which looks to rise opposition to overthrow leaders who are nervously supporting Ukraine.

Supporting Ukraine has led to adverse consequences for leaders in France and Germany, especially when this support entails significant measures that supersede their domestic priorities. The dynamics of such situations have produced troublesome outcomes for Ukraine's allies. The reality remains that Russian forces are killing Ukrainians and may not halt their atrocities there, underscoring why supporting Ukraine is a virtuous act. While providing aid to Ukraine may result in potential domestic electoral repercussions, it is crucial to recognize the imperative of being on the right side of history. European powers should consider their support for Ukraine at any price, prioritizing long-term ethical and strategic considerations over short-term political consequences.

Chapter 6

THE DIVIDED

Europe has a long history of independent kingdoms, duchies, city-states, and principalities, each with its own distinct culture, language, and governance. Its diverse geography, with its numerous mountain ranges, rivers, and peninsulas, has contributed to the emergence of distinct political entities. They are the roots of its historical fragmentation persisted through various periods, resisting unification under a single power to control the entire continent. That is not to say several powers have tried to bring it under their thumb but these attributes have had a complex dynamics in Europe's political identity, as it made alliances complex, resistance against aggression complicated and defending any state, to be thorny at best.

The first notable instance of cooperation among the governments of France, Germany, and Poland occurred even before the disbanding of the Soviet Union in December 1991, when the trio cooperated in the Weimar Triangle. It was a trilateral forum to facilitate dialogue and cooperation among France, Germany, and Poland. The forum contributed to promoting stability and reconciliation in Central Europe following the end of the Cold War. Fostering dialogue and cooperation between Europe's three larger states was the start of building trust and confidence in the new era of European integration.

The post-Soviet era facilitated cultural and educational exchanges that helped to deepen mutual understanding, fostered people-to-people connections, and promoted a sense of European identity among citizens of these three countries. The forum also addressed security issues within Europe, providing a platform for discussing regional security challenges and coordinating policies to address common threats, such as terrorism and organized crime. Poland's accession to NATO in 1999 and the European Union (EU) in 2004 furthered the cooperation. When it came to Ukraine, the leaders of the Weimar Triangle agreed their countries would provide military aid in long-distance artillery. German Chancellor Olaf Scholz and French President Emmanuel Macron were also looking to smooth over their own complex differences on how best to support Ukraine. The two great powers of Europe and Poland's newly elected Prime Minister, Donald Tusk, a former President of the European Council, wanted to boost the supply of ammunition to Kyiv.

Chancellor Scholz listed ways to achieve quick results. He wanted to procure even more weapons for Ukraine on the global market, believing the production of military equipment would be expanded through his own Ramstein Air Base as part of a new capability for long-range rocket artillery. What is evident is Scholz's reluctance to provide powerful missiles from Germany's stocks, fearing that President Putin might see his actions as an escalation of the war and produce a reality where Germany is directly at war with Russia. President Macron has called to send Western troops to Ukraine, but Scholz has ruled that out. Prime Minister Tusk has issued stark warnings about Ukraine's victory against Russia; he said that Europe had entered its pre-war era and that the war was a real threat to Europe. His comments in March 2024 came days after he met with his Ukrainian counterpart in Warsaw, where they discussed solutions to Ukrainian grain imports that are the subject of farmers' anger across Europe.

Tusk's predecessor, Mateusz Morawiecki's nationalist government, stopped supplying weapons to Kyiv due to the same issue. President Andrzej Duda corrected Morawiecki's stand in an interview where he said Warsaw would send weapons, just not new ones. Poland has already sent Ukraine 320 Soviet-era tanks and 14 MiG-29 fighter jets. Tension between Poland and Ukraine also includes Hungary and Slovakia, who also extended a ban on Ukrainian grain in the fall of 2023 as part of Polish farmers feeling threatened by imports of Ukrainian grain.

From the beginning of the war in Ukraine, the European Commission set up a few trade corridors for the sale and export of duty-free Ukrainian agricultural products to Africa and the Middle East, with one of these corridors passing through Poland. As Ukrainian grain was transported, 50% of it remained in Europe, and the rest went overseas. The price of Ukranian grain is much lower than that of wheat produced in the European Union (EU), particularly in Central Europe. The Ukrainian grain that was traded in Europe was destabilizing the local markets, affecting the income of farmers in Bulgaria, Hungary, Poland, Romania, and Slovakia. Together, the five blocked these imports in April 2023. Three months later, Russia refused to renew its agreement on grain exports through the Black Sea, which affected Central Europe even more. Tusk's government has worked well to mend such issues between Kyiv, but the rift has had a significant effect on Polish public opinion.

Differences over Ukraine between the Weimar Triangle may not look evident in the face of Russian aggression, but it is real and has the potential to derail the European project to support Ukraine. Within all the capitals of Europe, there is a concern about security, but when it comes to Ukraine, there appears to be more ceremonial support than actual economic, military and political backing. At a press conference, Prime Minister Tusk expressed an invitation to Macron and Scholz to Poland, but there are no guarantees that by then the differences will be mended. What is certain is the disagreements among the three will consume time, during which more Ukrainians will die of Russian aggression.

France, Germany, and Poland will need to sort out their major differences quickly, but that would be extremely hard to do given how they have come together in the 21st century, compared to how belligerent they were to each other only less than a century ago.

In the post-Soviet era, the process of European integration has posed challenges for all EU member states. Disagreements have arisen over issues such as budget contributions, the allocation of EU structural funds, and the governance of the Eurozone. Other issues, such as agricultural subsidies and labor migration, have also made things harder within the EU. Poland is one of the largest recipients of EU structural funds, and debates over the fairness and effectiveness of EU policies, particularly in addressing regional inequalities, remain a concern for Warsaw as it deals with Brussels.

Since the migration crisis in Europe in 2015, relations between EU member states have become strained. Disagreements over the distribution of refugees and asylum seekers, as well as border controls within the Schengen Area, a zone comprising 27 European countries and signed in the village of Schengen in Luxembourg in 1985, the area represents a significant step toward European integration. It is a zone that allows for the free and unrestricted movement of people, goods, services, and capital among the member countries, functioning essentially as a single jurisdiction for international travel with a common visa policy. The arrival of refugees and the EU's response, led to European tensions with disputes within the Schengen Area.

The European Union proposed a mandatory quota system to distribute refugees and asylum seekers among member states based on their population size and economic capacity. However, Poland, along with other Central and Eastern European countries, vehemently opposed the quota system, arguing that it infringed on national sovereignty and security concerns. Poland refused to accept any refugees under the quota system, and Polish officials cited security concerns as one of the primary reasons for rejecting the EU's refugee quotas. They argued that accepting refugees and migrants posed potential risks to national security, citing terrorist attacks in Western Europe and the need to protect Poland's borders.

Right-wing Polish politicians expressed concerns about the cultural and religious differences between Polish society and the predominantly Muslim refugees and migrants. They feared that the influx of migrants could disrupt social cohesion and undermine Poland's Christian identity.

In response, the European Commission launched legal proceedings against Poland, including Hungary and the Czech Republic, for their refusal to comply with the EU's refugee quota system. Poland remained steadfast in its position, rejecting any attempts to force it to accept refugees against its will. Since then, Berlin and Paris had particular concerns over the rule of law and democratic values in Poland, which have led to tensions between the Polish government and other EU member states. Issues such as judicial reforms, media freedom, and the independence of the judiciary have sparked debates within the EU and strained diplomatic relations with Poland. The election of Donald Tusk in December 2023, a senior pro-EU politician, has calmed some nerves, but to find a way to work together remains a challenge. Such tensions will produce unfavorable outcomes for pro-EU politicians.

As the only EU institution directly elected by voters from across 27 countries, the European Parliament serves as a critical link between European citizens and the EU's executive branch, the European Commission, as well as the Council, which comprises ministers from EU governments. This single position allows the Parliament to play a significant role in shaping the direction of EU laws and policies by amending and passing legislation, deciding on international agreements and enlargements, and endorsing the annual budget.

Members of the European Parliament (MEPs) have substantial influence over the legislative process. They can request the Commission to propose new laws, share the responsibility with the Council for adopting these laws, and oversee the activities of both the Commission and the Council. This oversight function ensures a degree of accountability within the EU's governance structure. MEPs typically align themselves with political groups that span the spectrum from left to right, rather than by nationality. This alignment necessitates balancing their commitments to their political groups and their national interests, often requiring complex negotiations and compromises.

For Ukraine, the actions and decisions of the European Parliament are particularly significant. The Parliament's legislative and budgetary powers can directly influence the EU's policies and funding related to Ukraine. For instance, if the Parliament supports increased financial aid or military assistance to Ukraine, it can advocate for such measures within the EU budget.

Furthermore, the European Parliament's role in international agreements and enlargements is crucial. As Ukraine seeks closer ties with the EU and potential future membership, the European Parliament's stance will be pivotal. MEPs can push for agreements that facilitate Ukraine's integration into European structures and support reforms necessary for its accession process.

The political composition of the European Parliament, therefore, has direct implications for Ukraine. A Parliament with a significant presence of right-wing and far-right parties might prioritize national sovereignty and tighter immigration controls, which could affect the nature and extent of support for Ukraine. Conversely, a more left-leaning or centrist Parliament might advocate for stronger collective EU action in support of Ukraine.

Ultimately, the European Parliament's ability to shape EU policies and its influence over the Commission and the Council positions it as a vital actor in the EU's relationship with Ukraine. The upcoming elections and the resultant political dynamics within the Parliament will thus play a crucial role in determining the EU's approach to Ukraine in the coming years.

Against the right-wing surge, the French President is sending a message to the opposition Jean-Luc Mélenchon's leftists and the far-right Marine Le Pen's National Rally (NR), a pro-Kremlin political group, that he is breaking with the status quo by threatening a direct confrontation with Russia. But by doing so, Macron is playing a dangerous political gamble by uniting the far-left and far-right against him. He is also placing the likes of his own centrist political party in difficulty, something that need not be heightened in the present climate. Already, the majority of Europeans are fed up with politicians unable to find solutions to economic inequality, unemployment, crime, security, immigration, integration, aging public services, healthcare, economic stagnation and globalization. Underneath Macron's move lies another aim. He hopes to prevent a vote of no confidence from the French Parliament in September, which could be triggered by his budget, especially given the status of his weak minority government. If that happens, there is no way the French President would survive and that is why it is so crucial to split both the Mélenchon leftists and the Le Pen right-wing coalitions.

It is almost certain, the vast majority of the European electorate wants to send far-right-wing groups to Brussels, not to do what previous politicians were unable to do, but to dent the functionality of the European parliament altogether.

The European Parliament is a cornerstone of the EU's democratic framework, playing a pivotal role in legislation, budgetary control, and oversight. Its evolving powers and responsibilities reflect ongoing efforts to enhance the democratic legitimacy and effectiveness of the European Union and shape the future of European integration. The June 2024 European Parliament elections will be a test of nerves, and it will also include a de facto referendum on Europe's stand against Russia.

Macron's Prime Minister Gabriel Attal has already laid the groundwork in labeling the opposition as "Putin's troops," but the far-right is already leading the polls. By distinguishing himself as the only French leader since Napolean to confront Russia militarily, Macron hopes to slow the far-right surge, but even if Macron does accomplish that, he also has to contain the outpouring support from his rivals in the Leftist Mélenchons. All this means that the problems for the French President will only grow, leading to political instability in France.

Most political commentators believe that after June, the European Parliament will have a greater far-right presence, but whether or not they will be able to form a governing coalition is questionable. The far-right parties are often focused on advancing their own national interests and agendas rather than prioritizing a political coalition at the parliamentary level, prioritizing domestic issues over pan-European unity, making it difficult to build consensus on common goals and strategies among a larger objective.

In Germany, Scholz has to handle a very tricky coalition with the Greens and the Free Democratic Party. Together, they form a strong 56% majority in the Bundestag. Scholz also knows public opinion in Germany is against sending weapons to Ukraine. Pacifist Germany also has a political makeup similar to that of the Baltic states. There are areas in Germany where Russian-speaking communities are still more prevalent due to historical migration patterns. Berlin has a significant Russian-speaking population, including ethnic Russians. They are the descendants of Russian immigrants who arrived in Germany during the pre and post-World War II era and the Cold War. Some areas in the former GDR (East Germany) have seen an influx of Russian-speaking immigrants since the end of the Cold War. The coastal areas along the Baltic Sea, such as Mecklenburg-Western Pomerania, have attracted Russian-speaking immigrants, including ethnic Germans from Russia and other former Soviet republics. These immigrants have settled in both rural and urban areas. Frankfurt, Munich, and Stuttgart have Russian-speaking communities among immigrants from Russia, Ukraine, Azerbaijan, Kazakhstan, and other countries of the former Soviet Union.

Like the perilous set of events in the previous century, Europe has to come together today to send a strong message to the Kremlin that they are united even when cracks are evident. The very nature of France, Germany, and Poland coming together is a success, but it is still in the beginning stages of a much-needed European cooperation setup. The intention to facilitate aid from the European Union (EU) for Ukraine and to jumpstart European security and defense cooperation is what the three agree in principle, but how each side conducts it in practice is another issue.

The June 2024 European parliamentary elections and the November 2024 American elections, will mark Ukraine's fate. This is why there needs to be a robust response from the Weimar Triangle to lead the way politically, militarily, and with committed economic aid to Ukraine, but time is running out.

Rheinmetall, a company headquartered in Düsseldorf, is an automotive and arms manufacturer. In 2023, the company announced it was going to build production facilities in Ukraine. In the 1930s, the same company, at that time called Rheinmetall-Borsig, began to rapidly increase production of firearms, anti-tank and artillery weapons, and as a result, became one of the main suppliers of heavy weapons to the Wehrmacht (German army) during WWII. On 3 March 2024, French Defense Minister Sébastien Lecornu hinted that tank maker KNDS, the holding structure formed by France's Nexter and Germany's Krauss-Maffei-Wegmann, is working with other companies including Rheinmetall to get supplies to Ukraine.

The members of the Weimar Triangle are all NATO members, but NATO does not want to get drawn into a conflict with Russia. The alliance has only provided Ukraine with old weapons to defend itself rather than having any new weapons or boots on the ground. Macron's recent stand to send troops to Ukraine is outside the alliance's status quo, but he has ruffled the feathers of his European counterparts. There is no doubt that neither Germany nor Poland would side with Macron, and a defensive NATO will never go to battle against Russia. These divisions will always be clouded under European ceremonies, much like the present Berlin March meeting when all the members of the Weimar Triangle met, and in the end, they refused questions from the media, perhaps fearing their differences would be fully exposed, resembling a European betrayal of Ukraine, but betrayal is a recurring theme in Europe.

One notable instance of a Polish betrayal is when France and Britain, as allies of Poland, had pledged to come to Poland's aid in the event of German aggression. However, when the Wehrmacht invaded Poland in September 1939, triggering the outbreak of World War II, France and Britain were unable to provide effective military assistance or response to Poland. This failure led to a host of events, including the Holocaust and Soviet occupation, something which many fear could resemble in Ukraine today.

France has its excuses. The French military strategy at the outset of World War II focused on defensive measures along with its border with Germany, known as the Maginot Line. French military planners were reluctant to launch a major offensive into Germany to relieve pressure on Poland, fearing a repeat of the trench warfare of World War I. While Britain and France declared war on Germany, their response was largely limited to diplomatic protests and no military action. There was a lack of a coordinated and decisive military strategy to support Poland effectively. Compounding Poland's plight, the Soviet Union, under the Molotov-Ribbentrop Pact, invaded Poland from the east on 17 September 1939, just over two weeks after Germany's invasion. This further divided Poland's defenses and left the country vulnerable to occupation by two powers.

While France and Britain did provide some material and financial support to the Polish war effort, their failure to mount a more robust military intervention has been criticized as a betrayal of their own commitments made under international treaties.

In the post-Soviet era, France and Germany have been instrumental in advancing European integration through cooperation, exemplified by the foundations of the Élysée Treaty in 1963, a cornerstone of European stability and progress. Together, they have spearheaded initiatives such as the European Coal and Steel Community (ECSC), the precursor to the European Union (EU), and have worked closely on major EU treaties and reforms.

The process of European integration has been difficult in the 21st century, especially at a time of divergent national interests, economic disparities, cultural differences, and political disagreements among EU member states. Catastrophic events of the 2008-09 financial crisis, the Eurozone debt crisis, and the challenges posed by Brexit, also added further pressures against integration.

While France and Germany have often worked together to address these challenges, they cannot dictate the outcomes unilaterally. The EU has expanded significantly since its inception from the Treaty of Paris in 18 April 1951, admitting new member states from Central and Eastern Europe, the Baltic states, and the Balkans. The integration of these diverse countries with varying historical experiences, economic conditions, and political systems have added complexity to the process of European unity. The rise of populist movements and nationalist sentiments in some EU member states has also posed a challenge to the idea of further European integration. These movements often emphasize national sovereignty and oppose deeper EU integration, complicating efforts to unite Europe. In the 21st century, Europe's position in the world and its ability to unite politically and economically are influenced by currents and trends often converging from both the East and the West, but mostly outside of Europe.

The Russian invasion of Ukraine, particularly the annexation of Crimea in February 2014 and the 24 February 2022 invasion had a significant impact on Europe. While the invasion did not lead to immediate and complete unity among all European countries, it has contributed to a greater sense of solidarity and cooperation within the EU. Some EU member states have bolstered their defense capabilities, enhanced military cooperation, and supported NATO's presence to deter further Russian aggression. The EU has provided political, financial, and humanitarian support to Ukraine in its efforts to resist Russian aggression and implement reforms. The support has included technical expertise and diplomatic backing, demonstrating solidarity with Ukraine's sovereignty and territorial integrity. However, the war has underscored the importance of energy security for Europe, particularly in reducing dependence on Russian energy sources. The EU has pursued diversification strategies, invested in renewable energy, and strengthened energy cooperation among member states to mitigate vulnerabilities to Russian influences. This has only partially worked. Bulgaria, Slovakia, and Hungary still harbor sympathies for Russia. Surveys show a majority of Slovaks would likely accept a Russian military victory over Ukraine. 67% of Bulgarians and 55% of Hungarians perceived Russia as a friend and would also likely accept a Russian victory.

Bulgaria's Euroskeptic President Rumen Radev and Hungary's

Prime Minister Victor Orbán are the only NATO and EU members to have officially refused to deliver arms to Ukraine. Bulgaria's previous Prime Minister, Galab Donev, secretly provided Kyiv with ammunition and fuel, concealing the fact from the public.

While the Slovak government supplied heavy weaponry to Kyiv, it has sided with Hungary in an exemption in the 2023 EU oil ban. The previous Slovak government of Prime Minister Eduard Heger and Hungary's Orbán, went against Brussels in purchasing Russian gas, going so far as to purchase Russian rubles. Prime Minister Orbán has repeatedly blocked sanctions against Russia.

As Europe was unsuccessful in integration, it was also successful in hiding the divisions from within. The end of Communism produced a greater appetite for capitalism, but that did not change centuries-old distrust and rivalry of East and West Europe. That division is often associated with religious differences, particularly between Western Christianity (Catholicism and Protestantism) and Eastern Christianity (Orthodoxy).

The historical event that solidified Europe's religious differences is known as the Great Schism of 1054. It was a gradual process that culminated in the formal split between the Roman Catholic Church in the West and the Eastern Orthodox Church in the East. One of the central issues was the question of ecclesiastical authority and the primacy of the Bishop of Rome (the Pope). In the West, the Pope asserted primacy over the entire Church and claimed authority over matters of doctrine and discipline. In contrast, in the East, the Patriarch of Constantinople, along with other Eastern patriarchs, emphasized the authority of the collective body of bishops (the "conciliar" model) and resisted the Pope's claims to supremacy.

The Western and Eastern churches developed distinct liturgical practices, theological emphases, and cultural traditions over centuries. Differences in language (Latin in the West, Greek in the East), liturgical rites, theological terminology, and religious art contributed to a sense of divergence between Western and Eastern Christianity.

The political division of the Roman Empire into the Western and the Eastern Roman Empire (Byzantine Empire) also played a role. Political tensions and rivalries between Rome and Constantinople, as well as disputes over territorial jurisdiction and ecclesiastical authority, exacerbated the theological differences between the two churches.

One of the theological issues that contributed was the "Filioque" controversy. The addition of the phrase "and the Son" (Filioque) to the Nicene Creed in the West signifies the procession of the Holy Spirit from both the Father and the Son, which was rejected by the Eastern churches. This theological dispute symbolized broader disagreements over doctrine, authority, and theological interpretation. The culmination of such theological, cultural, political, and ecclesiastical factors resulted in the formal excommunication of each other's leaders by the Western and Eastern churches in 1054, which marked a division that remained to this day.

The fall and renaming of Constantinople to Istanbul and the Ottoman conquest of the city in 1453 played a significant role in solidifying the divide between Eastern and Western Christianity, as well as in shaping the geopolitical and cultural landscape of Europe as well as the Middle East.

The end of Constantinople, the capital of the Byzantine Empire, by the Ottomans under Sultan Mehmed II, marked the end of the center of Eastern Christianity and Greek Orthodoxy, which had lasted for over a thousand years. Ottoman rule had profound cultural and religious implications for Europe and the Middle East. It resulted in the conversion of the Hagia Sophia, the iconic Byzantine cathedral, into a mosque, symbolizing the triumph of Islam over Christianity in the region. The renaming of Constantinople to Istanbul reflected the city's new status as the capital of the Ottoman Empire and its growing importance as a center of Islamic civilization. Through the trade routes, the Ottomans extended control into the heart of the Balkans and Eastern Europe and contributed to the polarization between East and West. The Ottomans altered trade routes between Europe and Asia, leading to the decline of traditional overland routes and the rise of maritime trade. This shift contributed to the economic decline of the Italian city-states, which had previously dominated Mediterranean trade, and facilitated the rise of maritime powers such as Portugal and Spain.

The Balkans were most profoundly impacted. The Ottoman empire gradually conquered territories inhabited by various Christian and Orthodox populations. Ottoman rule in the Balkans lasted for nearly six-centuries and resulted in profound demographic, cultural, and religious changes. Many regions converted to Islam, and the Ottomans governed through a system of religious and ethnic pluralism, with Muslims, Christians, and Jews living together, despite periodic uprisings and rebellions against Ottoman rule.

In areas of modern-day Ukraine, which was part of the Polish-Lithuanian Commonwealth, it was not directly ruled by the Ottoman Empire. However, the Ottoman expansion into southeastern Europe and the Black Sea had indirect effects on areas of Ukraine. The Ottomans competed with neighboring powers, including the Polish-Lithuanian Commonwealth, the Russian Empire, and the Crimean Khanate, for influence and control over the lands of Ukraine and the Black Sea. The Ottoman control over the Crimean Khanate brought the Ottoman-occupied southern border closer to Ukrainian territories, particularly in the region of modern-day southern Ukraine and Crimea. The Crimean Khanate, a vassal state of the Ottoman empire, conducted frequent raids and military campaigns into Ukrainian territories, especially in the border regions. These raids, known as "Tatar raids," targeted Ukrainian towns and villages, resulting in devastation, plunder, and the capture of prisoners for slavery, ransom and inflicting direct harm on communities.

The 17 July 1683 Siege of Vienna, and the Russia-Ottoman Wars, a series of conflicts beginning from 1676 to 1878, further weakened Ottoman control in Europe and led to the gradual expansion of Russian influence in the Balkans and the Black Sea. Territories, including Serbia and Greece, as well as the Caucasus and Crimea, now came under Russian control. Finally, it was the 1912 Balkan wars that marked the end of Ottoman rule in Europe. Comprising of Serbia, Montenegro, Greece, and Bulgaria, the coalition led the final dissolution of Ottoman control in all remaining European territories, with the exception of Constantinople (Istanbul) and a small strip of territory surrounding it. The near-quincentennial Ottoman rule of Europe's East had a lasting effect that is still very visible today, particularly in its differences from Europe's West.

Post-European integration failed to deliver the Western-model economies promised to subdue the Soviet remnants in the 21st century. Decrees were now received from Berlin and Paris rather than Moscow. In the last decade, the growth of social media and unregulated digital spaces tapped into disinformation and crafted a nostalgic Soviet era sentiments. It culminated in a pan-Slavic unity against Brussels. Increases in energy prices, the cost of living, and high inflation were mostly felt by the elderly and those who fared well during the Soviet era, now protested against anything that had roots in Western Europe.

Brussels, in particular, found itself in an East-West divide. It was unprepared for the war that came on 24 February 2022 in Ukraine and was even more underprepared to set the mechanisms for social media platforms, shaping the attitudes towards central events like the COVID-19 pandemic, terror attacks, and the 2015 migration crisis. It was also ill-equipped to take on Russian-sponsored disinformation campaigns, propaganda channels, and fake news.

A better-prepared Kremlin invested in online channels and targeted audiences, using a coalition of pro-Russian commentators at the heart of Western European cities, and pressed its propaganda against the mainstream media. Ukraine was the exception. President Zelenskyy's government has done a fantastic job not only in limiting Russian digital reach but also in leading by example in curtailing it.

From the beginning, the Ukrainian President realized his message was not reaching areas of Ukraine's East. All major television networks in Ukraine were controlled by Ukrainian oligarchs, many of whom opposed Zelenskyy's government and some of whom were allied with Russia. When he banned channels that were unleashing Russian propaganda, Brussels claimed Zelenskyy was going too far in limiting his citizens' freedom of speech. It was not until 2022 that Zelenskyy led his own response to the information war.

He took the airwaves over and treated them as national critical infrastructure as part of his defense. Analysts observed it as the President's Telemarathon against Putin. The Ukrainian President's team led the information on where the fighting was, where to shelter, when to evacuate, and how to survive, reaching every Ukrainian household.

Zelenskyy's information war is revolutionary. It is the first time a former Soviet state has taken on the information war against Russia. True, this has come at the cost of authoritarian measures in media regulation, but its effects will undo Russian propaganda.

When Ukrainian units consolidate former Russian-held areas, engineers have been quick to repair lines that have either hindered or halted Kyiv's reach. To counter this, fleeing Russian forces have destroyed television towers, satellites, cables, communication lines, and antennas. However, as the Ukrainian president has realized, there are areas he is simply unable to consolidate. Ukraine's forces found it hard to penetrate some Russian lines, and that was the case even before the six months of no American aid.

Residents in Russian-occupied areas, especially in the Donbas and surrounding areas, do not consider Kyiv's authority. There are populations that have grown up under not only Russian control but also the Russian language in radio, television, and other outlets who are fighting against Ukraine.

In Europe, the war in Ukraine has highlighted the danger of information. Brussels has to step up its digital literacy. Detection of fake news is a challenge, and getting populations to comprehend the differences during a time of severe polarization is a must for a divided Europe.

A genuine understanding between Macron, Scholz, and Tusk is that Europe is a success, but that also means one crucial outcome. The three have to understand each others' lines, length, and language despite differences in their political, military, and economic response to Europe, Russia, and assistance to Ukraine. It is crucial because, without it, Europe would be permanently divided, and Russia would succeed in re-installing its Iron Curtain.

One of the fundamental consequences of a divide within Europe is cultural and social fragmentation. Such divisions can exacerbate cultural and social differences, leading to increased tensions and conflicts. This fragmentation can manifest as discrimination, marginalization of certain groups, and an erosion of social cohesion. The rise of identity politics can become more pronounced, with groups emphasizing their distinct cultural, ethnic, or regional identities over a shared national identity, further deepening divides and hindering efforts to foster unity and cooperation. Europeans have become disillusioned with political and social institutions, leading to increased public discontent. A divided Europe will struggle to address the concerns of its population, resulting in further alienation and social unrest.

For Ukraine, a divided Europe will nullify its successes on the battlefield and undo the three-decades worth of progress rooted from the dark days of Soviet rule. Macron, Scholz, and Tusk may disagree on many things, but one issue on which they cannot afford to be divided is the necessity of supporting Ukraine at any price. Their unity is crucial to preventing Ukrainians from facing a perilous reality of a long Russian occupation.

Chapter 7

THE ANTI-WEST AXIS

The sudden disbanding of the Soviet Union changed the makeup of the geopolitical balance of power in the world. For the first time in centuries, a single nation, the United States, could exert its influence and power everywhere. Russia, the successor to the Soviet Union, was not a power at its inception on 26 December 1991, and it inherited a complex economic situation. The last decade of the 20th century was ending on a high note for the United States, but for China, it gave birth to its rise. Smaller regional powers like Iran and India too, looked to be on the ascendence.

The Soviet economy had been largely centrally planned, with the state controlling almost all aspects of production and distribution. However, by the late 1980s, it was plagued by inefficiency and public debt. By the time Russia inherited it, a necessary transition from a centrally planned economy to a market-oriented economy was badly needed. This transition, known as "shock therapy," involved liberalization, privatization, and deregulation. The process was tumultuous and led to economic instability, with widespread unemployment, inflation, and hyperinflation. Prices skyrocketed, and the value of the Russian ruble plummeted. It severely eroded the purchasing power of ordinary Russians and undermined confidence in the economy. Russia experienced a sharp decline in GDP, industrial output, and living standards. The transition to a market economy was accompanied by economic contraction, as inefficient state enterprises struggled to adapt to the demands of a competitive market. It led to economic upheaval, which fueled social unrest, with protests, strikes, and political instability becoming common. Many Russians experienced the much-hailed Soviet-era social services which were by now on the verge of deterioration.

As Russians suffered, its former rival China was experiencing robust growth and undergoing significant transformations, albeit with some challenges and complexities. China had been implementing economic reforms since the late 1970s under the leadership of Deng Xiaoping. By 1996, these reforms were well underway, with the gradual introduction of market-oriented policies, decentralization of economic decision-making, and opening up to foreign investment and trade. Throughout the 1990s, China consistently achieved high rates of economic growth, often surpassing 10% annually. The growth was driven by rapid industrialization, urbanization, investment in infrastructure, and the expansion of export-oriented manufacturing.

China's integration into the global economy further accelerated in the 21st century. The country became a major destination for foreign direct investment (FDI), particularly in manufacturing sectors such as electronics, textiles, and automobiles. Export growth was also significant, fueled by China's competitive advantage in low-cost manufacturing. The country continued its efforts to reform state-owned enterprises (SOE) to improve efficiency and competitiveness, which also included measures such as corporatization, partial privatization, and restructuring of inefficient enterprises. However, the process of SOE reform remained incomplete, with many state-owned firms facing challenges related to overstaffing, debt, and inefficiency.

Despite rapid economic growth, China faced social challenges such as income inequality, rural-urban disparities, and unemployment. The government implemented policies aimed at addressing these issues, including poverty alleviation programs, rural development initiatives, and social welfare reforms.

China's financial sector underwent gradual liberalization and modernization. Reforms included the establishment of stock markets, and the restructuring of state-owned banks. However, the financial sector remained relatively underdeveloped compared to Western economies, with ongoing concerns about non-performing loans and financial stability.

In the same decade, Iran's economy was undergoing a period of recovery and stabilization following the tumultuous years of the Iran-Iraq War (1980-1988) and the subsequent economic challenges that followed. Iran focused on rebuilding its infrastructure, industries, and economy, which had suffered significant damage during the decade of war. President Akbar Hashemi Rafsanjani's government invested in reconstruction projects to repair war-damaged areas, revive economic activity, and diversify its economy beyond its heavy reliance on oil revenues. Efforts were made to develop non-oil sectors such as agriculture, manufacturing, and services. However, the oil sector remained a crucial source of government revenue and export earnings. Tehran pursued policies to attract foreign direct investment (FDI) and expand its trade relations. The government implemented economic reforms to liberalize trade, encourage foreign direct investment, and facilitate joint ventures with international partners. However, Iran's economy continued to face challenges related to Western-backed sanctions and internal political tensions.

The country embarked on privatization programs aimed at transferring state-owned enterprises to the private sector and promoting entrepreneurship. Economic reforms were introduced to streamline regulations, improve the business environment, and enhance economic efficiency. However, progress in privatization and economic reform was gradual, and obstacles were faced due to bureaucratic inertia and political resistance.

Iran grappled with inflationary pressures and macroeconomic imbalances. The government implemented monetary and fiscal policies to control inflation, stabilize the currency, and manage public finances. Efforts were made to reduce budget deficits, enhance monetary policy effectiveness, and strengthen macroeconomic management. The Iranian government implemented social welfare programs to address poverty, unemployment, and social inequalities. These programs included subsidies on essential goods, employment, innovation, and social assistance programs aimed at supporting vulnerable and elderly populations.

As China, Iran and Russia, internally worked to consolidate to have its state infrastructures work in the 21st century, they also realized one crucial area of global dynamics. The reality of the United States as a hegemonic Superpower means it can dictate terms, but what it could not do, was halt the progress of international alliances that opposed its dominance.

Russian President Boris Yeltsin's Foreign Minister Evgeniy Primakov was the architect behind the policy of an anti-US alliance, that would counter the American hold on the international global order.

The Jewish Ukrainian-born Arabic-fluent Primakov, who grew up in Tbilisi was known for his significant contributions to Russian foreign policy. Primakov started his career as a journalist, working for the Soviet Union's official radio and later for the newspaper *Pravda*, specializing in Middle Eastern affairs. He was also a prominent scholar, contributing significantly to the fields of Oriental studies and international relations. He served as the Director of the Institute of Oriental Studies of the Russian Academy of Sciences and later, as the Director of the Institute of World Economy and International Relations. From 1991 to 1996, Primakov was the head of the Russian Foreign Intelligence Service (SVR), succeeding the KGB's First Chief Directorate after the disbanding of the Soviet Union. Yeltsin promoted him to Foreign Minister in 1996, and soon Primakov advocated for a multipolar world. He became known for his vocal opposition to NATO and its expansion after the disbanding of the Soviet Union. His subsequent warnings reached a new generation of post-Soviet Russian leaders, many who would become part of President Putin's inner circle.

Primakov's foreign policy make-up was interrupted in August 1998, when the Russian government devalued the ruble, a decision that led to rapid loss of confidence in the currency and a sharp depreciation. Additional problems related to the issue of short-term zero-coupon bonds, (GKO) were meant as a non-inflationary method of financing the deficit, but that too was affected. As a consequence of the ruble devaluation, it led to a spike in inflation, which eroded the purchasing power of Russians. The economy contracted sharply, with GDP falling significantly. Yeltsin's government declared a moratorium on its foreign debt, and also announced a restructuring of its domestic debt, which meant defaulting on its debt obligations, and GKO bonds. The crisis led to the collapse of many Russian banks, wiping out savings and causing widespread financial distress among Russians. Banks faced a severe liquidity crisis, and many could not meet their obligations to depositors and creditors. The economic crisis led to a rise in unemployment and underemployment, with many Russians falling into poverty as their savings were wiped out and prices for goods soared. The situation led to political instability, culminating in the resignation of Prime Minister Sergei Kiriyenko in August 1998. Yeltsin promoted Primakov to Prime Minister to deal with the crisis.

Immediately, Primakov assembled a broad-based coalition government that included representatives from various political factions, which helped to stabilize the political environment. He brought in experienced and pragmatic officials to key positions, such as Yuri Maslyukov as First Deputy Prime Minister and Viktor Gerashchenko as Chairman of the Central Bank of Russia. He further directed steps to stabilize the banking sector, and enhanced regulation to stabilize the ruble and control inflation. He prioritized focusing on fostering ties with non-Western nations as part of a new strategic economic alliance that would foster future foreign direct investment (FDI) in Russia. "Perevarivat' kamen'" translates to digesting stone and it was particularly relevant to Primakov's sentiments about financial aid from the International Monetary Fund (IMF).

Yeltsin's Russia received substantial financial assistance from the IMF and other Western institutions. However, the economic prescriptions that came with this aid, often referred to as "shock therapy," including rapid privatization, liberalization, and austerity, which led to significant economic and social upheaval in Russia. Primakov and his government were critical of the harsh austerity measures and market liberalization policies advocated by Western economists, which they believed exacerbated the economic crisis rather than alleviating it. He sought alternative economic partnerships and strengthened ties with other major economies such as China and India.

China's assistance came through a combination of trade, financial support, diplomatic backing, and strategic partnership initiatives. While not as high-profile as Western aid, China's role was nonetheless significant in providing Russia with the economic stability needed to navigate through the crisis and begin its path to recovery. It was in currency swap agreements, which allowed Russia to access the Chinese yuan without needing to rely solely on the US dollar, an arrangement which provided Russia with additional liquidity. Long-term contracts for the supply of Russian energy and raw materials ensured a steady stream of income. The establishment of joint ventures in energy, mining, and manufacturing facilitated technology transfer and industrial cooperation, further helped the Russian economy.

India's assistance came through a combination of trade, defense cooperation, energy deals, economic and technical assistance, strategic and diplomatic support, further providing Russia with the economic stability and revenues the country needed to navigate through the crisis.

While Primakov managed to stabilize the Russian economy, his cautious approach and resistance to rapid economic reforms were perceived by some, including Yeltsin, as contributing to an economic slowdown. His policies were more focused on economic stability and gradual recovery, which contrasted with Yeltsin's more aggressive agenda.

Friction between the Prime Minister and the President began in 1999 when the Russian economy stabilized. Primakov's growing popularity and his ability to unite various political factions, including the Communists and other opposition groups, made him a powerful figure in Russian politics. The NATO intervention in the Balkans, particularly the bombing of Yugoslavia, beginning in March 1999, for Primakov, was a unilateral U.S. action that disregarded Russian interests and international norms. It was a feeling that was very similar to what Putin felt in 2003, when the Americans invaded Iraq. Primakov wanted Yeltsin to take a stand against the American and NATO bombings against a fellow Slavic country, but Yeltsin remained silent. Where Yeltsin became particularly alarmed by his Prime Minister was in Primakov's government's anti-corruption investigations that targeted key figures within his inner circle, including members of his own family. Yeltsin feared a future President Primakov would put him, his family and his close associates to live the rest of their lives in some Autonomous Oblast and in a notorious prison as political convicts.

On 12 May 1999, Yeltsin fired Primakov and appointed Sergei Stepashin as Prime Minister, who was seen as a more loyal and less politically threatening figure, which temporarily gave Yeltsin some relief before other problems soon mounted.

Primakov's reign as both Foreign Minister and Prime Minister looks to emulate the groundwork of which Putin became the beneficiary. He was the chief architect of a project where Russia would reassert its influence on the global stage and create the foundations of a much more resurgent player in international affairs with its own interests. By 2004, Russia reached that milestone and in 2024, the Anti-West Axis is a reality of Primakov's vision from his 1998 proposal, which laid the foundations for a strategic triangle in Eurasia. Primakov had envisioned an economic coalition between Russia, China, and India. Iran later expressed its interest in joining it. Although Primakov's specific vision did not come to fruition to include India, pariah states like Iran, Venezuela, Nicaragua, North Korea, and Cuba, expanded his original Anti-West Axis.

These states have regularly defended each other at the UN and their votes are based on a myriad of strategic, ideological, and tactical reasons, as well as opposition to the American-led global order, which is undoubtedly at the center. Today, China, Russia, and Iran are taking on the United States in their own versions of strategic paralysis theory and deterrence.

For Russia, it played a waiting game for American democracy to weaken. China did the same until it was more economically stable and Iran held back for decades, until its proxies had enough, and it was forced to react. Rather than actively engaging with the United States, all three employed a strategy of observing American economic, political and military actions closely, looking for vulnerabilities, mistakes, and patterns of behavior. In 2018, there was a feeling that America would eventually disengage with the world and revert back to its political isolationism of early 20th century, but others argued that economically, it would surge decades ahead of its competition.

The beginning of the 21st century belonged to the United States, but the challenge to its supremacy began with the 2008-09 financial crisis. The episode revealed weaknesses in the U.S. financial system, particularly in the banking and mortgage sectors. Risky lending practices, such as subprime mortgages and the bundling of these mortgages into complex financial products, led to widespread defaults and a collapse in the housing market. It not only affected American homeowners but also reverberated throughout the global financial system, demonstrating the interconnectedness of economies worldwide and severely affecting markets in Asia and Europe.

The episode highlighted deficiencies in financial regulation and oversight. American regulatory agencies failed to adequately monitor and control risky financial activities, allowing practices that contributed to the crisis to go unchecked. It exposed flaws in the regulatory framework and raised questions about the effectiveness of government oversight in preventing such crises, as it underscored the interconnectedness of the global economy. Financial institutions and markets around the world were heavily interconnected, leading to the rapid transmission of financial shocks across borders. The crisis demonstrated that economic problems in one country could quickly spread to others, no matter how far they were, highlighting the need for coordinated international responses to address financial instability.

Leading G7 economies took on the vulnerabilities of their own economy, which was heavily reliant on debt-fueled consumption. Prior to the crisis, many Americans were borrowing beyond their means to finance consumption, leading to unsustainable levels of debt. When the housing bubble burst and asset prices plummeted, households faced financial distress, leading to a sharp contraction in consumer spending and further exacerbating the economic downturn.

In the aftermath, a political gridlock took hold, and challenges in policymaking began the first steps to polarization. Despite the severity of the crisis, partisan divisions and ideological differences hindered the US government's ability to implement timely and effective policy responses. Delays in decision-making and debates over the appropriate course of action prolonged the economic downturn and exacerbated its impact.

The 2008-09 financial crisis revealed vulnerabilities in the U.S. economy and financial system, challenging the perception of the United States as an invincible Superpower. During the same time, Russia had amassed significant reserves, largely due to high oil and commodity prices. These reserves provided a cushion against external shocks and allowed the government to implement counter-cyclical fiscal policies to stimulate the economy. Despite its heavy dependence on oil and natural gas exports, Russia's economy diversified compared to previous decades but at a very limited level. It helped mitigate the impact of the decline in oil prices during the crisis, as other sectors, such as agriculture and manufacturing, which contributed to some economic stability. The Kremlin implemented prudent financial policies in the years leading up to the crisis, including maintaining a relatively conservative approach to debt management and implementing reforms to strengthen the banking sector. These measures helped to build resilience in the financial system and limited the impact of the 2008-09 financial crisis on the domestic economy.

Russia allowed its currency, the ruble, to float freely during the crisis, which helped absorb external shocks and maintain competitiveness in international markets. While the ruble depreciated significantly during the crisis, the flexible exchange rate setup facilitated adjustments in the economy and supported export-oriented industries. The Russian government intervened actively to support the economy, including providing liquidity to banks, injecting capital into oil and gas industries, and implementing stimulus measures to boost domestic demand. These interventions helped stabilize the financial system, support employment, and mitigate the impact of the crisis on businesses and households. The domestic consumption in Russia remained prudent and a vital resilient factor during the crisis. It was helped partly due to the government's efforts to support household incomes through social assistance programs and wage subsidies, as well as the presence of a large "under-the-table" economy that provided a cushion against job losses.

China maintained robust domestic demand during the 2008-09 financial crisis, as the government implemented a massive fiscal stimulus package totaling around $586 billion, which included investments in infrastructure, social welfare programs, and subsidies for consumer spending. The stimulus helped support economic growth and offset the decline in external demand caused by the global recession. As China's exports were impacted by the decline in global demand during the crisis, its diversified export markets helped mitigate the impact. China has been expanding its trade relationships with emerging markets and other Asian economies to reduce its reliance on any single market. The diversification helped cushion the blow of reduced demand from traditional export destinations like the United States and Europe. The country maintained and managed a floating exchange rate, which allowed the value of the Chinese yuan to adjust in response to changing market conditions. While there were criticisms of China's exchange rate policies, the flexibility helped support export competitiveness and mitigate the impact of external shocks on the economy. Its banking sector remained relatively insulated from the financial turmoil experienced in Western countries. It was partly due to stricter regulations and oversight, as well as the limited exposure of Chinese banks to complex financial products that were at the heart of the 2008-09 financial crisis. Additionally, the Chinese government took proactive measures to bolster the capitalization of banks and provide liquidity support as needed. The government also demonstrated flexibility and coordination in its policy response to the crisis. In addition to the fiscal stimulus package, monetary easing measures, such as interest rate cuts and reductions in reserve requirements, to support liquidity and credit availability helped. The government also encouraged state-owned enterprises to increase investment and consumption to stimulate economic activity. The government was able to conduct such measures because it had been implementing structural reforms aimed at rebalancing its economy away from export-led growth towards greater domestic consumption and innovation. While these reforms were still ongoing during the 2008-09 financial crisis, they helped support resilience by reducing the economy's dependence on external demand and promoting sustainable growth drivers.

Iran was less exposed to the financial turmoil because of its relatively isolated from the global financial system since 1981, due to Western-backed sanctions and restrictions on its banking sector. Its extremely limited activities in the global financial markets helped insulate itself from some of the direct impacts of the 2008-09 financial crisis. Oil revenues, despite fluctuations, continued to benefit the government from exports, which provided a vital source of foreign exchange earnings that helped stabilize the economy and mitigate the impact of the global downturn. Iran's economy is heavily reliant on oil exports; it has diversified its trade relationships to some extent, including trade partnerships with countries in Asia, Africa, and the Middle East, which helped reduce its dependence on any single market and provided some resilience against fluctuations in global demand during the crisis.

The Iranian government implemented various subsidy programs and social welfare initiatives aimed at supporting low-income households and mitigating the impact of economic shocks. These programs provided a safety net for vulnerable populations and helped maintain social stability during periods of economic uncertainty. Like the Soviet Union, Iran's economy is characterized by significant state control and intervention, including state ownership of key industries and strategic sectors. The government has implemented policies aimed at promoting self-sufficiency, import substitution, and industrial development, which helped reduce reliance on external sources during the crisis. While Western-backed sanctions limited Iran's ability to access external funding during the crisis, it also reduced its exposure to risks associated with global financial instability.

China, Russia, and Iran did not suffer as badly in the 2008-09 financial crisis as the United States and their allies in Europe, but how they handled their own economies during the crisis were shaped by their own historical, geopolitical, and economic realities. All three have a rich history of empire-building, which influences their modern geopolitical thinking. All three had previous empires that marked their own ascendence as regional powers, an attitude that has not shifted entirely in their actions of today.

The Russian Tsar who employed a patient and strategic approach to governance was Ivan IV, also known as "Ivan the Terrible." He ruled as the Grand Prince of Moscow (1533 to 1547) and then as the first Tsar of Russia from 1547 until his death in 1584. His reign was marked by significant political, military, and social developments and is often credited with centralizing power in Russia, expanding its territory from within, and laying the foundation for modern-day Russia. He was not particularly careful about antagonizing the powers in Kyivan Rus, primarily because by this time Kyivan Rus had long fragmented and ceased to exist as a unified entity. Under the rule of the Varangians, had disintegrated into various principalities by the 13th century and was further devastated by the Mongol invasions. By the time Ivan IV came to power in the mid-16th century, the remnants of Kyivan Rus were divided among different states, including the Grand Duchy of Lithuania, the Kingdom of Poland, and the emerging Muscovite state. His main problems were within, including internal dissent. Ivan's approach could be interpreted as playing a waiting game and skillfully handling diplomatic relations with neighboring powers, particularly the Grand Duchy of Lithuania and the Crimean Khanate, to stabilize his rule. Rather than constantly engaging in costly military campaigns, Ivan often employed diplomacy and strategic patience to advance Russia's interests and avoid unnecessary conflicts. He signed a peace treaty with the Grand Duchy of Lithuania in 1552, which ended decades of border conflicts and established a period of relative stability along the western frontier. Similarly, he formed alliances with other European powers, such as Britain, to counterbalance the influence of the Ottomans. While Ivan was known for his military campaigns, including the conquest of the Khanates of Kazan and Astrakhan, he also demonstrated restraint when it served his strategic interests. Rather than launching reckless offensives, Ivan often waited for moments of siege warfare that would benefit his forces to wear down his opponents over time. He also implemented various long-term policies aimed at strengthening Russia's position and reducing its vulnerability to external threats by modernizing the military, fortifying border defenses, and promoting economic development to enhance Russia's resilience and capacity to withstand foreign pressure in his expansionism. It is a Kremlin attitude that has continued to this day.

Ivan's strategies of "playing a waiting game" competently mirrored that of Chinese King Wen of Zhou. During the 11th century BCE, King Wen was renowned for his contributions to the establishment of the Zhou state. He was the father of King Wu, who completed the conquest of the Shang dynasty. He is primarily remembered for his role in laying the groundwork for the overthrow of the Shang dynasty, a process that took decades to unfold. He focused on building his state's moral and ethical integrity, promoting virtues such as benevolence, righteousness, and humility. Through his exemplary conduct and leadership, he gained the respect and loyalty of his people, as well as support from neighboring states. He sought alliances and formed strategic partnerships with other regional powers that shared his vision of overthrowing the corrupt and tyrannical Shang dynasty. By aligning himself with like-minded allies, King Wen strengthened his position and laid the foundations for future military campaigns. He understood the importance of careful preparation and long-term planning. He spent years consolidating his power, building alliances, and gathering resources before launching a full-scale campaign against his enemies. This patient approach allowed him to bide his time and strike when the conditions were most favorable. Throughout his reign, he demonstrated adaptability and flexibility in responding to changing circumstances and unforeseen challenges. He adjusted his strategies and tactics as needed, always keeping his ultimate goal of overthrowing the Shang dynasty in mind. It is a visionary approach that has not escaped the leaders of the National People's Congress (NPC) of today, including the Chinese President Xi Jinping.

Like Ivan and King Wen, the present Shia theocracy in Iran cites Cyrus the Great, the founder of the Achaemenid Empire (559 to 530 BCE) as one who had his version of strategic paralysis in his approach to expanding his empire and dealing with rival powers. He was known for his policy of tolerance toward ethnic and religious groups within his empire. Rather than imposing a uniform religious identity, he allowed conquered peoples to maintain their customs, languages, and religious practices. This approach helped to mitigate resistance and foster stability within his empire. He was adept at forming alliances and coalitions with neighboring states to achieve his expansionist goals and often sought to exploit divisions among rival powers or leverage diplomatic means to secure favorable outcomes without resorting to outright military conflict. Against his key opponents in the Lydian Kingdom and the Babylonian Empire, he patiently approached to gradually expand his influence and consolidate his power.

While Cyrus was a capable military leader, he also understood the value of strategic patience and calculated restraint. Rather than launching reckless offensives, he sometimes waited for opportune moments to strike in his siege warfare to wear down his opponents over time. He had a long-term vision for his empire, which extended beyond mere conquest and territorial expansion. He focused on building a stable and prosperous realm, investing in infrastructure, trade, and governance systems to ensure the long-term viability of his empire. This patient and forward-thinking approach laid the foundation for the enduring success of his Achaemenid Empire. The leaders of Iran today, in their influential maneuvers in Iraq, Lebanon, Syria, Yemen and potentially in Gaza, do employ similar methods.

The commonality of the Chinese, the Russian, and the Persian empires says something about this Anti-West Axis. They are all regional powers and their status of enduring legacies in terms of empire, architecture, art, and literature, influencing their own subsequent dynasties and beyond, says they harbor ambitions beyond their present status quo. All three have experienced periods of fragmentation and confronted foreign adversaries throughout history, but the memory of their illustrious imperial past continues to resonate in their identities. All three have avoided direct confrontation with the

West and aim to minimize their campaigns to manageable escalations. By refraining from direct action, these three employ a strategy of alerting to opportunities to exploit their opponent's weaknesses. In the future, this could involve strategic maneuvers, disinformation campaigns, or alliances to further undermine their opponent's position, even as they conduct a waiting game while maintaining pressure and other forms of non-military coercion to weaken their opponent's position over time.

China is considered widely to be a power in the modern world with significant global influence and the ability to project power beyond its own borders, but it takes an extremely cautious approach to its next steps. More particularly, when it comes to strategic paralysis, it employs it to its core. It does not rest on its past legacy of a great empire; but rather, it is much more forward-thinking in how it perceives itself and how the world perceives it for its present and future.

The dangerous outcomes are linked in a protracted conflict. Russia with Ukraine, China with Taiwan, and Iran with Israel. As they take on their rivals, they are also taking on their common backer, the United States. The last decade of the 20th century may have ended on a high note for the United States, but the next century showed American blunders, particularly in military campaigns.

American military adventures in Afghanistan and Iraq were by no means a defeat but they left American allies in a much more vulnerable situation than they previously were. When the United States withdrew from Afghanistan in August 2021, its key ally that suffered significant consequences was the Afghan government itself. The abrupt withdrawal of U.S. military support and the subsequent rapid takeover of Afghanistan by the Taliban led to the collapse of the Afghan government and security forces, causing immense turmoil and instability in the country. President Ashraf Ghani, relied heavily on U.S. military and financial assistance to maintain security and stability in the country. The withdrawal of U.S. troops and the cessation of air support, logistics, and training programs severely weakened the Afghan security forces, making them vulnerable to Taliban advances. As the Taliban swiftly captured major cities and provincial capitals across Afghanistan, the Afghan government struggled to maintain control and had no choice but to abort, leading to a humanitarian crisis, with widespread displacement of civilians, loss of lives, and concerns about human rights violations, which still continue to this day.

Amidst the American power vacuum in Afghanistan, China stepped in. Despite Afghanistan's historical instability and security challenges, the country is still rich in natural resources, including minerals such as lithium, copper, gold, and rare earth elements. China, as a major global consumer of minerals and metals, sees investment in Afghanistan's mining sector as an opportunity to secure access to these valuable resources for its industrial needs. Investing in Afghanistan's infrastructure, such as roads, railways, and energy projects, could facilitate trade and transportation routes linking Central Asia with China and beyond, thereby advancing China's economic interests and expanding its influence in the region. To accomplish that, it needs the Taliban to halt the Islamic State–Khorasan Province (ISKP), which could threaten its own security interests. By investing in Afghanistan's economy and infrastructure, China aims to reduce the risk of instability spilling over into neighboring countries, many of whom are Chinese allies like Iran and Pakistan.

Afghanistan still has the potential to become a transit hub for trade and investment. China will use it to strengthen its ties with regional partners and assert its influence in shaping the geopolitical dynamics of Central Asia and demonstrate its commitment to supporting development and reconstruction efforts. Such measures will help China to take advantage of the unfinished business the United States had left over.

There are parallels to Afghanistan and another country. More than a decade back, when the United States withdrew from Iraq, one of its key allies that faced significant challenges was the democratically elected Iraqi government. The withdrawal of U.S. forces from Iraq in December 2011 left a security vacuum that contributed to increased instability and sectarian tensions within the country.

The Iraqi government, led by Prime Minister Nouri al-Maliki at the time, relied on U.S. military support and assistance in combating insurgent groups, maintaining security, and stabilizing the country. The phased withdrawal of U.S. troops created a void in security capabilities and left the Iraqi security forces without critical intelligence, and logistical support. Iraq experienced a resurgence of violence and insurgency, particularly from militant groups such as

ISIS (Islamic State of Iraq and Syria), exploiting the power vacuum and sectarian divisions to seize territory, including major cities like Mosul and Tikrit. When the terror group took these areas, they imposed a brutal kind of Sharia rule, based on their own interpretation of Islam. The Iraqi government struggled to confront the ISIS threat. They faced challenges in military capabilities, corruption, and political divisions. The rise of ISIS exacerbated existing tensions between Iraq's Sunni and Shia populations, deepened the sectarian divide and spread to neighboring countries, mostly affecting Syria. It also brought about the expansion of Russia and Iran's role in exerting influence over Damascus.

The United States found itself with frustrations in both Afghanistan and Iraq. Both President Obama and President Trump not only inherited Afghanistan's problems from President George W. Bush's administration, but felt the effects of how such conflicts destabilized the United States politically.

President Obama faced numerous challenges in managing the U.S. military presence in Afghanistan and implementing a strategy to stabilize the country. Corruption and governance were a deep concern within the Afghan government of President Hamid Karzai and even his successor, President Ashraf Ghani. It undermined efforts to build effective state institutions and win the trust of majority Afghans. It was particularly within the police force and judiciary, that corruption eroded the public confidence and hindered progress. This was not helped by significant investments in training and equipping Afghan security forces, who were supposed to help the security situation but did not have the capability to produce such results. The Afghan army struggled to contain the Taliban insurgency and other militant groups, leading to continued violence and instability.

The Obama administration was frustrated by the slow progress in building capable and reliable Afghan security forces that could take over responsibility from the American and NATO forces. The Afghan army was the prime victim of the political power struggles, owing its allegiance to different warlords or ethnic political factions, making it harder for the Afghan government in Kabul to build consensus and implement reforms. The failure of the Afghan army and a weak Afghan state fueled American public skepticism and war weariness, which forced the Obama administration to wind down its role in

Afghanistan.

When President Trump came to office, Afghanistan was not a priority, but it provided an avenue to vent out American frustrations. Trump often cited corruption as a reason to question the value of continued U.S. involvement in Afghanistan and was critical of Afghan leaders' handling of the security situation when the Taliban insurgency persisted. The President repeatedly called on Afghan leaders to contribute more to the cost of the U.S. military presence and voiced opposition to the idea of nation-building, arguing that the United States should focus on its own interests and prioritize domestic concerns over foreign interventions. He advocated for a more limited role for the United States in Afghanistan, including a potential withdrawal of all American troops.

The cost of Afghanistan, which amounted to trillions of US dollars over two decades, strained the U.S. economy and contributed to budgetary pressures. The financial resources allocated to the war effort diverted funds away from domestic priorities in healthcare, education, and infrastructure, leading to debates in Congress about the trade-offs.

Veterans returning from Afghanistan faced challenges such as physical injuries, post-traumatic stress disorder (PTSD), and difficulties reintegrating into civilian life. The human cost of the war raised moral and ethical questions about the justifications and the long-term consequences for those who served.

These consequences in Afghanistan were similarly felt in Pakistan. From 2005 to 2015, due to the spillover effects, Pashtun tribes on both sides of the border provided a safe haven for militant groups to operate along the porous border, often crossing into Pakistan to carry out attacks or seek refuge from the Afghan army and international forces. Infiltrations were also a common occurrence among rogue groups, including Islamic State–Khorasan Province (ISKP), which fostered the rise of other militant groups and spread extremism. Pakistan faced a wave of terrorist attacks perpetrated by militancy, including Tehrik-i-Taliban Pakistan (TTP), al-Qaeda, and other affiliated extremist organizations. These groups targeted civilians, security forces, government installations, and religious minorities, seeking to destabilize the country and undermine the government's authority. Suicide bombings became a hallmark of militant violence, with major cities such as Islamabad, Lahore, Karachi, and Peshawar, experiencing multiple attacks targeting crowded public places, markets, mosques, and government buildings.

The Pakistan Army launched several military operations and counterterrorism campaigns to combat militant groups operating within its territory. Operation Radd-ul-Fasaad targeted insurgent strongholds in the tribal areas along the Afghan border, aiming to dismantle militant networks and restore stability, but it had mixed results. The Pakistan army kept a delicate balance in entering South Waziristan, where many militants were sheltering. There was a short period of peace, and then violence again escalated. The volatility in peace sometimes exacerbated to security concerns and hindered efforts to address the root causes of the violence stemming from Afghanistan.

In November 2013, the Pakistan Army had a new Chief of the Army, General Raheel Sharif. Under his orders, the Pakistani military conducted several major raids against militant groups operating within the country, particularly in the tribal areas along the Afghan border. Operation Zarb-e-Azb launched in 2014, and subsequent offensives targeted insurgent strongholds, disrupted militant networks, and degraded the terror group's capabilities to carry out attacks. The Pakistan Army enhanced security measures, including increased intelligence gathering, border controls, and law enforcement efforts to counter militant threats. These measures helped disrupt terrorist plots and reduce the frequency of attacks in major cities and urban centers. With more units committed to its western border, the Pakistan army collaborated with the United States to address cross-border militancy and promote stability. Improved coordination and intelligence sharing helped disrupt militant networks, operating along the porous border. This was the beginning of a period of relative stability, beginning of 2015, as the Pakistan army continued its counterterrorism efforts and now had the upper hand to control its western border. Pakistan saw a significant reduction in violence after, but that was not the case for Afghanistan. One of the root causes of a persistent two-decade-long lack of authority in the Kabul government was that Washington since 2001, had shaped it to meet the West's counterterrorism interests, not nation-building or uplifting the lives of common Afghans. United States, NATO, and its other coalition members focused primarily on making the counterterrorism model work through Afghanistan. This also meant choosing its own class of warlords who remained unaccountable, even unreliable, and most who were no more different from the others who were also notoriously corrupt, lethal, and causing havoc among Afghan communities.

Under the payroll of Americans, these deceitful and unprincipled men prioritized the protection of their own ethnic tribes and regions. Men like the ethnic Uzbek leader Abdul Rashid Dostum, Atta Mohammad Noor, a prominent Tajik leader. Gul Agha Sherzai a Pashtun leader and former governor of Kandahar and Nangarhar provinces. Ismail Khan a former mujahideen commander and influential political figure in western Afghanistan and an Iranian ally. Mohammad Mohaqiq, a Hazara leader and former mujahideen commander. Haji Din Mohammad, a Pashtun tribal leader and also a former governor of Nangarhar province and the list goes on, were all American preferences of power brokers that were essential to the American project in Afghanistan.

It took the assassination of Ahmad Wali Karzai on 12 July 2011, the half-brother of then-Afghan President Hamid Karzai for an American introspection. There were suspicions that individuals within the Afghan security forces and government may have been complicit or had knowledge of the assassination plot. This incident underscored the challenges of relying on local power brokers and warlords, even those who were perceived as American allies, and the risks of their potential collusion with insurgent elements. The incident served as a wake-up call for American policymakers, highlighting the need for greater scrutiny and caution in their partnerships with Afghan factions and warlords. It was realized from then on that Afghanistan was not sustainable, and the absence of accountability was now heralding a time of unknown consequences. In some ways, the Obama administration realized that contracting out Afghanistan to Afghan leaders was just not working. At the basic level, Afghan leaders were not doing what they were tasked to do, maintain security. President Biden, who had personally witnessed the realities of Afghanistan as Vice President, prioritized the American exit.

Iraq, while deemed as the "unnecessary war," was not totally absolved from the sectarian crisis that awaited at its doorstep and the establishment of a functioning and prosperous autonomous Kurdish state in its north was the only American consolation, but it had existed for more than a decade before the US invaded Iraq in 2003. The real problem was the reservations of American ally and NATO member Turkey. Ankara had significant concerns about how the Kurdish government in Erbil could feasibly permit groups, identified as terrorists like the Kurdistan Workers' Party (PKK) and its affiliates, the Kurdistan Democratic Party (KDP) based in Iraq, to operate and use its positions to launch attacks on Turkey.

Turkish forces conducted cross-border military raids into Iraq to target Kurdish rebels, particularly members of the Kurdistan Workers' Party (PKK). Over time, such raids became frequent. Subsequent military operations included Operation Dawn (Şafak), Operation Sun (Güneş), and most recently, Operation Claw (Pençe), which openly defied the sovereignty of the autonomous Kurdish administrative entity within the Republic of Iraq.

Iraq still possessed significant oil reserves, and the United States sought to ensure access and stability to Iraq's oil production and exports. This included supporting efforts to rebuild Iraq's oil infrastructure, develop its energy sector, and attract foreign investment. Successive elected Iraqi governments tried to restore essential services such as electricity, water supply, and promoted economic growth in job creation as part of a long-term stability. As the Iraqi government in Baghdad was busy conducting such efforts, the US Army sought to prevent the resurgence of extremist groups, particularly al-Qaeda and its affiliates. To counter the insurgency, the US trained and equipped Iraqi security forces and promoted reconciliation among Iraq's various sectarian and ethnic groups to undermine support for extremist ideologies.

The turning point for the United States to rethink its strategy in Iraq and develop a plan to exit can be traced back to 2006. That year, Shia political parties (which also had militias of their own) emerged as key players in Iraqi politics. Many of them had ties to Iran. Parties such as the Islamic Dawa Party and the Supreme Islamic Iraqi Council (SIIC) often got their directions from their respective Ayatollah patrons in Iran.

The Muqtada al-Sadr's Mahdi army, which emerged as a significant armed group along with other Shia militias, received training, funding, and weapons from Iran. The rise of Nouri al-Maliki, a Shia politician, also with close ties to Iran, as Prime Minister of Iraq from 2006 to 2014 coincided with a period of growing Iranian influence within Iraq.

Nearly every major Iraqi military unit had some connection to the Quds Force, one of the five elite divisions of Iran's Islamic Revolutionary Guard Corps (IRGC). The establishment of military links between Iran and Iraq was the brainchild of General Qasem Soleimani. Soon Iraq, like Vietnam and Ukraine, became a proxy conflict and served as a battleground in an indirect war between Iran and the United States. By November 2008, an agreement was reached by the Iraqi parliament to withdraw U.S. forces. By December 2011, the US honored that commitment.

The Americans left Iraq without any authority in charge for the well-being of Iraqis. In 2010, a government in Baghdad was finally formed after several rounds of in-fighting within its own coalition, notably between the Allawi coalition that supported the Maliki government. Like a political move typical of Saddam, Maliki ruthlessly took over the defense, interior, and national security ministries, ultimately consolidating his hold on the Iraqi security forces. Within two years, Iraq descended back to sectarian conflict. Maliki's move to exclude Sunnis from political participation, sparked agitations from the Iraqi Sunni population, and soon, radical Sunni militants crossed over from the Syrian border. By April 2013, al-Qaeda, under its affiliate, the Islamic State in Iraq and the Levant (ISIL), openly were at war with the government in Baghdad.

Ten years later, ISIL's presence in Iraq had significantly diminished compared to its peak in 2013. However, remnants of its affiliated branches are still active in certain parts of the country, particularly in areas where Iraqi Shia militias are not present. Jihadist factions too, continue to operate under different names or as part of new alliances. Additionally, the rise of the Islamic State in neighboring Syria further marginalized influence in the region, as many Sunni militants and extremist sympathizers rallied around the ISIS self-proclaimed caliphate.

Today, Iraq's Prime Minister, Mohammed Shia al-Sudani, has no choice but to play a weak balancing act between Iran and the United States, while also defeating ISIS. For analysts who have seen what Iraq has become during the last two decades, and despite huge resources of oil, the country is an anathema. In most cases, Iraq looks worse than in the 1990s, which is considered one of the worst periods in Iraq's history in terms of political, social, economic, and humanitarian considerations.

While the United States made significant blunders in Afghanistan and Iraq, the outcomes of these interventions have been what critics argue has highlighted systemic failures in US foreign policy, military strategy, and the absence of nation-building.

By February 2022, Russia, China, and Iran became more active in their criticism of the only Superpower. This has been in the making for more than two decades. It began on 24 July 2001, when Russia and China signed the Treaty of Good-Neighborliness and Friendly Cooperation, underscoring a strategic partnership on broad economic and trade relations, in cooperation in technology and diplomatic relations. The intent was priorities on trade rather than military exercises. The 7 October 2001 American invasion of Afghanistan and the 10 March 2003 invasion of Iraq changed all that. From then on, Russia and China speeded up their offensive in their trade partnership to expand. They created the Shanghai Cooperation Organization (SCO) with the Central Asian states of Kazakhstan, Kyrgyzstan, Tajikistan, and Uzbekistan. At its inception, it was focused on security-related issues such as counterterrorism, fighting separatists, Islamic extremism, and drug trafficking. Since then, the Shanghai Cooperation Organization has expanded to include major Asian powers like India, Pakistan, and Iran. The organization has grown and is an important platform for military, economic, and energy cooperation.

Since China is a massive manufacturer, it requires enormous energy resources, and Russia supplies the demand, it was only natural to establish an energy partnership and in 2009, the two signed a deal to build the Eastern Siberia-Pacific Ocean oil pipeline, which started transporting oil to China in 2011. Furthermore, in 2014, both sides signed a 30-year gas deal worth $400 billion for the Power of Siberia pipeline. In 2019, the pipeline started delivering gas to China.

Russia has become key to China's Belt and Road Initiative as one of the important transit points connecting China to European markets. However, following Western-backed sanctions on Russia in 2014 after its annexation of Crimea and then on 24 February 2022, Russia was suspended from the Society for Worldwide Interbank Financial Telecommunication (SWIFT). As a result, the Kremlin accelerated their use of other currencies like the Indian Rupees, Chinese Yuan, and Cryptocurrencies. For China, this meant to go around Russia and develop direct trade links in the Balkans.

In November 2022, Russian Deputy Prime Minister Alexander Novak stated that the share of currencies from states considered friendly to Russia rose to 31% in the Russian foreign exchange market, with the Chinese yuan having the highest portion. This was not the result of a few months, but rather something that began in 2015. That year, Russia started selling its Su-35 fighters and S-400 air-defense systems to China. In September 2018, Russia conducted the Vostok 2018 military exercises, which included the Chinese army. Since then, the two countries have participated in joint military exercises. Under the auspices of the Shanghai Cooperation Organization, in 2022, Russia and China carried out joint naval and ground military exercises. Even though there have been tensions in military cooperation between the two countries, both have understood that they need each other to counter the American threat to their own regimes. However, successive developments produced mixed realities.

In 2022, the Russian state defense conglomerate Rostec accused China of theft of Russian military technologies. Rostec accused China of reverse-engineering Russian military technologies without authorization. This included allegations of China copying designs and producing similar equipment, which could compete with Russian products on the global arms market. The accusations centered around breaches of intellectual property rights, where Chinese firms allegedly used Russian designs and technologies to develop their own versions of advanced military hardware. One prominent example is the alleged copying of Russian fighter jet designs. China's J-11 fighter jet is often cited as being heavily based on the Russian Su-27, which China initially acquired from Russia. There have been similar accusations regarding missile technology, where China is suspected of reverse-engineering Russian systems to develop its own versions. The alleged theft of military technology could potentially harm Russia's defense industry by reducing its competitive edge and market share in the global arms trade. These accusations, if not managed carefully, could strain the strategic partnership between Russia and China. Rostec's accusations reflect broader concerns within the defense industry about the protection of intellectual property and the risks associated with technology transfers. While both nations benefit from their strategic partnership, issues like intellectual property theft pose significant challenges. How these disputes are resolved will likely influence the future of military and defense cooperation between the two.

In the Russia-China tension, Iran is a very useful buffer to mend such differences. While Russia and Iran have historically had problematic relations and competed for influence in the Caucasus, Central Asia, and the Caspian Sea, the Syrian civil war and Western-backed sanctions imposed on Russia in 2014 and 2022, brought them together. In 2014, Moscow and Tehran signed an oil-for-goods deal, reportedly worth $20 billion, which was part of Russia's purchase of 500,000 barrels of Iranian oil per day in exchange for Russian products. The transaction was a means to undo the pressure imposed by Western-backed sanctions on the economies of both countries. The Russia-Iran trade turnover has modestly but steadily increased since then, reaching more than $4 billion in 2022.

Political and military cooperation with Iran has been closely intertwined with the ambition of nuclear deterrence. One of the consequences of Iran's refusal to stop uranium enrichment was the U.N.-imposed ban on selling heavy weapons to Iran, which forced Russian then-President Dmitry Medvedev in 2009 to ban sales of S-300 air defense systems, military aircraft, armored vehicles, and other military supplies. In 2024, however, Russia and Iran have deepened their military ties significantly. Nowhere is this more visible than in the Syrian civil war in which both sides backed the Bashar Al Assad regime.

Since 2015, the Russian-Iranian economic and military aid provided the lifeline for Bashar Al Assad's regime. By May 2023, the Syrian President was welcomed back to the Arab League after a 12-year absence. Previously, Syria was suspended from the Arab League on 16 November 2011 due to the violent crackdown on anti-government protests that had erupted as part of the Arab Spring uprisings. It is the prioritizing of strategic interests in Syria that has kept Russia and Iran close to ensure that the Assad regime survives against the American aim of ousting him.

Syria provided Russia with much more than a foothold in the Middle East, added by an interconnected set of political links which served as a tonic to Russia's struggle in Ukraine. Compounded with military and economic Western-backed sanctions, which affected its foreign direct investment (FDI) and hindered its military production for a brief period, the Kremlin looked to Tehran for assistance. Their collaboration in Syria provided a smoother channel that shielded against any Western intervention.

Since September 2022, Iran has supplied sets of Shahid and Mohajer drones to Russia, which have been used in mass strikes on the Ukrainian infrastructure. There are unconfirmed reports that Russia is providing different non-sanctioned ports for Iran to sell its oil in exchange. It is also believed Iran has been receiving Russian Su-35 fighter aircraft as part of the deal. There is a feeling that the late hardline President Ebrahim Raisi's government was nervous to sell or provide ballistic missiles to President Putin, fearing further Western-backed sanctions.

Before the Trump administration pulled out of the 2015 nuclear deal (JCPOA) in May 2018, Iran was exporting approximately 2 million barrels of crude oil a day. In 2024, it is estimated that it exports between 300,000 and 500,000 barrels daily, goes mostly to China.

The Beijing-Tehran relationship only took a serious tone in 2011, when it was reported that China purchased exclusive rights to several oil and gas fields in Iran. Unofficial estimates of 5,000 Chinese troops present in these facilities speak to the sensitivity of the important Chinese economic cooperation with Iran. In 2021, both signed a 25-year strategic partnership treaty as China identified Iran as an alternative route for the Belt and Road initiative. In return, China has heavily invested in Iran's infrastructure by funding the construction of Tehran's subway system, dams, and factories while also playing a role in extracting Iranian coal, zinc, and copper. By 2022, the trade turnover between China and Iran exceeded $20 billion.

China, Russia, and Iran have come together because, among the three authoritarian states, they share a deep opposition to Western interference in their own affairs. All three have routinely condemned protests and opposition movements in their regions and believe America meddles in their internal affairs to suit the aims of having a monopoly. The three are convinced that the ultimate goal of the United States is to overthrow their regimes and to install pro-U.S. governments in their place.

In Putin's view, both Gorbachev and Yeltsin were too influenced by the West and succumbed to their pressures. This view is much more pronounced today as it emerged primarily among certain segments of

Russian society who opposed Gorbachev's policies of reform, particularly his efforts to liberalize the Soviet Union and improve relations with the West. Gorbachev's policies of *Glasnost* (openness) and *Perestroika* (restructuring), involved significant reforms to the Soviet system, including greater political freedoms, economic restructuring, and openness to Western ideas and influences. However, some critics in Russia argue that these reforms were too accommodating to Western interests and undermined the integrity and sovereignty of the Soviet Union. His efforts to improve relations with the West is something Russian politicians have expressed dismay, claiming Gorbachev's willingness to engage in arms control negotiations, such as the Intermediate-Range Nuclear Forces (INF) Treaty, and his commitment to détente and peaceful coexistence, were seen as giving in to American demands and weakening the Soviet Union's own position.

Gorbachev's leadership during the tumultuous final years of the Soviet Union culminated in its disbanding in December 1991. The disbanding or, some say, "the end" of the Soviet Union is often perceived by some Russians as a national tragedy, and Putin himself has stated that "The breakup of the Soviet Union was the greatest geopolitical tragedy of the 20th century." However, as the Soviet Union disbanded, Russian nationalists believed the United States took full advantage. Successive American presidential administrations expanded their influence in the newly independent states of Eastern Europe, the Caucasus, and Central Asia. This included promoting democratic governance, market-oriented economic reforms, and integration into Western institutions. The United States and other Western European countries provided economic assistance and technical expertise to support the transition to market economies in former Soviet bloc countries. In Russia, however, this was a different story. American companies and their activities played a role, but it was an unhappy experience for both sides.

American companies like ExxonMobil, Chevron, McDonald's, Coca-Cola, PepsiCo, Ford, Boeing, and many others contributed capital, expertise, and technology to various sectors of the Russian economy. This investment helped to modernize industries, create jobs, and stimulate economic growth in Moscow and St. Petersburg, but other areas remained neglected. Additionally, American businesses provided technical assistance, training, and capacity-building programs. Investment advisors, economists, and trade liaisons were all involved in advising Yeltsin's government on privatization and market reforms. The privatization of state-owned enterprises, however, was criticized for being opaque and prone to corruption, leading to the concentration of wealth in the hands of a select few and the emergence of crony capitalism as a result of oligarchs owning a number of state-owned companies.

American companies were also involved in Russia's energy sector, including oil and natural gas production and exploration. While these activities contributed to the development of Russia's energy resources and export capabilities, they also raised concerns about resource exploitation, environmental degradation, and the influence of foreign companies on Russia's strategic industries.

American financial institutions provided loans, investment capital, and expertise to Russian banks and financial markets. However, lax regulatory oversight, speculative investments, and financial instability, contributed to a series of banking crises and economic shocks in Russia, including the 1998 Russian financial crisis that had American executives weary of their time in Russia.

Political liabilities compounded over economic benefits. Previously in 1994, the United States imposed economic sanctions on Russia in response to human rights abuses in Chechnya and for additional concerns around nuclear proliferation. These sanctions, along with political tensions, contributed to economic uncertainty and investor caution, affecting foreign investment and trade flows in Russia.

24 March 1999 can be perceived as the day when Russian public opinion started gradually withdrawing from its amicable relations with the West. It was the beginning of NATO's bombing of Yugoslavia. In response to the failure of diplomacy and escalating violence in Kosovo, NATO launched a military intervention. The bombing campaign, known as Operation Allied Force, aimed to halt Serbian atrocities in Kosovo and compel Serbian leader Milosevic to withdraw his forces from the region.

Both Serbs and Russians are predominantly Orthodox Christians, sharing a common religious heritage that dates back to the Byzantine Empire. The Serbian Orthodox Church and the Russian Orthodox Church have maintained close ties over the centuries. The concept of Pan-Slavism, which advocates for the unity and solidarity of Slavic peoples, has played a significant role in fostering relations between Serbs and Russians. Both peoples have identified with the broader Slavic cultural and linguistic community, sharing common traditions, folklore, and historical experiences. Both also have a long history of interaction and cooperation, particularly during periods of Ottoman and Habsburg rule in the Balkans. Russia has historically supported Serbia with diplomatic and military assistance during crises. The most prominent example is Austria-Hungary's declaration of war on Serbia on 28 July 1914. Russia responded by mobilizing its forces in defense of Serbia. It wasn't until the German empire declared war on Russia that marked Russia's official entry into World War I on 1 August 1914. The situation was much different during NATO's bombing of Yugoslavia in 1999; Russia's ability to influence the situation was limited, as it lacked the military and economic capability to challenge NATO's actions directly to aid their Slavic ally.

Among the incidents during the NATO military campaign was the controversial 7 May 1999 bombing of the Chinese embassy in Belgrade. China condemned the attack vehemently, describing it as a violation of Chinese sovereignty and a war crime. NATO and the United States initially claimed the bombing was accidental, attributing it to outdated maps and erroneous targeting, stating that the intended target was a nearby military facility. Critics questioned the credibility of NATO's explanation, citing the precision of modern targeting systems and the embassy's well-known location. The U.S. and NATO eventually issued formal apologies, and the U.S. agreed to pay $28 million in compensation to the victims' families and $4.5 million for property damage to the Chinese government. Some analysts believe that this was the single incident when a younger generation within the Communist Party of China (CPC), who were previously pro-United States, began to oppose NATO and American military interventions.

At various points in its history, the relationship between the United States and China was marked by periods of tension and conflict. During the 22-years Chinese civil war that ended in 1949, the United States supported the Nationalist government led by Chiang Kai-shek against the Communist forces led by Mao Zedong. The Communist Party of China (CPC) won the civil war and viewed the United States as an imperialist power. On 7 December 1949, Chiang Kai-shek's government retreated to Taiwan and made Taipei its temporary capital. The nationalist leader brought with him nearly 2 million "waisheng ren" consisting mostly of soldiers, intellectuals, business elites and members of the ruling Kuomintang (KMT), also known as the Chinese Nationalist Party, adding to the island's 6 million population.

The KMT was not welcome on the Island. Two years prior, KMT-affiliated nationalist troops brutally suppressed Taiwanese protests about corruption, killing thousands in an episode now known as "the 228 Incident." The KMT was notoriously corrupt, and many of its members brought with them stolen treasures from the mainland, volumes of gold, and foreign currency reserves. Much of this helped in the development of the new currency of the Taiwan dollar and stabilized the pre-existing inflation in the island.

As the South China Sea provided the buffer to Chiang Kai-shek's government in Taiwan, the Chinese Communists in the mainland captured all Kuomintang strongholds in northwest China, Dachen Islands, and Yijiangshan. By 1958 all Kuomintang areas were under the control of Mao's Communists.

Chiang Kai-shek almost immediately, with the help of Kuomintang, imposed martial law with the intent to suppress any political opposition and Communist sympathizers. About 140,000 people were imprisoned or executed. He preferred to be called the President of the Republic of China, but the international community soon understood the underlying title; President of Taiwan. Chiang Kai-shek's government enforced rapid industrial development and had sufficient economic and military aid from Washington. He died on 5 April 1975, leaving behind a one-party dictatorial state.

By 1979, Washington had replaced Taipei, preferencing Beijing for greater economic relations with the mainland. That same year, the US Congress passed the Taiwan Relations Act, promising to help the island defend itself if China ever attacked. Some analysts believe that it was the beginning of Taiwan's ascendence to democracy, and in 1987, the state ended its martial law status, which allowed its population to travel overseas, including to China. However, among Communist historians, there is a feeling that had the United States stayed out from supporting Chiang Kai-shek, there would be no rogue island of Taiwan and seven decades of tensions between Beijing and Taipei would not have existed as we see today. They further attest that their populations would not be in harm's way.

Beyond Taiwan, China still had friction with the United States. In the 1950 Korean War, China intervened together with the Soviet Union in support of North Korea's Kim Il Sung. The conflict resulted in significant casualties on both sides, resulting in approximately 3 million deaths.

China was not spared of American sanctions when in 1989 the Tiananmen Square protests began. The Chinese government cracked down on pro-democracy protesters. The U.S. imposed sanctions on China in response to the crackdown, leading to a period of strained relations. China returned to America's good graces on the eve of the Sino-British Joint Declaration. The British Conservative Tory government of Prime Minister John Major handed over Hong Kong to China on 1 July 1997 after 156 years, as part of an old treaty since the end of the first 1842 Opium Wars. The event opened the door for the United States as President Bill Clinton pursued policies to deepen economic ties, including supporting China's accession to the World Trade Organization (WTO) in 2001, opening up China's markets to increased trade and investment, benefiting both the US and China economically.

President Clinton sought to engage China on strategic issues of mutual concern, such as regional security, non-proliferation, and counterterrorism. Despite tensions over issues like Taiwan and human rights, the Clinton administration recognized the importance of working with China to address global challenges and maintain stability in the Asia-Pacific region. His administration played a significant role in the normalization of diplomatic relations and gradually paving the way for increased cooperation and dialogue.

Clinton adopted a policy of "three no's" regarding Taiwan. He reaffirmed the United States' commitment to the One-China policy, no support for Taiwan's independence, and no support for Taiwan's membership in international organizations where statehood is required. This policy aimed to maintain stability in cross-strait relations while avoiding provocative actions that could escalate tensions with China. Two decades later, both trade and Taiwan are at the center of tensions between Beijing and Washington.

The United States' approach to both the One-China policy and the 2015 Iran nuclear deal (JCPOA) reflects a larger geopolitical strategy of containment with mixed results. Maintaining the One-China policy is essential for stable U.S.-China relations, as is preventing nuclear proliferation in the Middle East. Both the One-China policy and the JCPOA have significant implications for regional stability. The One-China policy affects the stability of the Taiwan Strait and East Asia, while the JCPOA impacts the security dynamics in the Middle East. China is a signatory to the JCPOA, along with France, Russia, the United Kingdom, the United States, and Germany, plus the European Union. China has consistently supported the agreement and its involvement positions itself as a key player of influence in global conflict resolutions. The United States withdrew from the JCPOA on May 2018; however what cannot be understated is the interaction between these policies reflects the complexities of a multipolar world where agreements and policies are interconnected.

When it came to Iran, the United States did provide significant ammunition to the Anti-West Axis claim that overthrowing "elected" anti-American leaders to install pro-US governments in their place is a key American policy. On 21 July 1952, Mohammad Mossadegh was appointed as Prime Minister of Iran by the West-backed Shah Mohammad Reza Pahlavi. The sexagenarian Prime Minister had previously pursued a policy of seeking Western support for Iran's economic development and political stability. He initially attempted to negotiate with the British government and its economic arm, the Anglo-Iranian Oil Company (AIOC), to secure better terms for Iran's oil industry. He also sought support from the United States, initially hoping that Washington would back his efforts for better terms and reduce British influence in Iran. The U.S. initially hesitated, partly due to concerns about the spread of the Soviet Union's leftists, intellectuals, students, labor unions, other grassroots movements, and Communists in Iran.

When negotiations failed, Mossadegh found himself using the one option that would lead to his demise. The Tudeh Party was the largest Communist party with close ties to the Soviet Union. It advocated for socialist policies and the nationalization of industries. While not a direct proxy of the Soviet Union, the National Front government of Prime Minister Mohammad Mossadegh pursued policies that were perceived as anti-imperialist and nationalistic, which aligned with the Soviet Union's interests. Mossadegh's confrontational stance towards

Britain drew support from leftist and Communist groups, including the Tudeh Party. However, Mossadegh's National Front government was committed to democratic principles and the rule of law. His party aligned with Western values. Mossadegh himself was seen as a champion of democracy in Iran and sought to strengthen democratic institutions during his time in office. However, without any other option but to nationalize Iran's oil industry, Mossadegh found himself under confrontation with Britain and the United States.

The British conservative government under 78-year-old Prime Minister Winston Churchill sought American support in overthrowing Mossadegh's government, fearing the loss of its oil interests in Iran. CIA and MI6 collaborated on a plan to remove Mossadegh from power and restore the Shah as a more pliant ruler who would protect Western interests in Iran. Churchill was also instrumental in replacing the Shah's father, Reza Shah, in September 1941, incorrectly believing the Shah had German sympathies, favoring his son Mohammad Reza Pahlavi to replace him.

Operation Ajax involved a combination of covert operations, propaganda, and political maneuvering to undermine Mossadegh's government. This also included funding opposition groups, spreading anti-Mossadegh propaganda, orchestrating protest demonstrations, and supporting Iranian military officers and politicians who were opposed to Mossadegh's government. On 19 August 1953, these forces staged a coup d'état, leading to Mossadegh's arrest and the installation of General Fazlollah Zahedi as Prime Minister. Following the success of the operation, the Shah Mohammad Reza Pahlavi consolidated power and ruled Iran as an authoritarian for nearly three decades. He was backed and funded by the United States. The Shah suppressed any political dissent and opposition to his regime and his authoritarian style of governance limited political participation, freedom of speech, and civil liberties, hindering the development of democratic institutions and civil society organizations that were essential for sustainable development and poverty alleviation in Iran.

The cardinal sin, as many of Iran's hardliners feel today, is that the Shah's repressive policies and close ties to Western powers, particularly the United States, fueled widespread discontent. President Jimmy Carter, who made human rights a key pillar of his doctrine, looked the other way at a time when SAVAK, the Shah's intelligence agency, trained by CIA and Mossad, was arresting, torturing, and murdering dissenting and innocent Iranians.

Some Iranian commentators would point out that the 1953 coup had far-reaching consequences for Iran's political trajectory, contributing to the illegitimacy of the Shah as a ruler and the rapid ascendence of the Islamic theocracy to replace him. The episode also sets the tone for shaping modern-day Iran's Shia theocracy. The Shah's departure on 16 January 1979 unleashed a set of events that spearheaded Iran from ally to enemy of the United States. Successive events in the 4 November 1979 takeover of the American Embassy in Tehran and the 1980 Iran-Iraq war were key events that set the hardline stance for the Islamic Republic to become a pariah to the West.

The suspicious death of President Ibrahim Raisi and his Foreign Minister Hossein Amir-Abdollahian in May 2024 due to a helicopter crash in Iran's East Azerbaijan province would not change Iran's status. It is no secret that the seat of the President of Iran, though elected, is a ceremonial position, with real authority lying with the octogenarian and ailing Supreme Leader Ayatollah Ali Khamenei. The hardline Raisi however, was an exception and was widely tipped to replace Khamenei. His end will test the country's Shia theocracy, where hardliners control all branches of power. It comes at a crucially sensitive time as the seat of a middle-ranking cleric has to be filled by the Assembly of Experts, the body that chooses the successor to Khamenei when the moment arrives.

For some time, the possibility of a 54-year-old Mojtaba Khamenei, the son of the Supreme Leader, the unofficial Commander of the Basij, a paramilitary volunteer militia within the Islamic Revolutionary Guard Corps (IRGC), has been seen as a potential successor.

Iran's hardliners need a young, loyal ideologist dedicated to the Islamic Republic with a following, and he fits that checklist. However, even within Iran's hardliners, there are factions consisting of hardheaded, moderate, strategic, and realistic leaders who will make Raisi's replacement and the heir to the Supreme Leader work hard to unify all levels of local to parliamentary layers of government. When it comes to Iran's relationship with China and Russia, it is the elite Islamic Revolution Guard Corps (IRGC) that wields the footwork of the Supreme Leader, and therefore, the next President of Iran will have to make significant improvements in several areas, provided that he is permitted to do so by the Supreme Leader. Raisi's reign consumed the struggle with Western-backed sanctions and state corruption, which caused severe financial hardship for Iranians. Inflation stood at 40%, and Iran's currency value continued to dwindle. Raisi's government also had to deal with the fallout resulting in protests from the detention and death of 22-year-old Mahsa Amini in September 2022 for allegedly violating Iran's strict dress code.

The Islamic Republic can point to Israel as their arch-enemy, but their biggest opponents are within. In addition to the separatist Kurds in the western part of the country, including the province of Azerbaijan where Raisi's helicopter crashed, there are insurgencies on both sides of the south, especially in the Balochistan province.

The energy-rich Balochistan is especially exceptional. Afghanistan, Iran, and Pakistan all have slices of their own Balochistan within their borders, which is largely considered "the Wild South." Iran took slices of the area in 1928 and Pakistan in 1948. The two countries have the longest border of the province, thereby inheriting cross-border tensions that had lasted for decades. Several militant groups are active in the area, with the objective of autonomy and independence. In January 2024, Iran attacked Pakistan's Balochistan, claiming to target Jaish al-Adl, an active militant group. Pakistan retaliated, the first since 1980, with a missile strike inside Iran's south, also claiming to target militant groups called the Balochistan Liberation Army (BLA) and the Balochistan Liberation Front (BLF). Both sides later disclosed the loss of lives of civilians. The two sides later conducted a set of diplomatic initiatives, with Raisi visiting Islamabad to calm tensions as Iran already had its hands full in Iraq, Lebanon, Syria, Yemen and now in Gaza.

The more lethal opponents of Iran's hardliners are a young generation of women who will not tolerate the restrictions imposed by the state on their lives. This group is a serious threat to the Supreme Leader as he will see his real sources of power, damaging at a time when he has to work with the very little at his disposal. Those limits will sharpen after the death of Foreign Minister Hossein Amir-Abdollahian, who was accompanying President Raisi. Iran's foreign minister was the voice of the Supreme Leader in world forums. At the same time, he had nowhere near the masterful communication skills of his predecessor, the Western-educated Mohammad Javad Zarif. He was however, part of the roundtable phone calls between Arab, European, and Palestinian leaders to what produced a near escalation containment of events in Gaza. His departure will not change Iran's position or its foreign policy flavor, but there is an important signal here of a dieing breed that has made Iran attractive to regimes that oppose the West.

Putin's first visit to Tehran came in October 2007, the first by a Russian leader since Joseph Stalin's attendance at the Tehran Conference in 1943 during World War II. China and Russia have repeatedly blocked attempts in the UN to hold their ally Iran accountable. In 2018, the Iranian regime ruthlessly put down protests. China's justification of its position at the UN provided evidence of how well the Anti-West Axis would align globally. Beijing's take was, "We should not discuss the internal affairs of any country, nor is it the venue for any discussion of the human rights situation in a country…The Iranian situation does not pose any threat to international peace or security, nor is it on the agenda of the Security Council." In many ways, it was the precursor to Russia's annexation and then invasion of Ukraine and China's detention measures against its Uyghur minority.

Between 2016 and 2020, the Trump administration announced its withdrawal from several key international agreements and organizations, which included the Paris Climate Agreement, the Iran nuclear deal (JCPOA), and the Trans-Pacific Partnership (TPP) trade agreement. These withdrawals signaled a shift away from multilateralism and global cooperation, pursuing an "America First" trade policy, imposing tariffs on imports, including China and the European Union (EU). These trade tensions escalated into strained relationships with trading partners, contributing to perceptions of American protectionism. The administration also publicly criticized traditional allies and questioned the value of long-standing alliances such as NATO. The Trump administration implemented significant cuts to the State Department and foreign aid budgets, leading to a reduction in diplomatic engagement and the closing of diplomatic posts around the world. The downsizing of diplomatic resources raised concerns about the United States' ability to effectively address global challenges and promote its interests around the world. The administration prioritized domestic issues, immigration, healthcare reform, and tax policy over foreign policy. While the United States remained engaged militarily in various regions, there were also instances of troop withdrawals and reductions. The administration announced plans to withdraw troops from Afghanistan, Iraq, and Syria, signaling a desire to end "endless wars" and reduce US military commitments abroad. As America withdrew from the global stage, China and Russia had already begun the footwork to fill that void.

On 10 March 2023, China rejoiced over what was considered a diplomatic triumph. Beijing brokered the Iran-Saudi deal in the absence of American and European officials. It brought together the two most powerful rival countries in the Middle East to make peace atlast. Under the agreement, Iran would stop encouraging Houthi rebels to attack Saudi assets, support Vision 2030, and open an embassy in Riyadh. In return, Saudi Arabia would open an embassy in Tehran, the first since 2 January 2016, after the execution of a prominent Shia cleric, Sheikh Nimr al-Nimr by Saudi authorities. Riyadh would also cut off funding for Iran International, the London-based Persian-language channel, the mouthpiece of Iranian dissent. It will also stop funding militant groups like Mujahedin-e Khalq and Jaish al-Adl in Iran's Khuzestan, Sistan and Balochistan province. Finally, a key condition; for Saudi Arabia to normalize diplomatic relations with Iran's key ally; Syria's Bashar Al-Assad, was also agreed.

The Iran-Saudi deal was a major success for China. It did what the United States was unable to do. The diplomatic triumph had the Anti-West Axis to have the upper hand. The Iran-Saudi deal looked to move the resource-rich Middle East away from the United States orbit and towards China, Russia, and Iran.

Confronting the United States is beginning to take shape in the Anti-West Axis, as it is at the center of the new emerging power bloc but as it stands, Russia and China do not want another nuclear power, and certainly will contain their ally Iran, only if all options have been exhausted. So far, they have been trying to find a delicate balance between preventing the regime in Tehran from developing a nuclear weapon and assisting them financially and diplomatically.

In 1992, Russia and China expressed an interest in helping Iran develop its civilian nuclear industry, but that had already begun since the Eisenhower administration in 1953. The United States promoted the Atoms for Peace program, which aimed to encourage the peaceful use of nuclear energy for civilian purposes while preventing the spread of nuclear weapons and developing nuclear energy for peaceful purposes. The Shah of Iran accepted the offer as the U.S. provided technical assistance, expertise, and equipment for the construction of nuclear reactors and the development of nuclear technology for peaceful purposes.

By 1992, Russia and Iran signed an agreement on cooperating to develop a peaceful atomic industry in Iran. In 1995, Russia pledged to build the Bushehr Nuclear Power Plant. Under American pressure, Russia agreed to halt weapon sales to Iran. Still, it went on with constructing the power plant in Iran, unlike China, which gave up its ambitions to build several power plants.

As the Iranian nuclear program gained more international attention in the 2000s, Russia and China were part of the group of countries seeking an agreement with Iran on certain restrictions on its nuclear program. Both worked remarkably well in this process. At first, they supported the resolution of the issue within the International Atomic Energy Agency (IAEA) rather than going to the United Nations Security Council. Then, China supported Russia's proposal to process uranium for Iran's nuclear industry in Russia, which Iran rejected. After that, Russia and China embraced a two-prolonged strategy toward negotiations with Iran. The two envisaged joining the sanctions regime against Iran while encouraging Tehran to negotiate. As the problem entered the realm of the United Nations Security Council, Russia and China cooperated to make sanctions less severe, and both condemned unilateral sanctions imposed by the United States and the EU.

After the Trump administration exited the Joint Comprehensive Plan of Action Agreement (JCPOA), China and Russia used the opportunity to deepen relations with Iran. But this did not stop the Kremlin from criticizing Iran for taking steps to enrich uranium while also criticizing the United States for opting out of the JCPOA. There have been reports that Iran is seeking Russia's support in developing its nuclear program in exchange for drones in the war in Ukraine. However, it is doubtful that Russia or China would assist Iran with developing a nuclear weapon as it would alter the balance of power in Eurasia.

Such limitations were brought into question when on 13 April 2024, Iran launched more than 300 drones and missiles (a fraction of its capabilities) as part of its first strike against Israel in response to a 1 April, an airstrike on the Iranian embassy complex in Damascus, which destroyed the building, killing sixteen, including eight Islamic Revolutionary Guard Corps (IRGC) officers and two Syrian civilians. Iranian missiles descended on Israel, fired from Iran and their allies in Iraq, Syria, and Yemen. They were downed by Israel and their allies, including the United States, Britain, and Jordan. Only a few missiles reached Israel. One missile "lightly hit" the Nevatim Air Force base in the Negev desert in southern Israel. It is strategically significant due to its capacity to accommodate various types of aircraft, including fighter jets, transport planes, and helicopters. It serves as a hub for training, operational deployments, and maintenance activities for the Israeli Air Force.

Iran called it a "restraint" attack. Within a few days, Israel struck an Iranian air defense system. An additional strike damaged a defensive battery near Natanz, a city in central Iran that is critical to the country's nuclear weapons program. The episode unveiled the four-decade-long Iran-Israel shadow war of assassinations and proxy fighting. Iran is projecting itself as the defender of the Palestinians, while Israel is looking to fight America's war against Iran. While Washington promised to defend Israel, it was adamant that it did not endorse Israel's military response against Iran. The episode has opened the door for confrontation and unexpectedly, a potential dialogue. As much as the regimes in Jerusalem and Tehran misunderstand each other, both realize the need to avoid escalating their conflict into an unmanageable war. Israel has its hands full in its campaign in Gaza, and potentially another war in Lebanon. Iran too is occupied in the Middle East and supporting a key ally Russia in Ukraine. It will also support its ally Hezbollah if Israel seriously decides to enter Lebanon. The four-decade-long shadow war is now a war of coordinated conflicts between two regional powers. It is said that before the 24 February Russian invasion of Ukraine, as Ukraine was shifting to the West, Israel was shifting to the East. Jerusalem was getting closer to Riyadh, and the pathway opened by China would undoubtedly force Israel and Iran to, at the very least, find common ground. After 7 October 2023, that prospect looks difficult to come to fruition.

Analysts have pointed out that the same drones that descended on Israel were no different from those that were falling on Ukraine. It is Ukraine that brought Russia and Iran closer together than ever before. Both countries are heavily sanctioned and share knowledge about working around sanctions to stay afloat economically. But even as geopolitical circumstances bring these two regimes close, their economic interests will clash. Western-backed sanctions prevent Russia from selling oil to its traditional European customers, it has turned east to sell its oil, which has reportedly caused Iranian oil exports to decrease. Russia and Iran may well find a way to divide markets between themselves. Still, oil exports bring crucial revenue to their struggling economies, which may make the relationship complicated and become an issue followed by conflict.

The war in Ukraine has also made Russia-Chinese relations more complicated. China is a vocal supporter of the principle of territorial integrity in international relations, but they have refused to condemn Russia for the occupation and annexation of Ukraine. Instead, they blame the US of the expansion of NATO towards the East as the cause of the war. The war has complicated the situation with regard to Taiwan and has prompted the US to increase its military support for the island, demonstrating that the West can mobilize when its strategic interests are at stake. This has arguably made China rethink any future military action. Moreover, the war in Ukraine has already resulted in billions of dollars of losses for Chinese companies due to logistics disruption. For instance, the Chinese steel and nickel giant Tsingshan Holding Group has lost $8 billion since the start of the war due to the increased price of nickel. On the other hand, Russia is selling its oil at a significant discount to China due to Western-back sanctions. While China buys Russian natural resources, the West remains its chief trading partner, and China will not give that up. China needs the West to get back to its 10% growth era, which is why there are limits to how much China can afford to antagonize the US, Europe and Japan, because those are the markets that drive the Chinese economy.

Russia has dominated Central Asia ever since Tsarist Russia captured the region during the 19th century, maintaining close ties with Central Asian republics through various international organizations such as the Commonwealth of Independent States (CIS) and the Eurasian Economic Union (EEU). Through its military alliance, the

Collective Security Treaty Organization, it has wielded significant influence and is not ready to just hand it over to China. A concern is that Central Asian countries, particularly the former Soviet state Kazakhstan, have sought to deepen relations with China, including military cooperation.

The largest country in Central Asia is rich in natural resources, especially oil, natural gas, and minerals. Its energy resources are crucial for both Russia and European markets. Russian companies are deeply involved in Kazakhstan's energy sector. It is also a transit country for oil and gas pipelines, connecting energy resources from Central Asia to Europe and other markets, reducing Russia's reliance on its own domestic energy supplies.

Kazakhstan has a large ethnic Russian population, especially in the northern regions. Russia views this as a cultural and political interest. The two share a long border (approximately 7,600 km) with Russia, making border security a priority. Kazakhstan's political stability is crucial to Russia's internal security, especially in the sensitive regions of southern Russia and the North Caucasus. The two countries are members of the Collective Security Treaty Organization (CSTO), a Russia-led military alliance where Kazakhstan plays a key role in the security architecture of the post-Soviet space, particularly in countering terrorism and extremism.

Even though, China's influence in Kazakhstan has not led to any public manifestation of competition between China and Russia, it is safe to assume that there is a potential for a conflict over strategically important areas between the two.

BRICS, which unites the Shanghai Cooperation Organization for economic potential, may add the layers of friendship among the Anti-West Axis but the limits are very visible. BRICS is a platform of economic cooperation among Brazil, Russia, Iran, China, and South Africa, but due to geographic and political distances, the economic integration within the organization has not been at the level as Russia had hoped. The Shanghai Cooperation Organization (SCO) can potentially become an alternative for Russia, from its previous European buyers. It could unite some of the most powerful Eurasian and Asian states. It also could be a new geopolitical space that could pose a fundamental challenge to the United States. SCO member states also conduct joint military drills. The organization promotes the state-centric vision of international order, which Russia, China, and Iran share, and what it may lack in capability, it will make up in its will.

The most successful and long-term alliances need to have an ideological foundation behind them. This was largely true for the Socialist bloc too, as its Marxist ideological foundation helped to survive until economic stagnation and feuding leaders led to the disbanding of the Soviet Union. Now, there have been alliances among states that no longer share ideological beliefs but only have common rivals. This is not enough for a strong economic or military coalition. A bulging example is Egypt in the lead-up to its peace deal with Israel.

Anwar El-Sadat, who had been in power since 1970 following Gamal Abdel Nasser's death, was steering Egypt towards a different political and economic path. He initiated the controversial *Infitah* (openness) policy, which aimed to liberalize the economy by encouraging foreign investment and reducing state control over the economy.

Egypt in 1973 lost its second war with Israel and there was a fear within Sadat's inner circle that unless a significant shift came either domestic or in foreign policy, he would soon be overthrown by the same military that supported his political rise.

The situation looked untenable when in January 1977, widespread riots erupted due to Sadat's decision to cut state subsidies on basic goods such as bread, rice, and cooking oil, under pressure from the International Monetary Fund (IMF) to reduce budget deficits. The riots were intense and led to several deaths and injuries, forcing the government to reinstate the subsidies temporarily. The economic difficulties and the rapid shift from Nasser's socialist policies to a market-oriented economy caused widespread dissatisfaction among the populace, particularly among the poor and the working class. It led to increased inequality, as the gap between the wealthy elite, allied with Sadat's military who benefited from the reforms and the poorer segments of society widened.

Sadat's unprecedented visit to Israel in November 1977 was a pivotal moment in Middle Eastern politics and set the stage for the 1978 Camp David Accords. The Egypt-Israel peace deal is a cornerstone of U.S. foreign policy in the Middle East, providing Egypt with approximately $1.3 billion in American military aid annually. Additional economic aid of approximately $815 million in the years immediately following the Oslo Accords strengthened Egypt's military to monopolize the economy. Over time, the American economic aid decreased as Egypt's economy developed and the U.S. shifted its focus to other regions. The 1978 Camp David Accords, followed by the Egypt-Israel Peace Treaty in 1979, flipped Egypt, one of the most advanced military in the Middle East, from a Soviet to an American ally. It is a true example of how ideologies in the face of new opportunities will not be sustained unless there is a deep conviction of alliances and principles.

Russia, China, and Iran will continue cooperating and supporting each other internationally, particularly in defending authoritarian regimes and protecting each other from attacks at the UN. However, to cement their relationship for the future, they need to develop a more plausible ideological foundation for their alliance beyond an Anti-West ideology. A lack of robust conviction can be detrimental to any alliance. Furthermore, the need to either delineate their spheres of influence or agree on one leadership would be a difficult path forward. Given China's economic power, it is the most plausible candidate for leadership, but differences will persist in how Russia and Iran perceive their future role as "junior partner" to China. Russia, being resource-rich, and Iran, with its own significant oil resources, may both seek prominent positions within the alliance.

Currently, the primary binding factor among these nations is the fear of the United States encroaching to replace their regimes. However, this shared apprehension may not be sufficient in the long term to forge a truly unified and effective alliance. The unwavering Putin's obsession for Ukraine at any price, demonstrates he needs an effective alliance, but that will be difficult to do given all his allies have separate objectives.

Chapter 8

COURTING TERROR

On 7 October 2023, the Palestinian militant group Hamas and its partnering militant groups launched a synchronized attack on Israel's south. The episode resulted in the deaths of more than 1,160 mostly Israeli civilians and 253 abductions. It is now called "the Simchat Torah Massacre" in Israel. The West denounced the attack as terrorism, but many Arab states, allies of the West, singled out that the occurrence was due to Israel's occupation of the Palestinian territories. 16 Russian citizens died, but Moscow did not condemn Hamas.

President Putin pointed to the United States and directed his attacks, claiming that the Americans were responsible for the crisis. He further compared the lockup of Palestinians in Gaza by Israel to Nazi Germany's siege of Leningrad, an event that shaped many Russians of his generation, including his own family.

Putin's blaming of the United States had long roots. When Vice President Joe Biden met with Putin in March 2011, the meeting took place during Biden's visit to Russia, and Putin was then serving as the Prime Minister under President Dmitry Medvedev. The meeting occurred during a period of tense relations between the United States and Russia, with discussions focused on bilateral and international issues. This included arms control, nuclear security, and regional conflicts. Biden's visit was part of a "reset" with Russia as part of the Obama administration's initiative. During that visit, Putin viewed the actions of the future American President with deep distrust over a speech Biden made at Moscow State University.

Biden said, "We will not recognize any state having a sphere of influence. And almost regardless of the difficulty, we don't support any state's decision to change the leadership of an elected —democratically elected individual through force." He went on to say, "Or put it this way, you don't get industrial modernization without political modernization. And I realize — I realize — it's been a short journey — a short journey since, as we say in the West, the wall came down. And I realize there is an awful lot that's been accomplished. But —but —modernization in every way is essential. I think that's why so many Russians now call on their country to strengthen their democratic institutions. Courts must be empowered to uphold the rule of law and protect those playing by the rules." Then came the real source of antagonism when Biden said, "So I urge all of you students here: Don't compromise on the basic elements of democracy. You need not make that Faustian bargain." Those words of "democracy," "sphere of influence," and a "Faustian bargain" did not sit well with Putin. The American reset did not last. One particular event further derailed the effort, the Arab Spring.

It was a series of pro-democracy protests and uprisings that swept across several countries, predominantly in North Africa and the Middle East, in the form of a protest against heads of state. The Arab Spring movement began in Tunisia in December 2010 when Mohamed Bouazizi, a street vendor, set himself on fire in protest against government corruption and harassment. It sparked widespread demonstrations and eventually led to the ousting of the pro-West President Zine El Abidine Ben Ali in January 2011.

Inspired by the events in Tunisia, during the same month protests erupted in Egypt, demanding the resignation of another Western-backed ally who had ruled for nearly three decades, President Hosni Mubarak. After weeks of demonstrations, Mubarak stepped down in February 2011. Three months later, the former Egyptian President was ordered to stand trial on charges of premeditated murder of peaceful protesters. This was followed by the arrests of his sons Alaa and Gamal. Former interior minister Habib el-Adly and six former top police officials were also arrested. For the next six years, Egyptian courts were marred by a revolving door of prosecutors who won cases to convict Mubarak and his inner circle, only to see the former President being released on technicality on several counts. By 2017, the Court of Cassation, Egypt's top appeals court, acquitted Mubarak of all charges. The former President had been in poor health even before the Arab Spring. He had a history of health problems and had undergone surgery several times in the years following his resignation from the Presidency. He died on 25 February 2020.

Mubarak was involved in efforts to broker peace between Israel and the Palestinians. Egypt played a crucial role in mediating the Camp David Accords in 1978, which led to the Egypt-Israel Peace Treaty in 1979. The treaty was the first between Israel and an Arab state and resulted in Israel's return of the Sinai Peninsula to Egyptian control. President Anwar El-Sadat, however, insisted Gaza remain under Israel. Mubarak, who succeeded Sadat after his assassination on 6 October 1981 by the Islamic Group, upheld the peace treaty and maintained diplomatic relations with Israel. Throughout his Presidency, he continued to serve as a mediator between Israel and the Palestinians. Since the 1993 Oslo Accords, every Israeli Prime Minister has visited Cairo to facilitate negotiations and to be part of mediated disputes, as Egypt had close ties with Israel and several Palestinian groups. Mubarak's government was, however, criticized for its role in enforcing the blockade of the Gaza Strip, particularly after Hamas won the Palestinian legislative election in January 2006. Following the June 2007 Battle of Gaza, a military conflict between Fatah and Hamas, resulted in the expulsion of Fatah from Gaza. Egypt's cooperation with Israel in restricting the movement of goods and people into Gaza drew condemnation from some Arab quarters for exacerbating humanitarian conditions in the besieged enclave.

Under Mubarak's successor, President Abdel Fattah el-Sisi, Egypt sought to diversify its international partnerships. Relations between Egypt and Russia improved, especially in the areas of trade, military cooperation, and diplomacy. One of the roots behind such development was due to a change of heart from Washington. Former President Trump was seen as more supportive of Sisi, praising his leadership and avoiding public criticism of human rights. The Biden administration, while continuing security cooperation, has taken a firmer stance on human rights issues, signaling a possible shift in the tone of bilateral relations. In April 2023, *The Washington Post* stated that Egypt secretly planned to supply rockets to Russia to assist in its war in Ukraine. It appeared Egypt was swinging back to its pre-1978 status as a Soviet ally.

During the Cold War, North Africa and the Middle East were regions of significant geopolitical interest and rivalry between the United States and the Soviet Union. Many nationalist regimes in these regions were closely aligned with the Soviet Union. The Kremlin aimed to expand its influence by supporting regimes that opposed Western imperialism and colonialism, promoting socialism, and providing military and economic assistance. The Soviets supplied their allies with military hardware, training, and advisors, helping to build strong, pro-Soviet military regimes. In addition to military support, they provided economic aid for infrastructure projects, industrialization efforts, and development programs, often tied to the implementation of socialist policies.

In the 1960s, many Middle Eastern countries had relatively low GDP per capita compared to Western nations. Economic activity was largely based on agriculture, with limited industrialization. High levels of poverty and underdevelopment were prevalent. Many of these states faced challenges such as low literacy rates, inadequate healthcare, and insufficient infrastructure. For very limited oil-producing nations like Egypt, Syria, Yemen, and with no oil in Jordan, their economies were primarily based on agriculture. These Middle Eastern states struggled with economic challenges in low productivity, high population growth, and limited access to capital and technology. Economic policies were often state-led and focused on land reforms and nationalization of key industries. Under such circumstances, Soviet aid was not only attractive but very much needed.

One Middle Eastern country that flipped from the pro-West camp to the Soviets was Libya. The pro-West regime of King Idris is remembered for stability during the early years of Libya's independence after nearly four decades of Italian colonial rule. During the Italian occupation of Libya, Idris led his tribe, the Senussi resistance against the Italians, although he eventually sought refuge in Egypt in 1922 to continue the two-decades-long struggle from abroad. During World War II, Idris allied with the British, who recognized him as the Emir of Cyrenaica and badly needed his help to build a coalition of tribes to push Mussolini's forces out of North Africa. As a reward, the Western allies gave him Tripolitania, and Fezzan, incorporated into his Cyrenaica (the key bastion of his powerbase), on 24 December 1951. Idris (a.k.a. Sayyid Muhammad Idris bin Muhammad al-Mahdi al-Senussi) became the first and only king of his new state of Libya.

Idris' 18-year rule is a mixture of stability and authoritarianism. His government was deeply conservative, part of a revivalist Sufi movement founded in the 19th century by his grandfather, Muhammad ibn Ali as-Senussi. He emphasized a return to the original teachings of Islam, focusing on piety, simplicity, community service and Islamic principles, with Sharia law as an integral part of the legal system in Libya. Despite his strong Islamic beliefs, Libya maintained relatively tolerant relations with its small Christian and Jewish communities. Under his reign, the country witnessed little to no significant religious persecution or forced conversions.

Oil was discovered in Libya in 1959. The first commercially viable oil field was discovered by Esso (now Exxon Mobil) at the Zelten oil field in the Sirte Basin. This discovery marked a turning point but despite the influx of oil revenues, were not evenly distributed, leading to economic disparities, particularly among the urban and younger populations. The monarchy was criticized for being autocratic and repressive, with limited political freedoms and opposition. A younger generation, particularly those exposed to modern education and new free-market ideas, often found the ailing septuagenarian Idris' conservative and religious approach out of touch with the times, leading to growing discontent. One such quote reflects the view of youthful Libyans of the time, "In the eyes of those suffering under King Idris' rule, even the Iblis (devil) would seem a more merciful ruler." They got their wish on 1 September 1969, when the monarch was overthrown in a bloodless coup by a group of young military officers, led by an unknown anti-West, Naseerist, Arab nationalist and socialist-leaning Colonel Muammar Gaddafi. At the time, Idris was in Turkey receiving medical treatment. He lived in exile in Egypt until his death in 1983.

The Soviet Union provided Gaddafi's regime with significant military support, including arms, equipment, training, tanks, aircraft, and missile systems. Overtime, however, the perks of the military slowly gravitated to Gaddafi's family and loyalists within the Libyan armed forces. Many of those perks went to Gaddafi's Revolutionary

Guard Corps, Internal Security Agency and the Khamis Brigade.

Gaddafi's Libya, with Soviet backing, supported various liberation movements and insurgencies around the world, especially in Africa. This included providing funding, training, and arms to groups fighting against colonial, Western-aligned governments. Gaddafi was a strong supporter of the Palestinian cause for statehood and against Israeli occupation. In the 1970s and 1980s, he provided both political and financial support to the PLO and its leader, Yasser Arafat. His regime trained Palestinian fighters and backed the PLO in international forums. However, Gaddafi's leadership style and revolutionary rhetoric often clashed with the more pragmatic approach of the PLO leadership. Arafat believed in a two-state solution and sought to establish an independent Palestinian state through negotiations with Israel. Gaddafi, however, often supported more radical and militant factions within the Palestinian movement and advocated for armed struggle against Israel, similar to Hamas.

Gaddafi's Libya lost a major patron at the disbanding of the Soviet Union in 1991. It was already a pariah to the West after its involvement in the Lockerbie bombing. Pan Am Flight 103 flying over the Scottish town of Lockerbie, exploded due to an installed bomb in 21 December 1988. The episode killed all 243 passengers, 16 crew members and 11 residents of Scotland. After serious international pressure and Western-backed sanctions, Gaddafi handed over the two men responsible including Libyan intelligence officer Abdelbaset al-Megrahi. Some analysts believe the occurrence of Lockerbie was a way for Gaddafi to derail the Reagan administration's dialogue with the PLO, fearing he was being replaced as their chief patron in favor of the American President.

However, for Gaddafi, the subsequent shift in global geopolitics reduced the strategic importance of the Soviet-Libyan alliance. Libya faced increasing international isolation due to its involvement in international terrorism and confrontations with the West. This isolation was exacerbated by sanctions and military actions, such as the U.S. bombing of Tripoli and Benghazi in 15 April 1986. Operation El Dorado Canyon was a response to Libya's involvement in the killing of two American servicemen, one Turkish woman, and injuring over 200 people in West Berlin's La Belle discotheque in 5 April 1986.

The relationship between Libya and Russia began to revive under

Putin. High-level visits and diplomatic engagements increased, Gaddafi visited Moscow in 2008, marking a significant step in strengthening bilateral ties. Russia forgave Libya's Soviet-era debt of $4.5 billion, a move that facilitated closer economic cooperation and the signing of new contracts in several arms deals. Libya purchased a variety of Russian military equipment, including fighter jets, tanks, and missile systems. Russian companies, particularly in the energy and infrastructure sectors, secured contracts in Libya for oil exploration, the construction of railways and other infrastructure projects.

During the Arab Spring, Libya provided a turning point for Putin. The situation concluded after NATO intervention, which led to the overthrow and the death of Gaddafi in October 2011, leading to significant instability and conflict in Libya, well into 2023.

Syria was another critical venue of the Arab Spring. It was the jewel of the Roman Empire due to its strategic location on the Silk Road, which became in the 20th century the only center of Russia's naval base in the Mediterranean Sea, in the port cities of Latakia and Tartus (the Syrian President's strongholds). The bases provide Russia with a critical foothold and allowed for the projection of Russian military power beyond its immediate borders. It is also a crucial terminal for Russian arms sales, and military contracts, showcasing Russia's military capabilities and expanding its influence in the global arms trade.

In 2011 Syria had a massive population movement problem due to severe drought which completely upset the fragile demographic balance. Its two major economic centers; the minority-dominated Damascus in the south and the Sunni-dominated Aleppo in the north, which have been in direct competition with the capital for centuries, now saw significant changes in their demographics.

Damascus is one of the oldest continuously inhabited cities in the world and served as the capital of various empires and civilizations, including the Umayyad Caliphate. Aleppo, similarly ancient, was a major trading hub along the Silk Road and served as the capital of the Aleppo Eyalet during the Ottoman rule. The two had very different characteristics. The Syrian capital, located in the fertile plains of the south, thrived on textiles, handicrafts, agriculture, and trade routes to the Arabian Peninsula. Aleppo, in comparison, was closer to Turkey and the Mediterranean Sea and a prosperous center of commerce and trade in soap and metalworks. The two cities have always competed for political power and influence within Syria. Residents of both cities often take pride in their local customs and heritage, further fueling the rivalry between them. As successive empires and dynasties rose and fell, control over the region often shifted between the two, with each seeking to assert its authority over the other. This competition for political dominance continued into the modern era. Damascus, with its proximity to key military installations, transportation hubs, and population centers, provided the authority for the Assad regime to exert its rule over the country. However, the drought in the north, which began in 2007 and lasted well into 2010, affected Aleppo significantly, and the area lost huge swaths of its population. The majority migrated to areas around Damascus. This was something the Assad government found hard to assimilate with housing and jobs. It also wrought havoc around a very delicate power structure within the regime.

The majority of Syria's population identifies as Sunni Arabs, but the country is home to large groups of minorities. Kurds are the largest ethnic minority, comprising around 10%-15%. Yazidis and Christians are present in the northeast along the border with Turkey. Aleppo has a large population of Syrians of Turkmen origin who speak Turkish as well as Arabic. Smaller ethnic minorities like Assyrians and Armenians reside in Aleppo and Damascus. Then there are even smaller groups of Druze, Christians (including Orthodox, Catholic, and other denominations), and Ismailis, who are concentrated in the north, particularly in the Alawite-majority areas along the Mediterranean coast, including the governorates of Latakia and Tartus. The Palestinian population in Syria lives in refugee camps established after the 1948 Arab-Israeli War by the United Nations Relief and Works Agency for Palestine Refugees in the Near East (UNRWA). The Yarmouk refugee camp near Damascus, which was one of the largest Palestinian refugee camps in Syria before 2011, accommodated approximately half a million Palestinians. Syria's minority communities have historically played significant roles in the turbulent political landscape, especially the ruling Alawites.

During the period of French colonial rule following World War I, under the League of Nations mandate, the French authorities implemented a policy of divide and rule, exploiting existing sectarian and ethnic divisions to maintain control over the territory. They favored minority groups such as the Alawites, Christians, and Druze over the Sunni Muslim majority. This resulted in the Alawites gaining significant influence over the majority Sunni-dominated groups and advancement in politics, the military, and provincial administrations. It helped foster a sense of loyalty among certain segments of the Alawite community toward the French colonial administration. The privileges accorded to minority groups, specially the Alawites, continued to shape Syrian society and politics. The effects of which are still present today. The power structure within the Syrian parliament is largely symbolic, with real political power concentrated in the hands of President Bashar Al-Assad and his inner circle. His regime relied on economic patronage and crony capitalism to maintain the loyalty of key business elites.

President Assad's small Russian-backed Levantine minority has ruled Syria since 1970 with an iron fist. A minority sect of Shia Islam, the secular Alawites celebrate Christmas and the Zoroastrian New Year, Nowruz. They are estimated to be around 3 million of the 22 million of the Syrian population. Among those who adhere to a strict practice of the Quran and the Hadith [the recorded sayings and practices of the Prophet Mohammed (Peace be upon him)], the Alawites are considered a heretic sect. Traditionally, the Alawites had conducted their practices in taqiyya (secret) for fear of persecution. It is a vulnerability that has deep roots within the sect. In modern times, it has become evident among the larger Syrian population after more than a decade of civil war.

In 2011, the Syrian demographic imbalance led to resource competition and created divisions within Syrian society, with identity mattering more than before. Previously, intermarriages between minorities were common, but after 2011, that began to change. When the Arab Spring began in Syria in the city of Daraa in March 2011, there was a serious crackdown by Syrian Security forces. In a few months, foreign interference led to a full-blown civil war. The opposing Free Syrian Army was supported by Qatar and Saudi Arabia, with other members of the Gulf Cooperation Council, such as Kuwait, the United Arab Emirates (UAE), and Bahrain, as well as the United States and the European Union (EU), weighing in.

Putin and his inner circle monitored reports and also saw how the

US Ambassador Robert Ford, during the early stages of the Syrian uprising, was actively engaging with Syrian opposition figures. His vocal criticism of the Assad regime's violent crackdown on protesters signalled alarm bells in the Kremlin. In a show of support for the demonstrators, Ford made a highly publicized visit to the city of Hama, which had become a focal point of anti-government protests. His tenure as U.S. Ambassador to Syria ended in 2014, and he subsequently became a prominent voice advocating for increased U.S. support for moderate Syrian opposition groups and efforts to address the humanitarian crisis.

On 30th September 2015, Russia entered the Syrian civil war after having been convinced by Iranian General Qasem Soleimani of the Quds Force (IRGC's foreign espionage and paramilitary arm) and the invitation of Syrian President Bashar Al-Assad. Putin has justified Russia's military involvement in Syria as necessary to combat terrorist groups such as ISIS and to prevent the spread of Islamist extremism, which could potentially threaten Russia's security interests. Together with Iran, they split Syria into two parts. Russia has consolidated the northwest, right next to opposing anti-Assad Turkish forces, which control northern Aleppo province, including the cities of Jarabulus and Al-Bab, as well as several smaller towns and villages along the Turkish border. Iran, with the Lebanese-Shia Hezbollah group, has done the same in the southwest.

The Syrian civil war and the Israeli-Palestinian conflict are distinct, but they are interconnected through proxy dynamics. The resolution of one conflict is likely to have implications for the other. Syria, like many other Arab countries, historically espoused solidarity with the Palestinians in their struggle for self-determination and statehood. For nationalist Arab governments, the view was part of the struggle against imperialism, which resonated with the Zionist regime in Tel Aviv. At the time, many in the Middle East viewed the British were replaced by an equally imperialist minded regime, resulting in the 1948 Arab–Israeli War. By aligning itself with the Palestinian national movement and opposing Israel's policies, Syria sought to counterbalance Israel's regional dominance but found itself in trouble in doing so. Like Egypt, which lost the Sinnai (recovering it later) and Jordan, which lost the West Bank (although on 31 July 1988, Jordan renounced its claims to the West Bank but with the exception of guardianship over the Muslim and Christian holy sites in Jerusalem), Syria has conducted talks to get back the Golan Heights, which it lost in the 1967 war against Israel, but without success.

The Golan Heights is a significant source of water, feeding into the Jordan River and the Sea of Galilee, which are crucial for Israel's water supply. Control of the Golan Heights helps Israel secure its water resources. The area is also a strategically critical plateau that offers a commanding view. Control of this high ground provides Israel with a significant military advantage, offering both a defensive buffer and a vantage point to monitor Syrian movements. Israel's suspicion with Syria is rooted in past actions before 1967, when Syrian forces used the Golan Heights to launch artillery attacks on Israeli civilian communities and farmers in the Galilee region. Control of the Golan Heights has since provided Israel with a security buffer against potential Syrian aggression. Israel effectively annexed the area in 1981, but without international support. In 2019, the Trump administration formally recognized Israeli sovereignty over the Golan Heights.

The Arab Spring raised hopes for democratic reform and social change but produced an aftermath that was no different from before. While the movement consisted of change from authoritarian rule, it transitioned from one authoritarian rule to another. Tunisia, where the movement began, went from the pro-West authoritarian President Zine El Abidine Ben Ali to another authoritarian, Kais Saied. Egypt went from a former Air Force General Husni Mubarak to another Field Marshal Abdel Fattah el-Sisi. Egypt's only ever democratically elected President, Mohamed Morsi, who presided for a little more than a year, was overthrown by the military and imprisoned on 3 July 2013. He died in Tora Prison on 17 June 2019.

The Arab Spring served as a backdrop for Russia's engagement in the Middle East and North Africa, shaping its foreign policy priorities and relations with regional actors. Putin saw the episode as countering what he perceived as Western interference in the region, happening again in 2014 when the EU offered a free trade and association agreement to Ukraine's President Viktor Yanukovych. This was followed by the Verkhovna Rada (Ukrainian parliament) overwhelmingly approving and finalizing the agreement with the EU on 27 November 2013 in Vilnius. Putin put pressure on Yanukovych to reject the EU Association Agreement. To show what would happen if Yanukovych did accept the EU agreement, in August 2013, Russia began restricting Ukrainian imports, which Ukraine's opposition parties described as "a trade war." In response, only a week before the signing, Yanukovych went against his parliament and chose to side with Putin. Pro-EU groups under the banner of Maidan People's Union went on large protests at Maidan Nezalezhnosti at the center of Kyiv, which became known as 'Euromaidan.' The protestors demanded Yanukovych fulfill his pledge to sign the EU Agreement or else resign. They also called for a return to Ukraine's 2004 Constitution, which would give more power to parliament over the president. Behind these protests were grievances around Yanukovych's government's links with oligarchs, corruption, abuse of power, and human rights violations.

On 21 February 2014, Yanukovych and the parliamentary opposition came to an agreement about an interim unity government, constitutional reforms, and early elections. This was followed by the Ukrainian parliament voting 386–0 to reinstate the 2004 Constitution. The adoption of the new constitution was seen as a victory for democracy and civil society, as it introduced key reforms aimed at strengthening democratic institutions, enhancing the rule of law, and promoting transparency and accountability. It also set provisions for greater decentralization of power, including the establishment of local self-government bodies and the devolution of certain powers from the central government to regional and local authorities. Pro-EU supporters viewed decentralization as a means of empowering local communities, promoting regional development, and ensuring greater representation in decision-making processes for Ukraine. The 2004 Constitution enshrines fundamental rights, including the right to freedom of speech, assembly, and association. Pro-EU supporters also see the 2004 constitution as a safeguard against authoritarianism, repression and as a foundation for building a more open and pluralistic society. It also includes a commitment to European integration. Pro-EU supporters also view the constitution as a reflection of Ukraine's aspirations to align itself with European values, norms, and standards and to deepen its integration with the EU. The document is a system of checks and balances between the executive, legislative, and judicial branches of government. Pro-EU supporters see this as essential for preventing the concentration of power in the hands of a single individual or institution.

On 22 February, Yanukovych disappeared, as did the acting prime minister, Serhiy Arbuzov. That afternoon, the Ukrainian parliament voted 328-0 (with 119 members either absent or abstained) to remove Yanukovych from his post and call for presidential election on 25 May. There were reports of U.S. Assistant Secretary of State Victoria Nuland visiting the Independence Square, where many were calling for the resignation of President Viktor Yanukovich, who bore a similar resemblance to US Ambassador Ford in Hama. Pictures on Twitter showed Nuland shaking hands with Ukrainian security personnel, who had confronted the protestors. Together with then EU foreign policy chief Catherine Ashton, Nuland tried to find a compromise with Yanukovich's administration and the opposition.

Yanukovych has always maintained that he was unfairly removed from the Ukrainian Presidency as he neither committed a crime nor did parliament debate and vote on the nature of his removal. Putin viewed the occurrence as a Western hand in the removal of an ally.

Russia's Permanent Representative to the United Nations, Vitaly Churkin, told the United Nations Security Council on 4 March 2014 that Yanukovych had asked Russia to send troops across the Russia–Ukraine border to protect civilians in a letter to Russian President Putin three days prior. As a result, Russian troops invaded Ukraine and annexed Ukraine's Crimean Peninsula in February 2014.

The fighting near Crimea by Russia and the subsequent conflict in eastern Ukraine has been closely interconnected, shaping the security environment in the region. Efforts to resolve the conflict and achieve a lasting ceasefire continued, but the situation remained volatile and unresolved till the beginning of 2022.

Three months into Biden's Presidency, there were already reports that Russia was amassing some 200,000 troops at Ukraine's northern border. Putin had not forgotten Biden's speech in 2011 at Moscow State University and was convinced that after the abysmal American withdrawal from Afghanistan, only six months prior, the American President would have no appetite for another war.

In contrast, Putin had a better relationship with Israel's Prime Minister Benjamin Netanyahu. Despite differences about Iran, Putin and Netanyahu have maintained cooperation on security matters of mutual concern, such as counterterrorism and regional stability. Both have coordinated their military activities in Syria to avoid unintended clashes. Israeli fighter jets have targetted Iranian proxies and Hezbollah, but maintain strong communication with Russian forces. Netanyahu has sought to persuade Putin to limit Iran's influence in Syria and prevent the transfer of advanced weapons to Hezbollah, which Israel considers a threat to its security. The two have explored opportunities for energy cooperation, particularly in the field of natural gas. Russian energy companies have expressed interest in participating in Israel's offshore gas projects, while Israel has sought to diversify its energy sources and export routes. The two have met on several occasions, with Netanyahu visiting Moscow multiple times to demonstrate the importance of the bilateral relationship. His government has refused to take part in Western-backed sanctions on Russia.

After the 7 October attack on Israel, that bond looks to have disappeared. During the first few weeks after, there was no call of condolence from the Kremlin to Jerusalem.

Since Russia invaded Ukraine in February 2022, more than 45,000 Ukrainians have sought refuge in Israel (*Source*: Central Bureau of Statistics and aid groups). Previously, the Biden administration had asked Netanyahu's predecessor, Acting PM Yair Lapid, to increase Israel's military aid to Ukraine. It is one of the crucial policy differences between Washington and Jerusalem. For some analysts, it looked like the centrist-liberal Lapid was coerced into changing his government's stand from neutral to a pro-Ukraine position. Israel has so far not supplied advanced weaponry to Ukraine.

Lapid, now a leader in the opposition, took a more hawkish stand against Russia. His then Defense Minister Benny Gantz approved the delivery of additional equipment to emergency and civilian organizations. Helmets, protective vests, hundreds of protective suits for mine clearance, gas masks, and other equipments were delivered.

In Israel, there is discomfort over Putin's "special military operation" largely due to the comparison of Ukraine's government to Nazis. On 3 May 2022, Russian officials accused Israel of supporting the "neo-Nazi regime" in Kyiv, followed by Russia's foreign minister, Sergei Lavrov's antisemitic conspiracy theory that Adolf Hitler "had Jewish blood," giving evidence of his own "deep-rooted anti-semitism." The Kremlin also cracked down on the Russian branch of the Jewish Agency, a charity organization in Moscow closely affiliated with the Israeli government that assisted Russian Jews to immigrate to Israel.

As Israel conducted its military response in Gaza with US aid, the Kremlin saw it as a positive outcome. Diverting attention and resources away from Kyiv and onto Jerusalem would certainly help the Russian military take on Ukraine's forces, which were short on cash and ammunition.

There are unconfirmed reports that some in the Kremlin saw the Israeli military and their intelligence blunders on October 7 as a result of overconfidence. It is a result of a delusional attitude toward security over the Gaza strip and a prioritized direction toward the West Bank, home to many of the supporters of the Netanyahu far-right government.

The Israel Defense Forces (IDF) has several units that include women. These units play important roles in various branches of the IDF and contribute to Israel's defense capabilities. Tatzpitaniyot is a unit where women serve in combat intelligence units, gather and analyze intelligence information on enemy activities, monitor border areas, and provide real-time intelligence to commanders in the field. Since the attacks, many have spoken out. They claim their superiors did not heed warnings of unusual activity inside Gaza, of guerrillas training with explosives, rehearsing attacks on a replica tank, and a mock observation post. In Nahal Oz, one of several kibbutzim attacks by Hamas, there were previous warnings of unusual activities, including groups sending drones several times a day along the Gaza border. Not only are their charges of chauvinism in the Israeli army, but they also feed a sense that the Israeli Prime Minister and his security establishment were complacent in taking their eye off the ball in Gaza.

Addressing the Russian parliament, Vyacheslav Volodin, the speaker of the Duma, said that Russians who fled the country to side with Ukraine should be charged with treason and sent to work in mines. In response, NATO Secretary General Jens Stoltenberg and Ukraine's president, Volodymyr Zelenskyy, likened Hamas's barbarity to Russia's aggression in Ukraine.

"The only difference is that there is a terrorist organization that attacked Israel, and here is a terrorist state that attacked Ukraine," Zelenskyy said.

There are also reports that of the approximately 3,000 billionaires in the world, three of them are Hamas leaders. They include 73-year old Musa Abu Marzouk with a networth of $2.3 billion, Deputy Chairman, 68-year old Khaled Mashaal ($2.6 billion), and 62-year old Ismail Haniyeh, the current chairman of Hamas's Political Bureau with a networth of $4 billion. They all reside in Doha and analysts believe the three wield significant influence in the Hamas leadership in Gaza.

Even after the horrific 7 October episode, Hamas leaders amassed significant wealth. Retired IDF Colonel Moshe Elad assesses, "From two directions; Legacies from the deceased. Money from charity funds," Money from the United States through independent Palestinian charitable branches is also a lucrative flow of revenue. There are at least 600 Hamas millionaires in the Gaza Strip with prime real estate near the coast.

After Hamas took out Fatah militarily on 15 June 2007, they consolidated their hold on fuel, mobile, and anything that brought profits from both inside and outside the strip. Investments from, as Colonel Elad mentions, "Turkey's banking system helps Hamas dodge American sanctions…a booming, lightly regulated crypto market makes things even easier. Many of Turkey's biggest banks have been accused by Israel and America of knowingly storing Hamas's cash," that "the risk is that Hamas's finances will improve. As Israel steps up its operations in Gaza, countries with pro-Palestinian populations may make life even easier for Hamas bankers."

Hamas may have even profited from the events of 7 October. There were reports of a significant spike in short selling in a principal Israeli company that had been traded a few days prior. This is part of a financial strategy where individuals borrow shares and sell them at a high price. They wait to buy them back at a low price and repay the loan when the price falls. To really make a profit from the transaction, individuals would need a guarantee that the share price will fall. There are reports that traders who were fed advanced information by Hamas made millions. There is a dangerous pattern developing. Profits in millions are made as rocket firings cross the border and disrupt market trends. In the Hamas-Israel conflict, there is no shortage of mediators who have facilitated dialogue in Doha, Paris, and even in Moscow.

Putin offered to serve as a mediator, and Hamas, according to Russian press reports, praised Putin's position on the Israeli-Palestinian conflict. The question begs, what would the Kremlin gain?

Putin's support of Hamas is a u-turn from his predecessor. President Yeltsin condemned acts of terrorism by Hamas in the 1990s. In 2002, Putin's government joined the Quartet, a group of four including the U.S., the UN, and the EU, with the aim of promoting a comprehensive and lasting resolution to the Israeli-Palestinian conflict. This also included diplomatic initiatives, political engagement, support for economic and institutional development in the Palestinian territories. Unlike the West, Russia did not label Hamas as a terrorist organization.

When Hamas won the Gaza legislative elections in January 2006, Putin invited then-Hamas leader Khaled Meshaal to Moscow. The visit looked like Putin was ready to claim that Russia was back as a key player in the world stage. Successive visits from Hamas leadership continued well into September 2022. Within the Kremlin, a few saw Hamas in the same way as the United States sees Israel. The former Foreign Minister Evgeniy Primakov reportedly said in 2006, that he considers Hamas a humanitarian organization but acknowledged the differences between its political and military wings. He did consider the military wing as terrorists.

To support a rogue group like Hamas for the Kremlin was important as it tried to balance its own ne'er-do-wells. The Kremlin has been engaged in counterterrorism efforts, including military operations in the North Caucasus and implementing security measures to prevent further attacks. The threat of terrorism remains a significant concern, particularly due to ongoing conflicts and instability in the region. Russia has also faced criticism for its heavy-handed approach, including allegations of human rights abuses and indiscriminate targeting of civilians in areas where it believes it needs to flush out militants in the Caucasus. These events particularly went on the upsurge after Putin came to power in 1999. One of those events was the 2002 Moscow Theater Hostage Crisis, when Chechen militants seized a crowded theater in Moscow, holding hundreds of hostages. Russian security forces stormed the building after pumping it with gas to incapacitate the militants, resulting in the deaths of over 100 hostages, mainly due to the effects of the gas thrown by Russian security forces. Then came the 2004 Beslan School Siege, when Chechen separatists took over a school in Beslan, North Ossetia, holding more than a thousand people hostage, mostly children. The siege resulted in the deaths of over 300, including 186 children. Another episode came in the 2010 Moscow Metro Bombings. Two female suicide bombers linked to Islamist insurgent groups in the North Caucasus detonated explosives on the Moscow Metro during rush hour, killing at least 40 people and injuring more than 100.

Further events followed. In 2011 there was a huge explosion in Moscow Domodedovo Airport, when a suicide bomber detonated explosives in the international arrivals hall, killing 37 and injuring over 170 others.

In Putin's home city of St. Petersburg in 2017, a suicide bomber killed 16 people and injuring dozens. The perpetrator was linked to radical Islamist groups.

Putin didn't associate Hamas with radical Islamist terror. Very few Russians were living in Gaza and worked at the Russian cultural center in Kalinka, under the auspices of the Russian foreign affairs ministry, which was considered an umbrella for the FSB to conduct its own information operations.

Realizing where Hamas stood in supporting a key Russian and Iranian ally in its reservations about Bashar Al-Assad of Syria, Hamas for the Kremlin remained a better option against a host of ineffectual, neutral, and pro-West sets of Palestinian groups.

In November 2015, Deputy Foreign Affairs Minister Mikhail Bogdanov restated his view that Hamas was not a terrorist organization. After the 7 October attacks, the Kremlin invited the group's leadership on 26 October. The Russian action shows that Putin sees Hamas as a way to wield some level of influence, at the very least, send a message to the West that Russia may be a pariah on the international stage because of the war in Ukraine, but it is still an important player on the global stage.

According to a 13 October *Wall Street Journal* report, Hamas-linked terrorist groups found ways to circumvent Western-backed sanctions by utilizing Russia's cryptocurrency exchanges through the Wagner Group, where mercenaries are involved in various conflicts, including the Syrian civil war, Ukraine, Libya, Sudan, Central African Republic, and others. It also has a finance wing that specializes in covert crypto transactions. Some analysts believe that Hamas received substantial covert financial assistance, including assault tactics, production of arms, and military maneuvers. For Putin, if the West can supply weapons to Ukraine, why couldn't he do so in Gaza? Gaza does have something that is very attractive for Putin.

In 1999, the discovery of large gas fields off the coast of Gaza provided some hope. According to the Oslo Accords II, the Palestine National Authority (PNA) has maritime jurisdiction up to 20 nautical miles of the Gaza coast. In November 1999, the Palestine National Assembly (PNA) signed a 25-year contract for gas exploration with a UK-based BGG group. Gaza was estimated to have 1 trillion cubic feet of natural gas.

In a move to prioritize peace, in 2000 summer, Israel withdrew from its 18-year occupation of southern Lebanon. Prime Minister Ehud Barak's government wanted to prioritize the economy and soon directed its attention to the BGG deal. Tel Aviv granted the company the drilling of the first wells of natural gas, which supposedly belonged to the residents of Gaza. When the short-reigned Barak's Labor government fell, the newly elected Likud government took a different direction. Prime Minister Ariel Sharon's tough stand against Palestinians led the way in March 2001 for the BGG deal to become a casualty and the government halted the deal. In 2002 summer, British Prime Minister Tony Blair negotiated an agreement on behalf of the Palestinian National Assembly (PNA) with the Sharon government. An annual supply of 0.05 trillion cubic feet of natural gas was allotted to the Palestinians for a maximum of 15 years. By 2003, the Israeli Prime Minister had changed his mind. Sharon's successor, Ehud Olmert reopened the negotiation and in April 2007, made the case that Palestinians will receive from 2009, 0.05 trillion cubic feet of natural gas for $4 billion annually. In 2007, when Hamas came to power, the group wanted 10% of the BGG profits. The Israeli government bypassed the Hamas government in Gaza, throwing out the BGG deal. In 2008, any hope of an agreement ended.

Putin's Gazprom can replace the BGG deal. The East Mediterranean Gas (EMG), the closest Russian pipeline near occupied Palestine, could do what the BGG deal couldn't. While the pipeline itself does not originate from Russia, it has had Russian involvement in its operations and ownership. The EMG pipeline was originally built to transport natural gas from Egypt to Israel, and it became operational in 2008, but issues remained over its operational consistency. Russian companies, notably the state-controlled Gazprom, have been involved in negotiations regarding the potential use of the EMG pipeline to transport natural gas from Israel's offshore fields in the Eastern Mediterranean. The Russian move could sway the dynamics of disenfranchised Palestinians. As Israel continues its military operations in Gaza, pushing Palestinians nearly out of the strip, it would be very difficult for Putin's Gazprom to begin work.

Given the results of decades of marginalization, which have by now made Palestinians radical, is a common characteristic in the Arab world. Other conflicts like the Syrian civil war, the after-effects of the American invasion of Iraq and the creation of ISIS in 2004, a splinter group from al-Qaeda, have given fuel to radicalism in the Middle East.

ISIS may be defeated but its propaganda has remained. The terror group portrayed Russia as an enemy of Islam, citing its actions in Chechnya, its support for heretic regimes like in Syria, and its treatment of Muslim populations within its borders. This narrative aims to rally support among Muslims worldwide against Russia. Some analysts suggest that ISIS may also target Russia for its resources, including its oil and gas infrastructures. Control over resource-rich territories has been a significant driver of conflict in the Middle East, and ISIS' territorial ambitions may extend to regions where Russia has economic interests.

Nowhere has this been more visible than in Syria's east. It is the real prize of the regime in Damascus, particularly in the provinces of Deir ez-Zor and Al-Hasakah. Some of the significant oil fields in this region include the Al-Omar oil field, as well as the Tanak and Jafra. The Al-Omar oil field is one of the largest in Syria. It has changed hands multiple times throughout the Syrian civil war. Initially, it was under the control of the Syrian government. However, it fell under the control of ISIS in 2014. Following ISIS's territorial losses, the Syrian Democratic Forces (SDF), a Kurdish-led militia alliance, captured the oil field in 2017, including Tanak and Jafra. Since then, the SDF has maintained control, which has been a significant source of revenue for the autonomous administration in northeastern Syria. While the SDF and the Bashar Al-Assad government have engaged in tactical cooperation against ISIS through Russian mediators, their relationship remains subject to change based on evolving circumstances.

One particular development was in May 2023, when Syrian President Bashar Al-Assad was welcomed back to the Arab League with open arms and kisses from Saudi Crown Prince Mohammed bin Salman. "The Arab world can now reposition itself" he said, "in a world of Western dominance that lacks principles manners friends and partners." Assad's return after more than a decade of war may help to be one of the first steps to end the Syrian civil war.

Other Arab leaders seemed content, while the Emir of Qatar, Sheikh Tamim ibn Hamad Al Thani, a staunch Assad opponent, walked out before the Syrian President could speak. In Northern Syria, hundreds protested what they called the normalization of Syria's President.

Middle Eastern regimes just didn't roll out the red carpet to the Syrian President for mere normalization. There was another purpose. Captagon, a highly addictive amphetamine-type drug largely produced and consumed in the Middle East, is coming from Syria. In the fall of 2023, Jordanian Foreign Minister Ayman al-Safadi said; "that trafficking of the addictive amphetamine Captagon from Syria to Jordan has only increased after normalization talks that led to Assad's return to the Arab League in May."

Jordan shares a perilous 233-mile border with Syria. As a result of non-conformist actors operating in the area, Amman is one of the main stops for Syria's drug trade.

"Jordan is fighting on the border to make sure drugs do not get into the country," said King Abdullah II (*Source:* Al-Monitor).

In exchange for rehabilitation, some Middle Eastern governments urged President Assad to help crack down on the whopping $57 billion Captagon trade. The Gulf is a key consumer destination. Trading the drug has made Syria into a narcotic-state, with the Assad regime getting more than a cut to restock its coffers despite war and Western-backed sanctions. The sale of Captagon serves as a key Syrian foreign policy goal as a bargaining chip against Arab states, but it also serves as a key Russian and Iranian aim. Damascus is really a button to unleash mayhem against oil-producing nations, which the United States needs.

Ensuring a steady and diversified supply of energy resources is a key U.S. energy security priority that has been in place since the end of World War II. Gulf nations are key partners in this security priority and in the global energy markets. By maintaining diplomatic and economic ties, the United States aims to secure access to these critical energy resources and mitigate the risks of supply disruptions or price shocks in the global market. The petrodollar system, established in the 1970s, the practice of oil-exporting countries pricing their oil in U.S. dollars has helped maintain the U.S. dollar's status as the dominant global reserve currency and has facilitated international trade and finance. Gulf nations play a significant role in the petrodollar system, reinforcing the interdependence between the United States and oil-producing countries in the region.

The stability of the Gulf region is of strategic importance to the United States due to its geopolitical significance and the presence of major global shipping routes, particularly the Strait of Hormuz, that ensure stability and security in the Gulf. It is essential for safeguarding maritime trade, preventing conflicts that could disrupt oil supplies, and countering threats. The route plays a role that indirectly impacts Syria, and this is where Iran's proxies, the Houthis, who run a de facto government in Yemen in opposition to the recognized government in Aden, come useful.

In response to Israel's military campaign in Gaza, the Houthis started sending intercepted drones and missiles towards Israel. On 19 November 2023, the group hijacked a commercial ship in the Red Sea, the beginning of a number of attacks. One victim was the Barbados-flagged cargo ship named True Confidence. On 6 March 2024, three crew members were killed in a missile attack. The Straits of Hormuz have become a dangerous and almost unusable shipping route.

The strategic waterway is not the only place where the Houthis are targeting their attacks, continuing at the Gulf of Aden, the Red Sea, and off the coast of Yemen. As they do so, they are slowly inching closer to confrontation with U.S. led naval forces. There is no doubt that the Houthis are conducting such attacks to cause economic disruption in ways to keep its patron, Iran's adversaries in check.

What Moscow and Tehran could not do with aid in economic and arms ammunition, they made up in other ways, in part to make Damascus stable. The Russian air power has given Bashar Al-Assad's army self-assurance from a battered set of units into a force to be reckoned with. Today, the Syrian army can hold its own against most of its opposition forces.

The view in Damascus is that the Arab League needs Syria much more than Syria needs them. What is evident is that the Assad regime has not had to seriously meet any conditions for return to the Arab League. Aspiring to be like the League of Nations, the Arab League is a regional organization that wants to mediate to halt any conflict. It is composed of Arab states in the Middle East and North Africa, established on 22 March 1945, with the signing of the Alexandria Protocol by seven founding members: Egypt, Iraq, Jordan, Lebanon, Saudi Arabia, Syria, and Yemen. The League has since expanded to include a total of 22 member states. One of its aims is to promote economic, cultural, political, and social cooperation among its members, with its primary goal of safeguarding the independence and sovereignty by coordinating their policies on regional and international issues, and promoting Arab unity and solidarity. However, there is another face of the Arab League which reveals deep-seated divisions among its member states, stemming from political, ideological, and sectarian differences, as well as rivalries for regional influence.

Disagreements over issues such as the Israeli-Palestinian conflict led to Egypt being temporarily expelled from the Arab League in 1979 in response to its signing of the Egypt-Israel Peace Treaty, also known as the Camp David Accords. After President Sadat's assassination, Egypt was admitted back under President Mubarak.

In 1990, Saddam Hussein's invasion of Kuwait led to Jordan, the PLO, and Yemen siding with Iraq, while the rest of the Arab League went so far as to join the American coalition (which included Egypt and Syria) to oust Iraqi forces from Kuwait.

In the lead-up to the 2003 American invasion of Iraq, Saudi Arabia, Egypt, Jordan, Syria, and Lebanon protested. Less publicly, Jordan allowed US and British Special Forces to operate from remote bases in the desert near the Iraqi border. Kuwait, Qatar, Bahrain (home to the U.S. Navy's Fifth Fleet), Oman, and the United Arab Emirates (UAE) provided their own bases, logistical support, access to their airspace and facilities for military operations against Iraq. Without their support, the 2003 Iraq invasion would have dragged on much longer than the six weeks it took for what President George W. Bush called "Mission Accomplished."

The Syrian Civil War too exposed rifts within the Arab League.

Syria was expelled in November 2011. Lebanon, Iraq, Algeria and Sudan opposed the expulsion. Some member states accused the League of being ineffective and beholden to the interests of more powerful outside forces like the United States.

What was happening in Syria was part of a sectarian war in the region that had its roots in Iraq. After the 2003 American invasion of Iraq and the Arab Spring, members of the Arab league criticized the organization's failure to address pressing regional issues, including climate change and carving the region into what we see today, with one side led by Saudi Arabia and the other by Iran.

Critics have warned that the Arab League has not lived up to the pace of modernization in the 21st century. Hence, the population in the Middle East has struggled, with economic prosperity always halted at the cost of disruption and conflict. A recent crisis showed a perfect example. The 2017 Gulf crisis, a diplomatic and political dispute that erupted among Gulf Cooperation Council (GCC) member states, led to a significant rupture in relations between Qatar and other Gulf states, primarily Saudi Arabia, the United Arab Emirates (UAE), Bahrain, and Egypt. The crisis has had far-reaching implications for the Gulf region and has underscored underlying tensions and rivalries among key states.

The crisis began on 5 June 2017, when Saudi Arabia, the UAE, Bahrain, and Egypt simultaneously announced the severing of diplomatic ties with Qatar. These grievances included Qatar's alleged support for terrorist groups, its interference in the internal affairs of other countries, and its close ties with Saudi Arabia's key rival, Iran. The four countries then went on to impose a blockade on Qatar, severing land, air, and sea links and restricting access to essential goods and services. Qatar, which relies heavily on imports for its food and other necessities, was forced to seek alternative supply routes from Baku, Tehran, and other capitals.

Several attempts at mediation were made to resolve the crisis, including those by Kuwait and the United States, but initial efforts were unsuccessful. Qatar refused to comply with the demands of the blockading countries, arguing that they infringed on its sovereignty and were unjustified.

The crisis drew international attention and concern, with the United States calling for a peaceful resolution and urging dialogue among the parties involved. The United States, which has military bases in both Qatar and some of the blockading countries, expressed its desire for a swift resolution to avoid further destabilization in the region. The episode had significant and lasting implications as it has exacerbated existing tensions and rivalries, reshaped regional alliances, dynamics, and heightened concerns about security and stability in the Arabian Peninsula. Despite occasional signs of thawing relations and diplomatic initiatives, while there have been some efforts at reconciliation and de-escalation, deep-seated grievances and geopolitical rivalries continue to complicate efforts to find a lasting solution to the crisis.

Under a divided Arab League, the Assad regime has conveniently maneuvered around a non-conditional return and without any accountability. More importantly, Assad knows that the League does not have a process to reprimand him for his violations. The regime in Damascus can comfortably conduct its booming Captagon trade, with middlemen traffickers using increasingly advanced technology to smuggle the amphetamine out to Arab states, which is exhausting the security services of these countries as they conduct drug raids and are unable to put resources on their borders. Elements of Captagon are found in everything from building panels to baklava shipments. Saudi security forces alone found 47 million amphetamine pills hidden in a flour shipment at warehouses in Riyadh. The UAE too, foiled an attempt, seizing 13 tons of Captagon hidden in shipments. King Abdullah II's security forces often find themselves shooting down drones carrying amphetamines.

The Syrian President is really showing his patrons in Moscow and Tehran that he is their man in the Arab League, and they can count on him to stand as a bulwark against the Western-backed Middle Eastern states. Even with American sanctions on Syria, the Assad regime continues to commit war crimes, and the return of Syria to the Arab League is seen as a triumph for Russia and Iran.

The Assad regime does not control all of Syria, but rather approximately 70% of the areas, with the richest controlled by the American-allied Kurdish SDF. Small-scale skirmishes continue in the north, but Syria, like Ukraine, has become a battleground between one side, including Russia, Iran, versus Turkey, Israel, and the United States, with ISIS as a weaker and fading third party, which still controls several pockets in the Syrian desert, near to the border of Iraq.

For Russia, the consequences of backing rogue groups and rogue regimes have now come to its own doorstep. On 22 March 2024, an attack at the Crocus City Hall was the sight of the deadliest attack on Russian soil. The large concert venue is located in the Crocus City complex in Krasnogorsk, a suburb of Moscow. It is one of the largest and most prominent entertainment venues in the country. The theater has a seating capacity of around 7,000, making it one of the largest indoor concert venues. It features a spacious main hall with tiered seating, state-of-the-art sound and lighting systems, designed to accommodate a wide range of events, from concerts and theatrical performances to conferences and corporate events. It boasts of modern and stylish architecture, with a sleek exterior and elegant interior design. The main hall features a stage with advanced technical capabilities, including hydraulic lifts and motorized platforms, allowing for dynamic and immersive performances. It also offers various amenities and services to enhance the visitor experience, including VIP lounges, luxury suites, bars, restaurants, and ample parking facilities.

Both Tehran and Washington, as early as 7 March, had warned Moscow of potential terrorist attacks, citing probable incidents on 9 or 10 March. Over a hundred people died, but the only thing the Kremlin could do was not address the main issue.

The Ajnad al-Kavkaz, part of the Al-Nusra terror group, was responsible. It is an al-Qaeda front organization that has been fighting Syrian forces. The group also known as Soldiers of the Caucasus, consists of fighters from the North Caucasus, including Chechnya, Dagestan, and Ingushetia, as well as other parts of the Caucasus. Many of its members have combat experience from previous conflicts, including the Chechen Wars. The group emerged in 2015, drawing fighters from various North Caucasus militant factions operating in Syria, where members share a common goal of establishing an Islamic state governed by Sharia law. Its primary objective is to participate in the Syrian civil war alongside other jihadist groups, including Jabhat al-Nusra (now Hayat Tahrir al-Sham). The group seeks to overthrow the secular government of Syrian President Bashar al-Assad. It espouses a Salafi-jihadist ideology, advocating for the establishment of an Islamic caliphate governed by strict interpretations of Islamic law. Its fighters are motivated by religious convictions and grievances against perceived injustices committed against Sunni Muslims in Syria and elsewhere.

The group has closely cooperated with other militant factions in joint operations, primarily in the northwestern province of Idlib and the surrounding areas. It has also clashed with Kurdish militias and rival rebel factions. Since the destruction of the Islamic State's so-called Caliphate in 2016, there are claims that a number of Central Asian jihadists also resettled in Ukraine, including the group's deputy minister for war, Caesar Tokhosashvili. The group's main leader, Rustam Azhiev, is a former Russian mixed martial artist (MMA) champion. In 2014, Azhiev was involved in a highly publicized incident during an ACA event in Moscow, where he engaged in a post-fight brawl with his opponent and members of the audience. The incident led to sanctions and suspensions for Azhiev. From then on, he has advocated for the liberation of Chechnya.

Azhiev's Chechnya was always at odds with the expansionist aims of the Russian Empire, the Soviet Union, and Putin's Russia. Chechnya is inhabited by an indigenous ethnic group with a distinct language, culture, and history. The Chechens have a long-standing connection to their homeland, which predates the arrival of the Russian state. Throughout their history, the Chechens have fiercely resisted attempts by external powers to impose control over their territory, manifesting in numerous uprisings and conflicts, including the Caucasian Wars of the 19th century, a bloody resistance against Russian imperial forces.

In 1817, the conflict was sparked by the resistance of the Chechen and Dagestani peoples to Russian encroachment into their territories. Led by prominent leaders such as Sheikh Mansur and Imam Shamil, the indigenous forces waged a guerrilla campaign against Russian imperial forces. Despite initial success, the Russian army eventually suppressed the resistance. In 1825, the Second Caucasian War was a more prolonged and protracted conflict characterized by sustained resistance from various ethnic groups. The war saw the emergence of Imam Shamil as a prominent leader of the resistance. The Russian Empire deployed significant military resources to subdue the rebellion, employing brutal tactics such as scorched-earth and mass deportations. The war culminated in the capture of Imam Shamil in 1859, effectively ending organized resistance in the region.

The Russian adventure had far-reaching consequences for both the indigenous peoples of the Caucasus and the Russian Empire. While the Russian Empire ultimately succeeded in incorporating the Caucasus into its territory, the wars resulted in immense human suffering, loss of life, and displacement of populations. Many Circassians, an indigenous ethnic group from the North Caucasus region, and other ethnic groups were forcibly resettled and fled as refugees, leading to the depopulation of large areas of the Caucasus. The memory of the wars and the suffering endured by the indigenous populations remain deeply ingrained in the collective consciousness of the region's inhabitants to this day, contributing to ongoing tensions and conflicts in the Caucasus.

Putin was successful in setting up his proxies in the region. Since the end of the Second Chechen War in April 2009, Chechnya has been under the de facto control of Ramzan Kadyrov, who serves as the head of the Chechen Republic. Kadyrov, a former rebel fighter turned politician, has maintained a close relationship with Putin. The term "Kadyrovtsy" refers to loyalists and supporters of Ramzan Kadyrov within Chechnya's security forces, and government institutions. These individuals are known for their unwavering allegiance to Kadyrov and his administration, as well as their enforcement of his policies and directives. These men are in Chechnya's police, military units, and special operations groups and are considered to be extensions of Kadyrov's authority, playing a significant role in maintaining order and suppressing dissent, sometimes employing heavy-handed tactics to achieve their objectives.

Like Ukraine's east, Chechnya is rich in natural resources. It has significant reserves of oil and natural gas, particularly in the Grozny oil fields. These resources have the potential to contribute to the region's economic development and generate revenue for the local government. It also has large deposits of minerals, including limestone, gypsum, and clay, which have applications in construction, manufacturing, and other industries.

Chechnya is endowed with extensive forests and is a valuable natural resource, providing timber for construction, fuelwood, and other forest products. With a fertile agricultural land suitable for cultivation and with the region's agriculture primarily focused on livestock farming, including sheep, cattle, and poultry, as well as the cultivation of crops such as grains, vegetables, and fruits, it has huge economic potential.

Chechnya is also traversed by numerous rivers and streams, including the Terek and Sunzha rivers. These water resources have the potential for hydroelectric power generation and irrigation.

Like Russia, Chechnya, too, has a link to Ukraine. For centuries, the Tartar raiders, who had roots in the Caucasus, had pillaged the agricultural lands of Europe's east in search of slaves for nearly two centuries. In the 15th century, the Crimean Khanate emerged as a successor state to the Golden Horde, establishing control over the Crimea peninsula and neighboring territories. The area was ruled by a dynasty of Turkic origin and served as a center of power and inhabited by a diverse population, including Tatars and Nogais, who were of Turkic and Mongol descent. These groups formed the core of the Khanate's population and played a significant role in its administration, economy, and military. Periods of migration and settlement from the Caucasus continued. Various ethnic groups from the Caucasus, including Circassians, Abkhazians, and others, migrated to Crimea, seeking refuge from conflicts and for economic opportunities. As a result, the Khanate became a melting pot of cultures, languages, and traditions, with influences from the Caucasus, Central Asia, the Middle East, and Europe.

During the 19th century, the Russian Empire captured the homelands of the Chechens, Ingush, and Dagestanis. Further east, the Khanates of Khiva and Khokand, the Emirate of Bokhara, and the Tartar centers of Geok-Tepe, were seized in a lightning campaign that began in 1865. The Khanate of Merv fell too, without a shot being fired. Imperial Russia's efforts to restrict the influence of Islam by limiting the number of Hajj pilgrims and choking religious endowments provoked multiple rebellions. Islam arrived in Chechnya through a gradual process of conversions between the 8th to 10th centuries. The exact timing and circumstances of Islam's introduction are not precisely documented, but it likely occurred through trade, cultural exchanges, and interactions with neighboring Muslim civilizations. For the Russian empire, Islam was an enemy to be crushed. It is for those reasons large Muslim groups from the Caucus fought alongside Nazi Waffen-Schutzstaffel divisions during

World War II against the Soviets. They were by no means effective as in the summer of 1944, Crimea's Tatars were collectively rounded up by the Soviet secret police, the KGB, accused of Nazi collaboration and deported to Central Asia. Thousands died during their long journey east in airless, sealed cattle wagons, and thousands more succumbed to malnutrition and disease in collective farms and Gulags.

Nearly five decades later, President Yeltsin's Russia found itself at war with its restive Muslim nationalities in Chechnya. However, this time, things were different. Many Chechen fighters like Shamil Basayev, an engineer by training before becoming involved in the Chechen independence movement, had learned his skills from the Soviet war in Afghanistan. With a significantly well trained and well armed Chechen fighters, Yeltsin's nearly bankrupt and demoralized Russian troops were hurdled in buses back to Russia to showcase their defeat.

One of the first acts Putin as President conducted was a return of Russian troops to Chechnya to gain back a Russian victory. The 1999 Russian campaign was brutal. For the next decade, the situation in Chechnya pulled in regimes in Uzbekistan, Tajikistan, and Kyrgyzstan, who all feared jihadist violence to spread into their already weak post-Soviet regimes.

Uzbekistan was unsettled by occasional terror attacks. Tajikistan saw civil war. Kyrgyzstan witnessed terror attacks in its south. Fighters from these areas soon descended on Syria in 2013, joining al-Qaeda and the Islamic State. They came in even bigger numbers after Russian entry into the Syrian civil war in September 2015. In 2016, there were claims that several movements of Russian-speaking jihadists from Syria moved to Ukraine, including in areas of Kyiv and Kharkiv, to work as transit points for attacks in Western Europe and also Russia. Compared to the rest of Europe, Ukraine is well prepared to prevent Russian-speaking jihadists from using their territory to attack Europe or Russia, but Putin believes otherwise. If the West can use jihadists against the Soviet Union during its near decade long occupation of Afghanistan, is it so inconceivable that it would not employ the same methods now against Russia.

Putin fears a repeat of what happened on 15 February 1989 in Afghanistan when the last Soviet troops withdrew. The last Soviet soldier to leave Afghanistan was Lieutenant General Boris Gromov, the commander of the Soviet 40th Army who was responsible for the withdrawal of Soviet forces. During his last days, Gromov led the final column of Soviet troops as they crossed the Friendship Bridge from Afghanistan into Soviet Uzbekistan. Gromov has served three terms as governor of Moscow Oblast with Putin's blessing. After Putin's Presidential victory in March 2024, Gromov's departure from the governor's post appeared imminent due to 12 years of accumulated problems from deficit to debt, all of which stemmed from Gromov's governorship.

What happened in Afghanistan could transpire in Ukraine. It is a kind of humiliation Putin can do without, but the Ajnad al-Kavkaz group may very well have opened a can of "chyervi" (Russian word for worms) which Putin for years did not want to address, but now may very well have to deal with. This would mean his military would be fighting on two fronts, the other being on Russia's Caucasus to neutralize the network of Russian-speaking jihadists. It's not the option he wanted, and he can't appear to aid the terrorists labeled by the West in Hamas and not expect a response from the West.

Putin's Russia has survived and avoided global isolation two years after invading a sovereign Ukraine. As the Russian President aligns closer with rogue regimes to push for his alternative versus the West, he is headed on a dangerous path. Can he afford to pay the cost of escalation? It is a setting where he may confront the reality of his own weakening grip on Russia.

Chapter 9

THE OTTOMANS STILL MATTER

The Ottoman Empire's Siege of Vienna in 1683, led by Grand Vizier Kara Mustafa Pasha, marked a turning point in Europe. The event represented the culmination of the Ottoman expansion into Central Europe, having previously conquered much of the Balkans, Eastern Europe, and Vienna's fall would have potentially opened up further conquests into Western Europe. The capital of the Hapsburg empire held immense symbolic significance as a bastion of Christianity, and its fall would have been seen as a major blow to Europeans. After the episode, the Ottoman Empire began to gradually recede from its European territories, leading to the plodding decline of its power in Europe. The Ottoman defeat contributed to shaping European identity and consciousness as it reinforced the idea of a distinct European civilization with a common Christian identity shared by European nations. The successful defense of Vienna was celebrated as a victory for Christian Europe against the forces of Islam, but today, approximately 1,300 kilometers away, the events in Ukraine might demonstrate otherwise.

Following the establishment of the Republic of Turkey in 1923, its President, Mustafa Kemal Atatürk, implemented sweeping reforms aimed at modernizing the country's economy. These reforms included the introduction of secularism, industrialization, and the adoption of Western legal and educational systems. In the decades following World War II, Turkey, the successor state to the Ottoman Empire, pursued a policy of import substitution industrialization (ISI), a strategy aimed at promoting domestic industrialization by substituting imported items with domestically produced goods. ISI policies led to the growth of domestic industries and helped lay the groundwork for future economic development. By the 1970s, Turkey faced economic challenges, including high inflation and external debt. In response, the government implemented economic stabilization programs, liberalized trade, and encouraged foreign investment. Following a military coup in 1980, the third after 1960, there was a question of how to allow the government in Ankara to operate without military interference. The coup of 12 September 1980 was the most significant and consequential in Turkey's history. The military, led by General Kenan Evren, intervened to end a period of political instability marked by violence between leftist and right-wing factions. It led to the suspension of political activities, the dissolution of political parties, and the implementation of a new constitution. Martial law was declared, and thousands were arrested, tortured, and disappeared. Civilian rule was eventually restored in 1983, but with hard conditions imposed by the military.

From then on, successive Turkish governments embarked on a period of economic liberalization and structural reforms. These reforms, guided by the International Monetary Fund (IMF) and World Bank, aimed to reduce state intervention in the economy, promote privatization, and liberalize trade and investment. The liberalization policies helped attract foreign investment and spur economic growth. The next two decades fueled increasing exports, foreign investment, and domestic consumption. Turkey sought to modernize its economy, boost industrial development, and achieve higher growth rates. Integration with European markets looked to meet such objectives. In 1959, Turkey first applied for associate membership in the European Economic Community (EEC), the precursor to the European Union (EU). This application marked the beginning of Turkey's long and complicated journey toward EU membership and its relationship with Europe. Turkey signed an Association Agreement with the European Economic Community in 1963 and a full membership application on 14 April 1987. EU membership remains uncertain, with accession talks stalled or suspended at different points and at times facing delays and opposition.

President Recep Tayyip Erdoğan's Justice and Development Party (AKP) came to power in 2002. As Prime Minister, Erdoğan soon implemented further economic reforms, and pursued policies aimed at attracting foreign direct investment (FDI) and promoting infrastructure development. The country's strong economic performance in the early 21st century led to its classification as an emerging market by international financial institutions. Turkey's growing middle class, youthful population, and strategic location further bolstered its attractiveness to investors.

Despite significant economic attraction and improvements, the EU has always seen Turkey's candidacy as "exceptional." While analysts believe Turkey leads in GDP growth beyond some of the new members of the EU, namely Bulgaria and Romania, and is twice the size of the two combined, it suffers from a distorted boom-and-bust economy and is crucially dependent on international finance markets. The EU is concerned about Turkey's human capital, which it suspects is below the wider European levels. The Turkish agriculture sector is significantly high-performing, but it takes up nearly half of its labor force. What cannot be ignored is the Turkish economy is significantly more vibrant than most EU member states. It has a strong manufacturing base, particularly in sectors such as automotive, textiles, machinery, and electronics. It is one of the world's largest producers of textiles and clothing, exporting goods to markets around the globe. The country has a relatively young population, which provides a demographic in terms of a large, youthful and productive workforce. However, it also poses challenges in terms of providing employment opportunities and ensuring economic growth. Ankara has invested in strategic sectors such as energy, transportation, and telecommunications to support economic development and infrastructure modernization. Projects like the Turkish Stream pipeline and upgrading the Istanbul Airport reflect these efforts. As an emerging market economy, Turkey offers opportunities for investors seeking growth potential. However, it also faces challenges related to economic volatility, political uncertainties, and structural reforms.

International conflicts can drive economic demand for military and defense. Turkey has a relatively large and capable defense industry, and it can capitalize on supplying arms, equipment, and military expertise to countries involved in conflicts, as it has done in Ukraine.

Turkey has pursued a policy of engagement with both Russia and Ukraine, seeking to balance its relations with both countries while advocating for a peaceful resolution. Ankara has emphasized the importance of maintaining Ukraine's territorial integrity and sovereignty while also engaging in diplomatic efforts to de-escalate tensions with Russia. The war in Ukraine has provided an opportunity for Ankara that may very well tilt certain conditions in favor of Turkey, particularly its relations with Europe.

During the last decade, Ankara and Brussels have clashed on several fronts. On 6 July 2017, the European Parliament called for the suspension of European Union accession negotiations with Turkey. The resolution was passed amid concerns about Turkey's human rights record, particularly following the attempted coup in July 2016 against President Erdoğan. The subsequent crackdown on perceived dissenters, which led to widespread arrests, dismissals, and the erosion of democratic institutions were cited as key concerns. The resolution also highlighted other issues, including the deterioration of the rule of law, freedom of speech, and the independence of the judiciary in Turkey. It emphasized that Turkey's accession negotiations could only proceed if there were substantial improvements in these categories.

While the European Parliament's resolution carries political weight, it does not have the authority to formally suspend accession negotiations with Turkey. That decision ultimately rests with the Council of the European Union. However, the resolution signaled the growing concerns within the European Parliament about the direction of Turkey's domestic policies and its compatibility with European values.

Europe has always looked at Turkey without a strategic lens, prioritizing its Islamic roots rather than its economic and military strengths. Europe's suspicions of Ankara have evolved over decades over its historical and cultural ties to the Islamic world and have sometimes led to perceptions of cultural differences and religious tensions with predominantly Christian Europe. This has fueled stereotypes and prejudices on both sides and contributed to a sense of the "other."

Centuries of conflicts, including wars between the Ottoman Empire, and European powers, have left a legacy of distrust against Turkey. There is a form of double standards in Europe for centuries which has seen numerous atrocities, conflicts, and human rights abuses, towards fellow Europeans through wars dating as far back as 1337 Hundred Years' War to World War II. Even today, the Ottoman influence on Europe is particularly visible in the Balkans and parts of southeastern Europe. Large Turkish and Balkan diaspora communities especially in Germany, Austria, and the Netherlands, maintain cultural and economic ties that are partly rooted in the Ottoman era. The Ottoman millet system promoted religious tolerance and diversity, a legacy of significant ethnic mixing, creating diverse populations in many Balkan states, and today, the complex ethnic compositions and cultural interactions are still present in countries like Albania, Bosnia and Herzegovina, North Macedonia, and Kosovo, where different religious communities co-exist. However, Europe has always applied a state of double standards against the Ottomans and their successor state, Turkey, a consequential move that may put Europe in a difficult position within its foreign policy in the 21st century.

While such judgment can reflect a complex interplay of political, cultural, and strategic factors, the underlying fact is Europe has not come to terms with the Ottoman presence in its history.

Beyond Cyprus, where Turkey has de facto partitioned the island, which resulted in the displacement of thousands of Greek Cypriots from the north and Turkish Cypriots from the south, Europe will not even entertain the idea that it was a necessary action as much for Greece as it was for Turkey. The Turkish intervention in 1974 is often framed as a peace operation intended to protect Turkish Cypriots from violence and potential ethnic cleansing. This perspective highlights the fears and actual incidents of attacks against the Turkish Cypriot community by Greek Cypriot nationalist groups. Proponents point to the long history of tension and conflict between the Greek and Turkish communities on the island, emphasizing that Turkish Cypriots had been marginalized and subjected to violence, particularly during the intercommunal conflicts of the 1960s.

Turkish leaders justified their country's invasion and initial occupation of 3 percent (later expanding to 36 percent) of the island as part of an attempt to protect its Turkish minority, which constituted 20 percent of the population. In 1983, the Turkish areas declared independence, calling itself the Turkish Republic of Northern

Cyprus (TRNC) —not to be confused with the Republic of Cyprus with northern Nicosia (Lefkoşa in Turkish) as its capital. It was not recognized internationally but only by Ankara. Today, it has gradually become a province of Turkey.

European historians point out that Cyprus was not a single incident but rather a similar Ottoman type past behavior. There were numerous instances in Ottoman history of severe repression and violence against various ethnic and religious groups. Among them include the 1892 persecution of the Yezidis, along with other Christian sects. 1915 was the year of the Assyrian genocide, conducted by the Ottomans in mass killings, forced deportations and starvation, resulting in the deaths of an estimated 250,000 to 300,000 Assyrians. Mass killings of Alevis began in the 1921 Kocgiri Massacre, with periodic intervals continued till the 1995 Istanbul Gazi Quarter Massacre, a horrific incident but one which looked to be the last of its kind. A Greek genocide was also conducted between 1913 to 1922.

Among these incidences, the Armenian genocide stands out due to its scale and plays a key part in Europe's calculations. 1915 is also known as the year of the beginning of mass extermination and deportation of Armenians by the Ottoman continueing till 1923. The deaths of an estimated 1.5 million Armenians, along with the displacement of many others, is widely recognized as one of the first modern genocides, characterized by systematic killings, forced marches, starvation, and other forms of atrocities. Despite overwhelming evidence, the government in Ankara has long denied that a genocide took place, instead characterizing the events as a consequence of wartime conditions. Many countries and international organizations, including the European Parliament and several national governments, have officially recognized the events as genocide. However, formal acknowledgment and widespread recognition of the Armenian genocide remain contentious issues, particularly in the context of diplomatic relations between Turkey and other nations.

France officially recognized the Armenian genocide in 2001 through a law that declared 24 April as a day of commemoration. The move strained relations between France and Turkey, as Ankara vehemently denies that genocide took place and has consistently lobbied against its recognition by other countries. France has also passed legislation criminalizing the denial of genocides. This has further exacerbated tensions with Turkey, which views such laws as an infringement on freedom of speech and an attempt to dictate historical narratives. The move led to a diplomatic confrontation between France and Turkey on multiple occasions. Turkey has protested against France's recognition of the genocide and its efforts to promote awareness and remembrance of the event, while France has defended its position and upheld the importance of acknowledging historical truths. The controversy surrounding the genocide has had a significant impact on bilateral relations. Turkey has threatened with diplomatic and economic reprisals in response to France's recognition, and some of its allies, including Azerbaijan, continue to downplay the event.

The reality is all powers conducted horrors during their reigns, and to make peace with the past is complicated. This difficulty has expanded when such a burden has fallen on the successor states, who have to balance their own history with historical truths.

Modern-day France, also known as the Fifth Republic, may not have conducted itself as "savoir-vivre," but unlike Turkey, it has fared much worse. During the Napoleonic Wars, numerous atrocities were committed by French forces and their opponents that involved significant civilian suffering. In Spain and Portugal, French troops committed widespread atrocities against civilians during the Peninsular War (1807-1814). Massacres, looting, and brutal reprisals were common as French forces faced fierce resistance from local populations and guerrilla fighters. The invasion of Russia in 1812 led to catastrophic losses for both the French army and Russian civilians. The scorched earth tactics employed by both sides resulted in widespread starvation and suffering. Such circumstances also affected populations in areas of modern-day Ukraine. Within France, Napoleon's regime suppressed political opponents, real or perceived, who were often imprisoned, exiled, or executed. If the argument goes that was then and contemporary times are much more relevant, here too France's historical truths speaks volumes of its own conduct.

France's role in Algeria, and the subsequent brutal eight years of bloody conflict is no different from what Paris accuses Ankara. Algeria had been a French colony since 1830, but the indigenous Algerian population faced significant discrimination, economic exploitation, and political marginalization under French rule. In 1945, French authorities killed an estimated 6,000 to 45,000 Algerians over several weeks in what was known as the Setif and Guelma Massacre. Systematic executions continued.

After World War II, Algerian nationalists realized the state of the battered French republic. Led by the National Liberation Front (FLN), the group initiated an armed revolt against French colonial rule on 1 November 1954. The war involved widespread atrocities and horrors inflicted upon the Algerian population by French military and colonial authorities. French forces conducted summary killings of suspected FLN members and sympathizers. Only recently, mass graves and execution sites have been discovered, revealing the scale of extrajudicial killings. Further techniques against suspected Algerians included electric shocks, waterboarding, severe beatings, and sexual abuse. Prominent French figures, including General Paul Aussaresses, later admitted to authorizing and participating in torture. Over 2 million Algerians were forcibly relocated into internment camps, known as "regroupement centers," where living conditions were harsh, and many died from disease and malnutrition. Thousands of Algerians were detained without trial in overcrowded prisons and camps. The French Air Force carried out bombings of rural areas, often indiscriminately targeting civilians, using Napalm (a toxic gelling agent and a volatile petrochemical), in some instances, causing severe burns and deaths. There were even instances of false flag operations where French forces disguised themselves as FLN fighters to carry out atrocities. Estimates of Algerian casualties vary widely, but it is believed that between 300,000 and 1.5 million Algerians died between 1954 and 1962. In recent years, there has been increasing recognition and acknowledgment in France of the atrocities committed during the war. French presidents, including Emmanuel Macron, have taken steps to address this dark chapter.

What should be noted is that despite some admission of the French-inflicted horrors on Algerians, the colonial impulse and lust remained to subdue the French horrors in Algeria.

Historians have cited the French involvement in the 1994 Rwandan genocide, considered one of the most catastrophic events in the 20th century. The foundations of it go back to European colonial policies implemented by Belgium, the former colonial power, which favored the Tutsi elite and created resentment among the Hutu majority. On 6

April 1994, an airplane carrying Rwandan President Juvénal Habyarimana, a Hutu, was shot down near Kigali, the capital of Rwanda. The episode served as the basis for the massacres to come. Radical elements within the Hutu-dominated government and military launched a coordinated campaign of violence against the Tutsi minority. Using militias known as the Interahamwe and the Impuzamugambi, as well as elements of the Rwandan Armed Forces, Hutu radicals began systematically targeting Tutsis and moderate Hutus. Within approximately 100 days, from April to July, an estimated 800,000 Tutsis and moderate Hutus were killed in massacres, systematic killings, and acts of violence, characterized by extreme brutality, with victims often being hacked to death with machetes or shot at close range. Western governments did nothing to intervene, including France which had considerable influence to put a stop to the atrocities that were ongoing.

Habyarimana's regime had a close relationship with President Mitterrand and Rwanda was considered part of France's network of Francophone countries to counter the spread of Anglophone influence in Africa. France provided extensive military support to Habyarimana's government, including arms, training, and even troops. French soldiers were even stationed under the guise of protecting French nationals and maintaining regional stability. France's military involvement increased during the civil war but it viewed its presence to prevent a perceived Anglophone insurgency.

Efforts to deploy peacekeeping forces and humanitarian aid were hampered by a lack of political will and concerns about the risks of intervention. Paris remained silent.

In 1995, the French government recognized for the first time France's responsibility for the Jewish deportations when President Jacques Chirac publicly acknowledged the Vichy government's collaboration with Nazi Germany and apologized to the Jewish people on behalf of the French Republic. The incident had roots in a case on 8 November 2001, when a New York judge threw out a legal suit against the SNCF, France's state-owned railway company by Holocaust survivors over compensation for the company's role in transporting 76,000 French Jews to German labor and extermination camps under French Vichy government during the German occupation of France from 1940 to 1944. In the European view, Vichy France was conveniently forgiven for its role in killing Jews.

In 2024, Europe and France will pay the price as it exacerbates tensions with Turkey. One of the policy changes that infuriated the EU was a 2017 Turkish referendum that gave President Erdoğan more executive powers. If the EU tolerated Hungary's Victor Orbán within the same standards, why the hypocrisy when it came to President Erdoğan? Orbán, in comparison, fares far worse. His far-right Fidesz, a populist party and his own national-conservative government, has implemented numerous changes to Hungary's constitution since coming to power in 2010. Orbán has centralized power in the hands of the executive branch, weakening checks and balances, and undermining the independence of key institutions such as the judiciary and the media. The changes gave the Prime Minister greater control over the appointment of key government officials, the allocation of state resources, and the implementation of policies without significant parliamentary oversight.

Critics argue that Orbán's government has undermined democratic institutions in Hungary, including the judiciary, the media, and civil society organizations. The outcome is the politicization of judicial appointments, the imposition of restrictions on media freedom, and the targeting of independent voices and dissenting opinions. Orbán used the COVID-19 pandemic as an opportunity to further consolidate power. In 2020, the Hungarian Parliament passed a law granting the government sweeping emergency powers to rule by decree indefinitely. The move undermined democratic norms and allowed Orbán to govern without meaningful parliamentary oversight. Orbán's government has implemented changes to Hungary's electoral laws that have been criticized for favoring his own MPs and limiting the ability of opposition parties to compete on a level playing field. These reforms include changes to the electoral system, campaign finance regulations, and the redrawing of electoral districts.

Europe's tolerance for Orbán over Erdoğan is rooted in what looks like a preference of a European versus an Islamic authoritarian. However, subsequent events have given alarm to how European institutions picks and choses their authoritarians they want to work with. The European tone shifted further to engagement with Erdoğan at the height of Europe's migration crisis in 2016. The EU agreed to disburse €6 billion to Ankara to halt the high numbers of refugees.

There is no doubt that the frustration Ankara has felt in EU ascension will now play out in several fronts, and the refugee crisis is one of them. Events in 2016 turned the tide in favor of Turkey and today President Erdoğan can now dictate terms and have European leaders visit his cities without any pre-conditions. There is however, a feeling that the Turkish President may have a change of mind when it comes to EU membership. This would mean the implementation of delegating powers to key state institutions like banks, judiciary, and the media, something the Turkish President could do without. True that the customs union and visa waivers would appeal to Turkish voters but it has little benefits for the Turkish President's agenda of a more dynamic Turkish economy than Europe.

When it comes to Russia, the European double standards are still evident. Hungary is deepening relations with Russia despite what is happening in Ukraine. On 7 April 2024, Peter Pellegrini, the pro-Russian populist leader, was elected as President of Slovakia, adding to the pro-Russia European faction, and yet Turkey is singled out.

After the Russian invasion of Ukraine, Finland and Sweden placed their bids to join NATO. For President Erdoğan, it was an opportunity to renew his country's petition to become a member of the European Union. He compared Sweden's bid to join NATO with Turkey's bid to join the EU, a mere quid pro quo. It is an indication of Turkey's troublesome relationship with Europe. The first 20 months saw the Turkish President blocking Sweden's membership. With Turkey, Hungary too opposed their membership as part of an arrangement where fellow NATO members have the right to veto when it comes to new member states.

The NATO admission is crucially significant for Swedish defense. Gotland, a Swedish Island in the Baltics, is known for its high-quality produce, including lamb, potatoes, and strawberries. It is also a strategic location that can be used by Russian forces to seal off the Baltic states and attack Sweden. Leaders of Sweden had to beg the Turkish President and persuade him to allow them into the alliance. Erdoğan made his objections known. Stockholm was doing too little against Ankara's chief enemy, the Kurdistan Workers Party (PKK), a group banned in Turkey. The EU too, considers the PKK a terrorist organization, but little attention was paid to Turkey's concerns. The matter became so heated that NATO Secretary General Jens

Stoltenberg made several trips to Ankara to petition Erdoğan to include Sweden.

The Turkish stance is certainly a payback for Europe to drag Turkey's membership to the EU for decades. There is no excuse for Brussels to exclude Turkey's approximately 85 million population in economic benefits and cultural links within the EU. Those EU member states who have expressed apprehension about the implications of integrating Turkey into the EU are now paying the price in NATO.

Ankara is in a unique position as it wants to extort more benefits, both from Europe and the United States. It has halted the smooth entry of Finland and Sweden as it found significant leverage to acquire F-16 fighter jets from Washington. Yet it is Washington that the majority of President Erdoğan's electorate and supporters believe to be their greatest threat. The vast majority of Turkey does not believe NATO is a force that can withstand a war against Russia, so it is no surprise that the Turkish President has fostered a friendly relationship with the Kremlin.

Since February 2014, the European Union (EU) has applied eleven rounds of sanctions against Russia after its annexation of Crimea. Ankara and the Kremlin have traded extensively since and even more after February 2022. Turkey doesn't support sanctions on Russia as it holds talks with President Putin. At the same time, Ankara didn't recognize the annexation of Crimea. It continues to support Ukraine in negotiations but maintains a direct line to the Kremlin. It coordinates energy, trade policy, and defense. Ankara has a close exchange with the Kremlin when it comes to military matters, both in Syria and Ukraine. This cozy Ankara-Kremlin relationship is something NATO has no choice but to tolerate. Turkey is the second largest military contingent after the United States in NATO. Its troop numbers are still more than those of Britain, France, and Germany combined. The real problem for Europe is Turkey doesn't need NATO as much as NATO needs Turkey. In a war with Russia, there are more reasons to believe that Ankara might hold back its approximately 690,000 active troops, and will not permit its soil to be used against any attacks on Russia.

Since the founding of the modern Turkish state on 29 October 1923, the country has been demonstrating its military strength in Africa, the Middle East, and in UN peacekeeping missions. Strategically,

Turkey will stay and use NATO, but it will also take a stand against what it considers a priority within its own foreign policy. It will play the United States, Britain, France, Germany, Ukraine, and Russia against each other as Ankara focuses on its own positions. For President Erdoğan, it is his "Balancing Act" to use NATO for his preferences in the global arena and leverage against Russia and Europe.

In 1913, after the conclusion of the First Balkan War, many in Europe thought the weak Ottomans were a shadow of their former triumphs. Their hold over areas in Serbia, Montenegro, Greece, and Bulgaria was not only withering away, but after the war, they will be permanently out of Europe. The Treaty of London recognized the territorial gains of the Balkan states and guaranteed the end of Ottoman presence in Europe, or so they thought. Then, the Second Balkan War erupted shortly after due to territorial disputes and rivalries among the Balkan League members, particularly between Bulgaria and its former allies, Serbia and Greece. Bulgaria, dissatisfied with its share of the spoils from the First Balkan War, within months, launched an attack on its former allies in June 1913. It was repelled by a coalition of Greece, Romania and Serbia, but they also needed the help of the Ottomans. August 1913 brought the Treaty of Bucharest to end the conflict, which forced Bulgaria to cede territory to its neighbors and re-established the pre-war borders in the Balkans.

The Ottomans had infact left a ticking time bomb in Europe, compressing different ethnic groups of character, class, culture, and cuisine, compressed in borders with new states and new realities in the post-Ottoman era. Yugoslavia was formed after World War I, initially as the Kingdom of Serbs, Croats, and Slovenes, later renamed the Kingdom of Yugoslavia in 1929. After World War II, it became a socialist federal republic under Croatian-born Josip Broz Tito. He maintained a delicate balance between the different ethnic groups consisting of Serbs, Croats, Bosniaks, Slovenes, Macedonians, Montenegrins, and Albanians; the ethnic and religious diversity included Orthodox Christians, Catholics, and Muslims, a reality which had roots to the remnants of Ottoman design.

During his 27 years as Prime Minister and then President (in 1974, he made himself President for life) Tito used his strong central government and a policy of "Brotherhood and Unity," as part of his suppression of nationalist movements. It was a way to keep a check on the various ethnic groups aimed to promote a sense of shared identity and solidarity among the diverse population. He suppressed nationalist movements, like the brutal crackdown of the 1971 Croatian Spring. He implemented constitutional reforms in 1974, in part to address some of the grievances of his population. The new constitution granted greater autonomy to the republics, to maintain federal unity. Tito's rule may have brought a spirit of Slavic brotherhood and kept a lid on brewing boiling ethnic tensions, but after his death on 4 May 1980 and the disbanding of the Soviet Union in 1991, conflict and chaos plagued the Balkans.

The institutions of the Yugoslav state were not strong enough to manage the competing demands of various ethnic groups and republics, leading to frequent government changes as coalitions formed and collapsed. Fifteen governments came and went in the space of twelve years after Tito's death, as a result of political fragmentation within the ruling League of Communists of Yugoslavia (LCY). The frequent changes in government prevented the implementation of consistent policies, exacerbating economic problems and ethnic tensions. The emergence of new political parties further complicated the management of a very delicate power structure. Different factions had conflicting agendas, making it difficult to form a stable government. It was also not helped by the dire economic conditions. The 1980s saw significant economic decline in Yugoslavia, including rising debt, inflation, and unemployment. These problems had existed since 1974, but the situation became significantly worse as no single leader could command the same level of authority as Tito. The absence of a strongman central figure led to a weakening of federal control and increased factionalism, neglecting the economic priorities that would destroy the state.

The economic hardship in particular fueled the rise of nationalism, weakening the central government's authority in Belgrade. Ethnic nationalist sentiments began to resurface and political leaders in different republics started advocating for greater autonomy for independence, which led to conflicts and instability. Notable figures like Slobodan Milošević in Serbia, Franjo Tuđman in Croatia, and Alija Izetbegović in Bosnia and Herzegovina found a platform they otherwise did not in previous years. The federal structure started to weaken as republics sought greater autonomy. The central government's inability to address economic and political grievances further fueled the desire for independence among various republics.

The problem with the complex federal structure, which gave significant autonomy to republics and provinces, made it difficult to implement cohesive national policies. The decentralized system hindered effective governance and facilitated political maneuvering by regional leaders. The richer provinces of Slovenia and Croatia resented the demands of poorer members of the union in Bosnia and Herzegovina, Macedonia, Serbia and Kosovo, demanding more control over local resources.

The political instability and rising nationalist sentiments eventually led to the disintegration of Yugoslavia. The country descended into a series of violent conflicts known as the Yugoslav Wars, resulting in the breakup of Yugoslavia into several independent states.

Some historians argue that the legacy of decentralized Ottoman governance influenced the challenges faced by the rise and fall of Yugoslavia. The ethnic and religious divisions that had been managed under Ottoman rule and later suppressed under Yugoslav Communism re-emerged with the weakening of central authority. The legacy of Ottoman administrative divisions contributed to the complex and often conflicting national aspirations within Yugoslavia. The resurgence of nationalist sentiments in the late 20th century can be partly traced back to the historical grievances and identities shaped during the Ottoman period. The view that the rise and fall of Yugoslavia were influenced by its Ottoman past and while the creation of Yugoslavia represented an attempt to move beyond the divisions of the Ottoman era, the eventual disintegration of the state can be seen as a resurgence of those historical divisions. While anti-Turkish politicians in Brussels can rest on the narrative that the rest of Europe will not meet a similar fate as Yugoslavia, Europe will however lose sleep over the rise of nationalism, and the weakening of its authority in Brussels. Finally, there is something they cannot blame the Ottomans but would need to look more from within.

As European governments and Brussels obsesses over immigration, climate change, security, and Ukraine, President Erdoğan sits alongside the most powerful countries in the world directing his interests.

As Europe seeks Turkey's cooperation to bring the Ukraine conflict to a close, European governments face a pivotal choice: either ignore the lasting effects of the Ottoman legacy and continue to struggle in their relationship with Turkey. It is a crucial step for Europe to understand Turkey. Without it, Europe could foreseeably face avoidable consequences, something especially at this time they can do without.

The successful defense of Vienna was celebrated as a victory for Christian Europe. However, while the Ottomans may have physically retreated, the impact of their historical presence continue to resonate today. The Ottomans were not just a Muslim Empire; they were also a European Empire that shaped southeastern Europe for centuries, something Europe had not come to terms with to this day.

The urgency of the situation, with President Putin wanting Ukraine at any price, underscores the necessity for European leaders to bridge historical and cultural gaps with Turkey. By comprehensively understanding Turkey's history and its influence on contemporary policies, Europe can foster a more effective partnership, crucial for resolving the Ukraine war. The alternative is a continued struggle in European-Turkish relations, which could lead to unnecessary complications and hinder efforts to achieve long-term peace not only in Ukraine but also in Europe.

Chapter 10

THE SO CALLED BETRAYAL

The disbanding of the Soviet Union in December 1991 marked the beginning of significant geopolitical shifts, setting the domino effect of Eastern European states and their integration into West European structures, particularly through membership in Europe's exclusive clubs. It was a means of enhancing their economic fortunes, and ensuring their own security in the post-Soviet era. Former Soviet client states may have believed that they had left the Soviet fold, but sizeable portions of their populations didn't. Europe's leaders may have also believed Eastern Europe left Russia's sphere of influence, but in reality, Russia did not leave them.

Poland served in parity with Ukraine as part of the Soviet priorities of geographical strategic significance. Control over Polish areas provided the Soviets with access to the Baltic Sea and facilitated its expansion westward. In the post-Cold War era, Poland's location served as a buffer between Russia and NATO. All that changed on 12 March 1999, when Poland joined NATO. This was an occurrence that pumped up the security anxiety of the Kremlin, and from then on, developments in Poland were watched even more closely.

The partitions of Poland in the late 18th century, the 1919 Polish-Soviet War, and the coordinated invasion of Poland by Nazi Germany and the Soviet Union, as outlined in the August 1939 Molotov-Ribbentrop Pact, shaped the Kremlin's view in the wider European context. Poland, the second most-populous Communist regime and the largest member of the Warsaw Pact, played a significant role in setting off a domino effect that contributed to the end of Communism in Europe.

Almost a decade prior to the disbanding of the Soviet Union, Poland experienced widespread social and economic unrest, primarily driven by dissatisfaction with the Communist regime. The Solidarity movement, led by Lech Wałęsa, emerged as a powerful force advocating for Polish workers' rights, political reforms, and greater freedom. It led to the historic Round Table Agreement between the Polish Communist government of Wojciech Jaruzelski and Solidarity, paving the way for partially free elections in June 1989. Solidarity won by a landslide, leading to the formation of the first non-Communist government in Poland for decades. At the end of the year, the Sejm (Polish parliament) approved the Mieczysław Rakowski's government's reform program to transform its economy rapidly from centrally planned to free-market, and also agreed to amend the constitution to eliminate references to the "leading role" of the Communist Party. The events in Poland emboldened opposition movements and reformist elements across Eastern Europe, leading to a series of revolutions and upheavals.

The fall of the Berlin Wall in November 1989 and the collapse of Communist regimes in countries like Hungary, Czechoslovakia, and East Germany were direct consequences of the momentum generated by Poland's example, which set off a chain reaction that significantly weakened the Soviet hold in other areas including Albania, Bulgaria, and Romania.

For many Russians, particularly those who had lived through the Soviet era, the collapse of the Soviet Union's superpower status represented the rise of economic upheaval, and the fragmentation of a vast geopolitical entity. Europe was changing and new forces were at play rooted in the increased demands of its population for openness, freedom and liberalization.

The collapse of super power status of the Soviet Union was not a result of America or Europe's actions, but rather the result of Soviet Union's own making. President Putin claims that, in exchange for allowing German reunification in 1990, Moscow received a binding promise that NATO would not expand "not 1 inch" eastward. It is a complicated subject marked by convenience and complexities that has been distorted by the pro-Kremlin voices.

What those around the Russian President do not speak about is after the Iron Curtain collapsed, Central and and Eastern European countries were pounding on NATO's door, asking for admission. While there was a general feeling of aligning with the free-market economy of the West, now that the Soviet Union was no longer there, there was another aim; that the former Warsaw pact countries wanted to create a military alliance of their own.

The establishment of the Visegrád Group, which consists of three Central European countries including Poland, then Czechoslovakia, and Hungary, formed in 1991, aimed to foster cooperation among its members on security, defense, and economic development. While the group is not a military alliance like NATO, it represents a regional partnership with shared interests. NATO ultimately became the beneficiary that would integrate former Warsaw Pact members into the broader Western security framework.

When the first class joined NATO on 12 March 1999, Putin was not in office, but upon taking over the Russian Presidency, he did view the development as both a threat and a betrayal of a promise. It was a breach of trust that justified Russia's attack on former Soviet states in the succeeding decades.

While historians and analysts have viewed the matter through different lenses, one perspective is certainly significant. A reunified Germany certainly pushed NATO borders 283 miles eastward. The German reunification and the conditions around it were itself very "hypothetical," which had nothing to do with NATO. Events around that time included the actions of then Secretary of State James Baker, who wrote in confidence to his German counterpart that discussion of NATO's range of jurisdiction should "be avoided in the future" after strong reservations from President George H.W. Bush.

If the Russian invasion of Ukraine is a response to the past, directed at the actions of the United States, then it should be clarified that Washington did not initiate NATO enlargement, but instead honored and complied with the "not 1 inch" eastward condition.

In 1989, revolutionary movements in Europe were slowly gathering momentum and that too played a part in the German reunification equation. Nearly five-decades prior, Germany had surrendered unconditionally after World War II. The four powers on the winning side, the United States, France, Britain, and the Soviet Union, still had differences over what they envisioned in a defeated and divided Germany.

France sought to ensure that Germany would never again become a military threat to Europe, especially to France itself. Paris advocated for the complete demilitarization of Germany, aiming to disarm the German military and dismantle its military-industrial complex. This was achieved through the Potsdam Agreement, which imposed strict limits on the size and capabilities of the German armed forces. France supported the division of Germany into occupation zones alongside the United States, the Soviet Union, and Britain. To weaken Germany's central authority and prevent it from posing a unified threat to its neighbors, all powers agreed to the French conditions. Additionally, France supported the establishment of a decentralized political system in Germany, with regional autonomy and power-sharing mechanisms. Crucially, France had a vested interest in exerting influence over the economic reconstruction of West Germany, particularly in the western areas under its control that would, by default, assist its own economy. Through initiatives such as the Marshall Plan, France aimed to rebuild the West German economy in a way that would prevent it from becoming too powerful in Europe.

Britain sought to maintain a balance of power in Europe, which included preventing any one country, including West Germany, from becoming too dominant, which involved supporting European integration efforts, as a counterweight through the creation of the European Coal and Steel Community, which laid the foundations for the European Union (EU).

The Soviet Union extracted reparations from Germany to help rebuild the Soviet economy, which had been devastated by the war. The Kremlin dismantled German industrial infrastructure in its zone of occupation (primarily in East Germany) and transported it back to the Soviet Union as reparations. Additionally, the Soviets sought to exert control over the economic reconstruction, aiming to create a socialist state that was politically aligned with the Soviet Union, creating the German Democratic Republic (GDR) in 1949 and maintaining tight control over its foreign, political, economic, and military affairs.

The prospect of German reunification was never in the cards, but when it came, it rattled all the powers with disagreements. French

President François Mitterrand reportedly said, "I love Germany so much that I'm glad there are two of them." When Mitterrand made this remark in the context of the reunification of Germany, it showed how France was so against the move.

British Prime Minister Margaret Thatcher said, "We have beaten the Germans twice. Now they're back!" She had mixed feelings about German reunification and was initially cautiously skeptical. She was concerned about the potential economic and political consequences of a united Germany, particularly given its historical role in European conflicts. Thatcher worried that a reunified Germany might seek to dominate Europe again through its economic arm and upset the balance of power in NATO.

The American President, George H.W. Bush, unlike his counterparts, was neutral on the matter. "A united Germany fully sovereign in its internal and external affairs. The Federal Republic of Germany will be German. That is what we want, and that is what the German people want."

Britain and France were not at odds with the Soviet Union, but if the United States spearheaded the reunification, they were cautious about what Mikhail Gorbachev would want in return for giving up East Germany. The Soviet Union still had a formidable military force, including a large standing army, a large nuclear weapons arsenal, and significant naval and air capabilities, posing a direct threat in a conventional and nuclear conflict. It also supported various proxy conflicts and revolutionary movements in different parts of the world, including in Africa, Asia, and Latin America, which could threaten European economic and strategic interests. West German Foreign Minister Hans-Dietrich Genscher was certain that Gorbachev would want some security assurances in return.

The prospect of Poland, whose borders stretched from central and Europe's east, positioning at the crossroads of various regional dynamics was a concern as well, as it could magnify the effects of a reunified Germany. Fears of Poland's four provinces including the industrial rich Silesia, Pomerania, East Brandenburg, and East Prussia, formerly German areas which were transferred to Poland as part of the Potsdam Agreement at the end of World War II, may opt to join a reunified Germany.

There was a feeling, however, that Wojciech Jaruzelski's Polish government and his successors had little appetite to give support to the prospect of a reunified Germany or join any Western European union. But while that was a Soviet safeguard, other states posed a similar problem. Landlocked Hungary looked to be a Soviet apprehension. The government of Miklós Németh permitted large numbers of East Germans to pass through his country and make their way into West Germany. It was a decision that ultimately led to events in the fall of the Berlin Wall on 9 November 1989.

Foreign Minister Genscher proposed the idea to Secretary of State James Baker whether the Soviet General Secretary could be given monetary options. Baker visited Gorbachev at the Kremlin on 9 February 1990 and the discussion centered around letting a part of Germany go. What was discussed was NATO's jurisdiction would move "not 1 inch" eastward. After the meeting, Baker flew back to Washington. President George H.W. Bush was not pleased. Negotiating the future of NATO was not on the cards. In the American President's view, NATO was fine just the way it was. After that meeting, Baker wrote to the West German Foreign Minister, apologizing for the confusion and saying that NATO was not a subject they should be talking about. Whatever offer was given to Gorbachev was no longer valid. Two weeks later, Bush invited West German Chancellor Helmut Kohl and his wife to Camp David. One of the subjects discussed was that the United States was not going to negotiate over the future of NATO. Chancellor Kohl did remind the American President that German reunification was a priority for his government, and to accomplish that, Secretary Gorbachev was going to want something in exchange for East Germany.

The Berlin Wall had fallen and Kohl's government was under pressure as population movements were frequent. The Soviets stood in the way to what the majority of Germans wanted. Foreign Minister Genscher's monetary option appeared as the only way forward and it would be West Germany to spearhead the effort of reunification, not the United States.

A "2 plus 4" negotiation involved discussions between the two Germanys (East and West) and the four wartime powers (United States, Soviet Union, Britain, and France) that would honor the terms and conditions of German reunification. The talks went on until 12 September 1990. It concluded with the signing of the agreement on the final settlement with respect to German reunification, commonly known as the "Treaty on German Unity." The agreement paved the way for the reunification of East and West Germany. It addressed issues such as borders, military matters, and Germany's international status.

In November 1990, Germany and Poland signed a separate treaty confirming the Oder-Neisse line as the definitive border between the two countries. This German-Polish Border Treaty was a clear indication that Germany accepted the post-World War II borders and had no intention of pursuing any territorial claims.

The German reunification signing ceremony took place on 3 October 1990 in Moscow and marked the formal end of Soviet presence in Germany. Chancellor Kohl's government agreed to pay the costs for withdrawing Soviet troops and resettling them back to their area of origin and authorized close to 94 billion Deutsche marks ($50 billion) for the Kremlin's acceptance of reunification, a decision made by the Gorbachev–Kohl meeting of 14-16 July 1990. However, even while negotiations were ongoing, nothing stood in the way of German reunification. The line "not 1 inch" eastward was not in any treaty. Even if Kohl had not paid Gorbachev, there is a feeling that the Soviets would not only have been driven out by popular protests and numerous uprisings to leave East Germany, but would have no choice but to retreat its forces. The outcome of a German payment was a mere gesture of a peaceful departure rather than a violent one.

The Treaty on German Unity, by default, explicitly set the domino effect which allowed NATO to enlarge across the former Cold War lines. Gorbachev's government signed, ratified, and accepted the payment. This is something Putin and his supporters do not mention.

As the Soviet Union disbanded, the Warsaw Pact was officially dissolved. Now that the Soviet Union was gone, what would the aims of NATO be? The most prominent argument was due to geopolitical realities. Just because the Cold War ended, there was no guarantee that the Soviet Union or its successor, Russia, was going to unfollow the path of confrontation with the West.

Former Iron Curtain states embarked on a journey of transformations. They delved into arms reduction, a process that intertwined with their newfound independence and aspirations to join Western Europe's most exclusive clubs, including the European

Union. The reduction of arms was not merely a dismantling of weapons; it was a reimagining of national priorities, where the resources once allocated to military were now redirected towards building their infrastructures and revitalizing their economies. This shift orchestrated a mosaic of peace efforts, with each country contributing its unique piece to the tapestry of regional stability. The intricate and often enigmatic process of arms reduction required international cooperation, elements that were crucial in transforming the once heavily armed regions into peace and development. In this kaleidoscopic period of change, there were investments in education and healthcare. The former Soviet republics reimagined their identities and roles on the global stage, moving away from their Cold War legacies towards a more interconnected Europe.

At the 1994 Budapest Memorandum, independent Ukraine, which was the world's third-largest nuclear power at the time, gave up its Soviet nuclear arsenal. It was a preferential demand of Britain, France, the United States, and Yeltsin's Russia. In exchange, Ukraine received "assurances" of its territorial integrity. Clinton and Yeltsin were the chief guarantors. China was not a signatory; it did however provide a separate statement in connection with the memorandum, expressing its support for the security assurances provided to Ukraine. There is evidence in 2022 that the Russians used some of the non-nuclear missiles relinquished to the Kremlin by Ukrainians as part of the Budapest Memorandum to attack Ukrainians. It is considered a key violation of the 1994 agreement.

Ukraine is perceived as the direct Putin response to the "not 1 inch" eastward betrayal, but Germany was at the receiving end of the real consequences.

West Germany began to depend significantly on Russian gas imports during the late 1960s and early 1970s, particularly after the conclusion of long-term gas supply contracts with the Soviet Union. This dependence grew steadily over the following decades, especially with the expansion of natural gas infrastructure and the gradual decline of German domestic gas production. By 2005, Russia had become Germany's largest supplier of natural gas. Almost two decades later, the German economy, which was far from a resilient system that could adapt to external disturbances, became overly dependent on cheap Russian gas, Chinese supply chains, and large foreign export markets.

After the 24 February 2022 invasion of Ukraine, steel, fertilizer, and chemical plants all closed or on the brink of shutting down. German automakers are being forced to consider moving domestic production to countries where energy is cheaper, potentially to the Middle East or southern Europe. Green hydrogen is looking to be the best option in a situation where cheap Russian gas is sanctioned. In response to the energy crisis, Chancellor Scholz unveiled a national subsidy that was not coordinated with European Union (EU) allies and was thus seen as sabotaging their own efforts. It is an outcome where Germany in the future, may become the untrusted and lonely financier of Europe.

From the 2008 Georgian war to the February 2014 annexation of Crimea, the hit on MH-17, and the harm to Russian opposition leader Alexei Navalny, Germany always had a special relationship with Russia, unlike any other country in Europe. German technology firms have found an exclusive relationship with energy-rich Russia. Such arrangements expanded to football sponsorships and German companies making large investments in Russian manufacturing, particularly in sectors like automotive, machinery, chemicals, transportation, telecommunications, and construction. Similarly, Russian companies have invested in Germany, particularly in sectors like technology, real estate, and finance.

The Russian military, as we see it today, despite their debacles in Ukraine, more than a decade earlier went through a thorough series of modernization cycles with the help of German firms. The sale of combat simulation systems in 2008 from Germany to Russia for €100 million, stirred controversy and raised concerns. It centered on the potential implications for European security and stability. Combat simulation systems are advanced military technologies that can be used for training purposes but can also have dual-use applications for military planning and invasions. The sale attracted criticism from especially the United States, drawing concerns of highly secure technologies being sold to Russia, which could undermine Europe's regional security or contribute to military aggression against NATO. Merkel's government eventually canceled the deal despite 95% having already been delivered. Georgia was at the receiving end of such German assistance that made a Russian army more lethal as it nearly took over Tbilisi during the 2008 Russian invasion.

2008 was not the start of Germany's waiver to Russia but rather a continuation of Soviet-era policies. In February 2014, after Russia annexed Crimea, Berlin not only did not join in the Western-backed sanctions but continued to do business as usual with the Kremlin. The murder of a Chechen rebel on German soil barely caused any diplomatic ruptures. President Putin had every reason to believe that Germany was playing lip service to the West in the Minsk agreement with Ukraine, ultimately producing a shallow deal that neither side had any impetus to honor. As he saw it, Germany was giving him an open playfield to do what he pleased in Europe, and so the Russian President took full advantage. The real consequence, in turn, was as Putin sent his forces to Ukraine, he also had an eye on Germany.

Soviet-occupied East Germany, officially known as the German Democratic Republic (GDR), was reunited with West Germany on 3 October 1990. Nearly 35 years later, cities and towns of the former GDR have faced economic challenges, including deindustrialization, unemployment, and disparities in economic development, compared to the prosperous western areas of the country. Under a reunified Germany today, the identities of residents in the former GDR areas are very much an East German identity. The residents of what used to be West Germany are today called "German," but those who come from East Germany are referred to as "the other." The sentiment of belonging to what was once East Germany among today's inhabitants in these areas is crucially strong. There are reports that among the youth, 20%-30% are proud of their East German or "the other" identity. The leftover Soviet relics, the pavements, the tower blocks, a difference in income levels, the less valued real estate, the lack of professionals and even to some level the use of German as a language, means the success of reunification has not entirely become complete.

There is a feeling among some quarters in Berlin that the so-called issues of "East Germans" are centered on the majority of its population moving to Cologne, Frankfurt and Stuttgart, leaving areas in Germany's east with little innovation. It has also not been helped by the poverty and the rise of the far-right political groups.

The Alternative for Germany (AfD) is a right-wing populist party that has gained significant traction, including in Germany's east. AfD's anti-establishment stance, skepticism toward immigration and anti-multiculturalism, and criticism of mainstream political parties have attracted support from voters disillusioned with the political status quo. In Germany's east, where economic challenges persist, and nationalist sentiments can be stronger, AfD has performed particularly well in elections, capitalizing on population grievances. It has 78 seats (out of 734) in the German parliament (Bundestag) and is part of the opposition.

Such grievances have direct links to the Soviet exit from GDR. When state-run industries closed after reunification, mass unemployment spread throughout the former GDR areas. Huge parts of the east never fully recovered. Under the Soviets, individuals, families and even single parents had state support, but after reunification, jobs, professional training, and a sense of a permanent income never truly materialized.

Germany's West in contrast composed of a state-of-the-art manufacturing sector, which encompasses automotive, machinery, chemicals, and engineering industries. It provides a diverse range of high-quality goods and services exported to markets worldwide with a network of globally competitive companies, a strong infrastructure, and a reputation for engineering excellence. It is at the forefront of technological innovation in renewable energy and pharmaceuticals, with heavy research and development (R&D), fostering collaboration between industry, academia, and governments driving innovation characterized by the presence of a large number of small and medium-sized enterprises (SMEs), known as the Mittelstand. These companies form the backbone of the German economy, contributing to job creation, innovation, and economic resilience. Areas of Germany's west consist of a highly skilled and well-educated workforce, supported by vocational training programs and a tradition of apprenticeships with low unemployment rates compared to many other European countries. The economy of Germany's west formed a robust social safety net, in contrast with a completely reversed state of the economy in Germany's east, which enabled the idea that reunification only brought German lands together and not Germans.

Putin has capitalized on this. To many Germans, Russian propaganda, which reaches many of the areas of Germany's east, has worked to make NATO the villain. The myth that the United States made the move, when in reality, it was West Germany that began a set of initiatives leading to reunification and later the disbanding of the Soviet Union is molded in numerous ways. Rarely is the truth discussed. The Russian propaganda has driven a wedge into German public opinion, sowing doubt about the German alliance with the United States, especially as Germans no longer have cheap Russian gas or either of the two Nordstreams to their disposal, and their Chancellor is siding more to the welfare of Ukrainians when the majority of Germans want to stay out of the war.

Germany, due to its historically close relationship with Russia, may hold a perspective that diverges from what Europe's leaders have believed for decades. While Eastern Europe ostensibly left the Soviet Union, in reality, Russia, has never left them. Similarly, Germany may have reunified its East, but in truth, its eastern regions have maintained enduring connections with the Soviet Union and its successor, Russia.

President Putin's obsession with taking Ukraine at any price, further complicates this dynamic, as Germany's unique position within Europe shapes its approach to the conflict. The deep-seated ties between Germany's east and Russia challenging the broader European narrative of complete political and economic separation from Moscow. This historical context influences Germany's current policies and its diplomatic stance, potentially causing friction within the EU as it seeks a unified strategy against Russian aggression in Ukraine and potentially in Europe.

Chapter 11

LIKE DRESDEN

On 18 February 2007, President Putin delivered a speech that was widely interpreted as critical of U.S. foreign policy. Putin expressed concern about what he perceived as the growing dominance of the United States in global affairs and its unilateral approach to international relations. He criticized U.S. military interventions, particularly in Iraq, and accused the United States of pursuing policies that undermined international stability and security.

"First and foremost, the United States has overstepped its national borders in the economic, political, and humanitarian spheres it imposes on other nations. Well, who would like this? Who would like this?" "It results in the fact that no one feels safe," said the Russian President. "I want to emphasize this… no one feels safe."

The atmosphere in the ballroom of the Munich Security Conference changed. American Senators John McCain and Joseph Lieberman were present along with then Secretary of Defense Robert Gates and several other European heads of state, including President of Ukraine Viktor Yushchenko and the German Chancellor Angela Merkel. Even those who shared Putin's criticism of the Iraq war reacted with surprise and concern.

Putin's words may have been a reaction to what happened a month prior. In January 2007, U.S. President George W. Bush announced a new strategy involving a significant increase in American troops in Iraq, commonly known as "the surge." This involved deploying an additional 20,000 troops, with the aim of improving security, especially in Baghdad and in Al Anbar Province. The surge was part of a broader counterinsurgency strategy led by General David Petraeus, which emphasized securing and protecting the civilian population to undermine insurgent support. Besides Britain and the United States, other coalition forces from various countries were involved in military operations and reconstruction efforts in Iraq, but as the surge went on, so too did troop withdrawals. Britain, America's chief partner, began withdrawing troops, reducing its levels from approximately 7,000 to 5,500 and aimed to lower this number further to about 2,500 by the end of the year. NATO member Denmark, withdrew its 460 troops stationed in southern Iraq by August, as did Poland and Lithuania.

Putin saw the invasion of Iraq conducted without explicit authorization from the United Nations Security Council. Russia believed that military action should only be taken with U.N. approval and felt that the George W. Bush administration acted unilaterally, undermining the authority of the U.N. If the Americans could go alone in Iraq and violate their own creation of international order, why couldn't he do so in Chechnya, Georgia, or even in Ukraine?

The message was clear, Putin was driving towards a new Cold War. It was an era that he knew personally from his time nearly two decades back from the same city in which he now made such a declaration.

Putin was stationed as a KGB intelligence officer in what is today Germany. The city of his birth, St. Petersburg, founded by Tsar Peter the Great in 1703, did have some German influences. Designed to showcase Russia's connection to Europe, in cultural exchanges and influences between German and Russian communities, particularly in areas in music, literature, and education. The Russian ruler Catherine the Great, was of German descent (born in Stettin, Prussia, now Szczecin, Poland) and ruled from 1762 to 1796. She played a significant role in the development of the city and the surrounding region. Her reign saw the continuation of cultural exchanges between Russia and German-speaking territories, influencing various aspects of Russian culture and society. Throughout the 18th and 19th centuries, German settlers migrated to various regions of the Russian Empire, including St. Petersburg and its surrounding areas. These settlers often brought with them their language, customs, and traditions, contributing to the cultural diversity of the city.

Like some families in St. Petersburg, the historical narrative of Germany's relationship with inhabitants of the city is marred by tragic episodes. Ekaterina Semenovna Tikhonova, Putin's maternal grandmother, allegedly of Ukrainian descent, fell victim to the brutal realities of World War II. In 1941, during the German occupation of the Tver region in northwest of Moscow, she was killed by German forces. This incident underscores the profound and personal impact of the war on Putin's family. The occupation of the Tver region, like many others, was marked by violence and oppression, with civilians often bearing the brunt of the conflict, shaping attitudes of a new generation of Russians and the KGB.

While stationed in Munich, Putin's primary responsibilities would have included gathering intelligence on political, economic, and military developments in Western Europe. West Germany was a key NATO ally; as a KGB officer, Putin would have operated under deep cover, meaning he likely used a false identity and worked discreetly to avoid detection. Putin would have been involved in intelligence-gathering activities, such as monitoring diplomatic communications, recruiting and handling agents, and conducting surveillance on individuals or organizations of interest to the Soviet Union. Munich's status as a major center of political, economic, and military activity in Western Europe would have made it a strategically important location for Soviet intelligence operations. Some sources claim his alias was Mr. Adamov, an employee of TASS (Telegrafnoye Agentstvo Sovetskogo Soyuza), which translates to the Telegraph Agency, at the time the official Soviet news agency. Some sources also attest that Putin was expelled from West Germany. In May 1983, it was widely believed that the West German intelligence, the Bundesnachrichtendienst (BND), penetrated a network that led to the expulsion of Soviet diplomats. It is said they were involved in gathering classified information, conducting surveillance on West German officials, military installations, and possibly engaging in other intelligence-gathering activities. The story goes that Putin was sent back to Moscow for further training. He goes on to graduate from the 401st Andropov Red Banner Institute (named after Brezhnev's successor) in 1984 and began his work in the KGB's 5th Directorate.

The primary mission of the 5th Directorate was to monitor and suppress any form of dissent or opposition to the Soviet regime that was perceived as ideological or political in nature. This included monitoring religious groups, political dissidents, intellectuals, writers, artists, and any other individuals or organizations deemed to be spreading ideas counter to the Communist Party's ideology. It employed a variety of tactics to carry out its mission, including surveillance, infiltration, censorship, harassment, intimidation, and imprisonment of dissidents. The 5th Directorate worked closely with other branches of the KGB, as well as with local security agencies and informants, to identify individuals and groups, including political dissidents, human rights activists, religious organizations, ethnic minorities seeking autonomy or independence, nationalist movements, and anyone else perceived as a threat to the Soviet regime's control. The activities of the 5th Directorate were a significant aspect of the Soviet Union's repressive apparatus. It also played a central role in maintaining the Communist Party's monopoly on power. Its methods and tactics were often brutal and resulted in the persecution, imprisonment, and sometimes even the death of those who dared to challenge the regime's authority. Following the disbanding of the Soviet Union in December 1991, the KGB was disbanded, and its functions were reorganized into various successor agencies in the newly independent states. The 5th Directorate was officially abolished in 1989 and renamed. Most of the division became the core of the new Tax Police, and many of its officers went into politics or the private sector, with others reassigned to other security posts. Some even made their way to the top of the Russian internal security services.

When Putin became President, this specific Directorate was tasked to remove individuals he considered a threat. Among them was Mikhail Khodorkovsky, a former Russian Oligarch and the founder of the Yukos oil company. The once richest man in Russia in July 2003 was charged with fraud, tax evasion, and other economic crimes. Khodorkovsky along with Platon Lebedev, the fourth largest shareholder in Yukos, was arrested on suspicion of illegally acquiring a stake in the state-owned fertilizer firm Apatit in 1994. Yukos was under investigation from the chief prosecutor's office. Its merger with Sibneft was delayed due to the Antitrust Commission's approval. Yukos was later acquired by the Russian state-owned energy giant

Gazprom in 2005. Khodorkovsky suffered a similar fate as Boris Berezovsky, another prominent Russian Oligarch, who amassed significant wealth and political influence during the chaotic years following the disbanding of the Soviet Union. He was a close ally of President Boris Yeltsin and played a key role in bringing Putin to power. However, Berezovsky later fell out of favor with Putin and went into self-imposed exile in Britain, where he became a vocal critic of the Putin regime. Berezovsky died in 2013 under mysterious circumstances. Other Oligarchs were targeted, followed by legal prosecution, harassment, exile, and, in some cases, assassination. This is a similar pattern to the operations of the dreaded East German Stasi, also known as The Ministry for State Security or the State Security Service of East Germany (GDR).

While Dresden may have provided a learning center for Soviet intelligence officers, it was still a sleepy town. The real center of Cold War intelligence was in divided Berlin, approximately 100 miles north. Dresden, by comparison, was home to a mere 6 to 13 KGB officers under the guise of diplomatic translators.

The architecture of the area was a mix of socialist modernism and restored Baroque structures. Iconic buildings like the Frauenkirche remained as ruins, preserved as a war memorial, while others like the Zwinger Palace and the Semperoper had been painstakingly restored. Many parts of the city featured utilitarian, prefabricated buildings known as "Plattenbau," typical of East German urban planning.

The Elbe River ran through the city, with its banks offering some respite from the industrial feel. Dresden was known for its rich cultural heritage, hosting art galleries, theaters, and a strong classical music scene. In everyday life, its inhabitants dealt with shortages of consumer goods, long queues, and limited freedoms, but residents of the larger East Germany (GDR) enjoyed higher living standards than the Soviet Union. While the GDR regime had significant limitations and faced criticism for its authoritarian nature and lack of political freedoms, there were some positives in living standards, particularly when compared to other Eastern Bloc states.

The GDR implemented extensive social welfare programs, including universal healthcare, education, and housing. Healthcare was provided free of charge to citizens, and the government invested heavily in education, with literacy rates and educational attainment levels comparable to those in Western countries. GDR made moderate strides in promoting gender equality compared to many other countries, including the West. Women in East Germany had equal access to education, employment, and political participation, and the government actively encouraged women to enter the workforce. Despite economic challenges, the GDR invested in infrastructure development, including transportation networks, public housing, and industrial facilities. The government prioritized infrastructure projects to support economic growth and improve living standards for their citizens.

The socialist state had a vibrant cultural scene, with significant contributions to literature, music, theater, and the arts. Additionally, the GDR invested in sports and achieved notable success in international sporting competitions. East Germany qualified for the UEFA European Championship in 1972, held in Belgium. It was their first and only time of participation. They reached the quarter-finals but were eliminated by the Soviet Union. It must have hurt for the GDR regime to see its rival, West Germany go on to win the tournament, beating the Soviet Union 3–0 in the final. They made amends in 1976, at the Summer Olympics in Montreal, when East Germany won the Men's Olympic football tournament.

Politically, East Germany differed from the Soviet Union and other Soviet blocs. It had a number of separate political parties, even though it was still firmly under Communist rule, albeit within a tightly controlled framework that ensured the dominance of the ruling Socialist Unity Party of Germany (SED), which exercised significant control over the political system, economy, and society. Other opposition parties operated within the parameters set by the SED and faced considerable constraints on their activities, including censorship and surveillance by state authorities. Additionally, there were other political parties and organizations that represented specific interests, such as the Liberal Democratic Party (LDPD) and the National Democratic Party (NDPD). These parties, while technically independent entities, were also subject to control and manipulation by the SED. Despite the presence of multiple political parties, East Germany remained a one-party state in practice, with the SED holding a monopoly on political power. The political system was characterized by authoritarianism, censorship, and limited political freedoms, with dissent or opposition to the ruling party often met with repression.

East Germany housed 380,000 Soviet troops and a few sets of intermediate-range missiles. It also served as an economic and industrial hub within the Eastern Bloc, with close economic ties to Soviet economic investment and assistance.

Dresden was also the second-largest East German city. Among intelligence networks, it was known for the illegal stripping of state resources and money laundering through the Coordinating Committee (Ko-Ko), the Communist Party wing that actually ran the transactional operations.

Of all the many inter-governmental bodies, the Joint Governmental Commission for Economic and Scientific-Technological Cooperation, established in 1966, presided over an imposing array of Soviet East German agreements between individual enterprises, industrial branches, scientific and technological cooperation. That was the formal arrangement, but underneath, an array of illegal activities was part of the state-sponsored means to do the Soviet's dirty work.

From 1984 onwards, money was flowing out of East Berlin through state-owned trading companies. KGB, the Ministry for State Security (i.e., Stasi) officials were covertly moving millions of East German Deutsche Marks through their channels, notably in banks in Austria and Switzerland, with the help of Austrian Communists and into a host of new accounts before anonymously investing it. The state-owned Novum bank is said to have transferred significant capital to then Österreichische Landesbank (ÖLB), one of the largest banks in Austria. By 1986, the KGB and the Stasi were active players in this practice.

The money laundering process has only matured today, but it began with a directorate of the KGB, which was in charge of overseeing many of these schemes and using shell companies that didn't even have to file any proper accounts from their pro-banking governments. These shell companies didn't pay taxes and didn't have to report their real profiting business activities. They often falsified their accounts, and billions of dollars came through untraceable bank accounts. Once the money got into private equity funds or what was the investment arm of banks, the money was used for investments. It was a big loophole in avoiding disclosure requirements. At the time, law enforcement was not empowered to look beyond certain jurisdictions.

The most local Western authorities could do was investigate the untraceable source of financing, but they could not go further beyond that.

Western intelligence agencies realized that in 1962, Nikita Khrushchev's government formally began the key ingredient that was the founding scheme of money laundering: narcotics. Cocaine was purchased from dealers in Latin America, shipped to the East German port city of Rostock, and transported to divided Berlin. The Stasi would then deliver it to their handlers, who transported it to their channels in West Germany. Both the Stasi and the KGB operated on two fronts. One, they took their cuts in the arrangement to bolster the East German currency, the East German Mark. Second, they laundered their profits in investments through several layers of middlemen, including Eastern Bloc bankers, who had ties to Western banking institutions.

By the time Gorbachev came to power in March 1985, the Stasi-KGB scheme had become so lucrative that it became a major stumbling block between *perestroika* ("restructuring") as a means to decentralize and improve economic decision-making. The Berlin Wall divided the city into East and West sections to prevent the mass emigration of Germans. It became the focal point of this Stasi-KGB arrangement. On 12 June 1987, President Ronald Reagan made a famous speech in which he said, "Mr. Gorbachev, tear down this wall!" at the Brandenburg Gate, a divided symbol of divided Berlin. His speech, written by Peter Robinson, became one of the most important symbols of the United States' commitment to the fall of the Berlin Wall. However, tearing the wall down would mean the demise of the Stasi-KGB coffers, and more importantly, the Stasi would lose control of their Seidenstraße (silk route).

KGB agents had made personal fortunes from the narcotics trade, but after 1987, they began dealing in Soviet arms. They sold weapons to their contacts in different parts of the world, who in turn sold them at much higher prices to their handlers in the Middle East, Latin America and other parts of Eastern Europe.

At the time, the KGB was also directing the Stasi to assist in developing foreign assets. However, these channels would later develop into what would become the center of international terrorism. The Stasi was able to get its hands on funding a training camp outside

East Berlin for members of Yasser Arafat's PLO and the more radical elements of George Habash's Popular Front for the Liberation of Palestine (PFLP). It was the beginning of the Stasi military advisors and their covert means of facilitating terrorist training camps in Europe and in the Middle East, facilitated by the KGB.

In West Germany, a group called the Red Army Faction (RAF), also known as the Baader-Meinhof Group, a left-wing Marxist-Leninist militant organization, active from the late 1960s, and founded by journalists Andreas Baader, Gudrun Ensslin, and Ulrike Meinhof. The group had an international wing, with connections to the Palestinian Liberation Organization (PLO) and Marxist revolutionary movements in Latin America, Nicaragua's Sandinista National Liberation Front (FSLN), and the Revolutionary Armed Forces of Colombia (FARC). The group emerged in the wake of student protests and social unrest, fueled by discontent with the political establishment of the Christian Democratic Union (CDU), perceived by the group as imperialistic and what they saw as fascism lingering in West German society. They carried out a series of bombings, assassinations, kidnappings, and other violent acts targeting political and economic institutions, as well as individuals whom they considered representatives of the capitalist system. Notable attacks included the assassination of leading figures in West Germany, such as industrialists and government officials, as well as attacks on U.S. military installations and personnel.

In 1977, the group killed the Dresdner Bank Chairman Jürgen Ponto while initially attempting to kidnap him as a bargain to secure the release of the imprisoned group's members. That same year, other prominent figures also met a similar fate. The Federal Prosecutor General Siegfried Buback and Daimler-Benz, CEO of Hanns-Martin Schleyer, were also killed. By 1985, the group went rogue and also bombed the U.S. military barracks in Frankfurt, which resulted in the deaths of two Americans and injuries of dozens of others. The RAF received Stasi protection, and the KGB had approximately half of a hundred military advisors to assist them in destabilizing West Germany. Whether or not Putin was one of those KGB officers advising the group is up for debate. Some accounts suggest that he did, but based on his role in overseeing the larger KGB operation in East Germany, he may have known significant details of their activity but maintained several layers of separation to make sure his cover was not blown to Western intelligence.

Putin arrived in Dresden, under alias Alexander Rybin. The German-speaking KGB agent was part of a shadow war for vital information for Moscow to counter West Germany. The Reagan Doctrine aimed to support anti-Communist movements and regimes around the world, a broader strategy to undermine Soviet influence. The real job of the KGB in responding to the Americans was to organize what Chancellor Helmut Kohl's government called a "massive propaganda campaign of interference in West German affairs." It came to fruition in 1998 when Kohl's Chancellorship ended over a donation scandal, and he was forced to resign from all his duties, including the leadership of his political party, the Christian Democratic Union (CDU).

Kohl's departure, as some analysts believe, had been in the making since 1982-84, around the same time Putin began his time in Dresden. The scandal and the investigations around it revealed that the CDU had been receiving illegal donations from various sources, including businesses and individuals, during Kohl's tenure as Chancellor since 1982. These donations were not declared to the authorities, as required by German law, and were kept hidden in "black accounts," secret slush funds that were used to finance the party's activities and election campaigns. They were kept off the party's official books, allowing the CDU to evade transparency and accountability.

While the Chancellor initially denied any wrongdoing, he later admitted to accepting cash donations and overseeing the party's illegal financing schemes. Kohl argued that the funds were necessary to maintain the CDU's political dominance and support German reunification efforts following the fall of the Berlin Wall in 1989.

In 2001, Kohl was fined by the CDU for his role in the scandal. He was also investigated by German prosecutors for breach of trust, but the statute of limitations expired, and he was not criminally charged. The episode tarnished Kohl's reputation and legacy as it also damaged the credibility of his political party. The incident led to calls for political reform and greater transparency in party financing. It further robbed the former Chancellor of the honorary chairmanship of his party. He was succeeded as Chancellor by the leader of the Social Democratic Party of Germany in 1998, the pro-Putin Gerhard

Schröder.

The CDU scandal bore the attributes of a classic Soviet disinformation campaign, a central element of a covert strategy aimed at influencing public opinion, and sowing discord.

In 1986, rifts were developing between the Stasi and the KGB. There were significant Stasi complaints about the behavior of Soviet soldiers in the Dresden area. One Soviet soldier apparently sold a grenade for 30 West German Deutsche marks, while others sold pornography and clothing materials. They used petty cash to purchase vodka. Soviet soldiers often stole vegetables from private gardens, and one even broke into a store window to take chocolate Easter bunnies. There are also police reports of intoxicated Soviet soldiers with uncontrolled behavior, which led to violent outbreaks in some neighborhoods in areas between East Berlin and Dresden. There were further embarrassment when, in 1986, three Soviet soldiers made the run to cross over to West Germany.

The situation got worse by 1988 when the KGB asked the Stasi to lodge three visiting KGB officials free of charge due to their lack of funds. Another time, the KGB asked the Stasi to provide 1,200 free stadium tickets for Soviet soldiers to watch the football match between Dynamo Dresden against Spartak Moscow.

In 1987, the Stasi wanted to recruit a man who lived next to a German Communist Party guesthouse in Dresden. They wanted to seek his help on spying on visitors. This incident is famously known as the attempt to recruit a waiter named Rainer Sonntag. The recruitment did not go ahead. Whether Putin and his men failed or whether his KGB bosses later aborted the mission is unclear. The Stasi went ahead anyway and approached Sonntag with an offer to work as an informant, leveraging his proximity to the guesthouse to gather information on visitors. However, Sonntag rejected the offer and instead decided to cooperate with the West German intelligence agency, the Bundesnachrichtendienst (BND). Some analysts believe Sonntag was a double agent and a self serving Neo-Nazi.

During this time, serious friction between the Stasi and the KGB began to surface. It began when the KGB tried to recruit star Stasi agents without their bosses knowing. Tension was brewing over posssibilities of German reunification and what that would mean for Stasi officers.

In 1989, KGB agents arrived at the East Berlin Hotel Bellevue for a meeting with their Stasi counterparts. The hotel was situated near the Spree River and offered scenic views of the city, including nearby landmarks such as the Berlin Wall and the Brandenburg Gate. The landmark was known for its luxurious accommodations and served as one of the primary hotels for foreign visitors. It hosted numerous international guests, including dignitaries, diplomats, and journalists, for official business, cultural exchanges, and media coverage. For the KGB, it played a symbolic role in East German propaganda efforts to showcase the country's hospitality and modern amenities to the outside world. The hotel was often used to project an image of prosperity and stability despite the political and economic challenges faced by the East German regime.

Putin's boss at the time, KGB General Vladimir Shirokov, denied his Stasi counterpart's request for elite Stasi officers to receive further training from Soviet military intelligence for wireless communications. Putin presumably worked with informants inside the GDR and knew very well of the economic conditions. He also had special knowledge of the activities and major economic law enforcement responsibilities of Stasi agents. Sensing a change in their attitudes, he may have tipped off his boss about desperate and nervous Stasi officers, who may have felt that they would be brought to trial after German reunification, which by now looked likely.

Nevertheless, a few Stasi officers remained loyal to Putin. Many of them became bankers in the post-German reunification era. They served as a small but pivotally concentrated channel, laying the foundation for Putin in the post-Soviet era. Some members of the Stasi who have influential links to their local Communist Party used party funds as capital and loans for new manufacturers. They bought banks and other real-estate holdings in Europe. Some of them would sit on the boards of Russian banks and companies.

In February 1988, Stasi boss Erich Mielke awarded Putin a bronze National People's Army service medal "in recognition and appreciation of service in the struggle for peace, in defense of socialist homeland and proletarian internationalism in years of fraternal cooperation between the Stasi's Chekists and the Soviet security organs against the common enemy." Some analysts interpreted this episode as a reward for opening up options for the Stasi in the post-

German reunification era. This also meant that other Soviet agents who received high-ranking gold and silver honors also did something much more than Putin. One episode in particular validated such rewards.

The "Flick Affair," or "the 1987 Flick-Bundestag scandal," centered around allegations of illegal political contributions and influence peddling involving the Flick Group, a prominent West German conglomerate, one of the largest industrial conglomerates in West Germany with interests in various sectors, including steel, mining, and chemicals. It was led by Friedrich Karl Flick, a powerful and influential businessman. It was later revealed that the Flick Group had made substantial illegal contributions to political parties and individual politicians in West Germany. These contributions were intended to influence government policies and gain favorable treatment for the Flick Group's business interests, from its executives to government officials on regulatory matters and business contracts.

The scandal rocked the West German political establishment and led to widespread public outrage over the perceived cozy relationship between big business and government officials. Numerous executives from the Flick Group and government officials were prosecuted and convicted for their involvement in the scandal. It led to changes in campaign finance regulations and increased scrutiny of corporate donations to political parties. The incident also served as a wake-up call for the demand to strengthen democratic institutions, enhance accountability, and combat corruption in West Germany. To the Stasi, it was a triumph to discredit the pro-reunification and former West German Chancellor Helmut Schmidt, who was implicated in the scandal. However, not even the KGB and the Stasi could stop the long arm of Schmidt's successor, the much-determined Helmut Kohl, who would consume East Germany into his fold.

Since 1982 until the fall of the Berlin Wall in 1989, Kohl implemented several strategic policies aimed at weakening East Germany (GDR) and advancing the cause of German reunification. One of those efforts included the broadcasting of Western television and radio programs into the GDR, which provided East Germans with alternative sources of information and exposed them to Western lifestyles and political freedoms, undermining the KGB and the Stasi disinformation campaigns. Kohl's government highlighted the human rights abuses in GDR, supporting dissidents through safe havens, and political backing, advocating for freedom and reform within the Soviet-controlled areas, and helping to bolster internal opposition within East Germany. The strongest and most effective stroke the Kohl's government used was in its economic leverage, providing General Secretary of the Central Committee, Erich Honecker's Soviet-backed East German government, with financial incentives and credits, but tied these financial packages to demands for greater openness and reform. Thereby increasing GDR economic dependence while promoting gradual liberalization. Kohl's soft power to encourage greater people-to-people contact between East and West Germans through cultural exchanges, family reunifications, and travel opportunities, provided the foundations to break down the ideological barriers between the two Germanys. The West German government further supported policies that encouraged East Germans to emigrate to the West, providing financial and logistical support to those fleeing East Germany, which not only weakened the GDR but also caused a brain drain. These measures accumulated to what resulted in the additional demands of East Germans to break down the Berlin Wall on 9 November 1989.

Beholden to the KGB in its final years, the Stasi's power and influence had waned amidst growing discontent and protests against the Communist East German governments of Erich Honecker and his successor Egon Krenz. As the peaceful protests gained momentum, culminating in mass demonstrations in East Berlin and other major cities, the Stasi's ability to suppress dissent became increasingly untenable. East Germans became braver everywhere and in December of that year, a small group of demonstrators decided to march to the local headquarters of the KGB. The guard at the gate disappeared but then a short "agitated" man appeared.

"Don't try to force your way into this property. My comrades are armed, and they're authorized to use their weapons in an emergency."

The demonstrators took no further action and ultimately dispersed, revealing their actions to be a bluff and a precarious gamble. The incident underscored the high-stakes environment of the demonstrators' decision to retreat without escalating their protest. The KGB man's gamble lay in projecting a threat of greater unrest, potentially compelling concessions or provoking a reaction. However, this approach carried significant risks, as any miscalculation could have led to severe repercussions. Amidst this volatile situation, and recognizing the potential for escalating chaos and violence, the man reached out to the headquarters of a Red Army tank unit.

"We cannot do anything without orders from Moscow," the voice at the other end replied. "And Moscow is silent."

"I think it's the key to understanding Putin," says his German biographer, Boris Reitschuster. "We would have another Putin and another Russia without his time in East Germany."

In early October 1989, a significant event occurred that illustrated the mounting pressures and unrest in East Germany. Hundreds of East Germans who had sought political asylum at the West German embassy in Prague were granted permission to travel to West Germany. This movement was orchestrated under strict conditions, involving sealed trains to prevent any unauthorized attempts to join the escape. As these trains crossed through Dresden, the passage of these asylum seekers, symbolizing a breach in the Iron Curtain, drew enormous crowds who yearned for the same freedom and opportunity. The scene in Dresden was one of heightened tension and desperation. Large numbers attempted to breach the security barriers in a bid to board the trains and flee. The episode vividly captured the widespread discontent and the intense desire for political and personal freedom that characterized the last days of East Germany.

The authorities' struggle to maintain control amidst the chaos highlighted the weakening grip of the East German regime. The episode in Dresden did not merely represent an isolated incident but rather a symptom of the broader systemic collapse of Communist regimes in Europe.

Wolfgang Berghofer, Dresden's Communist mayor at the time, says there was chaos as security forces began taking on almost the entire local population.

"A Soviet tank army was stationed in our city," he says. "And its generals said to me clearly: 'If we get the order from Moscow, the tanks will roll."

Moscow under Mikhail Gorbachev "was silent." The Red Army tanks did not arrive, and instead, two weeks later, West German Chancellor Helmut Kohl came to the city. He delivered a speech that rendered the prospect of German reunification seemingly inevitable and foreshadowed the imminent demise of the German Democratic

Republic (GDR). This pivotal address marked a turning point in the political landscape of the Soviet Union, effectively sealing the fate of the GDR as a separate entity.

The speech resonated profoundly, as it underscored the growing momentum towards German reunification, driven by widespread public dissatisfaction and escalating demands for democratic reforms within East Germany. Kohl's rhetoric captured the aspirations of millions who yearned for unity and freedom, capitalizing on the socio-political currents that had been steadily eroding the GDR foundations. The implications of the speech were far-reaching. It not only galvanized support for reunification but also signaled to international observers that the dissolution of the GDR was no longer a matter of if, but when. By articulating a vision for a reunified Germany, Kohl effectively delegitimized the GDR's political authority and accelerated the processes leading to its eventual collapse.

The period of upheaval, characterized by the rapid disintegration of the German Democratic Republic (GDR), had far-reaching consequences for the KGB. East Germany had been a critical outpost in the Soviet intelligence network, providing strategic advantages in espionage activities against the West. The sudden collapse of the GDR dismantled this intricate web of surveillance and operations, leaving KGB agents in a state of disarray. The once stable and familiar environment of East Germany, which had facilitated their clandestine activities, was now replaced by uncertainty, but far worse, by a NATO member.

This rupture affected not only KGB agents, their belief systems, their purpose and their professional futures and their personal lives. Many KGB agents had established deep roots in East Germany, with families, homes, and social networks intricately linked to the GDR's existence. The dissolution of the state forced a reevaluation of their existence as the security and privileges they had enjoyed under the socialist regime had now evaporated.

Furthermore, the geopolitical shift resulting from the GDR's collapse necessitated a rapid adaptation to new realities. The reunification of Germany and the consequent expansion of NATO's influence represented a strategic setback for the Soviet Union and its intelligence apparatus. KGB agents had to navigate the complex transition from operating in a friendly socialist state to dealing with a unified Germany aligned with the West.

Some KGB agents were recalled back to Moscow, while others sought to adapt to the new political realities and even other employment. For those KGB agents who remained in the former GDR, their roles and allegiances shifted. Some transitioned to working for the new German intelligence agencies, while others pursued different career paths which did not necessarily mean, a better standing than their time in the KGB.

One of Putin's key Stasi contacts, Major General Horst Boehm, the man who assisted Putin for much of his time in East Germany, committed suicide early in 1990. Dresden, in many respects, left a lasting mark on the Russian President. The events of German reunification that consolidated the GDR and the ripple effects on his group of KGB agents are a dangerous memory and reminder of what the West did in the Soviet bloc then and what it will do in Putin's Russia. Putin saw the parallels in the 2011 Russian winter, when a series of protests that lasted for nearly two years over the Russian election process, which was really fraudulent, echoed memories of Dresden.

2011 winter produced the largest series of protests in Moscow since the 1990s. The underlying factors centered around two events. Putin was running for President again from his position of Prime Minister. He was swapping places with his political partner, President Dmitry Medvedev, as part of his two-term limit that ended previously in 2008. The other factor was that by 2011, the wealthy Moscow middle class had achieved enough economic growth to find the confidence to undermine Putin's autocratic rule. They demanded new political rights.

Putin would have none of that. Ultimately, the protests did not result in significant political changes or the overthrow of the Russian government. Instead, the Russian authorities responded by tightening control over dissent and cracking down on protesters and opposition figures. The protests gradually dwindled as the Kremlin implemented measures to suppress dissent, including arrests of protest leaders and stricter regulations on public demonstrations. Additionally, the Kremlin undertook efforts to co-opt some of the protesters' grievances, such as launching investigations into electoral fraud and making minor concessions on political reforms. By the spring of 2012, the momentum of the protests had largely dissipated, and the government maintained its grip on power. Putin was re-elected as President in March 2012, following which he continued to consolidate control over the political landscape in Russia. The protests did serve to highlight dissatisfaction with the Russian political system and the growing desire for accountability.

Events in Dresden shaped Putin's layers of power as we see today. The Stasi-KGB relationship became the precursor to Putin's relationship with his Oligarchs, as he sought to balance control over wealthy individuals while also utilizing their resources to consolidate his own authority and advance his own political agenda, particularly linking Russia's oil and gas profits, for his foreign policy aims. Similarly, the Russian President has used his FSB to maintain relationships, as part of his war against the West, with Hamas, Hezbollah, the Ministry of Intelligence and Security (MOIS), Iran's principal intelligence agency, North Korea's Reconnaissance General Bureau (RGB), President Bashar al-Assad's government in Syria and the Venezuelan government, under President Nicolás Maduro and his predecessor Hugo Chávez.

Not all was lost in Dresden for Putin. Like most KGB agents, Putin also had interactions with future East German political leaders. Putin reportedly met with future German Chancellor Angela Merkel during his time in Dresden, who was working for the East German government as a physicist. Her office was reportedly located near Putin's KGB building in Dresden. While the details of their interactions during this period are not extensively documented, it is known that Merkel and Putin had some level of contact.

In Dresden, Putin had been part of a network of individuals who might have lost their Soviet roles but were well-placed to prosper personally and politically in the post-Soviet era. Nikolai Patrushev rose to the position of Director of the FSB before becoming Secretary of the Security Council of Russia. He is widely regarded as one of Putin's closest allies and advisors on security matters. Igor Sechin served in the KGB's Main Intelligence Directorate (GRU) before transitioning to a career in politics and business. He is currently the CEO of Rosneft, the state-owned oil company. Sergey Chemezov, a former director at Russia's arms export agency, now runs a state program supporting technology. Nikolai Tokarev, another former

KGB officer in Dresden, is now head of the state pipeline company, Transneft. Markus Wolf was a high-ranking official in the Stasi, serving as the head of its foreign intelligence service. After the fall of the Berlin Wall, Wolf relocated to Moscow, where he reportedly advised Russian intelligence agencies. He maintained close ties to Russian officials and Putin. Matthias Warnig, a former Stasi officer, is now managing director of Nordstream. Wolfgang Schwanitz, also a former Stasi officer, served as a cultural attache at the East German embassy in Moscow during the Cold War; after German reunification, Schwanitz remained in Russia and became a historian specializing in Russian-German relations. André Kempe, another former Stasi officer, later worked for the Russian energy company Gazprom.

Dresden was also the center of a ticking time bomb that the KGB left and one which is soundly advancing Putin's agenda now. The capital city of the German state of Saxony suffered extensive destruction due to Allied bombing raids in February 1945. The memory of these bombings has been exploited by far-right groups to foster feelings of victimhood and resentment towards the West, as well as to promote nationalist and revisionist narratives.

German reunification, deindustrialization, unemployment, and demographic changes, led to feelings of disillusionment and alienation among certain segments of the East German population, which far-right groups have exploited to gain support.

Dresden gained international attention in 2014 with the emergence of the Patriotic Europeans Against the Islamization of the West (Pegida) movement. The group organized weekly demonstrations against immigration, Islam, and multiculturalism, drawing thousands of participants. While Pegida originated in Dresden, similar movements emerged in other parts of Germany and Europe, reflecting broader far-right sentiments. Far-right political parties, such as the Alternative for Germany (AfD), have gained significant electoral support in Saxony and other eastern German states. Dresden has become the hotspot for violent far-right extremism, with neo-Nazi groups engaging in attacks on immigrants, left-wing activists, and other minorities. These incidents have raised concerns about the spread of extremism and the potential for radicalization in the region. The AfD has capitalized on anti-immigrant and anti-establishment sentiments, winning seats in 9 parliamentarians in the European parliament, 252 in regional parliaments, and in the Bundestag, the German federal parliament, with 78 out of 736 seats.

The roots of contemporary far-right and neo-Nazi groups go back to 1986, a time when Stasi operations intensified, particularly in response to growing internal dissent and external pressures against the GDR regime. The policies of *glasnost* (openness) and *perestroika* (restructuring) initiated by Soviet leader Mikhail Gorbachev had a ripple effect in the GDR, which emboldened critics of Gorbachev, with many in the Stasi fearing a German reunification could put them behind bars.

It was in 1986 that Stasi wanted to recruit a waiter named Rainer Sonntag. While Sonntag refused to join the Stasi, he kept close links with his KGB contacts. By the time the Berlin Wall fell, Sonntag had become one of the leading neo-Nazis in former East Germany. His followers would often target foreigners, immigrants, and local business owners who employed non-Germans. In one instance, his gang attacked the city's Vietnamese cigarette sellers and became infamous for their raids. Sonntag had come to Putin's attention due to George Johannes Schneider, a former Dresden police officer who was instrumental in expanding the number of KGB assets in the city. Sonntag was sent to West Germany as an informant in 1986. There are few documented records of his time in Frankfurt, but he blended well into the city's underworld circles. At the time, the city experienced socio-economic changes, urbanization, and immigration patterns, which influenced the high crime rates. Additionally, factors such as drug trafficking, organized crime activities, and political unrest, played a role in shaping the criminal landscape during that time. Frankfurt also served as a hub for various American military installations, including the home of American military families who lived on base and in nearby housing areas. Facilities such as schools, hospitals, and recreational amenities were often locations where Americans lived nearby. The Rhein-Main Air Base was situated near Frankfurt am Main, one of Germany's largest cities, and it is a major transportation hub in Europe, not far from Frankfurt. Its strategic location provided American forces, the U.S. Army (USAREUR), the U.S. Air Force (USAFE), U.S. Navy, and Marines, easy access to other parts of Germany and neighboring countries, with the primary mission to serve as a logistical and transportation hub in supporting troop deployments, airlift operations, and cargo transport across Europe. The base was equipped with various facilities to support its mission, including aircraft hangars, maintenance facilities, fuel depots, warehouses, administrative buildings, and housing for military personnel and their families. It also had a runway and taxiways to accommodate military aircraft of different sizes, primarily serving to defend West Germany and NATO allies against the potential threat of Soviet-backed forces, which also included a potential attack from East Germany.

Before long, Sonntag gravitated toward Frankfurt's underworld, and his reach infiltrated other groups. As he widened his network, he also kept in contact with his KGB handlers. The Stasi petitioned the KGB to get Sonntag within the corridors of political power. Instead, with KGB backing, Sonntag ran his National Assembly party as part of a far-right coalition in an anti-foreigners platform in the 1989 local elections. One of the parties in this alliance was the AfD. However, Sonntag's time was cut short in West Germany. After the sudden killing of neo-Nazi Gerald Hess, many within the far-right-wing political groups believed that Sonntag had a hand in it. He was forced to return to Dresden in 1990. With Putin and most of the KGB now gone, Sonntag was used by former Stasi officers to start making problems. His followers created trouble in Dresden, and the new German police often worked with them. Sonntag's return did inflame right-wing movements, but that did not resonate with parliamentary success. His reign only increased crimes against foreigners, gradually making Dresden the center of neo-Nazi groups.

Sonntag died during a struggle with a pimp who refused to pay him his cut. In death, he became a martyr to the neo-Nazi movement, and Dresden became the site of unimaginable violence. In the years that followed, right-wing marches in February (the month of Sonntag's death) became a tradition in Dresden.

The former KGB and the Stasi officers who had propelled Sonntag lived without any state prosecutions against them. In the post-reunification era, Germany had no political will to bring the Stasi men to trial nor the KGB. Their involvement in several incidents was never investigated at all. Berlin has a strong interest in keeping the lid closed; rooted in the excuse was a strong desire for reconciliation and stability. Germany was faced with the monumental task of integrating East and

West, both economically and socially. Pursuing widespread prosecutions of former Stasi officers could have destabilized this fragile process by exacerbating social tensions and fostering resentment. Prosecuting individuals for their involvement in Stasi activities presented significant legal challenges. Much of the evidence against former Stasi officers looked circumstantial, and proving direct involvement in criminal activities was difficult, especially given the secretive nature of Stasi operations and the destruction of many Stasi files, many of which were assisted by the KGB.

The transition from East Germany to a reunified Germany involved delicate political negotiations. There were concerns about alienating former East German elites and officials, including all with ties to the Stasi. Pursuing aggressive legal action against former Stasi officers could have been seen as provocative and potentially destabilizing the entire reunification project. German leaders made the unprecedented move to integrate guilty individuals into the mainstream German political landscape.

Wolfgang Schwanitz, a former Stasi officer, later became a politician in the newly reunified Germany. He was a member of the Christian Democratic Union (CDU) and served as a member of the Bundestag (German federal parliament) from 1990 to 1998. Schwanitz's political career was marked by controversy due to his Stasi past, but he remained active in public life. Similarly, Wolfgang Schnur, a lawyer and former Stasi informant, played a prominent role in the opposition movement in East Germany during the late 1980s. He co-founded the New Forum, one of the first opposition groups to emerge in East Germany. After reunification, he continued his legal career but faced public scrutiny and legal consequences due to his past Stasi connections. Those who did not have Stasi connections were also mended into German political life. Wolfgang Thierse, a key figure in East German civil society and an advocate for political reform, played a key role in the Round Table talks that paved the way for German reunification. Thierse was not a Stasi officer, but he had some involvement with the regime's structures, serving as a cultural functionary. After reunification, he became a prominent politician in the Bundestag, eventually serving as President from 1998 to 2005.

One of the problems in going after the most zealous Stasi officers was that in some cases, the statute of limitations posed a barrier to prosecuting individuals for crimes committed during the East German regime. Certain offenses, particularly those classified as less severe under East German law, were subject to limitations on prosecution. There was also another reason. The German government did not want its economic relationship with Russia disrupted by going after the most criminally and sadistic former Stasi officers.

In June 2010, then-Prime Minister Putin visited Berlin. He was courted by the crème de la crème of German businesses. Everyone wanted to do business with Russia, but few understood the consequences that lay ahead. Companies like Volkswagen, Siemens, and a host of banks were all extremely eager to find a niche in the Russian market. They were just a few of the 3,600 German companies who wanted to set up their presence in Moscow. German banks would go on to make huge profits because of the kinds of customers it was willing to accept and how much they were willing to look the other way when it came to regulations and compliance.

Beyond gas and oil, Germany's economic relationship with Russia runs the extent from Mercedes to muesli. Total trade with Russia totaled US$9.9 Billion during 2023, a staggering 83% deficit from pre-annexation Crimea years. Germany's determination to trade with Russia through thick and thin is attributed to Ost-Ausschuss, also known as "The East Committee," a lobbying arm of West German businesses in Eastern Europe founded in the 1950s. It was the brain child of Ludwig Erhard, the German economy minister. It did not matter that a slice of Germany was taken by the Soviets as West German leaders saw economic opportunity in the newly formed Eastern Bloc and beyond.

The East Committee secured trade deals for then West Germany in the 1950s with both Romania and China, and in the 1970s, played a significant role in negotiating gas deals with the Soviet Union. After the disbanding of the Soviet Union, the group sprinted to the doorsteps of the Kremlin to do what it does best, selling machinery and sophisticated engineering to modernize the economy.

German trade with the former Eastern bloc exploded, transforming the region. Starting in Poland, then Czechoslavakia but when it came to Russia, one hundred forty-four million of its inhabitants, nearly 20% the size of the EU and its natural resources beyond oil and gas, in minerals, timber, metals, fishing, hydropower, agriculture, and others were not just a trading opportunity, but profits German businesses could not live without. Providing economically viable opportunities for the Kremlin was a convenient German bag of sweets, in return for the deaths of nearly twenty-five million Russians who perished from the horrors of World War II.

If the Kremlin resisted temptations and stayed out of Western agitations in Libya, Syria, and Crimea, there is no doubt German businesses would not only have a higher presence in Russia, but for the Kremlin, it would mean much larger coffers than what they had in 2014 and after. Russia's annexation of Crimea diverted German investments to China, where the fear of Western-backed sanctions are extremely limited. China may have provided the convenient alternative path but the German appetite and lust for Russia did not go away. By 2016, several heads of German businesses, including the East Committee's new chair, Wolfgang Büchele, pressed the Merkel government for the removal of Western-backed sanctions against the Kremlin. The East Committee was particularly sensitive to the lifeline of Nordstream 2, the controversial successor to the original Nordstream pipeline, which became operational in 2011. Nordstream 2, designed to complement the existing pipeline by expanding the capacity for gas transportation directly from Russia to Germany via the Baltic Sea, bypassing traditional transit countries like Ukraine, Belarus, and Poland, was so lucrative that even when Putin critic Alexei Navalny was poisoned with a nerve agent in 2020, some German business leaders petitioned the Merkel government to not only stay out of the Western-backed sanctions, but remove existing sanctions that were harming their profits connected to the Kremlin.

The second most significant outpost for the East Committee is Munich, where the group sits with its largest network of German businesses that mostly advocate for a pro-Russia stance at the Munich Security Conference, the annual gathering of American and European political leaders, security officials, and business executives. After 2022, the East Committee changed its format and supported the Western-backed sanctions on Russia. It was not a move that came from their own choosing, but rather a combination of hard conditions imposed by their partnering companies in the West and the new government of Olaf Scholz.

When Putin was speaking at the same podium sponsored by the East

Committee on that February 2007 night in Munich, nearly 250 miles away, neo-Nazis were congregating in Dresden for their annual march. Perhaps, in his anger, the Russian President thought that as the West disregarded its own global norms, he would one day turn Tbilisi and Kyiv into Dresden.

Chapter 12

THE VALUE IN DEFEAT

It is true that the European Union (EU) can and will back Kyiv politically and monetarily but only to an extent, but what they don't understand is the Russian problem will remain within Europe. Politically, the EU is more nervous about its domestic agendas and it is deeply worried about gains from far-radical right-wing forces in the next European parliament and even in Europe itself. These developments can further complicate the urgent decisions when it comes to Ukraine, but what will Europe do if Ukraine can't make up the gains after six months of no aid from the United States? Will the lapse period contribute to unforeseen consequences? And how will this conflict end?

Brussels and the Kremlin know that the EU will never be able to fill the gap of any American aid, and in post-2024, if that becomes absent, the geopolitical and economic cost of Ukraine's defeat would have ripple effects across Europe. As much as it is about the future of the Ukrainians, it is also about how the EU expects to deal with Russia in the war's aftermath. It may very well have to deal with a foreseeably another Russian invasion. The EU would not like permanent Russian annexations, but this is a recurring theme in Europe. In Transnistria, officially known as the Pridnestrovian Moldovan Republic, the 1,600 square miles of an internationally unrecognized state is occupied by Russian forces. It is a defacto pro-Russian breakaway region, squeezed between Moldova and Ukraine, that mirrors the likes of Georgia's

Abkhazia, South Ossetia and Ukraine's Crimea, Donbask, and Luhansk. It has a presence of 1,500 Russian soldiers and is home to a half million Russian-speaking population. The government in Chișinău has always been nervous about how it treads between Brussels and Moscow with this break-away enclave. In 2023, Moldova imposed new customs duties on Transnistria's imports and exports. In response, the parliament of Transnistria appealed to the Kremlin for help. The Russian foreign ministry immediately responded with full backing of Transnistria.

Most analysts believe this is part of the Russian playbook. Signal the alarm to Moscow, followed by Kremlin support of solidarity against the besieged discriminated Russian-speaking population, then put the pro-European government on the back foot, followed by a justification for military intervention.

Similar to Georgia's and Ukraine's break-way regions, Transnistria offers Russia a strategic foothold. It offers economic leverage over governments in Moldova and is also a buffer against NATO. Transnistria hosts the Moldovan segment of the Dniester River, which provides a strategically lucrative hydroelectric power base and provides Russia a transit route for its natural gas exports to Moldova and indirectly, to other European countries. Exploiting this space may provide the Kremlin with options in their "special military operation" in Ukraine, but taking on Moldova is much more complex than Georgia and Ukraine. However, like a typical Putin playbook, the Russian President has a Viktor Yanukovych type proxy in Moldova.

Even before the disbanding of the Soviet Union, the people of Gagauzia, fearing cultural and political marginalization, declared an independent "Gagauz Republic" in 1990. This move was not internationally recognized, and tensions between the Gagauzia leadership and the Moldovan government continued. Gagauzia was one of a very few areas which wanted to remain part of the USSR

The inhabitants of Gagauzia are a Turkic ethnic group, primarily Eastern Orthodox Christians. Their origins are debated, with theories suggesting they descended from the Seljuks, Pechenegs, or other Turkic tribes that settled in the Balkans during the Ottoman Empire's rule. Following the Russia-Turkish War (1806–1812), the Gagauzians, along with Bulgarians, were encouraged to settle in the Russian

Empire's newly acquired territories of Bessarabia (which included parts of modern-day Moldova and Ukraine). Gagauzia was incorporated into the Moldavian SSR after World War II. During this period, the Gagauz, like other ethnic minorities, were subject to Soviet policies of collectivization and Russification. However, they maintained their distinct language and cultural traditions. An agreement in 1995 was reached with the central government in Moldova; Gagauzia was granted the status of an autonomous state, with control over its own education, language, culture, and their local administration in their capital Comrat.

In 2024, the Governor of Gagauzia, the 37-year-old Evghenia Guțul, has been accused by the state prosecutor of transferring large amounts of capital from Moscow to finance her Kremlin-backed political party, the Victory bloc. She has the support of Kremlin-backed Oligarch Ilan Shore, who is in exile in Russia and convicted in Moldova for financial embezzlement.

The Kremlin is using Guțul to counter Moldova's EU's ascension. Russian finances are paying for the small and poverty-ridden Gagauzia province in areas unmatched by the central government in Moldova, in the Gagauzia pension fund, and other state entities, galvanizing support to derail Moldova's admission to the EU by 2030.

In addition to Guțul, there are large political forces of opposition to the present administration of the pro-European President Maia Sandu. The opposition Socialist Party of Moldova (PSRM) has traditionally advocated for closer relations with Russia and has support among Moldova's Russian-speaking population. However, it also struggles with regional political power bases of the predominantly Romanian-speaking West, which is politically also very closely linked with NATO-member Romania.

Any Russian military actions or escalations in Moldova will have immediate security implications for Romania, and any threat to its security could invoke NATO's Article 5. Romania has been modernizing its military and increasing its defense budget in recent years. Ranked 10th in the NATO hierarchy of 72,000 active troops, its military capabilities, while not as extensive as Russia's, are supported by NATO's collective defense infrastructure. Romania and Moldova share deep historical and cultural ties, with approximately 7% of the 2.5 million population identifying themselves as Romanians (*Source*:

2014 Moldovan Census) and the majority of them have dual Romanian-Moldovan citizenship. There is a unionist movement in Moldova that advocates for reunification with Romania. Its supporters typically identify strongly as Romanians. This connection under a Russian attack, will drive Romania to take a more active role in defending Moldova. Any conflict involving Romania due to Russian actions in Moldova would likely involve NATO. However, within NATO, there is a deep sense of nervousness should former President Donald Trump win the 2024 November election.

Trump is the first former President to be found guilty of a crime and also the first former President to become a convicted felon. A status he has achieved from his May 2024 Hush-money trial. He has vowed that he would end his support for the Ukraine war. The former President's opponents in Congress have passed legislation in the National Defense Authorization Act (NDAA) that to halt aid for Ukraine; there would be a need for two-thirds approval from the Senate. However, President Biden's Democrats are defending more Senate seats than their Republican opponents in the 2024 November elections. Comparatively, Trump's Republicans are not defending any. Although some nervousness may sway on who the former President picks as his Vice President and whether that gives Europeans enough of an indication of things to come. Nevertheless, Europeans are nervous. The re-election of Trump will provide a boost to already present far-right-wing forces in Europe. For instance, Hungary's authoritarian leader Victor Orbán, will hold the rotational Presidency of the Council of the EU. It is a largely a ceremonial role but the position can be used to set Europe's agenda and cause significant problems for Ukraine at their hour of need. Orbán not only has been a thorn in Brussels' side, but has also slowed the military and economic aid to Ukraine. He made headlines when he said, "Trump's comeback as President is the 'only serious chance' for end of Ukraine war." He has labeled Ukraine "the land of nobody."

Like Hungary, in Italy, there are internal tensions between the pro-Ukraine stance of right-wing Prime Minister Giorgia Meloni and her junior coalition partner, the Kremlin-backed far-right League party leader Matteo Salvini. Meloni has consistently condemned Russian military aggression, while her deputy, Salvini, has had strong links with Putin's United Russia party since the signing of a 2017 cooperation agreement. There is a feeling the Kremlin is stepping up efforts to stoke public opposition to Meloni's pro-Ukraine stance. There is a showdown looming between political forces on the right and the left in another Italian election, the third time in six years. In the next election, Ukraine will be a central issue. Europe's war fatigue and a potential Trump Presidency would weaken Meloni's political capital.

Italy has traditionally been one of the founding members of the European project but recently, there are differing views within Italian public and politics regarding the pace and scope of European integration. As right-wing and far-right-wing forces find new ground in the political landscape, there are signs of a New Europe emerging.

At the foundation, New Europe is unwelcoming to refugees, bipolar in economic policies when it comes to Russia, and inconsistent on balanced budgets. Meloni looks to be the heir to Angela Merkel to lead in this era of New Europe. The right-wing Italian Prime Minister of the Brothers of Italy party, with roots in Benito Mussolini's far-right movement, looks to have control of Europe's right-wing forces. She has much in common in anti-immigration, anti-abortion, and anti-LGBTQ positions. She has won the hearts and minds of Marine Le Pen (France), Sebastian Kurz and Norbert Hofer (Austria), Andrzej Duda (Poland), Thierry Baudet (Netherlands), Santiago Abascal (Spain) and Jussi Halla-Aho (Finland). Such is the admiration from Europe's right and far-right that Meloni was successful in persuading Hungarian Prime Minister Viktor Orbán to stop blocking an EU aid package for Ukraine. Like Orbán, Meloni used to be very anti-EU but has come to work with it. She secured €200 billion from the EU, only to find ways to spend the money without successful results. She weighed her options with China too. Italy had been the only major Western nation to join China's signature Belt and Road Initiative. Meloni decided to pull out as a way to win the hearts of the West. Domestically, her approach reflects the growing consensus of turning away from fiscal restraint and free market reforms. She has embraced bigger deficits with higher spending and tax cuts for workers. She's tried to go after big business with price controls on airfares and an extra tax on banks, but it is a work in progress with few results. A constitutional reform with the aim of shoring up her own powerbase and guaranteeing 55% of seats in parliament to whichever group wins the most in an Italian parliamentary election is an unsuccessful ploy of her own making. It is the resemblance of a Mussolini-style fascist control of Italian politics which she has tried, and has not succeeded.

When it comes to immigration, Meloni has been the hawk of hawks. She recognizes that tough measures in Italy alone are inadequate to fix the problem. As African migrants continue to arrive on Italy's shores, Meloni has undertaken steps beyond measure to stop the flow. She made a deal with Albania to hold asylum seekers while they waited for their cases to be adjudicated. Italy's lower chamber of parliament approved the deal, followed by the Senate. Two processing centers are to be set up in Albania at a cost to Italy of more than €600 million over five years. She wanted to make another deal with Tunisia's Kais Saied, who like Orbán, is turning his country into a dictatorship. Since assuming absolute power in a 2021 coup, Saied has slandered, criminalized, and jailed his critics. He has been ruthless to his political opponents, reverting his country back to worse than pre-Arab Spring conditions. With help from the EU, Meloni offered Saied's government $120 million in "migration funding" to block migrants from crossing the Mediterranean. The deal, however, collapsed shortly due to more guarantees from Saied's government.

In January 2024, Meloni's government announced a $6 billion plan to strengthen its partnership with Africa at the Italy-Africa Summit aimed at placing barriers for those leaving their homes for Europe. Voters in Italy overwhelmingly approve of Meloni compared to voters in Britain, France, and Germany, who are unhappy with their elected officials. Meloni is bringing Orbán-style politics into the European normality, positioning herself as a link between the European establishment and the far-right. She has a visible podium closeness with Ursula von der Leyen, the President of the European Commission. As Orbán's influence with Leyen is problematic, Meloni's is on the upswing. The Italian prime minister is poised to become a "Queenmaker," shifting Brussels more to the right. She will be able to do this even at the cost of Italy's weak economy, and as Macron and Scholz, who shape European policy, need her help with dissenting quarters within Europe, especially the rising tide of right-wing and far-right forces, Meloni's political capital will only shine if Ursula von der Leyen gets a second term.

The next President of the European Commission will most likely have to deal with right-wing parties and will need the Italian PM to hold her parliament together. No other politician in Europe is flexibly better positioned than Meloni for a Biden or a Trump Presidency. In post-2024, if it is a Trump Presidency, the question is whether she will remain faithful to the pro-Ukraine camp or Europe's far-right. It looks likely that Meloni will preside over a broad coalition of conservatives, far-right-wing, and nationalist parties, much like her own center-right coalition. A Trump Presidency will cement the rise of the likes of Meloni. It will, however, cut NATO's capabilities as it takes on Russia.

The United States may opt for a reduced engagement with NATO from 2025 onwards, if Trump is elected. It will include fewer military communications, military drills and exercises, but dangerously, the United States will not share intelligence with its European partners. If a NATO member is attacked, like Poland, and the United States does not respond to its commitment to Article 5, it will be the beginning of a new reality of New Europe becoming vulnerable.

Washington may not even bother itself with imposing new Western-backed sanctions on Russia and decide to be silent. Former President Trump has always claimed that Europe and NATO members are not pulling their weight, at a 2% minimum commitment to their defense budget from their GDP. This is not entirely true. Poland has spent more than 4% of their GDP on defense. It has strengthened its armed forces in the Army, Air Force, and Navy. Poland is not alone. Britain, Estonia, Greece, Latvia, Lithuania, and Romania, consistently meet or exceed the 2% NATO defense spending target.

By supporting Ukraine, the West has come together after a first-term Trump Presidency. Between 2017-2021, Europe fell to the "America First" agenda, which included imposed tariffs on imports against key American allies such as Canada, Mexico, and members of the European Union. These tariffs sparked trade tensions and retaliatory measures, leading to concerns about the stability of global trade and economic relations among Western countries.

As one of the largest economies in Europe and a major trading partner of the United States, Germany felt the impact of tariffs on its steel and aluminum imports. Additionally, Trump's criticism of Germany's trade surplus created tensions in the bilateral relationship. France too, saw its agriculture and luxury goods sectors affected. President Trump's decision to withdraw from the Paris Agreement on climate change also strained relations with the Macron government, which strongly supports international efforts to combat global warming. Trump's criticism of Britain's approach to Brexit and his decision to impose tariffs on British steel and aluminum imports added complexity to the bilateral relationship. Italy too, faced trade uncertainties and tensions, particularly regarding tariffs on European goods. The European Union was criticized for its trade practices, skepticism towards multilateralism, and Trump's preference for bilateral deals, which also raised concerns about the future of transatlantic relations.

Trump's trade war destabilized America's key allies in Europe as it marked the imposition of tariffs and renegotiation of trade agreements, and promoted economic nationalism. This resonated with European right-wing and far-right-wing parties that advocate for protectionist measures to shield their economies from globalization. Emphasis on national sovereignty and control over their own economies echoed Trump's policies and rhetoric. European right-wing and far-right parties leveraged this to argue against EU regulations and for stronger national borders. Britain witnessed four Prime Ministers come and go from 2017 and well on to 2024. France's National Rally (NR), Germany's AfD, and Italy's League, capitalized on this narrative, arguing that their countries should prioritize national interests over international cooperation. Far-right-wing parties in Europe often cited Trump's policies as a model, advocating for similar measures such as renegotiating trade deals, imposing tariffs, and reducing immigration. This policy mimicry helped them gain traction among their voters.

The election of President Biden in 2020 was a welcome relief to Europe, but the "America first" hangover did not go away. In September 2021, the United States, Britain, and Australia announced the formation of AUKUS, a trilateral security partnership aimed at countering China's growing influence in the Pacific. As part of this agreement, Australia scrapped a $66 billion deal to buy French-designed submarines and instead opted for a new fleet of nuclear-powered submarines with technology provided by the United States and Britain. French officials, including President Macron, expressed strong dissatisfaction and disappointment over the way the deal was handled, as it effectively sidelined France, a NATO ally and EU member, in favor of the AUKUS partners. Macron termed the move a "stab in the back" and recalled France's ambassadors from the United States and Australia in protest. Although later he sent them back. Most observers believe the French have not healed from the affair. When it comes to Ukraine, the Biden administration is a trustable backer and rightfully did not want a wider war, which would have also meant another conflict just six months after the abysmal American withdrawal from Afghanistan.

With American boots on the ground, it would have also risked a nuclear showdown. Ukraine's success has also been an American success. Both have contained Russia and China but the real criticism comes on the battlefield. The American administration has armed Ukraine but stopped short of facilitating assembly lines and mechanical depots to service the tanks, transports, and weapons. It is quite visible that two years into the war, Kyiv looks more to Washington than those in Berlin, Paris, or London. However, Ukraine is a politically problematic subject in the United States.

The twice-impeached former President Trump did endure one of the articles of impeachment against him, related to his actions involving Ukraine. Trump was impeached on charges of abuse of power and obstruction of Congress, a charge that stemmed from allegations that he pressured the Ukrainian government and President Zelenskyy to investigate his political rival, then former Vice-President Joe Biden, and his son, Hunter Biden, in exchange for releasing military aid and granting a White House meeting. The obstruction of Congress charge was based on the Trump administration's refusal to cooperate with the House impeachment inquiry by withholding documents and blocking key witnesses from testifying. The American political problems with links to Ukraine did not end there.

Before the 2016 Presidential election, Paul John Manafort Jr. worked for Putin's ally, Ukrainian President Viktor Yanukovych. He came to the attention of federal prosecutors by a *The New York Times* report on August 2016 through what was known as the Black Ledger. It was an inventory of handwritten lists of secret payments by Ukraine's President Yanukovych's political party; Party of Regions to several individuals. Manafort was accused of receiving approximately $12.7 million, but this did not necessarily mean a confirmation that Manafort received the full amount as campaign manager to Trump. *The New York Times* report implicated Trump with Ukraine and because Yanukovych was a Putin ally, a link to Russia.

Manafort was indicted on 12 counts of money laundering, tax evasion, and lobbying violations in 2017, separate from *The New York Times* report.

Ukraine finds itself in the convenient American political blame game. The former President's troubles began from the Russian interference in the 2016 elections. It was further amplified by the fallout caused by Ukraine that pulled Trump into a toxic political space that consumed much of his Presidency. The truths of the episode came out when Yevgeny Prigozhin, head of the Wagner Group, admitted that Russia had intervened in the 2016 Presidential election.

Ukraine is equally damaging to President Joe Biden. Then Vice President Joe Biden pushed for the dismissal of Ukraine's prosecutor general, Viktor Shokin, revolving around concerns of corruption within the Ukrainian government and the prosecutor's office. Biden, as Vice President, along with other Western leaders and international institutions, called for the removal of Prosecutor General due to accusations of ineffectiveness in combating corruption and for not pursuing corruption cases aggressively enough. There was a widely reported incident in 2016 where Vice-President Biden threatened to withhold $1 billion in U.S. loan guarantees to then Ukraine's President Petro Poroshenko unless Shokin was removed from office. Biden's position was that Shokin's removal was necessary to help Ukraine address corruption within its government and institutions. This stance was in line with broader international efforts to support anti-corruption measures in Ukraine.

Shokin was not investigating Hunter Biden or the company Burisma that employed him. It developed into a political liability when Hunter Biden joined the board of Burisma Holdings, one of Ukraine's largest natural gas producers in April 2014. Burisma was owned by Ukrainian Oligarch and former politician Mykola Zlochevsky, who was facing a money laundering investigation. Hunter Biden's position on the board attracted scrutiny due to concerns about potential conflicts of interest, given his father's role as Vice President of the United States at the time. Critics raised questions about whether Hunter Biden's position on the board influenced U.S. policy towards Ukraine, particularly regarding anti-corruption efforts. Some also alleged that his role was a way for Burisma to gain favor with the U.S.

government.

As BBC's Sam Cabral investigated, in 2014, Hunter Biden joined the board of a Ukrainian energy company, Burisma Holdings, receiving a $1.2 million salary to help Burisma with corporate governance best practices. The President's second son was considered a reputational risk by some within the board of Burisma, but he completed his term in April 2019.

Biden's critics in the Republican party believe that then Vice-President Biden and Hunter Biden received $5 million payouts from Burisma executives in exchange for Mr Shokin's firing. The BBC stated that "a former business partner to Hunter also testified Joe had been on speakerphone several times during Hunter's calls with various contacts."

The discovery of an abandoned laptop at a Delaware repair shop and the contents of the hard drive found its way to harm the prospects of Biden's 2020 presidential campaign. It remained problematic as the Republican-controlled Congress on 13 December 2023, authorized the impeachment inquiry into President Joe Biden, with every Republican rallying behind the politically charged process despite lingering concerns among some in the party that the investigation will produce evidence of misconduct by the President.

There has been no evidence of wrongdoing by either the President or Hunter Biden in relation to their activities in Ukraine. Multiple investigations, including those by Ukrainian and U.S. authorities, have found no evidence of illegal conduct by either of them.

In 2024, Ukraine's political factions will do their utmost best to stay out of the American Presidential election, but that would be hard to do given how much of a pivotal role the United States is playing in Ukraine.

Two years into the war, Ukraine has become comfortable in its uncomfortable relationship with the United States, unlike its rapport with Europe. In the aftermath of the Russian annexation of Crimea in February 2014, Ukraine felt a sense of isolation from Europeans, as many in the EU and NATO were cautious in their response to Russia's aggression, often balancing between supporting Ukraine and maintaining their own economic and political ties with Russia. The conflict, particularly in the Donbas region, escalated into a protracted crisis and exacerbated Ukraine's isolation and frustrations with European partners as they struggled to find a unified approach to addressing the crisis.

Events in Ukraine unleashed the differences between West and East Europe. Despite decades of shared interest and economic success, Western Europe, particularly after the disbanding of the Soviet Union, could not measure up to the challenges. Wealthy Western Europe did not have an answer to the 1991 Croatian War, a conflict between Croatian forces and the Yugoslav People's Army (JNA). Europe needed American intervention. That same year, Slovenia declared independence from Yugoslavia, leading to a brief conflict between Slovenian forces and the Yugoslav People's Army (JNA). Europe could do very little to help the Slovenians.

In 1992, the Bosnian War involved ethnic Serbs, Croats, and Bosniaks (Bosnian Muslims) and resulted in widespread atrocities, including ethnic cleansing and genocide. European leaders remained distant in their intervention. During the 1998 Kosovo War, led by Slobodan Milošević and his Serbian security forces against the Kosovo Albanian guerrilla fighters, this time, European leaders badly needed American intervention.

Western Europe has been slow to rise to the challenge of prioritizing peace after the end of the Soviet Union. However, despite such shortcomings, Europe today is a success story. They have divisions among their ranks and differences in their views on domestic and foreign policy, but as a wealthy union, they are committed to their constitutional law and have been fantastic allies to the United States.

The 2008-09 financial crisis and the subsequent sovereign debt crisis in the Eurozone strained Europe and the British relationship with the EU. Britain opted to stay out of the Eurozone, but the economic turmoil in Europe fueled anti-EU sentiment and arguments for greater British independence from EU policies and regulations. As a result, the rise of populist and nationalist movements in Europe, including the UK Independence Party (UKIP), played a significant role in shaping the Brexit debate, capitalizing on public discontent with EU institutions and policies, framing Brexit as a means to reclaim British national sovereignty and control over immigration.

The decision for Britain to leave the European Union was the result of a host of reasons that had gathered momentum since the 2008-09 financial crisis. Many Brexit supporters argued that leaving the EU would restore Britain's sovereignty and regain control over its laws, borders, and immigration policies. Brexiters viewed EU membership as undermining British sovereignty by subjecting the country to the authority of EU institutions and regulations, and painfully, the direction of Brussels and not London. Some British voters were worried about the perceived lack of controls over immigration from other EU member states, particularly regarding the free movement of EU citizens. They believed that leaving the EU would enable Britain to impose stricter border controls and reduce immigration levels.

While some Brexiters argued that leaving the EU would allow the UK to forge new trade deals and pursue a more independent economic policy, others expressed dissatisfaction with the EU's economic policies and regulations. Some British businesses felt burdened by EU regulations and sought greater flexibility outside the EU's single market and customs union. Critics of the EU argued that it was undemocratic, bureaucratic, and unresponsive to the needs and concerns of ordinary citizens. For some Brexiters, leaving the EU was about asserting British identity and reclaiming national sovereignty. They viewed EU membership as incompatible with British values and traditions. Brexit was an opportunity to reaffirm British independence and autonomy.

Brexit showed the uglier side of the European integration project. Similar EU breakaway movements are brewing and may take hold after the June 2024 European parliamentary elections. In France, there is a hypothetical scenario where it can exit the EU, with political movements advocating for a renegotiation of France's relationship with the EU or even leaving it altogether. So far, there isn't a major political party dedicated solely to advocating for an EU exit with significant parliamentary representation or mainstream acceptance. However, there have been smaller parties and movements that have advocated for similar ideas. One of the most prominent figures associated with the EU exit movement is François Asselineau, who founded the Union Populaire Républicaine (UPR) in 2007. The UPR promotes French withdrawal from the EU, the Eurozone, and NATO. However, the UPR has struggled to gain significant traction in national elections, and its support base remains relatively small, with only four mayors in all of France, affiliated with the political party.

In the Netherlands, there isn't as strong a movement to leave the EU, but there are Eurosceptic parties that have raised the issue. Not only do they have representation in parliament, but they do have a significant following. The most prominent among them is the Party for Freedom (Partij voor de Vrijheid, PVV), led by Geert Wilders. While PVV has been critical of the EU and has called for reforms, including regaining control over Dutch borders and reducing EU influence, it hasn't explicitly campaigned to leave the EU. The PVV is the largest opposition party in the Dutch parliament. It can certainly wield enough support to disrupt the European project and pull support away from Ukraine. The PVV is not alone, as there are more extremist forces. The Forum for Democracy (Forum voor Democratie, FvD), led by Thierry Baudet, has also expressed Eurosceptic views and has criticized the EU's role in Dutch politics. They have three seats in the Dutch parliament and one seat in the European Parliament. For now, they are of little significance, but with the way the Netherlands is evolving, they could very well find themselves on a stronger side of political fortunes in the future.

Although the main purpose of the June 2024 European parliamentary elections is to determine the composition of the European Parliament, voters frequently use this opportunity to express their sentiments toward their national governments. Given the rising prominence of far-right parties across Europe, and in the Netherlands, for instance, a Dutch exit poll has already indicated that Geert Wilders' Freedom Party is nearly tied with a left-green alliance, highlighting the growing support for far-right ideologies and politics in Europe is changing.

Polls indicate that the two major right-wing groups, the European Conservatives and Reformists (ECR) and Identity and Democracy (ID), could potentially surpass the center-left and become the second-largest faction in the European Parliament. However, the expulsion of Germany's far-right Alternative for Germany (AfD) from the ID group due to a series of scandals underscores the volatility and internal conflicts within the far-right. Traditionally, the center-right European People's Party (EPP) has collaborated with the center-left to navigate legislative processes. However, a poor performance by the center-left may compel the EPP to seek alliances with other political factions, possibly including right-wing groups. This shift could significantly impact the EU's legislative agenda.

A rightward shift in the European Parliament could slow down or halt key priorities for Europe including Climate change, trade, defense, immigration and Ukraine. Far-right political parties often prioritize national interests and economic concerns over collective environmental action. Additionally, social and economic legislation may become more conservative, focusing on stricter immigration policies and reduced social welfare programs.

New Europe is an outcome of nearly three decades of globalization that has made the West significantly richer, but marginalized larger segments of its population. Frustration around a globalized economy where jobs from the West moved elsewhere in significant low-income labor economies in China, India, and Mexico, but allowed Western economies to prioritize innovation in education, high-tech, biotechnology, healthcare, and green energy.

Globalization had existed in the early side of the 1920s. It was a period in which Europeans and others who could afford, moved around the world. Money too, moved around the world as part of trade, transactions, and communications, which expanded enormously. The Telegram, a key instrument of the time, was comparable to today's internet. It meant one could find out what was happening on the other side of the world almost instantaneously. Communication lines that illustrated the global telegraph network allowed connectivity between different continents, enabling rapid communication over long distances for the first time in human history.

Compared to globalization today, where some consumers benefit due to cheaper products, the makers of such products in the early 20th century, like small, independent shops in several cities around Europe, faced stiff competition from department stores that offered a wider variety of goods at lower prices. Many small shops competed against such department stores. Under such fierce competition, their businesses failed. It was a result of consumer preferences, going to larger stores for variety and cheaper products. Tailors, dressmakers, milliners (Hat makers), cobblers (shoe repairers), butchers, grocers, toymakers, furniture makers, upholsterers and many other professions, suddenly couldn't work or find work. This is an example of people who were dispossessed by globalization and by the changes in production, now joined anti-semitic groups.

Jobs were disappearing as more mechanization and better technology became available. The generation of that time and even several generations after, who looked forward to satisfying jobs for the rest of their lives suddenly didn't have them. In an awful reality where they had to scramble for food and feed their families, they turned to fascist and totalitarian forces, just as today as Europe is shifting further right and far-right.

One of the causes of preferences for new and far-right politicians in the 1920s and the 1930s, who came along with their fragmented solutions and were treated much better compared to traditional, elite, and long-time office-bearers, was because they offered hope. Many of their rhyme and rhetoric were slightly distorted and often simplistic, which most of the time was not a solution, but rather adding to the larger problem. Yet, they were able to galvanize huge crowds through their message, diverting the electorate support from traditional politicians who followed a common line "that it is complicated" to Nationalist politicians who carried the line "we will fix it."

The French President of the (far-right) National Rally (NR), Marine Le Pen, uses globalization as a buzzword to show the French electorate the greed of large corporations, tuning it with her own far-right "White French" cultural narrative. It is a nostalgic story of an old industry and a pledge to bring it back. The simple truth is that it is not only difficult, but it will take generations to undo the effects of globalization. Le Pen's story is of volumes of no significant economic upward direction, instead, continuing the business of self-serving.

What she is successfully able to do is dig into the deep anxieties of workers who are under pressure from de-industrialization from technological change from globalization. A message that has resonated across the Atlantic in key American swing states for the 2024 November elections in Michigan, Ohio, Pennsylvania, and Wisconsin. Many of these areas are impacted by the decline of coal, labor, and manufacturing industries, as well as the effects of technological change from globalization. To honor the pledge to bring back old industries means to dent or manipulate multilateralism institutions in all of Europe to be ineffective.

It is about developing a broader nationalistic anti-immigration policy within the European Union in concert with several right-wing parties to plan for the mass deportation of foreigners. As despicable as it sounds, far-right political parties have found support among the same voters with anxieties who are under pressure from the effects of globalization. What supporters of New Europe are oblivious to is Europe, overall, has a labor shortage. It is in both categories of skilled blue-collar and white-collar jobs. A further reduction in labor shortages also means contractions in their present prosperous economies.

A few supporters of New Europe have come around to work with businesses to find ways to mend the shortages. Hungary's Victor Orbán introduced a flat tax to maintain a delicate balance between businesses and his own far-right supporters, with the Kremlin as a key collateral.

A flat tax system, where everyone pays the same percentage of their income regardless of how much they earn, does not generate economic growth. For a country like Hungary that is dependent on EU subsidies, since everyone pays the same rate, those with lower incomes end up spending a larger proportion of their earnings on taxes compared to high-income earners. This can reduce their disposable income, limit their ability to spend on basic needs and reduce overall consumer spending, which is a key driver of economic growth.

The argument that supporters of New Europe not only want to derail the European project, expel migrants, and conduct a reset in their economies means one dangerous objective: a global economic crises.

It is an old fascist playbook from the 1930s when through a combination of economic turmoil, political instability, social unrest, and adept manipulation of nationalist and populist sentiments, far-right political parties used democratic processes to take over European legislative branches.

Supporters of New Europe would need not just an emerging but a global economic crisis to tilt the one thing that has defended Europe's democratic institutions; Europe's social welfare mechanisms. The European Commission, through its Directorate General for Employment, Social Affairs and Inclusion, is the body that plays a leading role in coordinating and overseeing social welfare programs across Europe. If far-right parties are able to topple mainstream pro-welfare parties out of the way in the 2024 June European parliamentary elections, they are well placed to capitalize on their anticipated economic nightmare, which they hope parallels the 1929 Great Depression. Such an economic collapse, hopefully, can be averted, but only if Europeans don't fall for the bate.

The treacherous pathway is not just economic but cultural too. For almost a decade, far-right parties have stirred up passions within electorates to sway the importance of economics to the standing of a European "White culture", something that has unusually played a better hand than the effects of European economic prosperity. Across Western Europe mainstream center-right political parties really grapple with the challenge of populist and far-right parties. The far-right are appealing to smaller voter groups on the right, and they are losing the support of those voters in the center. They consistently favor the interests of white voters who fear migration and ethnic change. Thus, alienating the larger voter groups who are minorities and who are just as conservative as them on economic and social policies, but consider them to be too antagonistic to be worthy of their support. How much that will affect Europe in the future remains to be seen.

The outcome on 9 June 2024 will lay the course of the EU's support for financial and military aid to Ukraine. A stronger presence of far-right-wing parties in the European Parliament may lead to a reassessment of the EU's external commitments, including its support for Ukraine. These factions often advocate for reduced foreign intervention and a focus on domestic issues, which could result in decreased EU engagement in Ukraine.

There is no doubt that the divide in Europe is not just visible but are very noticeable among others outside of Europe and also the Zelenskyy government. It is a source of an uneasy relationship with Europe that could dangerously play a role in Ukraine's hour of need.

Despite what Europe is prioritizing now, it should not be forgotten that the positive aspects of the EU is not failure, rather a moral stroke to attempt to integrate former Soviet satellite states into a common European identity. The European union has been remarkably successful economically in doing so.

Poland became a member of the EU on 1 May 2004, and two decades on, it is looking to take Britain's former place in Europe. It was once considered a significant power during the Polish-Lithuanian Commonwealth of the late 16th century until the late 18th century. It was and still is one of the largest and most populous countries in

Europe. Poland played a significant role in European politics, culture, and military affairs, and it was known for its relative religious tolerance, parliamentary system (the Sejm), and its nobility's significant political power. Its empire was a vast multi-ethnic and multi-confessional state that encompassed much of present-day Austria, Poland, Lithuania, Ukraine, Belarus, and parts of Latvia, Estonia, Romania, Moldova, and western parts of Russia. Today, it is leading the Baltics, including Slovenia and Romania, in a club of its own that not only spends more than 2% of its GDP on defense but is the first to respond to Ukraine's defense.

One of the reasons why Europe is a much better place today than a century ago is because France and Germany no longer have a military-industrial complex, and Britain and Italy do not have an empire. Europe produced authoritarians, fascists, and imperialists that shattered the lives of Europeans and their colonial subjects. After 1945, European powers had neither powerful militaries nor superpower status. Today, as Eastern Europe meets the American definition of equal partners in NATO, Europe as a region and its businesses are integrated into the American supply chains. There are partners in technology, pharmaceuticals, (Covid-19 vaccines like Pfizer-BioNTech (Comirnaty), AstraZeneca-Oxford (Vaxzevria), Moderna (mRNA-1273), Johnson & Johnson (Janssen) and Novavax(NVX-CoV2373)) and joint ventures which has helped foster an integrated global economy. The wealthy EU is a group of pacifist nations and such is their deep roots in pacifism after the horrors of two World Wars that their active duty numbers in NATO do not come close to the American definition of actual active duty soldiers.

It is astonishing how Putin believes NATO to be a threat when the alliance is profoundly a defensive alliance. What is even more surprising is that a defensive group of Europeans is aiding a nation like Ukraine, which is not only defending well against the unprovoked Russian aggression, but Ukraine is setting the European military standards and principles when it comes to Russian aggression.

This is the primary reason why President Zelenskyy favors the United States over Europe. Reality dictates that Europe cannot fight a war, but the Americans can. Europe is very good at doing business and nation building. For Ukraine, their relationship with the EU can only mature once the war is manageable. Ukraine will have to distinguish itself to understand what victory looks like, especially if they are unable to consolidate the Russian occupied eastern areas and Crimea.

The successful defense of Kyiv and a valiant Ukrainian President after two years of war is a testament to being the only country that has stood in the way of Putin. It is now a "state of perpetual conflict," where hostilities, tensions, and military engagements persist without a clear path to an end of the conflict.

How does a country win a war in a state of perpetual conflict? One way is to address the underlying grievances. Both Putin and Zelenskyy are unwilling to back down. Putin wants all of Ukraine, and Zelenskyy wants all of Ukraine too, and Crimea. Both men have the willpower and both will continue the war until their aims are met. Both are also on the path to producing their own fighting capability through weaponry and international help. Strangely, nearly half a century ago, the United States and the Soviet Union engaged in similar methods.

The two Cold War rivals engaged in an arms race, continuously developing and stockpiling increasingly sophisticated nuclear weapons and conventional military capabilities. Like Ukraine, West Germany was at the center of it. Berlin, its capital and a divided city became a focal point of rivalry. Its location in the heart of Europe made it strategically significant as it was located deep within the Soviet-controlled territory in Eastern Europe. Berlin became a symbol of Cold War divisions between the Western and Eastern blocs. The construction of the Berlin Wall in 1961 further solidified this division, physically separating East and West, symbolizing the larger divide between Communism and Capitalism.

Ensuring access to West Berlin became a crucial priority for the United States to demonstrate its resolve and support for its allies. The Berlin Airlift, which took place from 1948 to 1949, was a significant event that highlighted the American commitment to the city. When the Soviets cut off supply routes, the United States and its allies organized a massive airlift operation to provide essential supplies to the city. This demonstrated Western determination to stand up to Soviet aggression and support the people of West Berlin.

Like Berlin, Kharkiv today is a city in eastern Ukraine, and could become the pivotal point of rivalry between Ukraine and Russia. However, unlike the Cold War, there are more dangerous concerns now than before. Modern warfare involves highly advanced and precision-based weaponry, including hypersonic missiles, cyber weapons, and advanced drone technology, causing significant destruction at a rapid pace and with little warning. The use of sophisticated nuclear arsenals too, made weapons more lethal and their delivery systems more advanced. Large-scale cyber attacks are causing crippling critical infrastructure, including power grids, communication networks, and financial systems. The integrated nature of digital infrastructure in today's society makes such tools challenging to prepare any safeguards. Then there is the spread of disinformation and propaganda through social media and other online platforms which can destabilize events and influence public opinion more rapidly and effectively than during the Cold War.

The global economy is highly interconnected today, meaning that any large-scale conflict will have devastating economic repercussions worldwide. Sanctions and economic warfare can lead to significant financial instability and hardship on a global scale, with disruption of global supply chains which have lead to shortages of essential goods, affecting not just the countries involved in the conflict but destroying the livelihoods of inhabitants of poorer nations.

During the Cold War, diplomatic channels and treaties (like the INF Treaty and the START treaties) were established that helped manage and reduce tensions. Many of these agreements have been weakened or abandoned, reducing the mechanisms available to prevent escalation. The erosion of trust and communication between major powers now will lead to misunderstandings and miscalculations, increasing the risk of conflict. Military technology and the speed of information flow today mean that decisions are made more quickly, leaving less time for deliberation and de-escalation, which can lead to rapid escalation before diplomatic solutions can be explored. All of this goes to say that the West should finish what it started in Ukraine.

Both Europe and the United States have to ramp up production of arms and ammunition. The assembly lines of the Cold War era simply do not exist anymore. Europe has no military-industrial complex, but the United States does. However, it has wound its production levels down from Cold War era levels. Refilling inventory remains a challenge, and it will become even more difficult as the Ukraine war continues. This is because getting inventory refilled requires several years. Additional problems around restocking, recruiting more

American troops for future campaigns and the military contractors that support them, are not just a supply issue but also a problem with innovation and logistics. The United States hasn't ramped up production because the understanding is that Western-backed sanctions on Russia were going to do the real damage, but they didn't. The Russian economy has survived and is not running out of arms and ammunition, which was supposed to be the real aim.

Russian forces are able to produce and go on the offensive and Ukraine's cities will soon require more defense. America's lazy maneuver to limit Russian ability has failed and the real casualties are Ukrainians, who are losing their capability to fight in the long term.

Washington was nervous about supporting Ukraine away from the insurgency and to incremental defense, wanting to contain the war and ensure Ukraine's fighters remain on Ukrainian soil, but if the war continues for a longer period, it will be hard to demand Kyiv to stay onside, much to Washington's dismay, they are inching further into Russian terriroty. That hasn't changed the much fixated image of a permanent Russian occupation which is also not dissimilar to some of the realities within Europe of today.

In the de facto partition of Cyprus with a Greek Cypriot-controlled south and Turkish Cypriot-controlled north, and the UN between them in the form of a buffer zone, this is a picture that could very well reflect Ukraine's and Russia's borders of tomorrow.

There is no doubt that there are major differences between Cyprus and Ukraine, but there are similarities. As Ukraine disentangled itself from its Soviet past, so too did Cyprus from its Ottoman history. Under such a similar conclusion, a reality of a Russian-occupied Ukraine, with Kharkiv as its capital and what is left of a sovereign Ukraine with its capital in Kyiv, could very well become a reality. The Cyprus example has similarities to Ukraine's border status for the future. True that Ukraine is significantly larger by landmass and a larger population, but in the future it may have to deal with the same struggles as the Cypriots.

There are also several similarities with the historical conflict in Northern Ireland, particularly in terms of underlying ethnic and political tensions, foreign involvement, and the impact on civilians. Like Ukraine, where conflict also involves significant ethnic and linguistic divisions, there are parallels, particularly between ethnic

Ukrainians and ethnic Russians in Donetsk and Luhansk. The roots of the Northern Ireland problems in deep-seated divisions between the primarily Protestant unionists and loyalists, who identified as British and wanted to remain with Britain, and the mainly Catholic nationalists and republicans, who identified as Irish and wanted to unite with the Republic of Ireland, is not too far from the Russia-Ukraine conflict.

Identity played a crucial role in whether Northern Ireland should remain part of Britain or join a united Ireland. Like Russia, the British government had a direct role in the conflict, both through its military presence and political policies. The Republic of Ireland provided moral and diplomatic support to the nationalist cause. The troubles led to widespread violence, including bombings, shootings, and riots, which affected the civilian population of Northern Ireland. Many were killed, injured, or displaced as a result of the conflict. The 1998 Good Friday Agreement was a significant milestone that largely brought an end to the fighting. It included provisions for power-sharing, disarmament, and constitutional changes, and it was supported by referendums in Northern Ireland and the Republic of Ireland. Today, the conflict is frozen in a very fragile peace. However, some recent events have indicated otherwise. In Ballymena on 3 May 2024, an attack involving two petrol bombs was thrown through the living room window of a house on Queen Street. Fortunately, neither of the bombs exploded, and the male occupant of the house, although shaken, was not injured. A similar bomb threat against the home of Helen McEntee, Ireland's Minister for Justice, on 28 April 2024 looked to disturb the fragile peace. Although no explosives were found, the threat was taken very seriously, leading to the evacuation of McEntee's family. These incidents highlight the sensitivities of the delicateness in Northern Ireland, something Ukraine is dealing at a significantly and higher combative level, but that could very well be part of its permanent state.

Two years into the war and six months of no economic and military aid to Ukraine has resulted in Russian forces advancing. These advances come at a time of large human toll on both sides. Thousands of Russian soldiers have been sent to Ukraine to fight, and the disparity between what's being reported in Russia in terms of the number of casualties and the numbers in Ukraine is difficult to verify. Russians are rallying around their President in this time of crisis. It is as if they don't want to believe Putin may have taken a fatal decision to go to war recklessly, but it is Russians who are paying the price. This is at odds with what the Kremlin wants Russians to believe, that Russian troops are in Ukraine in the interest of Russians and a necessity against NATO. Critics of the war are detained and fined under a new law for discrediting the Russian armed forces. Meanwhile, with the growing number of Russians killed and buried in Russian cemeteries, is only expanding. War graves are becoming a common sight, and they are growing, sometimes twice as much as before and some even more. This is the reality of all graveyards all over Russia since the start of the "special military operation." There are unconfirmed reports that Russia has lost 23% more troops in the second year of the war compared to the first. Since January 2023, Russia began sending thousands of inexperienced troops forward in waves to weaken Ukrainian positions and expose their location. Six months of no American military aid produced more Russian firepower against Ukrainian forces. This will only continue on as the Ukrainians struggle to shift that balance. Russia is taking areas across the front, but part of its success is in recruiting a different caliber of fighters. Prisoners in the Russian system have been crucial to these tactics and in return, for six months on the front line, they are promised an amnesty deal. However, many have died on the front lines.

In a state of perpetual conflict, it is important to estimate the value of defeat. If the US is not serious about ramping up production to support Ukraine, other problems will soon arise. If Ukraine is not going to win the war, Europe cannot help. If Ukraine is on the brink of defeat, where Ukraine doesn't get back every inch of its territory, what would that mean? Surprisingly, Europe has an answer.

Strasbourg, the capital of the Grand Est region, formerly known as Alsace, in northeastern France, is a city rich in history and culture, situated directly across from the German town of Kehl, a unique geographical location has profoundly influenced its identity, architecture, and cultural life, making the city appear distinct from many other French cities. The city has oscillated between French and German control multiple times, particularly during the 1870 Franco-Prussian War, World War I, and World War II. Like Ukrainians, many residents are bilingual, speaking both French and Alsatian, a dialect closely related to German. Street signs and public information are often in both languages, underscoring the city's bicultural nature.

THE VALUE IN DEFEAT

Like President Putin, French King Louis XIV pursued a policy of expansion known as the "Reunions," aiming to consolidate French territories and secure natural borders. This included efforts to annex cities and territories that were strategically important, and claimed under vague historical rights. In 1681, using the pretext of ancient claims and strategic necessity, French troops, under the command of Marshal François de Créquy, marched into Strasbourg and occupied the city without any significant resistance. The formal French annexation of Strasbourg came at the Truce of Ratisbon in 1684. The story of Strasbourg is a fairly decent indication of what may become of Kharkiv, Crimea, and other cities occupied by Russia, if Ukraine is unable to consolidate these areas.

Despite Ukraine's immediate negative consequences, a military defeat can present several valuable opportunities. Such an outcome can underscore the importance of international economic cooperation, paving the way for new partnerships that enhance various capabilities over time. A Ukrainian military defeat would not hinder an economic resurgence; instead, it would lead to full membership in the EU, thereby increasing political capital for the Zelenskyy government. The value of a Ukrainian defeat in a war with Russia would invigorate Europe to include Ukraine in key structures beyond economic, military, and political alliances.

Just like Strasbourg, which is one of the primary seats of the EU and hosts the official seat of the European Parliament today, symbolizes Franco-German reconciliation. Ukrainian cities under Russian occupation in the future could undergo a similar transformation. An imminent prosperous and thriving Ukraine could effectively nullify President Putin's ambitions of annexing Ukraine. It may not be apparent now, but if Putin's predecessor and successive Soviet leaders were unable to force Ukrainians under their fold, what makes the Russian President so sure that even with the threat of nuclear weapons, he can succeed where others have failed. To add to his frustrations, the practical implications of Ukraine's transformation from a battleground to a beacon of prosperity would serve as a powerful counter-reality to Russian expansionism, demonstrating that Putin's pursuit of Ukraine at any price is ultimately, recklessly futile.

END NOTES

PREFACE

"Aegis Ashore Scores in First Intercept Test" | Lagrone, Sam | USNI | 10 December 2015 | https://news.usni.org/2015/12/10/aegis-ashore-scores-in-first-intercept-test

"United States : Anniversaries of NATO Enlargement." | United States Department of State | 31 March 2014 | https://2009-2017.state.gov/secretary/remarks/2014/03/224228.htm

Farquhar, J. (2015). Aerial Reconnaissance, the Press and American Foreign Policy, 1950-1954. Air Power History, 62(4), 38-51.

"The Peculiar Timing Of Trump's Dismissal Of FBI Director Comey" | WBEZ Chicago | 10 May 2017 | https://www.wbez.org/wbezs-reset/2017/05/10/the-peculiar-timing-of-trumps-dismissal-of-fbi-director-comey

"A comparative analysis: Acts of cultural genocide in historic Nazi Germany to present day Afghanistan and China." | Turner, S. | 2021 | https://core.ac.uk/download/552657281.pdf

CHAPTER 1: Vigilance

"Russia's Medvedev warns of nuclear response if Ukraine hits missile launch sites" | WCTS Radio. | Reuters | 11 January 2024 https://wctsradio.com/russias-medvedev-warns-of-nuclear-response-if-ukraine-hits-missile-launch-sites/

Lamar, N. (2023). "BRICS threat against the US dollar rings hollow." Indianapolis Business Journal, 44(10), 21A.

END NOTES

The Comprehensive Nuclear-Test-Ban Treaty: a success story ready for completion | United Nations Information Service Vienna | October 2022 |
https://unis.unvienna.org/unis/en/pressrels/2022/unisinf585.html

"UNITED STATES POSITION TOWARDS IRAN' S NUCLEAR PROGRAM" | University of Baghdad | October 2019 | doi:10.13140/rg.2.2.26388.94088

"Chapter 1. Nuclear Disarmament1" | Hiroshima Report 2019 | Hiroshima for Global Peace |
https://hiroshimaforpeace.com/en/hiroshimareport/report-2019/hr2019disarmament/

"Trump's announcement to leave INF raises concerns" | The DONG-A ILBO | 23 October 2018 |
https://www.donga.com/en/article/all/20181023/1512924/1

"The Impact of the Proliferation of Small Arms and Light Weapons on West African States: An Analysis of the Sierra Leone Civil War." | Oluwadare, A. J.| 2014   https://core.ac.uk/download/229606464.pdf

"The INF Treaty Lapses Tomorrow. Trump & Putin Should Save It" | Corden, Pierce | Defense One | 1 August 2019 |
https://www.defenseone.com/ideas/2019/08/inf-treaty-expires-tomorrow-trump-putin-should-save-it/158852/?oref=d1-next-story

"Nuclear Safety and Security in the Arctic: Crafting an Effective Regional Governance System." | Lysenko, M., Vylegzhanin, A., & Young, O. | 2022 |
https://doi.org/10.23865/arctic.v13.3820

"Prohibition of the development, production and stockpiling of biological and toxin weapons and on their destruction" | University of Macedonia | 2019 | https://www.thessismun.org/participants-guide/documentation/study-guides-2019/1st-study-guide-topic-area-b/

"Why China has done better than Russia since 1989" | Bucknall, K. | International Journal of Social Economics | 1 July 1997 | https://www.emerald.com/insight/content/doi/10.1108/03068299710 178991/full/html#:~:text=Rising%20labour%20costs%20in%20dyna mic,little%20or%20nothing%20to%20offer.
"The work of the European Parliament July 1988-June 1989" | EU European Parliament Document | 2 May 2017 | https://aei.pitt.edu/86623/

"Paavo Väyrynen to the memorial ceremony of former Foreign Minister Hans-Dietrich Genscher of Germany" | Finnish Government Ministry for Foreign Affairs | 15 April 2016 | https://valtioneuvosto.fi/en/-/paavo-vayrynen-saksan-entisen-ulkoministerin-hans-dietrich-genscherin-muistotilaisuuteen

"Etched in Stone: Russian Strategic Culture and the Future of Transatlantic Security" | Rumer E. and Sokolsky R. | Carnegie Endowment for International Peace | 8 September 2020 | https://carnegieendowment.org/research/2020/09/etched-in-stone-russian-strategic-culture-and-the-future-of-transatlantic-security?lang=en

CHAPTER 2: Change of Fortunes

"RUMORS SUGGEST MAJOR RUSSIAN MILITARY REORGANIZATION IMMINENT" | Blank, S. | Jamestown Foundation | 8 February 2006 | https://jamestown.org/program/rumors-suggest-major-russian-military-reorganization-imminent/

"Prominent journalist says Russia's Surovikin dismissed as head of aerospace forces" | Reuters | 22 August 2023 | https://www.reuters.com/world/europe/prominent-journalist-says-russias-surovikin-dismissed-head-aerospace-forces-2023-08-22/#:~:text=Prominent%20journalist%20says%20Russia's%20Surovi kin%20dismissed%20as%20head%20of%20aerospace%20forces,-By%20Reuters&text=Aug%2022%20(Reuters)%20%2D%20A,of%2 0the%20country's%20aerospace%20forces.

"Do not repeat the tactics which have gained you one victory" | Sun Tzu | https://www.artofwarinbiz.com/weak-points-and-strong/methods-regulated-by-circumstances/

"Ukraine is running out of time against Russia" | Clarett Consulting | 2 January 2024| https://www.claretteconsulting.com/post/ukraine-is-running-out-of-time-against-russia

"Celebrating the Republic Day 2020 in Azerbaijan" | Sinalco Group | 29 May 2020| https://www.sinalcogroup.com/celebrating-the-republic-day-2020-in-azerbaijan/

"Only one side implementing ceasefire in Syria: Russia" | Iran Press TV | 16 September 2016 | https://www.globalsecurity.org/wmd/library/news/syria/2016/syria-160916-presstv01.htm

"Russia: Two Men Detained In Moscow Blast" | Radio Free Europe | 9 August 2000 | https://www.rferl.org/a/1094504.html

"Russia's Nord Stream 2 Natural Gas Pipeline to Germany Halted" | Congressional Research Service | 10 March 2022 | https://crsreports.congress.gov/product/pdf/IF/IF11138

"U.S. waives sanctions on Nord Stream 2 as Biden seeks to mend Europe ties" | Shalal, A., Gardner, T., Holland, S.| Reuters | 19 May 2021 | https://www.reuters.com/business/energy/us-waive-sanctions-firm-ceo-behind-russias-nord-stream-2-pipeline-source-2021-05-19/

"Nord Stream 2: Twists and turns of a controversial gas pipeline" | Clean Energy Wire | 4 January 2024 | https://www.cleanenergywire.org/news/nord-stream-2-twists-and-turns-controversial-gas-pipeline

"Hypertrophy as NATO's Masculinity: Out-of-Area Operations and Enlargements in the Post-Cold War Context" | González-Villa, C. , Radeljić, B. | Journal of International Women Studies – Bridgewater

State University | August 2023 |
https://vc.bridgew.edu/cgi/viewcontent.cgi?article=3140&context=ji
ws

"Finland and Sweden Apply to Join NATO: What's Next?" |
Unlühisarcıklı, O., Lesser, I., Berzina, K. | German Marshall Fund |
19 May 2022 | https://www.gmfus.org/news/finland-and-sweden-
apply-join-nato-whats-next

"Neutrality has Outlived its Usefulness: Finland and Sweden Pick a
Side" | Williams, C.J. | Post Alley | 16 May 2022 |
https://www.postalley.org/2022/05/16/neutrality-has-outlived-its-
usefulness-finland-and-sweden-pick-a-side/

"Explainer: Finland, Sweden weigh up pros and cons of NATO
membership" | Reuters | 13 April 2022 |
https://www.reuters.com/world/europe/finland-sweden-weigh-up-
pros-cons-nato-membership-2022-04-13/

"Pakistan's Secret Arms Deal with US: Key to IMF Bailout and
Political Fallout Revealed" | Democracy News Live | 18 September
2023 | https://democracynewslive.com/leadstory/pakistans-secret-
arms-deal-with-us-key-to-imf-bailout-and-political-fallout-revealed-
1249174

"Only 150 Troops Involved, but Stakes Are Much Bigger: Trump's
Syria Decision Seen as Significant Policy Shift: The Rundown" |
Johnson, J. | Newser | 7 October 2019 |
https://www.newser.com/story/281403/trumps-syria-decision-seen-
as-significant-policy-shift.html

"Russia's Gain Is Turning Out to Be China's Pain" | Pei, M. |
Bloomberg | 6 June 2024 |
https://www.bloomberg.com/opinion/articles/2024-06-06/ukraine-
war-russia-s-gain-is-turning-out-to-be-china-s-pain

"How to Improve China-US Trust" | Dingli, S.| The Diplomat | 4
March 2011 | https://thediplomat.com/2013/11/how-to-improve-

china-us-trust/

"China, Russia, and the War in Ukraine" | Stent, A. | Internationale Politik Quarterly | 28 August 2023 | https://ip-quarterly.com/en/china-russia-and-war-ukraine

"Nickel prices soar on Russia tension, tight supply" | People's Daily | 21 February 2022 | https://peoplesdaily.pdnews.cn/world/er/30001225236

"Is Trump coming back?" | Hard Facts | 28 February 2023| https://hardfacts.online/putins-criminals-2-3/

"Russia's Economy Grew in 2023, Despite War and Sanctions" | Garver, R. | Europe VOA | 8 February 2024 | https://www.voanews.com/a/russia-economy-grew-in-2023-despite-war-and-sanctions/7478952.html

"Ex-KGB spy and oil magnate dies in latest mystery high-profile Russian death" | WSTale.com | 23 February 2023 | https://wstale.com/science/ex-kgb-spy-and-oil-magnate-dies-in-latest-mystery-high-profile-russian-death/

"Radhakrishnan Got Stalin to Support India on Kashmir" | India West Journal News | 6 September 2022 | https://indiawest.com/radhakrishnan-got-stalin-to-support-india-on-kashmir/

"China seen through 'colored lens': Ambassador to EU" | Jing, F. | China Daily | 21 September 2011 | http://europe.chinadaily.com.cn/europe/2011-09/21/content_13747157.htm

"Russia and China have been teaming up to reduce reliance on the dollar. Here's how it's going" | Nikoladze, M., Bhusari, M. | Atlantic Council | 22 February 2023 | https://www.atlanticcouncil.org/blogs/new-atlanticist/russia-and-china-have-been-teaming-up-to-reduce-reliance-on-the-dollar-heres-how-its-going/

"January 2024 — Monthly analysis of Russian fossil fuel exports and sanctions" | Levi, I. | Center for Research on Energy and Clean Air | https://energyandcleanair.org/january-2024-monthly-analysis-of-russian-fossil-fuel-exports-and-sanctions/#:~:text=Crude%20oil%3A%20China%20is%20the,Russia%20on%205%20December%202022.

"Which countries are most reliant on Russian energy" | IAEA | https://www.iea.org/reports/national-reliance-on-russian-fossil-fuel-imports/which-countries-are-most-reliant-on-russian-energy

CHAPTER 3: A Price of Consequences

"WHAT WAS THE WARSAW PACT ?" | North Atlantic Treaty Organization | https://www.nato.int/cps/en/natohq/declassified_138294.htm#:~:text=The%20Warsaw%20Pact%20was%20a,(Albania%20withdrew%20in%201968).

"Myths & Pretexts: NATO and Origins of the Ukraine Crisis" | Roininen, A. | Prague Europen Summit | 22 May 2017 | https://www.iir.cz/lies-provocations-or-myths-pretexts-nato-and-the-ukraine-crisis

"Ukraine: the history behind Russia's claim that Nato promised not to expand to the east" | The Conversation | 14 February 2022 | https://theconversation.com/ukraine-the-history-behind-russias-claim-that-nato-promised-not-to-expand-to-the-east-177085

"Did Putin invade Ukraine because of NATOs "broken promise"?" | Zanchetta, B. | Kings College London | 18 March 2022 | https://www.kcl.ac.uk/did-putin-invade-ukraine-because-of-natos-broken-promise

"The Warsaw Pact's forgotten legacy" | Braw, E. | Engelsberg Ideas | 21 May 2024 | https://engelsbergideas.com/notebook/the-warsaw-pacts-forgotten-legacy/

"UK Offers Crash Course to Ukrainian Troops on Protecting Power Plants" | Gets Your News | November 2023 | https://www.getsyournews.com/news/uk-offers-crash-course-to-ukrainian-troops-on-protecting-power-plants/

"Trans Adriatic Pipeline Project (Translated version)" | European Bank | 19 December 2017 | https://www.ebrd.com/work-with-us/projects/psd/trans-adriatic-pipeline-project.html

"China threatens consequences over US warship's actions" | News Hunt Times | https://newshunttimes.com/china-threatens-consequences-over-us-warships-actions/

From Crimea To Donbas: Analyzing The Ongoing "New Cold War" Between Russia And Ukraine | Banga, S. | Vision of Sid | https://visionofsid.com/2023/02/22/analyzing-the-ongoing-new-cold-war-between-russia-and-ukraine/

"Georgia's love-hate affair with Russia" | Bobylev, S. | Le Monde diplomatique | October 2021 | https://mondediplo.com/2021/10/10georgia

"The febrile world of Georgian politics" | Daum, P. | Le Monde diplomatique | October 2021 | https://mondediplo.com/2021/10/11georgia-box

"A drilling rig straight to the Caspian Sea" | Doepgen, C. | International Transport Journal | 30 December 2020 | https://www.transportjournal.com/en/home/heavylift-breakbulk/artikeldetail/a-drilling-rig-straight-to-the-caspian-sea.html

"Caspian Sea shows promise and disappointments" | Drilling Contractor | https://drillingcontractor.org/dcpi/2002/dc-julaug02/jul2-caspian.pdf

Dupont, C., Schultz, T., Wahl, M. R., & Angın, M. | "Types of political risk leading to investment arbitrations in the oil and gas sector" | The Journal of World Energy Law & Business | 2015 | https://doi.org/10.1093/jwelb/jwv019

"Azerbaijan and Armenia Conflict" | NIGMA | https://nigma.global/azerbaijan-and-armenia-conflict/

"Explained: Why Azerbaijan Launched Attack On Armenia, History Of Conflict" | Just Bureaucracy | 19 September 2023 | https://justbureaucracy.com/explained-why-azerbaijan-launched-attack-on-armenia-history-of-conflict/

"Putin says he could send police to Belarus if necessary" | Rainsford, S. | BBC | 27 August 2020 | https://www.bbc.com/news/world-europe-53930796

"The Role of Belarus in the Russia-Ukraine Conflict: From Guarantor of Security to a Source of Instability" | Leukavets, A. | Wilson Center | 7 July 2022 | https://www.wilsoncenter.org/event/role-belarus-russia-ukraine-conflict-guarantor-security-source-instability

"Risk of military incidents on Belarus-Ukraine border quite high: Lukashenko" | Aljazeera | 25 Apr 2024 | https://www.aljazeera.com/news/2024/4/25/risk-of-military-incidents-on-belarus-ukraine-border-quite-high-lukashenko

"Turkey begins operation in Syria to establish buffer zone: Report" | Press TV | 11 May 2016 | https://www.presstv.ir/Detail/2016/05/11/465017/Turkey-Syria-military-operation-Jarablus-Kilis-Daesh

"Turkey's military operation in Syria and its impact on relations with the EU" | European Parliament | November 2019 | chrome-extension://efaidnbmnnnibpcajpcglclefindmkaj/https://www.europarl.europa.eu/EPRS/EPRS-Briefing-642284-Turkeys-military-operation-Syria-FINAL.pdf

"Turkey's military operations in Iraq and Syria" | Reuters | 21 November 2022 | https://www.reuters.com/world/middle-east/turkeys-military-operations-iraq-syria-2022-11-21/

"US had Intelligence of Ukrainian Plan to Attack Nord Stream Project" | Singh, K. , Ayyub, R. || Washington Post | 7 June 2023 | https://www.oedigital.com/news/505649-us-had-intelligence-of-ukrainian-plan-to-attack-nord-stream-project-washington-post

"Angela Merkel's self-justification on Russia does not add up" | Cliff, J. | New Statesman | 14 June 2022 | https://www.newstatesman.com/world/europe/2022/06/angela-merkel-former-german-chancellor-on-russia

"Merkel: There was nothing I could do about Putin" | Preussen, W. | Politico | 25 November 2022 | https://www.politico.eu/article/angela-merkel-germany-there-was-nothing-i-could-do-about-vladimir-putin-russia-ukraine/

"Angela Merkel says she lost influence over Putin as a lame duck leader" | Connoly, K. | The Guardian | 25 November 2022 | https://www.theguardian.com/world/2022/nov/25/angela-merkel-says-she-lost-influence-over-putin-as-a-lame-duck-leader

"Karski's reports: the story and the history" | Rappak, W. | University College London | September 2020 | https://core.ac.uk/download/477686044.pdf

CHAPTER 4: A Dependent Alliance

Chevreux, L., Plaizier, W., Schuh, C., Brown, W., & Triplat, A. (2014). NATO Forces. Apress EBooks. https://doi.org/10.1007/978-1-4302-6748-5_19

"NATO's Largest Military Exercise Since the Cold War- Steadfast Defender" | Helloscholar News | 14 September 2023 | https://news.helloscholar.in/natos-largest-military-exercise-since-the-cold-war-steadfast-defender/

END NOTES

"February 5, 2018: When the Berlin Wall had been up for 10,316 days" | The Hindu | 10 February 2018| https://www.thehindu.com/news/international/february-5-2018-when-the-berlin-wall-had-been-up-for-10316-days/article22716067.ece

"NATO and SHAPE" | Heinen | | https://www.heinen-doors.com/en/projects/nato-and-shape/

"Clipping the Eagle's Wings: The Limiting of the Korean Air War, 1950-1953" | Horky, R. K.| Office of Graduate Studies of Texas A&M University | 2013 | https://core.ac.uk/download/17050144.pdf

"Shyam Saran on Foreign Policy Challenges in 2022" | Saran, S. | CPR| 22 February 2022 | https://cprindia.org/shyam-saran-on-foreign-policy-challenges-in-2022/

"The Cold War and American Society" CHAPTER 21 – 3 | slideum.com | https://slideum.com/doc/4161401/the-cold-war-and-american-society

"Turkish PM warns companies against inking energy contracts with Cyprus" | Wilayat Times | 30 May 2024 | https://wilayattimes.com/turkish-pm-warns-companies-against-inking-energy-contracts-with-cyprus/

"Finland and Sweden Do Not Have the 'NATO Option' They Think They Have" | Hurt, M. | ICDS | 5 January 2022 | https://icds.ee/en/finland-and-sweden-do-not-have-the-nato-option-they-think-they-have/

"NATO: Strengthening Transatlantic Security and Cooperation" | The Global MUN | 29 November 2023 | https://theglobalmun.com/nato-strengthening-transatlantic-security-and-cooperation/

"The Russian Food and Agricultural Import Ban" | Khachaturyan,

M., & Peterson, E. W. F.| 2017 |
https://core.ac.uk/download/188117416.pdf

Sadeghi, S., Nzeza, P., Griffin, M., Amur, J., Fung, N., Hendel, J.,
Nicholson, P., Oetting, J., Zilk, C., & Schmidt, N. (2007). Index.
Index on Censorship. https://doi.org/10.1080/03064220701565906

"United States Sophistry on the Palestinian Resolution for Statehood"
| Mason, M. J. | 2012| https://core.ac.uk/download/215697033.pdf

"Syria, Hezbollah, Iran mobilising 'thousands of troops" | Al Bawaba
| 7 September 2013 | https://www.albawaba.com/news/syria-iran-
hezbollah-us-strike-518638

CHAPTER 5: Ukraine's Key Allies

"Skripal Case: UK Police Name 2 Russian Suspects, Moscow Calls
for Cooperation" | Sputnik International | 9 May 2018 |
https://sputnikglobe.com/20180905/uk-prosecution-skripals-suspects-
1067763246.html

"Russia not cooperating on Khangoshvili murder case, German
foreign minister says" | UNIAN | 12 August 2020 |
https://www.unian.info/world/khangoshvili-murder-german-foreign-
minister-says-russia-not-cooperating-on-probe-11109338.html

"Something is Rotten in the Heart Of Brussels" | EURACTIV PR | 12
December 2022 | https://pr.euractiv.com/pr/something-rotten-heart-
brussels-243774

"China's development of asymmetric warfare and the security of
Taiwan, Republic of China" | Jinn, G. W. | 2004 |
https://core.ac.uk/download/36694993.pdf

"The Allied unity and solidarity are strengthening Latvia's security" |
Ministry of Foreign Affairs Republic of Latvia | 27 February 2022|
https://www.mfa.gov.lv/en/article/allied-unity-and-solidarity-are-

strengthening-latvia-s-
security?utm_source=https%3A%2F%2Fwww.google.com%2F

CHAPTER 6: The Divided

"Europe Divided? Elites vs. Public Opinion on European Integration" | Hooghe, L | Institute for Advanced Studies, Vienna | April 2003 | https://aei.pitt.edu/531/2/pw_88.pdf

"Europe's Divided Left" | Taylor, R. | DISSENT | 2009 | https://www.dissentmagazine.org/article/europes-divided-left/

"Europe Divided Again: Wall Street Journal" | Pancevski, B. | YaleGlobal Online | 17 November 2019 | https://archive-yaleglobal.yale.edu/content/europe-divided-again-wall-street-journal

"Despite the recent cooling-off, Russia and Germany can still work together – if they see each other for what they really are" | Trenin, D.| The German Times | October 2018 | https://www.german-times.com/despite-the-recent-cooling-off-russia-and-germany-can-still-work-together-if-they-see-each-other-for-what-they-really-are/

"Creating the 4th Reich within the EU – Nazi plan for post-war dominance… 'plans of German industrialists to engage in underground activity' : THE RED HOUSE REPORT" | ADARA PRESS | 30 December 2019| https://adarapress.com/2019/12/30/the-red-house-report-nazi-plan-for-post-war-dominance-plans-of-german-industrialists-to-engage-in-underground-activity-creating-the-4th-reich-within-the-eu/

"The Eu Was Started with an Agreement of "| ALTERON REIT | 7 March 2023 | https://alteronreit.com/the-eu-was-started-with-an-agreement-of-3269.html#:~:text=The%20EU%20started%20with%20an,signed%20on%20April%2018%2C%201951.

END NOTES

"ENLARGING THE EUROPEAN UNION A FUTURE PERSPECTIVE" | Remond, J. | Paper presented at the Fourth Biennial Conference of the European Community Studies Association | 11-14 May 1995 | https://aei.pitt.edu/7005/1/redmond_john.pdf

"Pompeo wants NATO to take 'actions' to help Ukraine" | American Military News | March 2019 | https://americanmilitarynews.com/2019/03/pompeo-wants-nato-to-take-actions-to-help-ukraine/

"Coming Out Christian in the Roman World: How the Followers of Jesus Made a Place in Caesar's Empire" | Boin, D.R. | Bloomsbury Press; 1st edition | 3 March 2015 | https://books.google.com/books/about/Coming_Out_Christian_in_the_Roman_World.html?id=k-txBgAAQBAJ&source=kp_book_description

"CRISIS, IDENTITY AND URBAN CONTINUITY IN SEVENTH CENTURY BYZANTIUM: A HAGIOGRAPHIC REASSESSMENT" | Kelly, D. J. | 2022 https://core.ac.uk/download/524821817.pdf

"Byzantine heritage, archaeology, and politics between Russia and the Ottoman Empire: Russian Archaeological Institute in Constantinople (1894-1914)" | Üre, P. | 2014 | https://core.ac.uk/download/46517782.pdf

"Inside Zelensky's Plan to Beat Putin's Propaganda in Russian-Occupied Ukraine" | Shuster, S. | Time Magazine | 22 June 2023 | |https://time.com/6288904/ukraine-russia-propaganda-counteroffensive-zelensky/

"Kremlin runs disinformation campaign to undermine Zelensky, documents show" | Belton, C. | The Washington Post | 16 February 2024 | https://www.washingtonpost.com/world/2024/02/16/russian-disinformation-zelensky-zaluzhny/

"Victory in Ukraine Starts with Addressing Five Strategic Problems" | Jensen, B. and Hoffman, E. | Center for Strategic & International Studies (CSIS) | 15 May 2024 | https://www.csis.org/analysis/victory-ukraine-starts-addressing-five-strategic-problems

CHAPTER 7: The Anti-West Axis

"The Great Recession: A Self-Fulfilling Global Panic" | Bacchetta, P., and van Wincoop, E. | AMERICAN ECONOMIC JOURNAL: MACROECONOMICS VOL. 8, NO. 4, (pp. 177–98) | OCTOBER 2016 | https://www.aeaweb.org/articles?id=10.1257/mac.20140092

"Comparative Analysis of the 2008-2009 Financial Crisis and the Current Banking Crisis" | Gurdian, E. & Montanez, S. | Journal of Student Research | 30 November 2023 | https://www.jsr.org/hs/index.php/path/article/view/5508

"Disruptions and resilience in global container shipping and ports: the COVID-19 pandemic versus the 2008–2009 financial crisis" | Springer Link | Originally Published: 4 January 2021| https://link.springer.com/article/10.1057/s41278-020-00180-5

"President Kassym-Jomart Tokayev held talks with President of the People's Republic of China Xi Jinping" | akorda-kz | 17 October 2023 | https://www.akorda.kz/en/1-1792253#:~:text=October%2017%2C%202023&text=The%20officia l%20visit%20of%20Kassym,to%20respect%20the%20distinguished %20guest

"THE ROLE OF THE FINNISH SPECIAL OPERATIONS IN THE SPACE BETWEEN PEACE AND CRISIS" | Hilden, A. I. | 2018 | https://core.ac.uk/download/343436274.pdf

"The 2023 Financial Crisis is Likely to Be the Worst Economic

END NOTES

Downturn" | Delarno | Booboone.com | 6 January 2023 | https://booboone.com/2023-financial-crisis/

"How to measure China's true economic growth" | Finance News | 24 March 2023| https://financenews.expert/2023/03/24/how-to-measure-chinas-true-economic-growth/

"Relocating labour-intensive manufacturing firms from China to Southeast Asia: A preliminary investigation. Bandung: Journal of the Global South" | Yang, C | 2016 | https://doi.org/10.1186/s40728-016-0031-4

"Iran nuclear deal could make oil even cheaper" | CBS58 Staff | 17 March 2015| https://www.cbs58.com/news/iran-nuclear-deal-could-make-oil-even-cheaper

"News Update - Monday, Dec 20, 2021" | Afghan Report | 20 December 2021 | https://afghan-report.com/news/20211220/

"Ivan IV's Personal Mythology of Kingship" | Slavic Review, Vol. 52, No. 4. (Winter, 1993), pp. 789–809| Hunt, Priscilla

"Ivan the Terrible" | History Today (Mar 1953) 3#3, Vol. 3 Issue 3, pp. 170–73 | Menken, Jules

"Change in ISIS Threat Means Evolution in Long-Term U.S.-Iraq Relationship" | U.S. Department of Defense | Lopez, C.T. | 25 January 2024 | https://www.defense.gov/News/News-Stories/Article/Article/3656962/change-in-isis-threat-means-evolution-in-long-term-us-iraq-relationship/

"Turkish Deputy PM: Syria's Afrin should be cleared of terrorists" | Turkish Minute | 28 June 2017 | https://www.turkishminute.com/2017/06/28/turkish-deputy-pm-syrias-afrin-should-be-cleared-of-terrorists/

"Erdoğan says Turkey ready for new operation in Syria" | Turkish

Minute | 28 June 2017 |
https://www.turkishminute.com/2017/06/28/erdogan-says-turkey-
ready-for-new-operation-in-syria/

"The Shanghai co-operation organization : China's changing
influence in Central Asia"| Chung, C.P. | Lingnan University | 1
December 2004 | https://scholars.ln.edu.hk/en/publications/the-
shanghai-co-operation-organization-chinas-changing-influence-

" Xi Jinping Holds Talks with President Shavkat Mirziyoyev of
Uzbekistan" | Ministry of Foreign Affairs of the People's Republic of
China | 24 January 2024 |
https://www.fmprc.gov.cn/mfa_eng/zxxx_662805/202401/t20240128
_11234651.html

"Why Iran's Economy Has Not Collapsed Amid U.S. Sanctions And
'Maximum Pressure" | Northam, J. | NPR | 16 January 2020 |
https://www.npr.org/2020/01/16/796781021/why-irans-economy-
has-not-collapsed-amid-u-s-sanctions-and-maximum-pressure

"Russia's non-strategic nuclear forces. International Affairs" | Yost,
D. S. | 2001 | https://doi.org/10.1111/1468-2346.00205

"Russia and Ukraine: What to Know from a Historian" | McCarthy,
M.| 2022 | https://core.ac.uk/download/519863170.pdf

"Women's Vital Voices: The Costs of Exclusion in Eastern Europe" |
Foreign Affairs | Hunt, S.| 1997 | https://doi.org/10.2307/20048116

"Report to Congress on U.S. Sanctions on Russia" | USNI News | 14
January 2019 | https://news.usni.org/2019/01/14/report-congress-u-s-
sanctions-
russia?utm_sourc%EF%BF%BD%EF%BF%BD%EF%BF%BD

"The Bumpy Road Towards Judicial Independence: Past, Present and
Future Prospects of Mainland China" | Liu, H. | Brill | Nijhoff

END NOTES

EBooks| 2014 | https://doi.org/10.1163/9789004257818_030

"America's Arab Allies Should Work Together to Stop Iranian Cyberattacks" | Runkle, B. | Foreign Policy | 6 June 2017 | https://foreignpolicy.com/2017/06/06/americas-arab-allies-should-work-together-to-stop-iranian-cyberattacks/

"Comparative Analysis of China's Energy Activities in the Middle East and Africa" | Wu, L., & Wang, Y| Journal of Middle Eastern and Islamic Studies in Asia | 2009 | https://doi.org/10.1080/19370679.2009.12023122

"IAEA delegation to visit uranium enrichment center Mar. 20 – Ivanov" | RIA Novosti | 19 March 2007 | https://www.globalsecurity.org/wmd/library/news/iran/2007/iran-070319-rianovosti01.htm

"U.S. Says Deployed THAAD Missile Defense System To Israel" | Reuters | 4 March 2019 | https://en.radiofarda.com/a/u-s-says-deployed-thaad-missile-defense-system-to-israel/29802761.html

"Will The United States and NATO Wake Up To What Happened at the Meeting of the Shanghai Cooperation Organization? | The Gateway Pundit | Johnson, L.| 19 September 2022 | https://www.thegatewaypundit.com/2022/09/will-united-states-nato-wake-happened-meeting-shanghai-cooperation-organization/embed/

"Putin and Erdogan meet to discuss Ukraine grain deal" | Welle, D. | The Telegraph Online | 19 June 2024 | https://www.telegraphindia.com/world/putin-and-erdogan-meet-to-discuss-ukraine-grain-deal/cid/1887006

"China's Ukraine Conundrum: Why the War Necessitates a Balancing Act" | Xuetong, Y | Foreign Affairs | 2 May 2022 | https://www.foreignaffairs.com/articles/china/2022-05-02/chinas-ukraine-conundrum

"Russia's new soft power: The mir card system" | Gricius, G | 2020 | https://doi.org/10.47305/JLIA2020032g

CHAPTER 8: Courting Terror

"Opinion: Joe Biden update: He's late, reviews Russian-U.S. relations and screws up some names" | Los Angeles Times | 11 March 2011 | https://www.latimes.com/archives/blogs/top-of-the-ticket/story/2011-03-11/opinion-joe-biden-update-hes-late-reviews-russian-u-s-relations-and-screws-up-some-names

"Rethinking the 'Arab Spring': The Root Causes of the Tunisian Jasmine Revolution and Egyptian January 25 Revolution" | International Journal of Islamic Thought | 2018 | https://doi.org/10.24035/ijit.13.2018.007

"The 'secretive sect' in charge of Syria" | BBC | 17 May 2012 | https://www.bbc.com/news/world-middle-east-18084964

"Report of the Commissioner-General of the United Nations Relief and Works Agency for Palestine Refugees in the Near East (1 January - 31 December 2013)" | Official Records | 2014 | https://doi.org/10.18356/129f0331-en

"Both French, Russian Draft Counter-Terrorism Resolutions Could Be Adopted" | Sputnik International | 19 November 2015 | https://sputniknews.com/20151119/french-russian-draft-counter-terrorism-resolutions-1030425196.html

"Jordan Condemns Israel's Decision To Build New Settlement In Occupied East Jerusalem" | MENAFN | 5 December 2023 https://menafn.com/1107540603/Jordan-Condemns-Israels-Decision-To-Build-New-Settlement-In-Occupied-East-Jerusalem

"NATO PA sends President Zelenskyy message of strong support "until victory is achieved" | NATO Parliamentary Assembly | 9

END NOTES

October 2023 | https://www.nato-pa.int/news/nato-pa-sends-president-zelenskyy-message-strong-support-until-victory-achieved

"General Lavigne Addresses the NATO Parliamentary Assembly" | NATO-OTAN | 9 October 2023 | https://www.act.nato.int/article/general-lavigne-addresses-nato-pa/

"Hamas's blood-soaked billions: How does the terror group stay rich?" | The News Intel | 6 January 2024 | https://thenewsintel.com/hamass-blood-soaked-billions-how-does-the-terror-group-stay-rich/

"Russia's Relationship with Hamas and Putin's Global Calculations" | Borshchevskaya, A. | The Washington Institute | 6 November 2023 | https://www.washingtoninstitute.org/policy-analysis/russias-relationship-hamas-and-putins-global-calculations

"Putin thanks Trump for intelligence that prevented St Petersburg terror attack" | World Defense | https://world-defense.com/threads/putin-thanks-trump-for-intelligence-that-prevented-st-petersburg-terror-attack.4728/

"Who is Yevgeny Prigozhin, the leader of the Wagner Group?" | Rogers, P. | Samtana | 25 January 2023 | https://samtana.com/who-is-yevgeny-prigozhin-the-leader-of-the-wagner-group/

"Syria's drug problem casts shadow over Assad's rehabilitation | Pay For Desire | 30 September 2023 | https://payfordesire.com/index.php/2023/09/30/syrias-drug-problem-casts-shadow-over-assads-rehabilitation/

"Efforts of the Arab League in Resolving the Arab Spring Conflict in Libya and Syria in 2010-2012" | Maulidya, A. D. | 2020 | https://doi.org/10.19109/jssp.v4i1.5410

"International indifference on Idlib complicates Turkey's position" |

Kose , T. | Daily Sabah | 31 August 2019 | https://www.dailysabah.com/columns/talhakose/2019/08/31/international-indifference-on-idlib-complicates-turkeys-position

"Crimea Unravelled: a Deep Dive Into the History, Russian Occupation, and Ukraine" | UkraineWorld | 10 August 2023 | https://ukraineworld.org/en/articles/infowatch/crimea

"Moscow Presses in the Mediterranean" | Frattini II, C. and Casagrande, G. | ISW | 10 October 2017 | https://www.iswresearch.org/2017/10/moscow-presses-in-mediterranean.html

"How to Stabilize Ukraine Long Term? Securitize Well-Being" | Buckley, C., Clem, R. and Herron, E. |War on the Rocks | 4 December 2019 | https://warontherocks.com/2019/12/how-to-stabilize-ukraine-long-term-securitize-well-being/

CHAPTER 9: The Ottomans Still Matter

"The Effects of the Latest Modifications on Electoral Laws in Turkey" | Didem, Y. | Heinrich Böll Stiftung | Niwêneriya Tirkiyeyê | 13 September 2022 | https://tr.boell.org/en/2022/09/13/effects-latest-modifications-electoral-laws-turkey

"Back in the 1970s, British socialists made a free-trade case against the EU" | Wirtz, B. | 11 December 2018 | https://wirtzbill.com/2018/12/11/back-in-the-1970s-british-socialists-made-a-free-trade-case-against-the-eu/

"After 'Brexit:' The Western Balkans in the European Waiting Room" | ERIS – European Review of International Studies | Belloni, R., & Brunazzo, M.| 2017| https://doi.org/10.3224/eris.v4i1.02

"Two Rights and A Wrong: On Taner Akçam" | The Nation | 13 March 2013 | https://www.thenation.com/article/archive/two-rights-

and-wrong-taner-akcam/

"Could Cyprus Hold the Answer to the War in Ukraine?" | Hader, L. | The National Interest | 3 February 2023 | https://nationalinterest.org/feature/could-cyprus-hold-answer-war-ukraine-206165

"Preventive War against Iraq, Strategic Insight" | Russell, J. A., & Wirtz, J. J. | 2002 | https://core.ac.uk/download/36736039.pdf

"The Sustainable European Union Own Resources System" | Cieslukowski , M. | Centre for Studies on Federalism | 2016 | http://webarchive-2009-2021.on-federalism.eu/index.php/articles/236-the-sustainable-european-union-own-resources-system.html

"French Genocide Bill Angers Turkey" | Dechian, S. | HISTORICAL JUSTICE AND MEMORY NETWORK | 2011 | https://historicaldialogues.org/2011/12/20/french-genocide-bill-angers-turkey/

"Europe at Schools in South Eastern Europe - Country Profiles. ZEI European Studies and South Eastern Europe Papers, SEE 4," | Borissova, O., Domović, V., Gehrmann, S., Horvatić, I., Husi, G., Milososki, A., Petravić, A., Porumb, E. M., Stanković, D., & Todorova, S. | 2003 | https://core.ac.uk/download/5074984.pdf

"Russia's Fortress strategy is not for free" | Atradius | 14 September 2021 | https://group.atradius.com/publications/economic-research/russia-fortress-strategy-is-not-for-free.html

CHAPTER 10: The So Called Betrayal

"China and a Nuclear Weapons-Free Zone in Northeast Asia" | Zhenqiang, P. | Nautilus Institute for Security and Sustainability | 15 May 2012 | https://nautilus.org/napsnet/napsnet-special-reports/china-and-a-nuclear-weapons-free-zone-in-northeast-asia/?view=print

"Twenty Years After The Economic Restructuring Of Eastern Europe: An Economic Review" | Giannaros, D. | 2008 | https://doi.org/10.19030/iber.v7i11.3306

"Racial Violence in the New Germany 1990–93. Contemporary European History" | Panayi, P.| 1994 | https://doi.org/10.1017/s0960777300000898

"Thirty Years of U.S. Policy Toward Russia: Can the Vicious Circle Be Broken?" | Rumer, E., & Sokolsky, R. | Carnegie Endowment for International Peace | 2019 | https://carnegieendowment.org/research/2019/06/thirty-years-of-us-policy-toward-russia-can-the-vicious-circle-be-broken?lang=en

"Occupying the Rhineland" | The Weimar Republic / 1918 / Interbellum | 1918 - 1936 | The Second World War. https://www.thesecondworldwar.org/interbellum-1918-1936/the-weimar-republic/occupying-the-rhineland

"Trump's National Security Strategy: A New Brand of Mercantilism?" | Salman, A., & Bick, A. | Carnegie Endowment for International Peace | 2017 | https://carnegieendowment.org/research/2017/08/trumps-national-security-strategy-a-new-brand-of-mercantilism?lang=en

"European Coal and Steel Community!" | Lechelle, Y. | Scaleway | 6 May 2021 | https://www.scaleway.com/en/blog/digital-europe-needs-to-draw-inspiration-from-the-founding-fathers-of-the-european-coal-and-steel-community/

Interview with Willy Claes (Hasselt, 21 October 2010) — Excerpt: The fall of the Berlin Wall on 9 November 1989 and the political consequences of this historical event - CVCE Website.

https://www.cvce.eu/de/obj/interview_with_willy_claes_hasselt_21_october_2010_excerpt_the_fall_of_the_berlin_wall_on_9_november_1989_and_the_political_consequences_of_this_historical_event-en-ffee4b4b-f3e4-4dd8-9a54-37560d8011b6.html

"The Last Piece Of East Germany - Ernst Thälmann Island" | Robinson, M. | 6 April 2021 | https://www.berlinexperiences.com/the-last-piece-of-east-germany/

"One more time on avoiding a new Cold War" | Pifer, S. | Brookings Institute | 27 October 2015 | https://www.brookings.edu/articles/one-more-time-on-avoiding-a-new-cold-war/

"2010 NPT Review Conference and Nuclear Disarmament" | Kurosawa, M. | http://ir-lib.wilmina.ac.jp/dspace/bitstream/10775/903/1/d2010_05.pdf

"A comparison of British and German banking strategies in the context of European financial integration between 1993 and 2003" | Janssen, S. | 2007 | https://core.ac.uk/download/161923196.pdf

CHAPTER 11: Like Dresden

"PUTIN PRISONER OF PEOPLES POWER: His formative years as spy in East Germany saw how patriotic feeling, combined with yearning for democracy, proved so much more powerful than communist ideology" | https://www.fijileaks.com/home/putin-prisoner-of-peoples-power-his-formative-years-as-spy-in-east-germany-saw-how-patriotic-feeling-combined-with-yearning-for-democracy-proved-so-much-more-powerful-than-communist-ideology

"A New Twist in Russia's Yukos Oil Affair" | Arvedlund, Erin E.| The New York Times | Retrieved 24 May 2013 | https://www.nytimes.com/2004/04/16/business/a-new-twist-in-russia-s-yukos-oil-affair.html

"Khodorkovsky's gamble: from business to politics in the YUKOS conflict" (PDF) | LSE Research Online. London School of Economics | Retrieved 24 May 2013. | https://eprints.lse.ac.uk/3689/1/Khodorkovsky%E2%80%99s_gamble-from_business_to_politics_(LSERO).pdf

"Stasi Files Shed Light on Putin's KGB Past" | Tanner, A. | The Moscow Times | 27 February 2001 | https://www.themoscowtimes.com/archive/stasi-files-shed-light-on-putins-kgb-past

"What does the future hold for the CDU following Annegret Kramp-Karrenbauer's resignation?" | Walsh-Führing, M. | LSE | 18 February 2020 || https://blogs.lse.ac.uk/europpblog/2020/02/18/what-does-the-future-hold-for-the-cdu-following-annegret-kramp-karrenbauers-resignation/

"How Germany Inc. played Russian roulette — and lost" | Karnitschnig, M. and Nöstlinger, N. | POLITICO | 13 April 2022 | https://www.politico.eu/article/germany-inc-played-russian-roulette-and-lost-ukraine-war-energy-gas-trade/

CHAPTER 12: The Value in Defeat

"Kais Saied's Tunisia is becoming a failed state" | Guesmi, H. | Opinions | Al Jazeera | 5 May 2023 | https://www.aljazeera.com/opinions/2023/5/5/kais-saieds-tunisia-is-becoming-a-failed-state?traffic_source=KeepReading

"Trump's rise raises fears for NATO" | TrumpsCrimes.com | 10 February 2024 | https://trumpscrimes.com/index.php/2024/02/10/trumps-rise-raises-fears-for-nato/

"Cambodian PM says AUKUS becoming concern for ASEAN over nuclear proliferation" | Xinhua News Agency | 5 June 2023 |

https://cambodianess.com/article/cambodian-pm-says-aukus-becoming-concern-for-asean-over-nuclear-proliferation

"Marjorie Taylor Greene Says Intel Leaker is Being Treated 'Like a Traitor and Criminal' — Calls Biden 'The Real Enemy'" | Surley | News Views | 13 April 2023 | https://newsviews.online/2023/04/13/marjorie-taylor-greene-says-intel-leaker-is-being-treated-like-a-traitor-and-criminal-calls-biden-the-real-enemy/

"The fall of Rudy Giuliani: How 'America's mayor' tied his fate to Donald Trump and got indicted" | SISAK, M.R. | AP News | 17 August 2023 | https://apnews.com/article/giuliani-trump-election-indictments-georgia-eb2ff2ca7a94f9f80e95e897584c8e7d

"A committee of the US House of Representatives announces that it will hold a hearing next Thursday (June 20) to examine" | Offstream News | 11 June 2019 | https://offstream.news/feed/2019/06/11/a-committee-of-the-us-house-of-representatives-announces-that-it-will-hold-a-hearing-next-thursday-june-20-to-examine.html

"House Republicans invite President Biden to testify at public hearing as impeachment inquiry stalls" | Amiri, F. | Associated Press | 28 March 2024 | http://bucknermelton.com/author/farnoush-amiri-associated-press

"Introduction: Germany and European Integration" | Gilbert, M. R., Oberloskamp, E., & Raithel, T. | German Yearbook of Contemporary History | 2019 | https://doi.org/10.1353/gych.2019.0000

INDEX

INDEX